ULL ITEM BARCODE

19 1646912 1

D1429069

The Humanities

Library Science Text Series

The Humanities:
A Selective Guide to Information Sources

Second Edition

A. Robert Rogers

Dean, School of Library Science
Kent State University

SHL
WITHDRAWN

1979
Libraries Unlimited, Inc.
Littleton, Colorado

Copyright ©1979, 1974 A. Robert Rogers
All Rights Reserved
Printed in the United States of America

No part of this publication may be reproduced, stored in a retrieval system, or transmitted, in any form or by any means, electronic, mechanical, photocopying, recording, or otherwise, without the prior written permission of the publisher.

LIBRARIES UNLIMITED, INC.
P.O. Box 263
Littleton, Colorado 80160

Library of Congress Cataloging in Publication Data

Rogers, A   Robert, 1927-
    The humanities.

    (Library science text series)
    Includes index.
    1. Humanities--Bibliography. I. Title.
Z5579.R63   1979   [AZ201]   016.0013   79-25335
ISBN 0-87287-206-8 (cloth)
    0-87287-222-X (paper)

PREFACE TO THE SECOND EDITION

The response to the first edition of *The Humanities* from reviewers, library school faculty, and reference librarians was very encouraging. Rapid developments in the field and specific suggestions for improvement made plans for an early second edition desirable. The creation of the Machine-Assisted Reference Section (MARS) in the Reference and Adult Services Division of the American Library Association, and its growth to more than 1,650 members by 1978, indicated the increasing importance as well as the general acceptance of computerized reference service in the study of the humanities. Meanwhile, the printing presses continued to pour forth a plethora of new reference books. Perusal of sources like *American Reference Books Annual, Booklist, Choice, College and Research Libraries, Library Journal, RQ,* and *Wilson Library Bulletin* revealed approximately 350 new titles published between late 1973 and the end of 1977 that should at least be considered for inclusion in a new edition. The percentages by discipline were: philosophy—1 percent; religion—11.5 percent; visual arts—18 percent; performing arts—37.5 percent; language and literature—32 percent. Imprints from 1978 and 1979 increased the total but did not greatly alter the relative proportions.

The first edition grew out of my experience in teaching L.S. 60628 (Literature of the Humanities) at Kent State University. Plans for the second edition included consultations with library school faculty and reference librarians in order to broaden the perspective and, it is hoped, correct any myopic elements.

These consultations began in the spring of 1976, when questionnaires were sent to approximately one hundred faculty members in United States and Canadian library schools (identified in the 1976 Special Issue of *Journal of Education for Librarianship* as teachers of courses in the literature/bibliography of the humanities). The individual comments of the respondents (including two course syllabi with bibliographies) provided many helpful suggestions. There was substantial agreement that the introduction should be revised to include more specific information about user studies and suggested general readings in the humanities. There was strong agreement that the chapter on "The Computer and the Humanities" should be updated to include newer studies — a view with which I concur. Inclusion of greater depth on societies and information centers was recommended by a substantial number, and this has been attempted. Most respondents agreed that the bibliography chapters should be left largely as in the first edition, except for new titles and new editions. A substantial number favored longer, more comparative, and more critical annotations. There was strong agreement on the need for a new bibliographical chapter on major information sources in the humanities that cover several disciplines. A new chapter has been created to remedy this deficiency. A large number favored inclusion of sample reference questions for each discipline, with questions incorporated in the text but with a separate pamphlet for the teacher containing answers, sources, and strategy notes. (I have finally decided not to comply with this request for three reasons: 1) the need to tailor such questions to the reference collections of individual libraries if they are to be effective in teaching and not simply sources of student frustration; 2) the rapidity with which new titles and new editions appear; 3) the amount of time that might be taken away from more central purposes relating to improvement of the book.)

The second round of consultations began in the fall of 1977 and continued through the winter and spring of 1978. Several reference librarians with special subject expertise were invited to offer critiques of the book and to make suggestions for inclusion of new titles published since the first edition and valuable older titles that had been overlooked. Those who agreed to participate were sent complimentary copies of the book and forms to complete on which an evaluation of each title in the appropriate field could be given, using the following code:

V   Vital. Heavily used by reference librarians in this subject field. Every student should know thoroughly. Deserving of a major annotation in the book.

R   Recommended. Used with some frequency by reference librarians in this subject field. Each student should know something about this title. It probably should receive a separate entry with a brief annotation in the book.

P   Used only occasionally in prolonged searches. Need not have a separate entry, but can be included in an annotation.

NR Not Recommended. Reference librarians have found this work to be inadequate. If mentioned at all, it should be only within the text of an annotation warning of its deficiencies.

I wish to express deepest appreciation to those who responded to this survey: Hans E. Bynagle, Director of the Library, Friends University, Wichita, Kansas (philosophy); Glenn R. Wittig, Ph.D. Candidate, School of Library Science, University of Michigan (religion); William J. Dane,

Supervising Librarian, Art and Music Department, Newark Public Library (visual arts); Jacqueline D. Sisson, Head, Fine Arts Library, Ohio State University (visual arts); Julia Sabine, Special Assistant to the Director, Munson-Williams-Proctor Institute, Utica, N.Y. (visual arts); Dorothy L. Swerdlove, First Assistant, Performing Arts Research Center, New York Public Library at Lincoln Center (performing arts); Carol Bradley, Music Librarian, State University of New York at Buffalo (performing arts); Dorothy E. Litt, Assistant Branch Librarian, Douglastown Branch, Queens Borough Public Library (literature); Colby H. Kullman, Department of English, University of Kansas (literature); and L. Zgusta, Professor of Linguistics and Classics, University of Illinois (language). Their evaluations and suggestions have been extremely helpful; nevertheless, I have had to make my own judgments and decisions.

Of the 1,376 titles in the first edition, respondents rated 680 as "vital." (There was some disagreement, so the range of "vital" books is really somewhere between 530 and 680.) These reference librarians also suggested nearly 200 titles previously published but not included in the first edition. With the number of potential titles rapidly rising toward 2,000, I became alarmed because four years of using *The Humanities* as a text had convinced me that:

1. the number of titles receiving separate annotations should be reduced rather than increased;

2. students should be given more guidance in differentiating the most important titles from those of value but of lesser importance;

3. the inroads of inflation should be counteracted by making the text more compact or producing a paperback edition for student purchase, or both.

These considerations led to the following decisions:

1. the introductory first chapter should be revised to incorporate suggested readings and more specific information on user studies;

2. the "trends" chapters should be eliminated and suggested readings should be substituted in the chapters on accessing information;

3. the exposition of subject headings with examples should be given in detail once, in the philosophy section, and omitted or condensed to reflect only unusual features in the following chapters;

4. the bibliographical chapters should concentrate on works that serve either a selection or a reference function:

   a. general introductions and histories should be omitted unless of selection or reference value;

      b. periodicals without major reviewing sections or features of major reference . value (e.g., biographies, dates of performances, etc.) should be eliminated;

      c. information about librarianship in special fields should be transferred to the chapters on accessing information;

5. the references to publishers (especially well-known domestic publishers) should be shortened (e.g., "Bowker, 1977" rather than "New York: R. R. Bowker Co., 1977");

6. lengthy titles should be shortened whenever possible without loss of clarity;

7. citations to reviews should be provided on a very selective basis, mainly confined to situations in which there is disagreement about the worth of a reference work.

In the course of preparing this book, certain standard reference aids have been especially valuable: *Encyclopedia of Associations, Subject Directory of Special Libraries and Information Centers, Research Centers Directory, Subject Collections, Computer-Readable Bibliographic Data Bases: A Directory and Sourcebook*, and *Encyclopedia of Information Systems and Services*. Abbreviations for titles of periodical indexes have been taken from *Ulrich's International Periodicals Directory* when available or have been formed in accordance with the *American National Standard for the Abbreviation of Titles of Periodicals* (ANSI, 1970).

I am particularly indebted to Kosette Kies (Peabody) and Paul Winckler (Long Island) for suggested background readings in the humanities, to Lois Bebout, Donald Davis, and Donald Oehlerts for "User Studies in the Humanities; A Survey and a Proposal," *RQ* 15 (Fall 1975): 40-44, and to Cynthia McLaughlin for her chapter on "The Computer and the Humanities." Greg Byerly, of the Kent State University Libraries Reference Department, has helped with the computer searching of several databases. My debt to faculty in other library schools and to the reference librarians who assisted in the title-by-title evaluation has already been acknowledged. My greatest debt, however, is to my wife, Rhoda, who has typed this manuscript, helped with the index, and patiently endured the tribulations imposed by my work habits.

TABLE OF CONTENTS

LISTS OF ABBREVIATIONS

"Frequency of Publication" Abbreviations

Ann. — Annual

Ann. cum. — Annual cumulation

Bi. — Biennial

Bi-mo. — Bi-monthly

Mo. — Monthly

Q — Quarterly

S-Ann. — Semi-Annual

Tri. — Triennial

2/yr. — Two times per year

Wk. — Weekly

Abbreviations for Abstracting and Indexing Services

A&HCI — *Arts & Humanities Citation Index*, 1978- . 3/yr. Ann. cum. Institute for Scientific Information (hereafter cited as ISI).

A.B.C.Pol.Sci. — *Advance Bibliography of Contents, Political Science & Government*, 1969- . 6/yr. American Bibliographical Center/Clio Press (hereafter cited as ABC/Clio).

ABR.R.G. — *Abridged Reader's Guide to Periodical Literature*, 1935- . Mo. Ann. cum. Wilson.

Abstr.Eng.Stud. — *Abstracts of English Studies*, 1958- . 10/yr. National Council of Teachers of English.

Abstr.Folk.Stud. — *Abstracts of Folklore Studies*, 1963- . Q. American Folklore Society.

Am.Lit.Abstr. — *American Literature Abstracts*, 1967- . 2/yr. Department of English, San Jose State College.

Amer.Hist.&Life — *America: History and Life*, 1964- . 7/yr. ABC/Clio.

Arch.Ind. — *Architectural Index*, 1963(?)- . Ann. Denver, CO.

Art Ind. — *Art Index*, 1929- . Q. Ann. cum. Wilson.

ARTbibliog. — *ARTbibliographies Modern*, 1969- . S-Ann. ABC/Clio.

A.S.&T.Ind. — *Applied Science and Technology Index*, 1958- . Mo. Ann. cum. Wilson.

Avery Ind.Arch.Per. — *Avery Index to Architectural Periodicals.* 2nd ed. G. K. Hall, 1973. Suppls. 1975, 1977.

Bk.Rev.Dig. — *Book Review Digest*, 1905- . Mo. Ann. cum. Wilson.

Bk.Rev.Ind. — *Book Review Index*, 1965- . Bi-mo. Ann. cum. Gale.

Br.Arch.Abstr. — *British Archaeological Abstracts*, 1968- . S-Ann. Council for British Archaeology.

Br.Ed.Ind. — *British Education Index*, 1961- . Q. Ann. cum. British Library.

Br.Hum.Ind. — *British Humanities Index*, 1962- . Q. Ann. cum. Library Association.

Bull.signal.:art — *Bulletin Signalétique. Part 526: art et archéologie*, 1961- . Q. Centre National de la Recherche Scientifique (hereafter cited as CNRS).

Bull.signal.:hist.sci.lit. — *Bulletin Signalétique. Part 523: histoire et science de la littérature*, 1961- . Q. CNRS.

Bull.signal.:lit. — *Bulletin Signalétique. Part 523: histoire et science de la littérature*, 1961- . Q. CNRS.

Bull.signal.:phil. — *Bulletin Signalétique. Part 519: philosophie*, 1961- . Q. CNRS.

Bull.signal.:sci.lang. — *Bulletin Signalétique. Part 524: sciences du language*, 1961- . Q. CNRS.

Bull.signal.:sci.rel. — *Bulletin Signalétique. Part 527: sciences religieuses*, 1961- . Q. CNRS.

Bull.signal.:soc. — *Bulletin Signalétique. Part 521: sociologie-ethnologie*, 1961- . Q. CNRS.

Can.Per.Ind. — *Canadian Periodical Index*, 1948- . Mo. Ann. cum. Canadian Library Association.

Canon Law Abstr. — *Canon Law Abstracts*, 1959- . S-Ann. Canon Law Society of Great Britain.

Cath.Ind. — *The Catholic Periodical and Literature Index*, 1930- . Bi-Mo. Catholic Library Association.

CIJE — *Current Index to Journals in Education*, 1969- . Mo. S-Ann. cum. Macmillan, 1969-79. Oryx, 1979- .

Christ.Per.Ind. — *Christian Periodical Index*, 1958- . Q. Ann. & quinq. cum. Christian Librarians' Fellowship.

Curr.Biog. — *Current Biography*, 1940- . Mo. (exc. Aug.) Wilson.

Curr.Bk.Rev.Cit. — *Current Book Review Citations*, 1976- . Mo. Ann. cum. Wilson.

Curr.Cont. — *Current Contents/Social and Behavioral Sciences*, 1969- . Wk. ISI.

DSH Abstr. — *DSH Abstracts*, 1960- . Q. Deafness, Speech and Hearing Publications, Inc., Gallaudet College.

Ed.Ind. — *Education Index*, 1929- . Mo. Ann. cum. Wilson.

Eng.Ind. — *Engineering Index*, 1906- . Mo. Ann. cum. Engineering Index, Inc.

Film Lit.Ind. — *Film Literature Index*, 1973- . Q. Ann. cum. Filmdex, Inc.

Film Rev.Dig. — *Film Review Digest*, 1975- . Kraus-Thomson.

Hist.Abstr. — *Historical Abstracts*, 1955- . Q. ABC/Clio.

Hum.Ind. — *Humanities Index*, 1974- . Q. Ann. cum. Wilson.

I.B.Z. — *International Bibliographie der Zeitschriftenliteratur*, 1896- . F. Dietrich.

Ind.Bk.Rev.Hum. — *Index to Book Reviews in the Humanities*, 1960- . Ann. Phillip Thomson.

Ind.Jew.Per. — *Index to Jewish Periodicals*, 1963- . 2/yr. Cleveland, OH.

Int.Ind.Film Per. — *International Index to Film Periodicals*, 1972- . Irregular. St. Martins.

Int.Ind.Mult.Med.Inf. — *International Index to Multi Media Information*, 1970- . Q. Audio-Visual Associates.

Lang.Teach.&Ling.Abstr. — *Language Teaching and Linguistics Abstracts*, 1968- . Q. Cambridge University Press.

Lib.Lit. — *Library Literature*, 1936- . Bi-mo. Ann. & 2 yr. cum. Wilson.

LISA — *Library and Information Science Abstracts*, 1969- . Bi-mo. Library Association.

LLBA — *Language and Language Behavior Abstracts*, 1967- . Q. Sociological Abstracts, Inc.

Med.Rev.Dig. — *Media Review Digest*, 1970- . Q. Ann. cum. Pierian Press.

MLA Abstr.Art.Sch.J. — *MLA Abstracts of Articles in Scholarly Journals*, 1971- . 3/yr. Modern Language Association of America (hereafter cited as MLA).

MLA Int.Bib. — *MLA International Bibliography of Books and Articles on the Modern Languages and Literatures*, 1922- . 3/yr. MLA.

Multi-Med.Rev.Ind. — *Multi-Media Reviews Index*, 1970- . Ann. Pierian Press.

Mus.Ind. – *Music Index*, 1949- . Mo. Ann. cum. Information Coordinators, Inc.

New Test.Abstr. – *New Testament Abstracts*, 1956- . 3/yr. Weston School of Theology.

P.A.I.S. – *Public Affairs Information Service Bulletin*, 1915- . 44/yr. (Cum. 5/yr.). Public Affairs Information Service, Inc.

Phil.Ind. – *The Philosopher's Index*, 1967- . Q. Philosophy Documentation Center, Bowling Green State University.

Psych.Abstr. – *Psychological Abstracts*, 1927- . Mo. American Psychological Association.

Rel.&Theol.Abstr. – *Religious and Theological Abstracts*, 1958- . Q. Religious and Theological Abstracts, Inc.

Rel.Ind.:One – *Religion Index: One*, 1949/52- . S-Ann. American Theological Library Association.

Rép.bibliog.phil. – *Répertoire bibliographique de la philosophie*, 1949- . Q. Editions de l'Institut Supéricure de Philosophie.

R.G. – *Reader's Guide to Periodical Literature*, 1900- . Semi-mo. Q. & Ann. cum. Wilson.

RILA – *Répertoire internationale de la littérature d' art / International Repertory of the Literature of Art*, 1975- . S-Ann. College Art Association of America.

RILM – *Répertoire internationale de la littérature musicale / RILM Abstracts of Music Literature*, 1967- . Q. International Association of Music Libraries.

SCI – *Science Citation Index*, 1961- . Q. Ann. cum. ISI.

Soc.Abstr. – *Sociological Abstracts*, 1952- . 6/yr. Sociological Abstracts, Inc.

Soc.Sci.Ind. – *Social Sciences Index*, 1974- . Q. Ann. cum. Wilson.

SSCI – *Social Sciences Citation Index*, 1973- . 3/yr. Ann. cum. ISI.

Subj.Ind.Child.Mag. – *Subject Index to Children's Magazines*, 1949- . Mo. (exc. Je-J.) Semi-Ann. cum. Madison, WI.

Theol.Abstr.&Bibliog.Serv. – *Theological Abstracting and Bibliographical Services*, 1972- . Q. Harrogate, Yorkshire, England.

Of making many books there
is no end; and much study is
a weariness of the flesh.
(Ecclesiastes 12:12)

1   INTRODUCTION

In our media-saturated time when men must take refuge from the stimuli that daily bombard the senses, how dare a writer put pen to paper and start yet another book? The accusation is the more devastating when one reflects that the words quoted above were written nearly two millenia before the invention of printing. Like Eliot's Prufrock, one must indeed ask, "And should I then presume? And how should I begin?"

Through more than 3,000 years of civilization, the humanities have nourished the spirit of man. They have a message for our own time as well—if we can find our way through the contemporary clutter. Our problem is not scarcity, but overabundance. Librarians and other users of libraries need road maps to guide the search for the knowledge that is of most value. The need for some additional mapmaking is perhaps greater in the humanities than in the natural and social sciences, which are already somewhat better charted.

But which disciplines constitute the humanities? In classical and early Christian times, the scope seemed to be very broad. Literature (especially the epic poems of Homer) constituted the core, but virtually any discipline relating to the mind of man (even including mathematics) was, at one time or another, considered part of the humanities. In the Renaissance period, the term "humanities" was used in opposition to the term "divinity" and seemed to embrace virtually any area of study outside the field of religion. In the nineteenth century, the term was used to include those disciplines that could not be considered part of the natural sciences. In the twentieth century, the term "social sciences" has come into use for a body of disciplines (economics, sociology, anthropology, political science, etc.) that espouse "scientific" methods of investigation but deal with social rather than natural phenomena. History, long considered a humanistic field, has increasingly adopted methods of investigation that place it closer to the social sciences. For the purposes of the present book, "humanities" will be construed to include philosophy, religion, the visual arts, the performing arts, language, and literature.

The student interested in exploring the nature of the humanities has access to many resources. At the level of a general overview, one may begin with "Humanistic Scholarship, History of" and "Humanities" in the *Encyclopaedia Britannica: Macropaedia* (15th ed., 1974), v. 8, pp. 1170-81. More reflective treatment may be found in *One Great Society*, by Howard Mumford Jones (Harcourt, 1959), and in the volumes of *The Princeton Studies: Humanistic Scholarship in America* (Princeton, 1963-). Reference should also be made to the *Report of the Commission on the Humanities* (ACLS, 1964) and to "The Future of the Humanities" [*Daedalus* 98 (Summer 1969):605-869]. Walter Kaufmann's *The Future of the Humanities* (Crowell, 1977) is concerned primarily with the teaching of the humanities. Of particular interest to librarians are ch. 2, "The Art of Reading," and ch. 3, "The Politics of Reviewing and the Ethics of Translating and Editing." The articles "Humanism Today," by H. M. Jones [*Harvard Library Bulletin* 23 (October 1975):365-78], and "Objective Knowledge in Science and the Humanities," by H. L. Brown [*Diogenes* no. 97 (Spring 1977):85-102], should also be noted. Of more practical bent are pieces like H. S. Bailey's "The Economics of Publishing in the Humanities" [*Scholarly Publishing* 8 (April 1977):223-31] and Charles Bolte's *Libraries and the Arts and Humanities* (Gaylord, 1978). Mention should also be made of publications generated from projects funded by the National Endowment for the Humanities and the monitoring of federal legislation dealing with the arts and humanities reported by Congressman Fred Richmond (D. NY; 1707 Longworth Building, Washington, DC 20515). Finally, it should be noted that a new organization, the American Association for the Advancement of the Humanities (Suite 601, 918 16th St., N.W., Washington, DC 20006) — aided by grants from the Exxon, Ford, Rockefeller, and Dyson-Kissner foundations — began lobbying for the humanities in 1979.

The remainder of this introductory chapter will be devoted to the nature of scholarship in the humanities and the types of literature available to the librarian seeking to meet user requests for information, inspiration, and enlightenment.

At the outset, it should be remarked that humanistic research is differentiated most sharply from research in the natural sciences by the constant intrusion of questions of value. To the scientist *qua* scientist, such considerations are, indeed, intrusions. They interfere with and damage the quality of research concerned with objective, empirically verifiable data and with experimental results that can be replicated by other researchers. "Informed judgment" might play a part in deciding what experiments to conduct, but "refined sensibility" would have no impact on the outcome. Yet these are the "bread of life" for the humanistic scholar, whether dealing with a poem, a piece of music, a painting, a religious doctrine, or a philosophical theory. Thus, humanistic scholarship has traditionally been intimately intertwined with considerations of value.

One consequence of this connection between scholarship and value systems is the peculiarly personal and individualistic nature of humanistic research. Unlike colleagues in the natural sciences or even, to a lesser degree, in the social sciences, the humanist finds research to be such an intimately personal matter that it is more difficult than in other disciplines to function effectively as a member of a team. The results of team effort are more likely to be compromise and mediocrity than productive division of labor. Collaborative efforts are, of course, possible. But they require special planning and are not nearly as "normal" as in the natural sciences.

A further result of this state of affairs is the general lack of ability on the part of the humanistic scholar to delegate bibliographic searching to others. The interconnections within the researcher's mind are so subtle and complex that it is necessary to examine personally the index entry or abstract to identify an item of potential relevance and the original book or article to determine its actual relevance. The problem is, of course, compounded by the lack of standardized and controlled vocabularies of the sort that have become increasingly common in the pure and applied sciences. Yet the humanistic scholar needs help in the form of access to a wide variety of finding aids.

Part of the problem faced by the humanistic scholar also relates to the nature of "knowledge" in the humanities. It is not likely to consist of hard, identifiable facts like formulas in chemistry, or population and income statistics from census data. Facts there are, aplenty, but their sum total is considerably less than what the humanist is looking for. To know the number of times that Shakespeare uses the word "mince" in *Hamlet* is to tell us very little of importance about *Hamlet*. Yet the patient accumulation and analysis of factual data (often with the aid of the computer) can lay the foundation for knowledge of a higher order.

Closely related to the nature of "knowledge" is the question of "progress." In the natural sciences, knowledge tends to be "progressive." Each significant experiment either confirms, modifies, or overturns some piece of existing "knowledge." This is true whether the item in question is a new virus that has been detected through more sophisticated laboratory equipment or a far-ranging perception of relationships, such as the replacement of Newtonian physics with Einsteinian. In the humanities, no such "progress" is observable. Sophocles' *Antigone*, the Bhagavad-Gita, Michelangelo's "Pietà," or Mozart's *The Magic Flute* are not superseded as was the "phlogiston" theory in chemistry. Perception of beauty, insight into the human condition, and artistic creativity are not cumulative, though patterns of influence can be traced. Indeed, there is often a tendency for a work of artistic genius to be followed by a host of inferior imitations — not by new works that refine and improve it!

The factors noted in the preceding paragraphs have their impact on patterns of use of library materials. For the humanist and the social scientist, the library is the heart of the research enterprise. For the natural scientist, the laboratory is at the center, with the library in a supporting role. In this respect, the position of the creative artist (as distinct from the researcher) in the humanities may more nearly resemble that of the scientist — as anyone who has witnessed "dialogue" between a sculptor and an art historian can testify!

The centrality of the library for the humanistic researcher is still accompanied by the centrality of the monograph as distinct from the periodical article. Although there have been fewer use studies in the humanities than in other fields, the pattern of preference for books and pamphlets continues to emerge — in sharp contrast to the preference of the natural scientist for journal articles, reprints, and preprints.

Another characteristic reported in such few user studies as we have is the greater spread of individual titles used by researchers in the humanities. Whereas a relatively small number of journals contain a high proportion of the frequently cited articles in fields like chemistry and mathematics, the same high degree of concentration in journal or monographic titles has not been observed in the humanities. This is not to deny that critical studies tend to cluster around certain landmark works like Milton's *Paradise Lost* or Kant's *Critique of Pure Reason*, but the spread of titles is greater and the concentration much less intense.

A third use pattern that distinguishes humanistic from scientific researchers is a much greater time spread in materials. Whereas publications of the last five years are crucial to scientific research, with usage dropping off rapidly after that, the humanist is likely to be equally interested in publications of 20, 40, or 50 years ago. Indeed, if one considers the "classics" in each field (as distinct from modern editions or reproductions), the range of interest may readily extend to items two or three thousand years old.

Mention should be made, at this point, of some user studies that will clarify, and perhaps correct, the preceding general remarks. The best single starting point is the seminal article "User Studies in the Humanities: A Survey and a Proposal," by Lois Bebout, Donald Davis, Jr., and Donald Oehlerts [*RQ* 15 (Fall 1975):40-44]. The authors review a number of citation studies as well as interlibrary loan, circulation, and use studies of individual libraries. They then formulate a series of hypotheses concerning user behavior in the sciences, the social sciences, and the humanities. Their Table IV (p. 43), "Generalized Profile of Information-Seeking Behavior," deserves particularly careful study. The notes at the end of the article refer to practically every study of consequence.

An article of more general scope, but relevant here, is "Obsolescence and Change in the Use of Literature with Time," by M. B. Line and A. Sandison [*Journal of Documentation* 30 (September 1974):283-350]. The following hypotheses are advanced by the authors (pp. 317-18):

Literature may decline in use *faster* when
- (a) it deals with data of ephemeral relevance (e.g., prices, stocks, experimental data filling in a theory)
- (b) it is in the form of a 'report,' thesis, 'advance communication,' or preprint (which may be written up more fully or in more accessible form later)
- (c) it is in a rapidly advancing technology.

Literature may decline in use *more slowly* when
- (a) it is descriptive (e.g., taxonomic botany, properties of materials, basic methodology)
- (b) it deals with concepts (e.g., philosophy, political theory, new or seminal ideas)
- (c) it is critical (e.g., literary criticism, historiography).

Other studies are also enlightening. In a study reported in "Article Citations and 'Obsolescence' in Musicological Journals" [*Notes* 33 (March 1977:563-71], R. M. Longyear found no pattern of obsolescence in materials in musicology comparable to that in the sciences. In "Citations in the Humanities: A Study of Citation Patterns in Literary Criticism in English, French and German" [*IPLO Quarterly* 14 (July 1973):20-40], M. S. Batts notes the language barrier to be particularly significant in that area. Partially funded by the British Library Research and Development Department, the University of Sheffield's Center for Research on User Studies surveyed the entire field in *User Studies: An Introductory Guide and Select Bibliography* in 1977, edited by Geoffrey Ford. In addition, a follow-up study by Cynthia Corkill and Margaret Mann, *Information Needs in the Humanities: Two Postal Surveys* (Sheffield, 1978), suggests that works in the humanities do not become dated as quickly as those in the sciences, although user patterns do vary among disciplines. And finally, *The Arts and Humanities Citation Index* (ISI, 1978-) should facilitate additional studies that will clarify information-seeking behavior by scholars in the humanities.

The working scholar in a humanistic discipline tends to perceive the materials with which to work as falling into three broad categories: 1) original texts or artifacts, 2) critical literature, 3) literature designed for specific groups or purposes. Each of these categories requires further elaboration.

The heart of all humanistic study is the original creative work, whether this is an epic poem, a piece of sculpture, a symphony, a devotional psalm, or a discourse on the nature of the good life. Without the outpourings of creative genius and the lesser efforts at creativity, there would be no enduring contribution to the illumination of the human condition — and nothing for humanistic scholars to analyze and interpret.

The second major category, utterly dependent upon the first, is critical literature. Normally, this takes the form of analysis, interpretation, or commentary on a particular creative work, on a group of creative works, or on the output of a given historical period. It may also include efforts to develop general theories of criticism and even histories of critical theories.

The literature designed for specific groups or purposes may be further subdivided into popularizations, access tools, and professional literature. Popularizations have been common in the field of religion for centuries. In other disciplines, their advent is more recent. The rise of the art museum movement in the nineteenth century, for example, and the twentieth-century addition of an educational role to the curatorial function have created demand for inexpensive books with reproductions of acknowledged masterpieces and simple commentary. Books on music appreciation now reach wide audiences. Ironically, philosophy and literature, once scarcely in need of popularization, became increasingly narrow and technical in the early years of the twentieth century, necessitating special efforts to bridge the gap. A good popularization should simplify without distortion or misinformation.

Access tools cover most of the items commonly thought of by reference librarians: bibliographies, indexes, abstracts, encyclopedias, dictionaries, handbooks, atlases, etc. The exponential growth of knowledge in the twentieth century has been in no small measure dependent on the increasing availability and sophistication of these access tools.

The professional literature is designed by practitioners within each discipline for their mutual enlightenment and the advancement of knowledge. Typically, it is created through the efforts of one or more major professional societies at the national level in each country and a host of specialized, regional, or local groups. Journals, indexes, and abstracts are the most typical outputs, although conference proceedings and current awareness (tables of contents) services are also common. In recent years, international cooperation has become increasingly widespread, often with the aid of subventions from Unesco.

Bibliographic organization has been the subject of numerous conferences and publications since the end of the Second World War. Only a few items closely related to the humanities can be cited here. The 1950 Conference on Bibliographic Organization, sponsored by the Graduate Library School of the University of Chicago, produced, among other useful papers, a valuable survey by Karl H. Kraeling entitled "The Humanities: Characteristics of the Literature, Problems of Use, and Bibliographic Organization in the Field" [In: Jesse H. Shera and Margaret Egans, eds., *Bibliographic Organization* (University of Chicago Press, 1951), pp. 109-126]. Sixteen years later, an excellent update was provided by Conrad H. Rawski ["Bibliographic Organization in the Humanities," *Wilson Library Bulletin* 40 (April 1966):738-50]. The Department of Library Science, Queen's College (Flushing, NY), sponsored a Conference on Access to Knowledge and Information in the Social Sciences and Humanities on April 5-6, 1972. The papers by Joseph Raben on "Computers and the Humanities" and Walter S. Achtert on "Abstracting and Bibliographical Control in the Modern Languages and Literatures" are particularly relevant [In: *Access to the Literature of the Social Sciences and Humanities* (Queen's College Press, 1974), pp. 49-54 and pp. 55-68]. The topic was also discussed by John Phillip Immroth in "Information Needs for the Humanities" [*Information Science: Search for Identity* (Dekker, 1974), pp. 249-62] and in "Humanities and Its Literature" [*Encyclopedia of Library and Information Science* (Dekker, 1974), v. 11, pp. 71-83].

Library resources in the humanities have been reviewed in "Humanities Libraries and Collections," by Thomas D. Gillies [*Encyclopedia of Library and Information Science* (Dekker, 1974), v. 11, pp. 64-71]. The *Handbook* of the Center for Research Libraries (1978) should also be consulted. An example of professional involvement at the regional level is the work of the Southwestern Library Association which resulted in publication of *Guide to Humanities Resources in the Southwest* (distr. ABC-Clio, 1977). Other dimensions of the topic have been explored by D. W. Langridge in *Classification and Indexing in the Humanities* (Butterworths, 1976). B. O. Aboyade recommends improved bibliographical control and use of microforms to facilitate scholarly access to primary materials in the humanities ["Access to Primary Source Materials in the Humanities," *International Library Review* 8 (June 1976):309-316]. Access to serials ["National Serials Data Base in the Humanities in Machine-Readable Form," *Information News and Sources* 7 (November 1975):258] and translations ["John Crerar Library, under a Grant from the National Endowment for the Humanities, Will Investigate the Feasibility of a Translations Information Center for the Humanities," *Bibliographical Society of America Papers* 71 (January 1977): 109] have also been discussed.

The student of librarianship will still find much information of great value in *The Humanities and the Library*, by Lester Asheim (ALA, 1957). The marriage of classification, cataloging, and subject content continues to be a fruitful approach.

Information Sources in the Humanities, compiled by Thomas Slavens (Campus Publishers, 1968), is an annotated bibliography of a few of the major sources of information in each of the five disciplines (philosophy, religion, art, music, literature) commonly included in humanities courses. There are test questions to assist the student in consolidating knowledge, and the annotations are excellent.

A new work, edited by Thomas Slavens and reported to be comparable in the humanities to Carl M. White's *Sources of Information in the Social Sciences: A Guide to the Literature* (2nd ed. ALA, 1973), is in preparation.

Reference Books in the Social Sciences and Humanities, by Rolland E. Stevens and Donald G. Davis, Jr. (4th ed. Stipes, 1977), has excellent annotations that are particularly helpful to students.

Eugene P. Sheehy's *Guide to Reference Books* (9th ed. ALA, 1976) devotes approximately one-third (pp. 244-596) of its space to the humanities. Similarly proportionate coverage will be found in Sheehy's annotated lists of new reference books in the January and July issues of *College and Research Libraries*.

A. J. Walford's *Guide to Reference Material* (3rd ed. Library Association, 1973-77. 3v.) gives extensive coverage to the humanities, partly in volume 2 (*Social and Historical Sciences, Philosophy and Religion*), but mainly in volume 3 (*Generalities, Languages, Arts and Literature*).

Paul A. Winckler's *Humanities: Outline and Bibliography* (Palmer Graduate Library School, Long Island University, 1971) is extremely comprehensive, but lacks annotations except for a few titles.

American Reference Books Annual (Libraries Unlimited, 1970-) provides comprehensive coverage and critical reviews of new reference books. About 25 percent of approximately 1,500 reviews in a typical year are devoted to the humanities. Because of the classified arrangement and detailed table of contents, reviews in the various humanities disciplines are easily located.

Since the use of computerized data bases has become common in reference work, it is appropriate that the concluding portion of this introductory chapter contain some mention of sources of information. Anthony T. Kruzas and his associates have compiled a comprehensive listing of American, and a selective listing of foreign, information systems and services in *Encyclopedia of Information Systems and Services: A Guide to Information Storage and Retrieval Services, Data Base Producers and Publishers, Online Vendors* . . . (3rd ed. Gale, 1978). Even more useful is *Computer-Readable Bibliographic Data Bases: A Directory and Data Sourcebook*, 1976- (American Society for Information Science). This is kept up to date by replacement pages every six months. The basic arrangement is alphabetical by names of data bases, but there is a subject index.

It should also be noted that many indexes available in print format (like *Arts and Humanities Citation Index*, 1978-) are also available for online searching. Most of these data bases are now available through large commercial vendors like Lockheed, Systems Development Corporation (SDC), and Bureau of Research Services (BRS).

2 GENERAL REFERENCE AND SELECTION AIDS IN THE HUMANITIES

1. **American Humanities Index**, 1975- . Q. Ann. cum. Whitston.
Designed for the scholar who needs access to the less well-known periodicals in the humanities, especially those with new poetry and short stories, this publication does not duplicate coverage in *The Humanities Index* (see item 10) or other major indexes. Beginning with 100 titles and 20,000 entries for 1975, coverage has been expanded to more than 300 periodicals. Subject entries are in full caps; author entries are in upper and lower case. Reviews are given under both the author of the work reviewed and the reviewer. Only articles dealing with reviewing in general will be found under "LITERARY CRITICISM," but individual poems are listed under "POEMS" and individual stories, under "STORIES" as well as under the authors' names.

2. **American Reference Books Annual**, 1970- . Ed. by Bohdan S. Wynar. Libraries Unlimited.
In a typical year, some 1,500 signed reviews of American reference books (and foreign works distributed in the United States) in all fields are included, as well as citations to reviews in ten periodicals heavily used by librarians. About 25 percent of the space is devoted to reviews of reference books in the humanities. These are easily located through the detailed table of contents, which directs the user to chapters on fine arts, applied arts, music, theatre, films, religion, philosophy, mythology, linguistics, and literature. Reviews of individual known titles can easily be found through the index. One can also consult *Index to American Reference Books Annual 1970-1974: A Cumulative Index to Subjects, Authors and Titles*, ed. by Joseph W. Sprug (Libraries Unlimited, 1974), and *Index to American Reference Books Annual 1975-1979: A Cumulative Index of Subjects, Authors, and Titles* (Libraries Unlimited, 1979), by Christine L. Wynar. The humanities take up approximately one-third of the space in *Best Reference Books: Titles of Lasting Value Selected from American Reference Books Annual 1970-1976*, ed. by Bohdan S. Wynar (Libraries Unlimited, 1976), which follows the classified arrangement of the parent work. Another source of annual evaluation, which always includes some titles in the humanities, is "Reference Books of 19--," compiled by the Outstanding Reference Books Committee, Reference and Adult Services Division, American Library Association, and published each year in the April 15 issue of *Library Journal*.

3. **Arts and Humanities Citation Index,** 1978- . 3/yr. (incl. ann. cum.). Institute for Scientific Information.

Follows the pattern established by *Science Citation Index* and *Social Sciences Citation Index*. Each issue includes a "Citation Index," a "Source Index," a "Corporate Index," and a "Permuterm Subject Index." If one already has the name of an author from a footnote, bibliography, or other source, check the "Citation Index" to determine who may have cited the work in question. More complete bibliographic information about any items of interest thus discovered will be found in the "Source Index." The "Corporate Index" is arranged by institutions or organizations first and then by authors. The theory behind this approach is that precision searching is possible because later authors will cite only those studies relevant to their research. Unlike the *Humanities Index* (item 10), subject indexing is done from key words in titles of articles rather than from a subject heading list. The result is less standardization, but more points of access. Some 800 journals are covered (compared to 260 in the *Humanities Index*). Issues are scheduled for June and October, with annual cumulations the following May. In addition, a retrospective volume for 1977 has recently appeard and further retrospective coverage is planned. General background information may be found in "Citation Indexes," by Marvin Weinstock, *Encyclopedia of Library and Information Science* (Marcel Dekker, 1971), v.5, pp. 16-40. New publications announced by the Institute for Scientific Information include *Current Contents/Arts and Humanities* (1979- .W.) and *Index to Social Sciences and Humanities Proceedings* (1979- . Q. Ann. cum.). The former displays tables of contents from about 950 journals and 125 books in "literature, history, literary reviews, philosophy, arts, music, humanities, religion, linguistics, poetry, theatre, film/radio/TV, classics, folklore, architecture and dance" (publisher's announcement). Each issue also contains a weekly subject index. The latter covers approximately 1,000 proceedings a year and provides six indexes (author, sponsor, general category, meeting location, title words, author's organizational affiliation) to approximately 20,000 individual papers annually.

4. **British Humanities Index,** 1962- . Q. Library Association.

Covers over 350 scholarly and popular periodicals dealing with the humanities (very broadly interpreted). Quarterly issues are arranged by subject. Annual cumulations have an author section in the back. Supersedes, in part, the *Subject Index to Periodicals*. Because it is confined to British titles, there is less overlap with the *Humanities Index* (item 10) than might otherwise be expected.

5. **Chicorel Index to Abstracting and Indexing Services: Periodicals in Humanities and Social Sciences.** Chicorel, 1974. 2v.

Tells where some 33,000 periodicals are indexed or abstracted. Covers 135 abstracting or indexing services, with addresses given in the back of the second volume. Dates of coverage are not given. Basic arrangement is alphabetical by title of periodical abstracted or indexed. There is no systematic differentiation between abstracting and indexing services, though many services provide the necessary information by including the word "abstract" or "index" in the title. Somewhat critically reviewed in *Choice* 11 (Oct. 1974):1106 — " . . . while there is some overlap with *Ulrich's*, Chicorel lists more services under individual serials; on the other hand, Chicorel's coverage is sometimes spotty. . . . Large libraries with very extensive reference collections will want the set since it does provide information not readily available elsewhere. . . ." Similar, though less critical, reviews appeared in *RQ* 14 (Winter 1974):165 and *Wilson Library Bulletin* 49 (Sept. 1974):89.

6. **Choice: Books for College Libraries,** 1964- . Mo./Bi-mo. (July-Aug.). Association of College and Research Libraries.

Reviews are done by librarians and college faculty. Subjects in the humanities regularly covered include: art, humanities (general), language and literature, performing arts, philosophy, and religion. The "Reference" section should be checked for new reference books in the humanities (as should issues of *Booklist, Library Journal, RQ,* and *Wilson Library Bulletin*). Though planned for college libraries, *Choice* has also proved useful for many public and university libraries. The earlier volumes are now available in *Choice: A Classified Cumulation,* ed. by Richard K. Gardner and Phyllis Grimm (Rowman and Littlefield, 1976-77, 9v.). Also useful for selection is *Books for College Libraries* (2nd ed., ALA, 1975, 6v.). Part I deals with the humanities and part II, with language and literature.

7. **Dictionary of the History of Ideas: Studies of Selected Pivotal Ideas,** ed. by Philip Wiener. Scribners, 1973-74. 5v.

Compiled by the editor of *Journal of the History of Ideas,* this interdisciplinary work contains over 300 articles (many of considerable length), arranged alphabetically and supplemented by an analytical table of contents and an alphabetical list of article titles. Articles are written by noted scholars and contain bibliographies. There are many cross references. The index volume appeared in 1974. Complementary coverage of twentieth-century ideas will be found in *The Harper Dictionary of Modern Thought,* ed. by Alan Bullock and Oliver Stallybrass (Harper, 1977). Coverage in a different format is provided by *Great Treasury of Western Thought,* ed. by Mortimer J. Adler and Charles Van Doren (Bowker, 1977), which is halfway between an anthology and a book of quotations. There are 20 chapters on major themes like man, family, love, etc. These are subdivided into 327 sections that contain prose and verse from 200 authors ranging in time from classical Greece to the twentieth century. The classified arrangement is supplemented by both an author index and an alphabetical subject and proper name index of some 50,000 entries. Useful for inspirational browsing as well as reference, this work generally does not duplicate standard books of quotations.

8. **Essay and General Literature Index, 1900-1933: An Index to about 40,000 Essays and Articles in 2,144 Volumes of Collections of Essays and Miscellaneous Works,** ed. by Minnie Earl Sears and Marian Shaw. Wilson, 1934. Suppls., 1934- .

Although heavily oriented toward literature, this index is also useful for searches in other areas of the humanities. The original work was a successor to *ALA Index . . . to General Literature* (2nd ed., ALA, 1901-1914). There is some overlap for the years 1900-1910. *EGLI* is kept up to date by semi-annual, annual, and quinquennial supplements. The dictionary arrangement (authors, titles, and subjects all in one alphabet) is supplemented by numerous cross references and an alphabetical listing by main entry of works indexed. A vital reference tool, especially for students who may need to read a particular essay in a limited period of time, *EGLI* is also used by many libraries as a selection device. It is supplemented by *Works Indexed 1900-1969* (Wilson, 1972). Another useful work for reference and selection purposes in the humanities is *The Reader's Adviser* (12th ed., Bowker, 1974-77, 3v.), especially v.1 (*The Best in*

American and British Fiction, Poetry, Essays, Literary Biography, Bibliography and Reference and v.2 (*The Best in American and British Drama and World Literature in English Translation*). Evaluative comments are particularly helpful in answering questions like, "Can you suggest a good book on _____?"

9. Harzfield, Luis A. **Periodical Indexes in the Social Sciences and Humanities: A Subject Guide.** Scarecrow, 1978. 174p.
Coverage includes approximately 200 sources, principally indexes and abstracting services, but also journals that reproduce tables of contents, some serial bibliographies, and some library catalogs that contain analytics and are updated regularly. It is divided into 48 subject sections, with good cross references.

10. **Humanities Index,** 1974- . Q. Ann. cum. Wilson.
Subtitle: "An author and subject index to periodicals in the fields of archaeology and classical studies, area studies, folklore, history, language and literature, literary and political criticism, performing arts, philosophy, religion and theology, and related subjects." Indexes 260 periodicals, of which 117 are from the *Social Sciences and Humanities Index* (1965-74) and 143 are new. Good, basic coverage of major journals, selected by librarians in the field. A first choice and first source unless it is known that the question is likely to involve little-known creative writers (*American Humanities Index* [item 1]), British topics and persons (*British Humanities Index* [item 4]), or alternative approaches to conventional indexing (*Arts and Humanities Citation Index* [item 3]).

11. Sheehy, Eugene P. **Guide to Reference Books.** 9th ed. ALA, 1976.
Beginning with the eighth edition in 1967, the arrangement of this massive standard source of information about reference books was modified to permit easier access to broad groups of related fields. The part on "The Humanities" (pp. 244-596) occupies approximately one-third of the volume and is subdivided into sections on philosophy, religion, linguistics and philology, literature, fine arts, applied arts, theater arts, and music. These are easily found through the detailed table of contents. Each entry has a subject code (letters and numbers) and LC classification number. Known works can be located through the index, which "includes author and subject entries, and most, but not all, title entries." Annotations are concise, usually descriptive. Updating is accomplished by columns in the January and July issues of *College and Research Libraries* and by biennial supplements. *Reference Books in the Social Sciences and Humanities*, by Rolland E. Stevens and Donald G. Davis, Jr. (4th ed. Stipes, 1977), is less comprehensive in its coverage of the humanities, but its excellent annotations are particularly helpful to students.

12. Walford, A. J. **Guide to Reference Material.** 3rd ed. Library Association, 1973-77. 3v.
Like Sheehy, this major compilation of information about reference books has been a standard source for several years. The humanities receive extensive coverage, partly in v.2 (*Social and Historical Sciences, Philosophy and Religion*) and mainly in v.3

(*Generalities, Languages, the Arts and Literature*). Entries are annotated and frequently cite reviews. British and European reference sources in the humanities are somewhat more heavily covered by Walford than by Sheehy.

13.   Young, Margaret Labash. **Subject Directory of Special Libraries and Information Centers.** 2nd ed. Gale, 1977. v.4 — **Social Sciences and Humanities Libraries.**
Some 14,000 libraries in the United States and Canada are described in *Directory of Special Libraries and Information Centers.* Here, the information is rearranged in a subject classification, with volume 4 covering the humanities and related areas. Within each subject category, U.S. libraries are given first, then Canadian libraries. Each sequence is arranged alphabetically by name of institution and name of library. Note that the table of contents is alphabetical rather than by order of appearance of the various subjects. Young's classified approach offers an alternative mode of access to the alphabetical subject arrangement of Lee Ash's *Subject Collections* (5th ed., Bowker, 1979), which is arranged by LC subject headings and then by states. Size of collection, nonbook holdings, and any photocopying or loan restrictions are given by Ash. Although relatively little will be found under general headings like "humanities," a wealth of information can be located under more specific headings in the various humanities disciplines. There is considerable, but by no means complete, duplication between Ash and Young. Small libraries may prefer Ash, but larger libraries will need both for reference and interlibrary loan purposes. Large libraries will also need Richard C. Lewanski's *Subject Collections in European Libraries* (2nd ed. Bowker, 1978), which is arranged in classified order, following the eighteenth edition of Dewey. About 12,000 libraries are included, with information on such topics as name, address, size of collection, date of founding, director, catalogs, and any restrictions on use.

3 ACCESSING INFORMATION IN PHILOSOPHY

MAJOR DIVISIONS OF THE FIELD

Although the term "philosophy" is derived from two Greek words usually translated as "love of wisdom," there is reason to believe that the original usage of the term was somewhat broader, connoting free play of the intellect over a wide range of human problems and even including such qualities as curiosity, shrewdness, and practicality. A gradual narrowing of meaning began in antiquity and has proceeded in stages until modern times. Socrates differentiated his activity from that of the sophists by stressing the raising of questions for clarification in the course of discussion, as distinct from giving authoritative answers or teaching techniques for winning arguments. This emphasis on critical examination of issues remained central to philosophic method in succeeding centuries. Encyclopedic concepts of philosophy were finally shattered by the rise of modern science in the seventeenth century. First, the natural sciences emerged as separate disciplines. Somewhat later, the social and behavioral sciences also effected their separation from philosophy.

What, then, is left? First, there are questions about the nature of ultimate reality. Then there is the matter of knowledge as a whole as well as interrelationships of the various specialized branches. Also, there are questions about the methodology and presuppositions of individual disciplines. The term "philosophy of . . ." is frequently assigned to this type of endeavor. Finally, with certain normative issues, no scientifically verifiable answers are available.

Philosophy today is customarily divided into five areas: metaphysics, epistemology, logic, ethics, and aesthetics. Metaphysics may be further subdivided into ontology and cosmology. Ontology is concerned with the nature of ultimate reality, or sometimes referred to as "being." It includes consideration of whether reality has one basic component (monism), two (dualism), or many (pluralism). Monistic philosophies discuss whether reality is ultimately mental or spiritual (idealism), or physical (materialism). Dualistic philosophies commonly regard both matter and mind as irreducible ultimate components. Cosmology is concerned with questions about origins and processes. The nature of causality has been a frequent topic for debate. Although a few have argued for pure chance, more philosophers have emphasized either

14

antecedent causes (i.e., preceding events that cause the event under consideration to happen) or final causes (ends or purposes that exert an influence on the
outcome of events). Many of the former persuasion are convinced that there is
no room for either chance or freedom in the chain of causality. These
determinists are called mechanists if they also believe that reality is ultimately
physical. Philosophers who emphasize final causes are known as teleologists.

Epistemology is concerned with the scope and limits of human
knowledge. What can we know? With what degree of certainty? Rationalists
stress the role of human reason. Empiricists emphasize the importance of data
derived from experience. It is generally agreed that there are two types of
knowledge: *a priori*, which is knowable without reference to experience and
which alone possesses theoretical certainty (e.g., the principles of logic and
mathematics); and *a posteriori*, which is derived from experience and possesses
only approximate certainty (e.g., the findings of the sciences).

Logic deals with the principles of correct reasoning or valid inference. It
differs from psychology in that it does not describe how people actually think
but prescribes certain canons to be followed if they would think correctly.
Deductive logic (sometimes known as Aristotelian or traditional logic) arose in
antiquity and is concerned with the process by which correct conclusions can
be drawn from sets of axioms known or believed to be true. Its most familiar
form is the syllogism, which consists of three parts: a major premise, a minor
premise, and a conclusion:

> All men are mortal.
> Socrates is a man.
> Therefore, Socrates is mortal.

Inductive logic is a result of the development of modern scientific methods. It
deals with the canons of valid inference, but is concerned with probabilities
rather than certainties and frequently involves the use of statistics. It is, in a
sense, the opposite of deductive logic (which proceeds from the general to the
particular) in that it attempts to reach valid generalizations from an enumeration of particulars.

In ethics, the questions relate to matters of conduct. Can certain actions
be considered morally right or wrong? If so, on what basis? Should the interests of the self have priority (egoism)? Or the interests of others (altruism)? Or
is there some greater good (*summum bonum*) to which both should be subor-
dinate? Ethical theories may be classified by the manner in which criteria for
right actions are discovered or by the nature of the highest good. In the first
group, authoritarians stress submission to the will of God or some other external authority. Rationalists stress the free activity of the mind in examining all
aspects of a question. Intuitionists stress the importance of obedience to cons-
cience. Emotive theorists stress feeling as the proper ground for ethical
decision-making. In the second classification, hedonists regard pleasure as the
highest good. Eudaemonists pursue happiness. Perfectionists seek the ideal

fulfillment of human life. Kantians stress purity of motive and universalizability of individual ethical decisions.

The nature of beauty is the subject matter of aesthetics. The concerns of the philosopher may be differentiated from those of the psychologist and those of the critic. The psychologist concentrates on human reactions to aesthetic objects. The critic focuses on individual works of art or on general principles of criticism, usually within the confines of a particular discipline. The philosopher is broadly concerned with beauty per se, whether in art or nature. Does beauty inhere in the beautiful object? Are there objective criteria by which it may be determined? Or is beauty a subjective experience, with no universally valid norms? Classical theories tend to stress objectivity. Romantic theories emphasize individualism and subjectivity.

The student desiring a concise introduction should read the article "Philosophy," by C. I. Lewis, in the *Encyclopedia Americana* (1978 ed.), v. 21, pp. 769-77 or the article "Philosophy," by John Passmore, in *The Encyclopedia of Philosophy* (Macmillan, 1967), v. 6, pp. 216-26. More depth on the history of philosophy is given by the authors of "Philosophy, History of Western" in *The Encyclopaedia Britannica: Macropaedia* (15th ed., 1974), v. 14, pp. 247-75 and by S. N. Hampshire's "Philosophy, History of" in the *Encyclopedia Americana* (1978 ed.), v. 21, pp. 777-82. A more specialized aspect is covered by John Passmore's "Philosophy, Historiography of" in *The Encyclopedia of Philosophy* (Macmillan, 1967), v. 6, pp. 226-30. In the same volume of *The Encyclopedia of Philosophy*, William Gerber's three articles will be found to be of special importance for librarians: "Philosophical Bibliographies," pp. 166-69; "Philosophical Dictionaries and Encyclopedias," pp. 170-99; and "Philosophical Journals," pp. 199-216. There are also articles on related topics, like the philosophy of education, law, and religion. The chapter on "Philosophy" in Lester Asheim's *The Humanities and the Library* (pp. 61-99) is especially valuable.

Many of the best introductions and histories in philosophy are so technical as to be forbidding to the average layperson. An exception is Bertrand Russell's *A History of Western Philosophy* (Simon & Schuster, 1945), which is competently written in the lively, opinionated style for which Russell was justly famous. Less competently done, but very popular, is Will Durant's *The Story of Philosophy* (Simon & Schuster, 1926).

MAJOR CLASSIFICATION SCHEMES

Utilization of shelf arrangement as a tool for philosophic information retrieval must be considered secondary to other approaches, but some knowledge of the major library classification schemes will be advantageous. In order of approximate frequency of use, these are: The Dewey Decimal Classification (DDC) and the Library of Congress Classification (LC).

From the standpoint of user needs, there are three principal approaches to the arrangement of philosophic writings: 1) By individual philosophers. This approach is particularly helpful for those who wish to study either the total thought system of a philosopher or a particular work. It is doubly helpful if secondary works (commentaries, criticism, etc.) are also shelved with the primary sources. 2) By specialized branches of the discipline (metaphysics, epistemology, logic, ethics, aesthetics). 3) By interrelationships and influences (periods, schools of thought, language and nationality groupings, etc.). Most classification systems attempt to achieve some balance among these differing (and somewhat conflicting) approaches.

First devised by Melvil Dewey in 1876, the Decimal Classification (DDC) has been frequently updated and expanded. The section on philosophy (100-199) is the least successful; the latest edition (19th), by its inclusion of psychology, still reflects a late nineteenth century view of the world. It is frequently criticized for its separation of philosophical viewpoints from the sections on ancient, medieval, and modern philosophy, and for its failure to include a section on aesthetics (which DDC places with the arts in the 700s). Nevertheless, it is the most commonly used library classification system. Examples illustrating the major divisions and selected subdivisions are shown below.

100	PHILOSOPHY AND RELATED DISCIPLINES	142	Critical philosophy
101	Theory of philosophy	143	Intuitionism and Bergsonism
103	Dictionaries of philosophy	144	Humanism and related systems
105	Serials on philosophy	145	Sensationalism and ideology
106	Organizations of philosophy	146	Naturalism and related systems
107	Study and teaching of philosophy	147	Pantheism and related systems
109	Historical treatment of philosophy	148	Liberalism and other systems
		149	Other systems and doctrines
110	METAPHYSICS		
111	Ontology	150	PSYCHOLOGY
113	Cosmology		
114	Space	160	LOGIC
115	Time	161	Induction
116	Evolution	162	Deduction
117	Structure	165	Fallacies and sources of error
118	Force and energy	166	Syllogisms
119	Number and quantity	167	Hypotheses
		168	Argument and persuasion
120	EPISTEMOLOGY, CAUSATION HUMANKIND	169	Analogy
121	Epistemology	170	ETHICS
122	Causation	171	Systems and doctrines
123	Determinism and indeterminism	172	Political ethics
		173	Ethics of family relationships
130	PARANORMAL PHENOMENA AND ARTS	174	Economic, professional and occupational ethics
		175	Ethics of recreation and leisure
		176	Ethics of sex and reproduction
140	SPECIFIC PHILOSOPHICAL VIEWPOINTS	177	Ethics of social relations
141	Idealism and related systems and doctrines	178	Ethics of consumption
		179	Other ethical norms

(List continues on page 18)

180	ANCIENT, MEDIEVAL, ORIENTAL PHILOSOPHY	190	MODERN WESTERN PHILOSOPHY
181	Oriental	191	United States and Canada
182	Pre-Socratic Greek	192	British Isles
183	Sophistic, Socratic and related Greek	193	Germany and Austria
184	Platonic	194	France
185	Aristotelian	195	Italy
186	Skeptic and Neoplatonic	196	Spain and Portugal
187	Epicurean	197	Russia and Finland
188	Stoic	198	Scandinavia
189	Medieval Western	199	Other countries

The Library of Congress (LC) schedule for philosophy was first published in 1910 and revised in 1950. LC includes psychology, but otherwise is generally superior to DDC. Subclass B is designed to keep the works of individual philosophers together and to place philosophers in relation to periods, countries, and schools of thought. The general pattern for individual philosophers is 1) collected works, 2) separate works, 3) biography and criticism. LC also has sections for the major divisions of the field (including aesthetics). The principal divisions are shown in the synopsis below:

B	**PHILOSOPHY (GENERAL)**
	Serials, Collections, etc.
	History and systems
BC	LOGIC
BD	SPECULATIVE PHILOSOPHY
	General philosophical works
	Metaphysics
	Epistemology
	Methodology
	Ontology
	Cosmology
BF	PSYCHOLOGY
	Parapsychology
	Occult sciences
BH	AESTHETICS
BJ	ETHICS
	Social usages, Etiquette

Although some special philosophy classifications have been developed, their use appears to have been confined to the arrangement of certain bibliographies.

SUBJECT HEADINGS FREQUENTLY USED

Searching library catalogs (whether in card, book, or computer form) continues to play an important role in the retrieval of philosophical information. Although many subject indexes in recent years have been constructed on the basis of key words from document titles, or from text, most library subject catalogs use a controlled or standardized vocabulary embodies in a list of subject headings. Such lists usually include guidance on choice of main headings, methods of subdividing major topics, and cross references to lead the user to the headings chosen or to related topics.

The overwhelming majority of large American libraries today follow the *Subject Headings Used in the Dictionary Catalogs of the Library of Congress* (8th ed. LC, 1975) or its machine-readable counterpart. These headings enable the reader looking for a specific topic in philosophy to go directly to that heading. The disadvantage is that philosophic topics are scattered throughout an entire alphabetical sequence. This is true whether the library uses a "dictionary" catalog (in which entries for authors, titles, and subjects are interfiled in one alphabetical sequence) or a "divided" catalog (in which author and title entries are separated from the alphabetical subject portion).

This chapter includes some information that will not be repeated in later chapters on accessing information. Examples of subject headings in philosophy are provided, reproduced from the eighth edition of *Subject Headings Used in the Dictionary Catalogs of the Library of Congress*. These examples are followed by a discussion (see page 24) of the basic principles, based on *Subject Headings: A Practical Guide*, by David Judson Haykin (GPO, 1951) and updated from information contained in *Library of Congress Subject Headings: Principles and Application*, by Lois M. Chan (Libraries Unlimited, 1978). Haykin, as chief of the Subject Cataloging Division of LC, helped to shape the system he described.

Library of Congress Subject Headings in Philosophy

Philosophers *(Direct)*
  sa Alchemists
    Logicians
  x Philosophy—Biography
  — Biography
  — Correspondence, reminiscences, etc.
  — Relationship with women
Philosophers, Ancient *(B108-708)*
  — Anecdotes, facetiae, satire, etc.
Philosophers, Islamic
  See Philosophers, Muslim
Philosophers, Medieval *(B720-785)*
Philosophers, Modern
  x Modern philosophers
Philosophers, Muslim
  x Islamic philosophers
    Muslim philosophers
    Philosophers, Islamic
Philosophers' egg
  See Alchemy
Philosophers' stone
  See Alchemy
Philosophical analysis
  See Analysis (Philosophy)

Philosophical anthropology *(BD450)*
  sa Fallibility
    Humanism
    Man—Animal nature
    Man (Theology)
    Mind and body
    Persons
  x Anthropology, Philosophical
    Man (Philosophy)
  xx Civilization—Philosophy
    Humanism
    Life
    Man
    Ontology
    Persons
Philosophical grammar
  See Grammar, Comparative and general
Philosophical literature
  xx Philosophy—History
Philosophical theology *(BT40)*
  x Theology, Philosophical
  xx Christianity—Philosophy
    Natural theology
    Philosophy
    Philosophy and religion
    Religion—Philosophy
    Theology, Doctrinal

(Example continues on page 20)

Library of Congress Subject Headings in Philosophy (cont'd)

Philosophy *(B-BJ)*
  sa Act (Philosophy)
    Aesthetics
    Agent (Philosophy)
    Alienation (Philosophy)
    Analysis (Philosophy)
    Atomism
    Authenticity (Philosophy)
    Axioms
    Banality (Philosophy)
    Belief and doubt
    Causation
    Comparison (Philosophy)
    Consciousness
    Constitution (Philosophy)
    Construction (Philosophy)
    Contradiction
    Convention (Philosophy)
    Cosmology
    Creation
    Criticism (Philosophy)
    Cycles
    Depth (Philosophy)
    Description (Philosophy)
    Difference (Philosophy)
    Dualism
    Egoism
    Ends and means
    Epiphanism
    Essence (Philosophy)
    Ethics
    Evidence
    Exact (Philosophy)
    Experience
    Expression (Philosophy)
    Extension (Philosophy)
    Facts (Philosophy)
    Fate and fatalism
    Free will and determinism
    Gnosticism
    God
    Good and evil
    Hedonism
    Humanism
    Hylozoism
    Idea (Philosophy)
    Idealism
    Ideals (Philosophy)
    Ideology
    Immortality (Philosophy)
    Individuation
    Infallibility (Philosophy)
    Interaction (Philosophy)
    Intuition
    Irrationalism (Philosophy)
    Isolation (Philosophy)

Knowledge, Theory of
Law (Philosophy)
Logic
Many (Philosophy)
Materialism
Mean (Philosophy)
Meaning (Philosophy)
Meaningless (Philosophy)
Mechanism (Philosophy)
Metaphysics
Mind and body
Monadology
Monism
Mysticism
Naturalism
Negativity (Philosophy)
Neoplatonism
Nihilism (Philosophy)
Nominalism
Object (Philosophy)
One (The One in philosophy)
Ontology
Opposition, Theory of
Optimism
Order (Philosophy)
Organism (Philosophy)
Panpsychism
Pantheism
Participation
Peace (Philosophy)
Perception
Personalism
Perspective (Philosophy)
Pessimism
Phenomenalism
Philosophical theology
Platonists
Pluralism
Polarity (Philosophy)
Positivism
Power (Philosophy)
Practice (Philosophy)
Pragmatism
Principle (Philosophy)
Process philosophy
Psychology
Purity (Philosophy)
Quality (Philosophy)
Quantity (Philosophy)
Rationalism
Reaction (Philosophy)
Realism
Reality
Reflection (Philosophy)
Relation (Philosophy)
Relevance (Philosophy)

Library of Congress Subject Headings in Philosophy (cont'd)

Repetition (Philosophy)
Scholasticism
Self (Philosophy)
Situation (Philosophy)
Skepticism
Soul
Space and time
Spiritualism (Philosophy)
Structuralism
Style (Philosophy)
Subject (Philosophy)
Sufficient reason
Teleology
Theism
Theory (Philosophy)
Thomists
Thought and thinking
Tradition (Philosophy)
Transcendentalism
Truth
Universals (Philosophy)
Utilitarianism
War (Philosophy)
Whole and parts (Philosophy)
Will
Wonder (Philosophy)
subdivision Philosophy *under subjects,*
    e.g. Art—Philosophy
x Mental philosophy
xx Cosmology
    Ontology
— Authorship
— Biography
    See Philosophers
— Book reviews
— Historiography *(B51.4-6)*
— History *(Indirect)* *(B69-4695)*
    sa Philosophical literature
— — Methodology *(B53)*
— Introductions *(BD10-28)*
— Methodology
    See Methodology
— Miscellanea *(B68)*
— Pictures, illustrations, etc. *(B51.8)*
— Quotations, maxims, etc.
— Study and teaching *(Direct)* *(B52)*
— Terminology *(B49-50)*
Philosophy, American *(B851-945)*
  sa Mercersburg theology
    Messianism, American
Philosophy, American, [Arab, Chinese, etc.]
  x American [Arab, Chinese, etc.]
    philosophy
— Book reviews
Philosophy, Analytical
  See Analysis (Philosophy)

Philosophy, Ancient *(B108-708)*
  Here are entered works dealing with ancient philosophy in general and with
  Greek and Roman philosophy in particular.
  sa Ataraxia
    Atomism
    Diaeresis (Philosophy)
    Eleatics
    Gnosticism
    Manichaeism
    Megarians (Greek philosophy)
    Neoplatonism
    Peripatetics
    Platonists
    Pythagoras and Pythagorean school
    Science, Ancient
    Skeptics (Greek philosophy)
    Sophists (Greek philosophy)
    Stoics
  x Greek philosophy
    Philosophy, Greek
    Philosophy, Roman
    Roman philosophy
— Oriental influences
  xx Civilization, Oriental
Philosophy, Arab *(Medieval, B740-753)*
  sa Philosophy, Islamic
  x Arabic philosophy
    Philosophy, Arabic
Philosophy, Arabic
  See Philosophy, Arab
    Philosophy, Islamic
Philosophy, Buddhist *(B123)*
  sa Abhidharma
    Anātman
    Ātman
    Buddha and Buddhism—Early
      Buddhism, ca. 486 B.C.-ca. 100 A.D.
    Buddha and Buddhism—Philosophy
    Buddhist doctrines
    Buddhist logic
    Cosmogony, Buddhist
    Cosmology, Buddhist
    Knowledge, Theory of (Buddhism)
    Mādhyamika (Buddhism)
    Man (Buddhism)
    Matter (Buddhism)
    No-mind (Buddhism)
    Philosophy, Indic
    Pratyaya
    Sunyata
    Time (Buddhism)
    Truth (Buddhism)
    Vijñaptimātratā
    Wisdom (Buddhism)

(Example continues on page 22)

Library of Congress Subject Headings in Philosophy (cont'd)

Yogācāra (Buddhism)
  x Buddhist philosophy
  xx Buddha and Buddhism
     Philosophy, Hindu
     Philosophy, Indic
  — Introductions
Philosophy, Chinese
  sa Neo-Confucianism
     Philosophy, Confucian
     Philosophy, Taoist
     Tao
  — 20th century
Philosophy, Comparative *(B799)*
  sa Ethics, Comparative
  x Comparative philosophy
  xx East and West
     Philosophy, Oriental
Philosophy, Confucian *(Direct)* *(B128.C8)*
  sa Confucianists
     Jen
  x Confucian philosophy
  xx Confucianism
     Philosophy, Chinese
Philosophy, Czech
  — 19th century
Philosophy, Doctor of
  See Doctor of philosophy degree
Philosophy, East Indian
  See Philosophy, Indic
Philosophy, English
  xx Philosophy, Modern
  — 13th century
  — 16th century *(B776.E5)*
  — 17th century *(B1131-1299)*
  — 18th century *(B1300-1559)*
  — 19th century *(B1573-1612)*
  — 20th century *(B1614-1674)*
Philosophy, French
  sa Libertines (French philosophers)
  xx Philosophy, Modern
  — 16th century
  — 17th century *(B1815-1818)*
  — 18th century *(B1911-1925)*
  — 19th century *(B2185-8)*
  — 20th century *(B2421-4)*
Philosophy, German
  xx Philosophy, Modern
  — 18th century
Philosophy, Greek
  See Philosophy, Ancient
Philosophy, Hindu
  sa Advaita
     Anātman
     Ātman
     Cosmology, Hindu
     Dharma
     Dvaita (Vedanta)

Hindu logic
  Knowledge, Theory of (Hinduism)
  Lokāyata
  Maya (Hinduism)
  Nyaya
  Philosophy, Buddhist
  Philosophy, Indic
  Yoga
  xx Philosophy, Indic
  — Terminology
Philosophy, Indic *(B130-133)*
  sa Avidyā
     Mokṣa
     Philosophy, Buddhist
     Philosophy, Hindu
  x East Indian philosophy
     Indic philosophy
     Philosophy, East Indian
  xx Philosophy, Buddhist
     Philosophy, Hindu
  — Modern period, 1600-
  — 20th century
Philosophy, Islamic *(Direct)* *(B163;*
     Medieval, B740-753)
  sa Cosmology, Islamic
     Islam and philosophy
     Islamic ethics
     Knowledge, Theory of (Islam)
  x Arabic philosophy
     Islamic philosophy
     Muslim philosophy
     Philosophy, Arabic
     Philosophy, Muslim
  xx Philosophy, Arab
  — Greek [etc.] influences
Philosophy, Italian
  — 17th century
  — 18th century
  — 19th century
  — 20th century
Philosophy, Jaina *(B162.5)*
  sa Jaina logic
  x Jaina philosophy
Philosophy, Japanese
  sa Kokugaku
     Mitogaku
     Yōmeigaku
  — 19th century
  — 20th century
Philosophy, Jewish
  sa Cosmology, Jewish
     Hasidism—Philosophy
     Judaism and philosophy
  x Jewish philosophy
     Jews—Philosophy
  xx Bible—Philosophy
Philosophy, Mechanistic
  See Mechanism (Philosophy)

Library of Congress Subject Headings in Philosophy (cont'd)

Philosophy, Medieval *(B720-785)*
 sa Scholasticism
  Summists
  Thomists
 xx Scholasticism
Philosophy, Modern *(B790-4695)*
 sa Evolution
  Existentialism
  Humanism—20th century
  Humanism, Religious
  Neo-Scholasticism
  Phenomenology
  Positivism
  Pragmatism
  Semantics (Philosophy)
  Transcendentalism
  Philosophy, English, [French, German, etc.]
 x Modern philosophy
 — 16th century
  See Philosophy, Renaissance
 — 17th century *(B801)*
 — 18th century *(B802)*
  sa Enlightenment
 — 19th century *(B803)*
 — 20th century *(B804)*
Philosophy, Moral
 See Ethics
Philosophy, Muslim
 See Philosophy, Islamic
Philosophy, Natural
 See Physics
Philosophy, Oriental *(B121)*
 sa Philosophy, Comparative
 x Oriental philosophy
Philosophy, Patristic
 See Fathers of the church
Philosophy, Polish
 sa Messianism, Polish
Philosophy, Primitive *(GN470)*
 sa Classification, Primitive
  Indians of South America—Philosophy
Philosophy, Renaissance *(B770-785)*
 x Philosophy, Modern—16th century
  Renaissance philosophy
Philosophy, Roman
 See Philosophy, Ancient
Philosophy, Shinto *(B162.6)*
 x Shinto philosophy
Philosophy, Sikh
 sa Sikh ethics
 x Sikh philosophy
 xx Sikhism
Philosophy, Taoist *(B163)*
 x Taoist philosophy
 xx Philosophy, Chinese
Philosophy and astronomy
 See Astronomy—Philosophy

Philosophy and Islam
 See Islam and philosophy
Philosophy and Judaism
 See Judaism and philosophy
Philosophy and religion
 sa Buddha and Buddhism—Philosophy
  Catholic Church and philosophy
  Faith and reason
  Islam and philosophy
  Judaism and philosophy
  Philosophical theology
  Religion—Philosophy
 x Christianity and philosophy
  Religion and philosophy
 xx Religion—Philosophy
 Note under Faith and reason
Philosophy and science
 See Science—Philosophy
Philosophy and the Catholic Church
 See Catholic Church and philosophy
Philosophy and the Koran
 See Koran and philosophy
Philosophy in literature *(PN49)*
 sa Existentialism in literature
Philosophy of history
 See History—Philosophy
Philosophy of international law
 See International law—Philosophy
Philosophy of language
 See Languages—Philosophy
Philosophy of law
 See Law—Philosophy
Philosophy of literature
 See Literature—Philosophy
Philosophy of medicine
 See Medicine—Philosophy
Philosophy of nature *(BD581)*
 sa Cosmology
  Natural theology
  Nature (Aesthetics)
  Nature—Religious interpretations
  Nature (Theology)
  Uniformity of nature
 x Nature—Philosophy
  Nature, Philosophy of
 xx Cosmology
  Natural theology
 — Early works to 1800
Philosophy of psychiatry
 See Psychiatry—Philosophy
Philosophy of rhetoric
 See Rhetoric—Philosophy
Philosophy of teaching
 See Education—Philosophy
Philosophy, Hindu
 sa Vaiśeṣika

(Text continues on page 24)

To use these headings as a guide in the formulation of a search strategy, it is helpful to understand the basic forms subject headings may take:

1. **Simple nouns as headings.** This form is the most direct, immediate, and uncomplicated. If adequate to the task, it is normally preferred. The most obvious example, in this context, is "Philosophy."

2. **Adjectival headings.** These may be in natural or inverted form. An example of the natural form would be "Philosophical anthropology"; an example of the inverted form would be "Philosophy, American." The choice is determined by the need to emphasize those search words of greatest importance to the intended user. In the first example, the word "philosophical" is more significant to the philosophy student than the word "anthropology." In the second example, the word "American" would be of significance to the person seeking information on American philosophy, but the natural order would bury the topic among dozens (perhaps hundreds) of other entries beginning with "American." Since the prime topic is philosophy, with American philosophy as one variety, the inverted form is chosen.

3. **Phrase headings.** These usually consist of nouns connected by a preposition. An example would be "Philosophy in literature." Sometimes, it is necessary to invert the natural word order to emphasize a key search term. There is no ready example from the philosophy list, but an example from another field would be "Plants, Protection of." Another type of phrase heading is the so-called "compound heading," which is made up of two or more coordinate elements connected by "and." An example from the list would be "Philosophy and religion."

It frequently happens that the approaches described above do not result in headings that are sufficiently specific. In such cases, further division of the topic will be required. The techniques most frequently used for division are as follows:

1. **By form.** This plan of division is not based on the content of a work but on its manner of arrangement or the purpose it is intended to serve. Examples would include:

> Philosophy—Bibliography
> Philosophy—Dictionaries
> Philosophy—Directories
> Philosophy—Outlines, Syllabi, etc.
> Philosophy—Study and teaching.

2. **By political or geographic area.** Formerly, there were two principal methods of local division: direct and indirect. If the direct method was used, the name of a specific place occurred immediately after the dash, indicating a division of the main heading. If the indirect approach was chosen, the name of

a country or larger unit was inserted between the main heading and the specific place. Places likely to be familiar to American users were entered directly. Places less likely to be familiar will be entered indirectly. The lack of clear criteria for differentiation and the advent of machine-readable cataloging records produced pressure for greater uniformity. Since 1975, the Library of Congress has moved to the indirect method of subdivision with a few minor exceptions. Philosophy is not the best subject to choose for examples, since the need for geographic subdivision in philosophy is largely achieved in another way — namely, by use of the inverted form of adjectival headings, such as "Philosophy, English," or "Philosophy, French." There is one area of philosophy, however, in which the principle of local or geographic division can be illustrated. From the list on page 21, we note that "Philosophy — History" is to be further subdivided by using the indirect method. Thus, a book dealing with the history of philosophy in Padua would appear under the subject heading "Philosophy — History — Italy — Padua."

3. **By period.** This represents a departure from the customary alphabetical approach in that headings for generally accepted historical periods are arranged *chronologically*. In philosophy, this technique is used to subdivide under the different countries. Thus, we find that "Philosophy, French — 17th century" precedes "Philosophy, French — 18th century" although an alphabetical arrangement would have reversed that order. It should be noted, however, that very broad periods for philosophy as a whole are filed in *alphabetical* sequence. Thus, "Philosophy, Ancient" precedes "Philosophy, Arab," and "Philosophy, Medieval" follows "Philosophy, Jewish."

It should also be noted that any formal list of subject headings will not include one very large category of subject entries — individual names as subjects. These may be personal (e.g., "James, William") or corporate (e.g., "American Philosophical Association"). In the case of very prominent or prolific writers, the entries may be further subdivided — e.g., "Dewey, John — - Addresses, essays, lectures."

A subject heading system must make provision for the user who may choose as his initial search term a word or phrase other than the one used in the system. Usually this will be a synonym for the term chosen. The necessary connections are provided by means of "see" references, which direct the reader from headings not used to those that are used. In the list of LC subject headings provided above, the chosen terms are given in bold type and other terms in lighter type. The cross reference "Philosophy — Biography. *See* Philosophers" is given in light type. The heading "Philosophers" appears in bold type. Under this heading in bold type is the following entry in light type: "*x* Philosophy — Biography." The symbol "*x*" is used to indicate that a "see" reference has been made from "Philosophy — Biography" to "Philosophers."

A subject heading system also provides the user with access to other headings that might lead to relevant information. This is done by means of "see also" references. These may direct the user to other topics of equal breadth and scope, or they may direct him to more specific subjects. A good example of the latter type is the list of more than 75 specific "see also" references under "Philosophy." (The symbol "*sa*" preceding this list indicates that these are "see also" references.) It is customary to enumerate all of these specific headings, which will be found elsewhere in the catalog. Sometimes, a more generalized kind of "see also" references are given after the full enumeration of specific "see also" references. An example of this type of heading from the philosophy list occurs under "Philosophy, Modern." After an enumeration of 10 specific "see also" references, this general "see also" reference is given: "Philosophy, English [French, German, etc.]."

The symbol "*xx*" is used to indicate the reverse pattern of "see also" references and is sometimes defined as "see also from." Thus, under "Philosophy," there occurs "*xx* Cosmology." This means that there will be a cross reference "Cosmology. *See also* Philosophy" in the catalog.

To remove doubt or confusion about what may or may not be covered by certain subject headings, scope notes are provided. These are relatively infrequent, usually noting limitations and sometimes referring to other entries. An example from the 1975 list may be found under "Philosophy, Ancient."

Comparison of the list reproduced above with the subject catalog of a medium-sized or larger library will make it apparent that many more headings are used in practice than are enumerated in the list. Most of these headings are formed in accordance with the principles already discussed and can readily be anticipated by the searcher who understands these principles. Checking the *Library of Congress Catalogs: Subject Catalog* will reveal examples. It should be noted, however, that new terms are constantly coming into use and older terms are being revised or deleted. Even in a relatively stable field like philosophy half a dozen to a dozen changes will typically be reported in each new supplement to *Subject Headings Used in the Dictionary Catalogs of the Library of Congress*. One such change was the cancellation of the heading "Philosophy, Mohammedan" and the substitution of the more modern "Philosophy, Islamic."

Ease and precision in philosophic information retrieval will be greatly facilitated by understanding the filing system used in a particular library. The dictionary catalog or the subject portion of a divided catalog will normally follow an alphabetical arrangement, but a chronological arrangement is used wherever a division by date seems more logical than a strictly alphabetical sequence.

Alphabetical arrangements usually follow one of two patterns. The first is the so-called "letter-by-letter" method used in many reference tools, including several indexes and encyclopedias. With this method, all the words in the heading are treated as parts of one unit. Filing proceeds strictly on the basis of the order of the letters in the unit as a whole, regardless of whether they are in separate short words or in a single long word. Thus, "Newark" would precede "New York." Libraries have not favored this method because it tends to scatter closely related topics. Instead, most libraries have adopted the "word by word" or "nothing before something" approach, in which each word is treated as a separate unit for filing purposes. Using this method, "New York" would precede "Newark" in the catalog. Within this general framework of "word by word" filing, the Library of Congress has developed the following sequence for subject headings:

1. Main heading alone;
2. Main heading plus time subdivisions (if applicable) — indicated by dashes;
3. Main heading plus form and subject subdivisions (interfiled alphabetically) — indicated by dashes;
4. Main heading plus geographic subdivisions (if applicable) — also indicated by dashes;
5. Inversions, indicated by commas;
6. Phrases.

As noted above, a chronological arrangement is used whenever a division by date seems more logical than a strictly alphabetical sequence. In philosophy, the practice is not altogether consistent. Broad periods, with definitely assignable names, are filed in alphabetical sequence with other inverted headings (e.g., "Philosophy, Ancient," "Philosophy, Medieval," and "Philosophy, Modern"). But the last-named is then subdivided chronologically (e.g., "Philosophy, Modern — 16th century," "Philosophy, Modern — 17th century," etc.). Period subdivisions are also used under the headings for philosophy in different countries (e.g., "Philosophy, French — 20th century").

MAJOR PHILOSOPHICAL SOCIETIES, INFORMATION CENTERS, AND SPECIAL COLLECTIONS

It has become a truism to say that the competent reference librarian will utilize information sources beyond the collections of one library. The role of bibliographies, indexes, and union catalogs in this process is already familiar and need not be elaborated here. What may be of assistance, however, is some discussion of supplementary information sources. In philosophy, these may be roughly grouped into three categories: philosophical societies, information centers, and special collections. Each of these will be examined. No attempt at completeness will be made; rather, a sampling of major sources will be offered, together with some suggestions about where additional information may be found.

Unesco has supported international philosophical activities in a variety of ways. In 1946, it recognized the International Council of Scientific Unions (The Hague) as a coordinating body. One of its branches is the International Union of the History and Philosophy of Science (Paris), which in turn has national committees in over 25 countries and which maintains affiliations with a variety of national and international organizations. Another organization recognized by Unesco is the International Council for Philosophy and Humanistic Studies (Paris). This Council is composed of many international non-governmental organizations, such as the International Union of Academies (Brussels) and the International Federation of Societies of Philosophy (Brussels). The latter, composed of approximately 90 philosophical societies in more than 35 countries, sponsors international congresses every five years. Unesco also provides grants for the activities of some of these groups and for certain philosophical documentation centers.

Further details concerning international philosophical societies and leading national philosophical groups outside North America may be found in *International Directory of Philosophy and Philosophers 1979-81*. Current information concerning philosophical congresses can be found in the "Chroniques" section of *Revue philosophique de Louvain*.

The most comprehensive philosophical society in the United States is the American Philosophical Association, founded in 1900 to promote not only the exchange of ideas among philosophers but also creative and scholarly activity in philosophy. Its membership (about 3,800) is restricted to those qualified to teach philosophy at the college or university level. In addition to the national officers (chairman and secretary), there are officers for three regional divisions (Eastern, Western, and Pacific), each of which sponsors an annual conference. Publications include *Proceedings and Addresses of the American Philosophical Association*, *Jobs in Philosophy*, and *APA Bulletin*.

Phi Sigma Tau was founded in 1931 to promote ties nationally between philosophy students and departments of philosophy. It publishes *Dialogue* and a *Newsletter*.

Another major organization is the American Catholic Philosophical Association, founded in 1926, with a current membership of over 1,600. Its publications include *The New Scholasticism* and *Proceedings of the American Catholic Philosophical Association*.

There are also many specialized societies. Sometimes, the interest centers on a particular philosopher (e.g., Hegel, or Dewey); sometimes, it is focused on a particular topic (like phenomenology and existential philosophy). A number of local, state, or regional groups complete the picture. Further details may be found in the "Societies" section of the *Directory of American Philosophers 1978/79* or in subsequent issues of this biennial publication.

There are several information centers actively at work in philosophy. In a number of cases, advanced computerized techniques are used for information retrieval and/or production of publications.

The Philosophy Documentation Center (Bowling Green State University, Bowling Green, Ohio 43404) exists to collect, store, and disseminate bibliographic data in philosophy. It issues a quarterly publication (cumulated annually) entitled *The Philosopher's Index*, which is a subject and author index with abstracts. Computerized searches of the data base are also possible.

The Philosophy Information Center (Philosophy Institute, University of Düsseldorf, Düsseldorf, West Germany) cooperates in the production of *The Philosopher's Index* by providing subject headings and abstracts of articles published in all German journals. The Center also makes use of a Siemens computer to produce its own series of bibliographies and indexes, such as *Gesamtregister zur Zeitschrift für Philosophische Forschung 1-21 (1946-1967)* and *Gesamtregister der Kant-Studien* (v. 1, 1897-1925; v. 2, 1926-1969).

Le Centre Nationale de la Recherche Scientifique, through its Centre de Documentation, Sciences Humaines (54, Boulevard Raspall, Paris VIe, France), lists or abstracts periodical articles in its *Bulletin signalétique—Section philosophie*, a quarterly publication with annual cumulative indexes. The Director of this center, Mme. L. Cadoux, also supervises the Cercle Internationale de Recherches Philosophiques par Ordinateur (CIRPHO), a new organization to promote philosophical research which arose out of the Montreal Congress (1971) of the Congrès des Sociétés de Philosophie de Langue Francaise.

Over 25 national centers participate in the work of L'Institut International de Philosophie (173, Boulevard Saint-Germain, 75-Paris-06, France), which publishes a quarterly bulletin entitled *Bibliographie de la philosophie* with the aid of a grant from Unesco and which cooperates with L'Institut Supérieure de Philosophie de l'Université Catholique de Louvain in publication of *Répertoire bibliographique de la philosophie*, which is also subsidized by Unesco.

Although not concerned solely with philosophy, the Institute of East European Studies (University of Fribourg, Switzerland) is a major source of information on Marxist philosophy.

Another major source of such information is Zentralstelle für die philosophischen Information und Dokumentation (GRD-108 Berlin, Taubenstrasse 19/23), which tries to cover all Marxist philosophical literature in *Bibliographie Philosophie* (1967-).

More detailed coverage of philosophical research and publication projects (especially those making use of computers) is contained in "L'informatique au service de la philosophie; réalisations et projects," by Christian Wenin [*Revue philosophique de Louvain* 6 (May 1972):177-211].

Special collections in philosophy may attempt to cover the discipline as a whole, some period in the history of philosophy, some special topic, or the works of an individual philosopher:

• The House Library of Philosophy at the University of Southern California contains more than 40,000 volumes and covers virtually every period from medieval manuscripts to the latest contemporary publications. A catalog of this collection was published in 1968 by G. K. Hall.

• The Professor Don C. Allen Collection at the University of California, San Diego, concentrates on the Renaissance period.

• The General Library of the University of Michigan has a large collection dealing with Arabic philosophy.

- The Weston College Library (Massachusetts) attempts to be comprehensive in Catholic philosophy, while the Dominican College Library (Washington, DC) specializes in Thomist works and attempts to collect all works by Dominican authors.

- The Van Pelt Library of the University of Pennsylvania has a collection of nearly 3,000 manuscripts dating from the fifteenth to the nineteenth centuries and dealing mainly with Hindu philosophy, religion, and grammar.

- The Special Collections Department of the Columbia University Libraries and the Jewish Institute of Religion Library of Hebrew Union College (Cincinnati) have distinguished Spinoza collections.

- In 1968, McMaster University Library (Hamilton, Ontario, Canada) acquired the papers of Bertrand Russell — more than 250,000 items. Information is now being disseminated in *Russell: The Journal of the Bertrand Russell Archives.*

The foregoing examples are merely illustrative of the many collections available in the field of philosophy. Others may be located by consulting Young, Ash and Lewanski (see item 13).

4 PRINCIPAL INFORMATION SOURCES IN PHILOSOPHY

BIBLIOGRAPHIC GUIDES

14. DeGeorge, Richard T. **A Guide to Philosophical Bibliography and Research.**
Appleton-Century-Crofts, 1971. 141p.
Compiled by the chairman of the Department of Philosophy, University of Kansas, and
published in the Century Philosophy Series (edited by Justus Buchler), this classified,
annotated bibliography is the best single volume currently available. It is much more
comprehensive than *The Bibliography of Philosophy*, by Charles L. Higgins (Campus
Publishers, 1965), though Higgins has more detail on bibliographies and bibliographic
patterns up to the time of compilation. Intended for graduate students, Henry J.
Koren's *Research in Philosophy* (Duquesne, 1966) is less crisply professional than
DeGeorge and more given to "fatherly advice," but often does contain supplementary
coverage. D. H. Borchardt's *How to Find Out in Philosophy and Psychology*
(Pergamon, 1968) is an extended bibliographical essay with evaluative as well as descrip-
tive comments, which the author has updated in "Recent International Documentation
in Philosophy: A Survey of Select Reference Works," *International Library Review* 4
(April 1972):199-212.

15. Jasenas, Michael. **A History of the Bibliography of Philosophy.** Georg Olms
Verlag, 1973. 188p.
Covering the period from 1592 to 1960, this work concentrates on bibliographies that
cover the whole of philosophy. Attention is given to major figures and influences.
Appendix I arranges the bibliographies discussed both chronologically and alphabetically, with a second section on other bibliographies. Appendix II is a list of major
philosophical works. There is a name index.

16. Lachs, John. **Marxist Philosophy: A Bibliographical Guide.** University of
North Carolina Press, 1967. 166p.
Compiled by a professional philosopher whose prime concern is substantive issues
rather than niceties of bibliography, and limited to works in English, French, and German (with emphasis on English), this guidebook is divided into 38 chapters, mostly
representing various aspects of Marxist and Marxist-Leninist thought. Each chapter
begins with a short, critical essay. About 1,500 items are lited. There are chapters on
documents, journals of special relevance, bibliographies, and reference works. This is
still the best work available in English, although *Guide to Marxist Philosophy: An
Introductory Bibliography*, edited by I. M. Bochenski (Alan Swallow, 1972) is more recent and serves as a useful supplement. Bochenski, Director of the Institute of

East European Studies (Fribourg), made selections and prepared annotations that some American reviewers regarded as rather biased. More comprehensive coverage of an important segment of Marxist philosophy will be found in *Bibliographie der sowjetischen Philosophie* (D. Reidel, 1957-68, 7v.), which includes Soviet books and articles in philosophy from 1947 through 1966. This is continued by bibliographies in *Studies in Soviet Thought.* Another attempt to cover Marxist philosophy comprehensively is the bimonthly *Bibliographie Philosophie mit Autoren und Sach Register*, 1967- (Zentrallstelle fuer die Philosophische Information und Dokumentation).

17. Magill, Frank N. **Masterpieces of World Philosophy in Digest Form.** Harper, 1961. 1166p.
Magill summarizes 200 major works from ancient times to the middle of the twentieth century. The chronological arrangement is supplemented by an alphabetical list of titles (front)and authors (back). The work also includes a "Glossary of Common Philosophical Terms" (pp. xvii-xxx).

18. **Philosophy,** by Roderick M. Chisholm, and others. Prentice-Hall, 1964. 560p.
Part of the series, The Princeton Studies: Humanistic Scholarship in America, this book provides a general survey of trends in American philosophical scholarship from 1930 to 1960, followed by chapters on metaphysics, theory of knowledge, ethical theory, and philosophy of science. Most chapters are heavily bibliographical, and there is a select bibliography at the end.

19. Plott, John C., and Paul D. Mays. **Sarva — Darsana — Sangraha: A Bibliographical Guide to the Global History of Philosophy.** Brill, 1969. 305p.
Worldwide coverage is attempted as a corrective to the traditional emphasis on Western philosophy. Intended for upper level undergraduates and graduate students in philosophy, it is also useful for those in area studies. In this classified and annotated work, items of special importance are starred. The introduction explains spelling and alphabetization. The compilers tend to slight the analytic tradition. Works in foreign languages are cited rather selectively. Appendix I is "A Syllabus Outline to the Global History of Philosophy." Appendix II (folded in the back) is "A Synchronological Chart to the Global History of Philosophy." The name index (pp. 293-305) includes cross references. Another corrective to the traditional Western bias will be found in Wing-tsit Chan's *An Outline and Annotated Bibliography of Chinese Philosophy* (Yale, 1969), which is chronologically arranged in the first part, with items of special importance starred. The second part is annotated and arranged alphabetically by author. There is a list of Chinese characters and a subject index. Chan has also compiled *Chinese Philosophy. 1949-1963: An Annotated Bibliography of Mainland China Publications* (East-West Center, 1967).

BIBLIOGRAPHIES (CURRENT AND RETROSPECTIVE)

20. Albert, Ethel M., Clyde Kluckhohn, and others. **A Selected Bibliography on Values, Ethics and Esthetics in the Behavioral Sciences and Philosophy, 1920-1958.** Free Press, 1959. 342p.
Some 2,000 books and articles are classified by discipline. A detailed guide (pp. 3-41) assists the user in locating pertinent references through a topical approach. There is also

an alphabetical index of authors. A more recent work, which attempts to promote an interdisciplinary approach, is Sebastian A. Matczak's *Philosophy: A Select, Classified Bibliography of Ethics, Economics, Law, Politics, Sociology* (Nauwelaerts, 1970). On a related topic, *Bibliography of the Philosophy of Technology*, by Carl Mitcham and Robert Mackey (University of Chicago Press, 1973), gives selective international coverage from 1925 to 1972 and is the first such bibliography in English. Another related specialty is covered on a current basis by *Bibliography of Bioethics*, 1973- (Gale).

21. **Bibliographie de la philosophie**, 1937-1953. Vrin.
Except for World War II (1940-1945), when it did not appear, this was a polylingual quarterly, compiled by the staff of the Institut Internationale de Philosophie, which often translated titles from little-known languages and tried to cover philosophy exhaustively. In the postwar years, 730 journals (100 of them French) were scanned. The arrangement is complex, with two general divisions. In the *first* are: 1) geographical arrangement of publishers; 2) directory of periodicals, reviews, newspapers, etc., under country of origin; 3) alphabetical author arrangement of all books and periodical articles published in the period covered. The *second* division includes: 1) alphabetical index of philosophers who are the subject of books and articles in the first part; 2) systematic classification of materials in the first part; 3) alphabetical arrangement of philosophic terms and concepts, with applicable book and periodical articles under each. Current coverage is given by *Bibliographie de la philosophie/Bibliography of Philosophy*, 1954-date.

22. **Bibliographie de la philosophie/Bibliography of Philosophy**, 1954- . Vrin.
The revised editorial policy of the successor publication is to list books only and to annotate each entry with an objective description of the contents and the aspect under which each book deserves attention. Summaries of English, French, German, Italian, and Spanish books appear in the languages in which the books are written. Other languages are summarized in French or English. The arrangement is classified, with three annual indexes: books, authors, and publishers. It is published by the International Institute of Philosophy, aided by Unesco and CNRS (the French National Centre for Scientific Research).

23. Brie, G. A. de. **Bibliographia philosophica**, 1934-1945. Editiones Spectrum, 1950-1954. 2v.
A major effort, subsidized by Unesco, this bibliography contains 48,000 entries (both books and periodical articles) gleaned from 400 journals. V. I covers history of philosophy in five major sections: General; Greek and Roman; Patristic and Medieval; Recent; Oriental. Each is further subdivided by period, area, or individual. Material by and about individual philosophers is grouped first by birth date of the philosopher, then by date of publication. V. II is a systematic survey: General; Logic; Theories of Knowledge; Psychology, etc. The literature of cognate fields is well represented. A critical study of a specific work will be found in v. II. A biography or an evaluation of a philosopher will be found under the individual's name in v. I.

24. Guerry, Herbert, ed. **Bibliography of Philosophical Bibliographies.** Greenwood, 1977. 332p.
International coverage (primarily in Western languages) is given for the period from

about 1450 to 1974. The scope is mainly confined to separately published bibliographies and those appearing in journals, with only a few major bibliographies that appeared as appendices to monographs. The first part is arranged alphabetically by individual philosophers and schools bearing their names. The second part is arranged alphabetically by topic. There is a name index, which refers to entry numbers, and there are cross references. Most entries are unannotated. There is no entry or cross reference under "Confucianism" in the subject part, though relevant items may be found under "Chinese philosophy." On the other hand, there is a cross reference "Hinduism. See Indian philosophy and Hinduism." There is only one entry under "African philosophy," but much that is relevant may be found under "Islamic or Arabian philosophy."

25. **Repertoire bibliographique de la philosophie,** 1949- . Editions de l'Institut Supérieure de Philosophie.
From 1934 to 1948, its predecessor appeared as an appendix to *Revue néo-scholastique de philosophie.* From 1939, it also appeared as a supplement of the Dutch *Tijdschrift voor Philosophie* entitled *Bibliographisch Repertorium.* As such, it appeared even during World War II, when *Revue néo-scholastique* was suspended. Since 1949, it has been an independent supplement to *Revue philosophique de Louvain,* assisted by grants from Unesco. Koren calls it "perhaps the most important single tool for assembling a bibliography on a particular subject." Coverage is attempted for all books in Catalan, Dutch, English, French, German, Italian, Latin, Portuguese, and Spanish, as well as philosophical articles from more than 300 periodicals. Entries are arranged in classified order, and each entry is assigned a number. There are cross references by number and topic from the thematic part to works listed in the historical part. The first three issues each year cover books and periodicals. The final one (November) lists book reviews and also contains an index of names (authors of books, articles, and reviews; editors; translators; etc.). Complete instructions for use (in French, English, German, Spanish, and Italian) appear in the February issue.

26. Totok, W., and H. Schroer. **Handbuch der Geschichte der Philosophie.** Klosterman, v.1, 1964; v.2, 1970- .
The title is misleading. Actually, this is a major bibliography. V. 1 covers ancient philosophy as well as Indian and Chinese and is arranged by periods. The author index has about 5,000 entries. There is a brief subject index and a list of journals cited. V. 2 covers the Middle Ages, and v. 3 and v. 4 are to cover the modern period.

27. Varet, Gilbert. **Manuel de bibliographie philosophique.** Presses Universitaires de France, 1956. 2v.
A selective bibliography, this covers the entire field of philosophy with special emphasis on 1914-1934, providing a foundation for Brie's *Bibliographia philosophica.* V. I treats the subject historically, beginning with Oriental philosophy and coming to the present. There are subdivisions by period and by individual. Works in all languages are included. For voluminous authors, the most important editions are mentioned. V. II is concerned with the development of systematic thinking. One section covers philosophy of art, religion, and history; another, philosophy of the sciences; and a third, political philosophy, educational philosophy, etc. There are many brief annotations. A general index of names is given at the end of v. I. Retrospective coverage of some 60,000 books and periodical articles up to 1902 will be found in Benjamin Rand's *Bibliography of Philosophy, Psychology and Cognate Subjects* (Macmillan, 1905; repr., 1949), which originally appeared as v. 3 of Baldwin's *Dictionary of Philosophy and Psychology.*

INDEXES, ABSTRACTS, AND CURRENT AWARENESS SERVICES

28. **Bulletin signalétique 519: philosophie**, 1947- . Q. Centre Nationale de la Recherche Scientifique.
Through several title changes, this work has remained a quarterly. It attempts to be exhaustive in coverage of the serial literature of philosophy, including philosophy of history and political philosophy. Religion was included prior to 1970. Worldwide index-ing coverage of 4,400 serials (24,000 entries) is provided. It does *not* list books, but is primarily an *abstracting* journal. Abstracts explain the scope, viewpoint, argumenta-tion, and conclusion. The arrangement is classified. Book reviews are indexed, and digests of reviews are given.

29. **The Philosopher's Index: An International Index to Philosophical Periodicals**, 1967- . Q. Ann. cum. Philosophy Documentation Center, Bowling Green State University.
A quarterly index (with annual cumulations) to approximately 300 philosophy periodicals, including all of the major ones in English, French, German, Italian, and Spanish, with more selective coverage of other languages. Assisted by the International Institute of Philosophy (Paris) and the Philosophy Information Center (Düsseldorf, West Germany). Each issue contains five parts: Subject Index; Author Index with Abstracts; Book Review Index; Philosophy Research Archives; and Translations in Progress. Instructions precede each part. Computerized searches and custom bibliographies with abstracts, formerly available through the Philosopher's Information Retrieval System (PIRS) though not through standard commercial sources, became available through DIALOG in 1979. Approximately 15,000 U.S. books from 1940 through 1976 are covered in *The Philosopher's Index: A Retrospective Index to U.S. Publications from 1940* (Philosophy Documentation Center, 1978, 2v.). More interna-tional coverage was given by *Philosophic Abstracts* (Moore, 1939-54), which was arranged by country of publication and was supplemented by author, title, and subject indexes to v.1-12.

DICTIONARIES AND ENCYCLOPEDIAS

30. **Enciclopedia filosofica.** 2nd ed. Sansoni, 1968-69. 6v.
The arrangement is dictionary-style, with individuals, places, ideas, schools, and movements in one alphabet. Articles are signed and accompanied by reading lists. Books, monographs, and periodical articles are listed. Greatest prominence is given to Continental European languages. Works are often listed in Italian translations. Suitable for the advanced student, the new edition is a complete revision of this scholarly work. The index is in v. 6.

31. **The Encyclopedia of Philosophy**, ed. by Paul Edwards. Macmillan, 1967. 8v.; repr. Macmillan, 1972. 8v. in 4.
The compilers of this monumental set tried to cover the whole of philosophy (East and West) and its points of contact with other disciplines. The *Encyclopedia* contains nearly 1,500 articles, some the length of small books and most with copious bibliographies. There are excellent articles on philosophical movements (both ancient and modern), major ideas (e.g., progress), the philosophy of various subject fields (e.g.,

history, law, religion, science), the history of philosophy in different countries (e.g., Indian philosophy, Russian philosophy), and biographies of major philosophers. Coverage of ancient, medieval, and early modern philosophers is generally good. Coverage of contemporary philosophers is better for Western Europe, North American, and India than for the Soviet bloc and the People's Republic of China. Reference librarians will find the articles on philosophical bibliographies, dictionaries, encyclopedias, and journals of particular value. The editor has tried to minimize editorial bias, but his own outlook is influenced by the Anglo-Saxon empirical and analytical approach. Thus, some topics that a Hegelian or an existentialist would omit may be discussed, and vice versa. Articles are long. The integrated approach has been preferred to a series of short articles. Small topics can be located by means of a detailed index in v. 8 (pp. 387-543). More than 1,500 philosophers from all over the world contributed; their names and brief credentials (including major publications) occupy over 30 pages. Over 150 scholars from the United States, Britain, and Europe served on the editorial board. This is likely to remain the definitive encyclopedia of philosophy for many years to come. It has largely superseded J. M. Baldwin's *Dictionary of Philosophy and Psychology* (Macmillan, 1901-1905; repr., Smith, 1957) except for historical treatment and biographies.

32. **Filosofskaya Entsiklopediya**, ed. by F. V. Konstantinov. Sovetskaya Entsiklopediya, 1960-70, 5v.
A general encyclopedia of philosophy written from a Marxist standpoint. The major articles carry lengthy bibliographies. It is especially valuable for the theoretical basis of communism and for biographical material.

33. Lacey, Alan Robert. **A Dictionary of Philosophy.** Routledge, 1976. 239p.
"The book aims to give the layman or intending student a pocket encyclopedia of philosophy, one with a bias toward explaining terminology" (preface). Individual philosophers of major stature are treated briefly. Articles on terminology discuss philosophical issues clearly and frequently cite sources of more extended discussions. More emphasis is given to epistemology and logic than to other branches of philosophy. Cross references (in FULL/CAPS) may occur within articles or independently. One may need to exercise some ingenuity in finding information. For example, there is no entry or cross reference for "logical positivism," but the topic is explained in detail toward the end of the article on "positivism." There is no entry or cross reference for "analytical philosophy," but it is discussed in "philosophy and analysis." The cross reference "Analysis. See PHILOSOPHY" seems insufficient. The author is strong on contemporary British philosophy and familiar with other modern movements. For more extensive treatment, the *Encyclopedia of Philosophy* should be consulted.

34. Lalande, André. **Vocabulaire technique et critique de la philosophie.** 12th ed. Presses Universitaires de France, 1976. 1323p.
Defines current philosophical meanings of terms and gives history of usage as well as German, English, and Italian equivalents. Paul Foulquié's *Dictionnaire de la langue philosophique* . . . (2nd ed., Presses Universitaires de France, 1969) lists words in groups under the main root word, with cross references from derivative forms.

35. Peters, F. E. **Greek Philosophical Terms: A Historical Lexicon.** New York University Press, 1967. 234p.

Designed for the "intermediate" student rather than the beginner or the mature philosopher. The basic arrangement is alphabetical in the main part. English words, with references to appropriate Greek terms in the main section, are given in the index at the end. Liberal references are made to passages in books of the Greek philosophers to clarify and illustrate usage and to aid further study.

36. Ritter, Joachim, ed. **Historisches Wörterbuch der Philosophie.** Vollig neubearb. Ausg. Basel, Schwabe; Darmstadt, Wissenschaflich Buchgesellschaft, 1971- . v.1:A-C, 1971; v.2:D-F, 1972; v.3:G-H, 1974; v.4LI-K, 1976.

Over 700 scholars have contributed to this revision of Rudolf Eisler's *Wörterbuch der Philosophischen Begriffe*. Some subjects covered in the earlier work (e.g., psychology) have been dropped and new material added. Other topics are revised and updated. "The articles, ranging in length from a few sentences to several pages, treat the historical development of philosophical terms and concepts in a very scholarly manner. Documentation is abundant and up to date. An index and list of abbreviations is to be included in each volume. It should be noted that articles on individual philosophers are not within the scope of this dictionary, although schools of thought based on the teachings of a single man are discussed"—*College and Research Libraries* 33 (January 1972):42. Also reviewed in *Australian Journal of Psychology* 50 (May 1972):100-101; *Archives de philosophie* 34 (July-September 1971):503-506; and *Revue philosophique de France* 97 (January-March 1972):114-16.

37. Urmson, James Opie. **The Concise Encyclopedia of Western Philosophy and Philosophers.** 2nd ed. Hutchinson, 1975. 319p.

Articles by about 50 scholars, mostly British. Written for "intelligent laymen." Coverage is selective. Biographies, general descriptions of trends, and definitions. No bibliography. More specialized in focus is Bernard Wueliner's *Dictionary of Scholastic Philosophy* (2nd ed., Bruce, 1966).

SOURCES OF DIRECTORY AND BIOGRAPHICAL INFORMATION

38. **Directory of American Philosophers,** 1962/63- . Bi. Philosophy Documentation Center. Ed. by Archie J. Bahm and Richard H. Lineback. 9th ed. (1978-79).

The main part is alphabetical by states and names of universities, with a separate section by provinces for Canada. There are sections on assistantships, societies, journals, and publishers. Indexes include: names and addresses of philosophers; universities; centers and institutes; societies; journals; and publishers. There is a brief statistical section at the end.

39. **International Directory of Philosophy and Philosophers, 1978-1981.** 4th ed. Ed. by Ramona Cormier and others. Philosophy Documentation Center, 1978. 275p.

Because it is intended to supplement the *Directory of American Philosophers*, this work excludes the United States and Canada. The main part is an alphabetical listing by countries, with sections on their universities, institutes, societies, journals, and publishers. Supplementary access is provided by indexes of philosophers, universities, institutes, societies, journals, and publishers.

40. Ziegenfuss, Werner. **Philosophen-lexicon. Handwörterbuch der Philosophie nach Personnen.** DeGruyter, 1949/50. 2v.
This is a useful biographical dictionary of philosophers, with emphasis on the nineteenth and twentieth centuries. Under each name, the following information is given: biographical data; a critical and descriptive digest of an author's contribution to the field; a catalog of the philosopher's principal published works, and a section that cites books and periodical articles that evaluate the philosopher's works.

HISTORIES OF PHILOSOPHY

41. Armstrong, Arthur Hilary, ed. **The Cambridge History of Later Greek and Early Medieval Philosophy.** Cambridge University Press, 1967. 711p.
Despite some unevenness of treatment, this has become a standard work in the field. Reference features include an excellent bibliography, an index of ancient and medieval works referred to in the text, a general index, and an index of Greek terms.

42. Brehier, Emile. **The History of Philosophy.** Tr. by Joseph Thomas and Wade Baskin. University of Chicago Press, 1963-69. 7v.
The author was professor of philosophy at the Sorbonne, and the set was published earlier in France. Bibliographies are useful for reference and selection. Contents: v.1, The Hellenic Age; v.2, The Hellenistic and Roman Age; v.3, The Middle Ages and the Renaissance; v.4, The Seventeenth Century; v.5, The Eighteenth Century; v.6, The Nineteenth Century: Period of Systems, 1800-1850; v.7, Contemporary Philosophy: Since 1850.

43. **Contemporary Philosophy: A Survey.** Ed. by Raymond Klibansky. Mario Casalini, 1968-71. 4v.
Klibansky, of McGill University, was president of The Institut Internationale de Philosophie, and this set was sponsored by that body. Contents: v.1, Logic and Foundations of Mathematics; v.2, Philosophy of Science; v.3, Metaphysics, Phenomenology, Language, and Structure; v.4, Ethics, Aesthetics, Law, Religion, Politics, Historical and Dialectical Materialism; Philosophy in Eastern Europe, Asia, and Latin America.

44. Copleston, Frederick Charles. **A History of Philosophy.** Search Press, 1975. 9v.
Covers the entire period from ancient times to the twentieth century. Written from "the standpoint of the scholastic philosopher," each volume has an extensive bibliography and an analytical index. Vols. 1-8 were originally published in 1946-66 by Burns and Oates.

45. Gilson, Etienne Henry, ed. **A History of Philosophy.** Random House, 1962-66. 4v.
Contents: v.1, Ancient Philosophy, by Anton Pegis [unable to verify publication]; v.2, Medieval Philosophy, by Armand Augustine Mauer; v.3, Philosophy: Descartes to Kant, by Etienne Gilson and Thomas Langan; v.4, Recent Philosophy: Hegel to the Present, by Etienne Gilson and Thomas Langan. LC classifies and catalogs the various volumes separately. Another major scholarly work by Gilson is *History of Christian Philosophy in the Middle Ages* (Randon House, 1955).

46. Guthrie, William Keith Chambers. **A History of Greek Philosophy.** Cambridge University Press, 1962- . 5v.
Reviewers of the first four volumes agree that this work is erudite, technical, and detailed, yet remarkably lucid. Some regard it as the best work available in English. It includes bibliographical references and indexes.

47. Passmore, John. **A Hundred Years of Philosophy.** Rev. ed. Duckworth, 1966; Basic Books, 1967.
Written from a British viewpoint, this work "restricts itself to epistemology, logic and metaphysics . . ." (preface). Excellent professional coverage is supplemented by bibliographical footnotes and suggestions for further reading. Reference access is provided by name and subject indexes.

48. Russell, Bertrand. **A History of Western Philosophy.** Simon & Schuster, 1945. 895p.
Written in the lively, opinionated style for which Russell was famous, this book is unusual for its emphasis on social, economic, and political conditions, and for the inclusion of some thinkers not ordinarily regarded as philosophers.

49. Schilpp, Paul A., ed. **The Library of Living Philosophers.** Northwestern University Press, 1939-49 (v.1-7); Open Court Pub. Co., 1952- (v.8-).
A major series in contemporary philosophy. Each volume is devoted to a single twentieth century philosopher. In addition to biographical and bibliographical information, there are critiques by other philosophers and a reply by the subject of the book. Several volumes have been updated or reprinted. Some 15 volumes are available from the current publisher. LC catalogs and classifies volumes separately.

50. Schneider, Herbert Wallace. **A History of American Philosophy.** 2nd ed. Columbia University Press, 1963. 590p.
This standard work includes a "Guide to the Recent Literature" and a name index. It is but one example of several histories of philosophy in various countries. One of the most scholarly of these is Yu-lan Feng's *History of Chinese Philosophy* (Princeton, 1952-53, 2v.), which has such reference features as chronological tables, bibliographies, and an index in each volume. *The Philosophical Traditions of India*, by P. T. Raju (University of Pittsburgh Press, 1972), is written at a more introductory level, but it includes a glossary of Sanskrit terms, a selective bibliography, and an index.

51. Ueberweg, Friedrich. **Grundriss der Geschichte der Philosophie.** 12 aufl. Benn Schwabe & Co., 1965- .
Excellent bibliographies supplement encyclopedic treatments by eminent scholars. Now in process of being published in a new edition. The last edition (1923-28 in five volumes) was a landmark.

PHILOSOPHY PERIODICALS

52. American Catholic Philosophical Association. **Proceedings,** 1926- . Ann. Catholic University of America.
Indexed: *Cath.Ind., Phil.Ind., Rép. bibliog.phil.* Also, cum. ind. v.1-39 (1926-65). Valuable for papers and activities.

53. American Philosophical Association. **Proceedings and Addresses,** 1927- . Ann. Antioch Press.
Indexed: *Phil.Ind., Rép.bibliog.phil.* Major professional association in the United States. Valuable for information about activities, presidential addresses, and informal notes on the teaching of philosophy.

54. **Archiv für Geschichte der Philosophie,** 1918- . 3/yr. deGruyter.
Indexed: *Phil.Ind., Rép.bibliog.phil.* Articles on history of philosophy and book reviews.

55. **Archives de philosophie: recherches et documentation,** 1923- . Q. Beauchesne.
Indexed: *Phil.Ind., Rép.bibliog.phil.* Original articles, historical surveys, book reviews, bibliography.

56. **British Journal for the Philosophy of Science,** 1950-. Q. Cambridge University Press.
Indexed: *Phil.Ind., Br.Hum.Ind., Curr.Bk.Rev.Cit., Rép.bibliog.phil., Bull.signal.:phil., Ind.Bk.Rev.Hum.* Official publication of the British Society for the Philosophy of Science. Lengthy, technical papers. A major journal in this field. Contains book reviews and conference information.

57. **British Journal of Aesthetics,** 1960- . Q. Thames & Hudson.
Indexed: *Phil. Ind., Br. Hum.Ind., Abstr.Eng.Stud., Art Ind., Curr.Bk.Rev.Cit., Rép.bibliog.phil., RILM, Ind.Bk.Rev.Hum.* Official publication of the British Society of Aesthetics. Most articles are by philosophers, though some are by practitioners in the arts. Includes book reviews and conference information.

58. **Dialectica: International Review of Philosophy of Knowledge.** 1947- . Q. Association F. Gonseth.
Indexed: *Phil.Ind., Rép.bibliog.phil.* Text in English, French, and German. Book reviews.

59. **Dialogue (Canada): Canadian Philosophical Review/Revue Canadienne de philosophie.** 1962- . Q. Canadian Philosophical Association.
Indexed: *Phil.Ind., Rép.bibliog.phil., Ind.Bk.Rev.Hum.* Covers all aspects and periods of philosophy. Articles in English and French. Book reviews.

60. **Ethics: An International Journal of Social, Political and Legal Philosophy,** 1890- . Q. University of Chicago Press.
Indexed: *Phil.Ind., Soc.Sci.Ind., Bk.Rev.Ind., Ind.Bk.Rev.Hum., Curr.Bk.Rev.Cit., Rép.bibliog.phil.* Articles by social scientists as well as philosophers. Book reviews.

61. **History and Theory: Studies in the Philosophy of History,** 1960- . 3/yr. Wesleyan University Press.
Indexed: *Phil. Ind., Hist.Abstr., Curr.Bk.Rev.Cit., Hum.Ind., Rep.bibliog.phil.* Long scholarly articles and book reviews. Some special bibliographical issues.

62. **International Philosophical Quarterly,** 1961- . Q. Foundation for International Philosophical Exchange, Fordham University Press.
Indexed: *Phil.Ind., Cath.Ind., Bk.Rev.Ind., Hum.Ind., Rep.bibliog.phil., Ind.Bk.Rev.Hum., Curr.Bk.Rev.Cit.* Encourages contemporary exchange of ideas across national boundaries and among different schools of thought. Long scholarly articles, with book reviews, and short selections on recent trends.

63. **Journal of Aesthetics and Art Criticism,** 1941- . Q. Cleveland Museum of Art.
Indexed: *Art.Ind., Music Ind., Psych.Abstr., Phil.Ind., Rep.bibliog.phil., Bk.Rev.Ind., Ind.Bk.Rev.Hum., Curr.Bk.Rev.Cit.* Published by the American Society for Aesthetics. Scholarly articles, replies, news of Society activities, membership lists, and book reviews.

64. **Journal of Philosophy,** 1904- . Fortnightly. Philosophy Hall, Columbia University.
Indexed: *Phil.Ind., Bk.Rev.Ind., Hum.Ind., Rep.bibliog.phil., Ind.Bk.Rev.Hum., Curr.Bk.Rev.Cit.* Wide circulation among philosophers. Stresses analytical philosophy and philosophy of science. Scholarly articles and replies, book reviews, and news of philosophical activities.

65. **Journal of Symbolic Logic,** 1936- . Q. Association for Symbolic Logic.
Indexed: *Phil.Ind., Ind.Bk.Rev.Hum., Hum.Ind., Curr.Bk.Rev.Cit., Rep.bibliog.phil.* Specializes in original technical papers. Includes conference activities (with abstracts of papers) and reviews (articles as well as books).

66. **Journal of the History of Philosophy,** 1963- . Q. Philosophy Department, Claremont Graduate School.
Indexed: *Hum.Ind., Ind.Bk.Rev.Hum., Curr.Bk.Rev.Cit., Rep.bibliog.phil., Phil.Ind.* International coverage. Articles mostly in English. Descriptions of movements and trends rather than original philosophic speculation. Also includes notes, discussion, and book reviews.

67. **Mind: A Quarterly Review of Philosophy,** 1876- . Q. Blackwell.
Indexed: *Phil.Ind., Br.Hum.Ind., Ind.Bk.Rev.Hum., Curr.Bk.Rev.Cit., Rep.bibliog.phil.* Throughout most of its long history, this journal has included broad coverage of virtually all aspects of philosophy. Articles in recent years reflect British interest in problems of language and logic. Also includes book reviews, discussions, and notices of conferences.

68. **Philosophical Books,** 1960- . 3/yr. Leicester University Press.
Indexed: *Ind.Bk.Rev.Hum., Rep.bibliog.phil.* Has signed reviews, each about 1,000 words. Covers about 20 books per issue (English-language only).

69. **Philosophical Review**, 1892- . Q. Sage School of Philosophy, Cornell University.
Indexed: *Phil.Ind., Bk.Rev.Ind., Hum.Ind., Ind.Bk.Rev.Hum., Curr.Bk.Rev.Cit., Rép.bibliog.phil.* Book reviews.

70. **Philosophische Rundschau: Zeitschrift für Philosophische Kritik**, 1953- . Q. J.C.B. Mohr.
Indexed: *Phil.Ind., Rép.bibliog.phil.* Book reviews.

71. **Philosophy**, 1931- . Q. Cambridge University Press.
Indexed: *Phil.Ind., Br.Hum.Ind., Ind.Bk.Rev.Hum., Psych.Abstr., Rép.bibliog.phil.* Broad coverage of all phases and schools of philosophy. Articles, discussions, and book reviews.

72. **Philosophy and Phenomenological Research**, 1940- . Q. Department of Philosophy, State University of New York at Buffalo.
Indexed: *Phil.Ind., Rép.bibliog.phil., Ind.Bk.Rev.Hum., Curr.Bk.Rev.Cit.* Published for the International Phenomenological Society. Articles and discussions appeal to the educated lay person as well as the professional philosopher. Variety of philosophical topics. Numerous book reviews. Brief notes of conferences and other activities.

73. **Philosophy, East and West**, 1951- . Q. University of Hawaii Press.
Indexed: *Phil.Ind., Rép.bibliog.phil., Curr.Bk.Rev.Cit., Ind.Bk.Rev.Hum.* Covers a wide range of philosophical topics, with emphasis on a comparative approach. Major source in English for information on Asian philosophy. Includes articles, commentaries, replies, book reviews, and news of philosophical activities.

74. **Philosophy of Science**, 1934- . Q. Department of Philosophy, Michigan State University.
Indexed: *Phil.Ind., Hum.Ind., Rép.bibliog.phil., Curr.Bk.Rev.Cit., SCI, Ind.Bk.Rev.Hum.* Original articles, historical surveys and book reviews. Official publication of the Philosophy of Science Association.

75. **Review of Metaphysics**, 1947- . Q. Philosophy of Education Society, Catholic University of America.
Indexed: *Bk.Rev.Ind., Hum.Ind., Rép.bibliog.phil., Ind.Bk.Rev.Hum., Curr.Bk.Rev.Cit., SSCI, Bk.Rev.Ind.* Includes book reviews, abstracts, bibliographies, and announcements. Cumulative index 1947-67.

76. **Revue internationale de philosophie**, 1938- . Q. Nauwelaerts.
Indexed: *Phil.Ind., Rép.bibliog.phil.* Text in English, French, German, Italian, and Spanish.

77. **Revue philosophique de Louvain**, 1894- . Q. Editions de L'Institut Supérieur de Philosophie.
Indexed: *Phil.Ind., Rép.bibliog.phil., Cath.Ind.* Original papers (mainly by Roman Catholic philosophers) and historical surveys. Book reviews. Extensive "chroniques" section includes brief obituaries, reports, and announcements. A quarterly supplement, also available separately, is *Répertoire bibliographique de la philosophie* (see item 25).

78. **Studies in Soviet Thought,** 1961- . Q. Reidel.

Indexed: *Phil.Ind., Rép.bibliog.phil., SSCI.* Jointly published by the Institute of East European Studies, University of Fribourg; the Russian Philosophical Studies Program, Boston College; and the Seminar for Political Theory and Philosophy, University of Munich. Includes book reviews and *Bibliographie der sowjetischen Philosophie/Bibliography of Soviet Philosophy,* which was published separately before 1967 (see item 16).

5 ACCESSING INFORMATION IN RELIGION

MAJOR DIVISIONS OF THE FIELD

Religions are commonly classified as being predominantly sacramental, prophetic, or mystical. Sacramental religions place great emphasis on the observance of ritual and on the sacredness of certain objects. Eastern Orthodoxy and Roman Catholicism are familiar examples. Prophetic religions emphasize communication of the Divine Will in verbal form, often with a strong moralistic emphasis. Islam and Protestantism reflect this approach. Mystical religions stress direct encounter with God and view words, rituals, and sacred objects as auxiliary aids at best, or hindrances at worst, to that full communion which is seen as the ultimate goal of all religious striving. Certain branches of Hinduism and Buddhism are examples of this type.

The literature generated by the religions of the world may be conveniently analyzed under the following headings: 1) personal religion; 2) theology; 3) philosophy of religion; 4) science of religion.

Personal religion is the primary and most direct source of religious writing. It is intimately related to the experiences of the individual and reflections about their significance. A major class of documents in this category would be the sacred scriptures of the world's great religions. Closely related to the sacred writings are those documents of explication and interpretation commonly known as commentaries. Finally, there is a much larger body of literature that does not have the same authoritative standing as the sacred scriptures and their commentaries. Works in this category may be devotional, autobiographical, or biographical. In this group also would be included a large number of popularizations.

Theology is an attempt to express in intellectually coherent form the principal doctrines of a religion. It is the product of reflection upon the primary sources of religion. It differs from philosophy in that the basic truth of the religious position is accepted, and attention is given to its systematic and thoughtful exposition. The field has many subdivisions. Within the Christian tradition, systematic (or topic-oriented) theology and biblical theology have been especially important, but there is also a substantial body of literature on moral, ascetic, mystical, symbolic, pastoral, philosophical, liturgical, and natural theology as well.

The philosophy of religion is an attempt to relate the religious experience to other spheres of experience. It differs from theology in that it makes fewer assumptions about the truth of a religious position, at least in the beginning. It differs from philosophy in its selection of religion as the area for speculative investigation. Perhaps it could best be described as a bridge between philosophy and theology.

The science of religion has also generated a substantial body of literature. Here, emphasis is placed on a comparative and historical approach, with no presuppositions about (and possibly no interest in) the truth or falsity of the religions being examined. Whereas the locus of interest in the first three categories is usually one of the world's living religions, this is not usually the case in the scientific study of religion, where a purely objective approach to the description and comparison of religious phenomena represents the ideal.

Although somewhat dated, John R. Everett's article on "Religion" in the *Encyclopedia Americana* (1978 ed., v. 23, pp. 342-50) provides a brief overview. More current and much better are the articles in *The Encyclopaedia Britannica: Macropaedia* (15th ed., 1974): "Religion, Philosophy of" (v. 15, pp. 592-603), "Religion, Social Aspects of" (v. 15, pp. 604-613), and "Religions, Classification of" (v. 15, pp. 628-34). There are also articles on related topics like religious dress and religious experience. The article on "Religion" in the *Encyclopaedia of Religion and Ethics*, edited by A. J. Hastings (Scribners, 1910-27, v. 10, pp. 662-93), represented sound scholarship at the time, but now it is seriously outdated. Good general studies of book length include *Religion: A Humanistic Field*, by Clyde A. Holbrook (Prentice-Hall, 1963), *Religion*, edited by Paul Ramsey (Prentice-Hall, 1965), and *Religion in America*, by Winthrop S. Hudson (2nd ed., Scribners, 1973).

The chapter on "Religion" in Asheim's *The Humanities and the Library* (pp. 1-60) still repays careful study. Charles Harvey Arnold's bibliographical article on "Philosophy and Religion" in *Library Trends* [15 (January 1967):459-77] is still useful. Recent bibliographical articles to aid college libraries include P. Schlueter's "Building a Basic Collection in Religion and Literature: A Suggested Collection for Academic Libraries" [*Choice* 12 (February 1976):1533-36+] and G. V. Henthorne's "Religion in the Small College Library" [*Choice* 8 (November 1971):1141-46 and 8 (February 1972):1562-66]. J. Cobb's "Recent Religious Reference Works in English [*Catholic Library World* 46 (March 1975):334-37] is now updated annually in the December issue. D. S. Marsh has given attention to the needs of public libraries in three articles: "Religious Book Selection in the Public Library: Principles and Problems" [*Catholic Library World* 49 (November 1977):174-75]; "Popular Religious Books: A Selected Bibliography" [*Library Journal* 102 (June 1, 1977):1248-50]; and "Popular Religious Books for Public Libraries" [*Library Journal* 102 [June 1, 1977):1243-47]. The headings "Religious Literature—Bibliography" and "Religious Literature—Book Lists" in *Library Literature* are productive sources of current information for librarians.

MAJOR RELIGIOUS ORGANIZATIONS, INFORMATION
CENTERS, AND SPECIAL COLLECTIONS

Religious organizations are major sources of information. These may be denominational, ecumenical, or academic. The number of denominational organizations (especially in the United States) is immense. Certain useful generalizations can be made about the larger religious groups. Generally, they maintain national offices and have extensive publishing programs. Much of their publishing is designed to serve the needs of local congregations for devotional and educational materials; but a number of denominations maintain research staffs at the national level, and nearly all of them gather such basic statistics as size of church membership and Sunday school attendance. Most also issue a variety of directories as well as reports of national, regional, or state conferences and other activities. Most support theological seminaries, and some have parochial schools and colleges as well. Many maintain collections of historical and other materials pertaining to the denomination. Some are active in promoting church libraries among their local congregations. Although the Lutherans, Southern Baptists, and United Methodists have such organizations, the Catholic Library Association (461 West Lancaster Ave., Haverford, PA 19041) probably has the widest range of activities, including publication of *Catholic Library World* and *Catholic Periodical and Literature Index*.

Ecumenical cooperation is exemplified by the work of the National Council of Churches of Christ in the U.S.A. (475 Riverside Drive, New York, NY 10027), which includes publication of the *Yearbook of American and Canadian Churches*, and by the activities of the Church and Synagogue Library Association (P.O. Box 1130, Bryn Mawr, PA 19010), which publishes *Church and Synagogue Libraries*.

The oldest of the academic organizations in this country is the Association for the Sociology of Religion (6525 N. Sheridan Road, Chicago, IL 60626), which was founded prior to World War II and which publishes a journal entitled *Sociological Analysis*. The largest of the academic groups is the Society for the Scientific Study of Religion (Box U68A, University of Connecticut, Storrs, CT 06268), which publishes *Journal for the Scientific Study of Religion*. Smaller and more recent are the Religious Research Association (P.O. Box 303, Manhattanville Station, New York, NY 10025), which publishes *Review of Religious Research*, and the American Society of Christian Ethics. The role of special congresses, such as the International Congress of Learned Societies in the Field of Religion held in 1972 in Los Angeles, should not be overlooked.

In response to a need for greater coordination of research and improved dissemination of religious information, an organization known as the Association for the Development of Religious Information Systems (ADRIS) came into existence. Major publications to date include *International Directory of Religious Information Systems* (Milwaukee: Marquette University Department of Sociology and Anthropology, 1971) and the *ADRIS Newsletter*.

In Europe, a major source of coordination is the International Federation of Institutes for Social and Socio-Religious Research, with headquarters in Louvain, Belgium. This organization published a *Directory of Centers for Religious Research and Study* in 1968.

Only a few of the major information centers can be mentioned. The Office of Research, Evaluation, and Planning of the National Council of Churches is noteworthy for its extensive research efforts and for its computerized inventory of more than 2,000 documents in the H. Paul Douglass Collection of research reports. The American Theological Library Association (5600 S. Woodlawn, Chicago, IL 60637) publishes *Religion Index One*. A major Catholic research effort is conducted by the Center for Applied Research in the Apostolate (P.O. Box 29150, Washington, DC 20017). The Centre Protestant d'Études et de Documentation (8, Villa du Parc Montsouris, Paris 14e, France) publishes a *Bulletin* and cooperates closely with a similar research center in Strasbourg. IDOC/North America (145 E. 49th St., New York, NY 10017) is part of an international religious documentation network that operates in 32 countries.

The number of special collections in the field of religion is immense. The best starting point for a search is under "Religion" in *Subject Collections*, by Lee Ash. Related headings cited by Ash and the names of individual religions (e.g., "Buddha and Buddhism"), denominations (e.g., "Baptists") and religious leaders (e.g., "Wesley, John") will prove fruitful for more specialized inquiries. G. K. Hall & Co. have published catalogs of some of the more outstanding collections, such as the American Jewish Archives (Cincinnati), the Klau Library of Hebrew Union College — Jewish Institute of Religion (Cincinnati), the Pontifical Institute of Medieval Studies (Toronto), Union Theological Seminary (New York), Dr. Williams' Library (London), and Institut des Études Augustiniennes (Paris).

Some local or regional surveys of special collections in religion as well as descriptions of individual collections have appeared in the library press. The most useful headings in *Library Literature* are "Special collections — Special subjects — Religion" and "Special collections — Special subjects — Religious literature."

The Center for Research Libraries (5721 South Cottage Grove Ave., Chicago, IL 60637) has acquired microfilms of several major research collections, including copies of the official yearbooks, annual reports, minutes, and statistics of groups ranging from the American Baptist Convention to the Seventh-Day Adventist Church. Further details may be found on pages 96-97 of the Center's *Handbook*.

6 PRINCIPAL INFORMATION SOURCES IN RELIGION AND MYTHOLOGY

INTRODUCTORY WORKS AND BIBLIOGRAPHIC GUIDES

79. Adams, Charles J., ed. **A Reader's Guide to the Great Religions.** Rev. ed. Free Press, 1977. 521p.
This collection of scholarly bibliographical essays is the most authoritative guide available. There has been substantial revision and expansion. The first edition had chapters on: primitive religion, religions of China, Hindiusm, Buddhism, religions of Japan, Judaism, Christianity, and Islam. The revised edition divides Judaism into two chapters and adds the following new ones: the ancient world, religions of Mexico and of Central and South America, the Sikhs, the Jainas, and an appendix entitled "The History of the History of Religions." Each chapter, by a different specialist, contains a good, brief introduction followed by authoritative evaluations of many of the works cited. There are name and subject indexes. A recent work that duplicates, but also supplements, Adams is *The Religious Life of Man: Guide to Basic Literature*, compiled by Leszek Karpinski (Scarecrow, 1978).

80. Capps, Donald, Lewis Rambo, and Paul Ransohoff. **Psychology of Religion: A Guide to Information Sources.** Gale, 1976. 352p.
This is a classified, partially-annotated bibliography of some 5,000 books and articles primarily since 1950 and with special emphasis on the period 1960-1974. There are author, title (for books), and subject indexes. Its purpose is different from W. W. Meissner's *Annotated Bibliography in Religion and Psychology* (Academy of Religion and Mental Health, 1961), but the latter should also be consulted for publications in the 1950s.

81. Fitzmyer, Joseph A. **The Dead Sea Scrolls: Major Publications and Tools for Study.** Distr. Scholars' Press, 1975. 171p.
This authoritative guide supersedes earlier efforts. It provides a new classification of both texts and sites. Unpublished reports are noted, as well as lists of surveys, bibliographies of scrolls, and auxiliary aids such as dictionaries and concordances. There are cross indexes to biblical passages.

82. Kennedy, James R., Jr. **Library Research Guide to Religion and Theology: Illustrated Search Strategy and Sources.** Pierian, 1974. 53p.
Designed for undergraduates who need to write term papers in religion, this small book is primarily an exposition of search strategy rather than a bibliography, but a brief, selective bibliography is given at the end. A more comprehensive approach for

writers of term papers will be found in *Religions: A Select, Classified Bibliography*, by Joseph F. Mitros (Learned Publications, 1973). *The Atid Bibliography: A Resource for the Questioning Jew* (United Synagogue of America, 1977) is designed to introduce young people to the classics of Judaism and related information.

83.   Parrinder, Edward Geoffrey, ed. **Religions of the World, from Primitive Beliefs to Modern Faiths.** Grosset, 1971. 440p.
The compiler has assembled a collection of concise, accurate essays on the world's major religions. Illustrations (some in color) have been well chosen and are of excellent quality. Other reference features include a bibliography and an index. A popular presentation, noted for its excellent pictures, is *The World's Great Religions* (Time, 1957). A more recent work, with excellent color illustrations and concise commentary, is *Great Religions of the World* (National Geographic Society, 1971).

84.   Regazzi, John J., and Theodore C. Hines. **A Guide to Indexed Periodicals in Religion.** Scarecrow, 1975. 314p.
Includes 17 abstracting and indexing services (strictly confined to religion) and some 2,700 periodicals covered by these services in four parts: list of abstracting and indexing services, with abbreviations; alphabetical list of periodical titles, with all abstracting and indexing services for each title; inverted title list, with comparable information; and listings by services. Only titles and abbreviations are given.

85.   **Religion**, ed. by Paul Ramsey. Prentice-Hall, 1965. 468p.
This useful work covers historical, philosophical, philological, and theological studies in biblical religions.

86.   Rosten, Leo, ed. **Religions of America: Ferment and Faith in an Age of Crisis; A New Guide and Almanac.** Simon & Schuster, 1975. 672p.
Part I consists of essay-type replies to questions (e.g., "What Is a Baptist?") by leaders of the 16 largest denominations in the United States, plus three other essays. Part II (Almanac) is a compilation of statistical and other information, arranged alphabetically by such broad topics as "Abortion," "Belief in God," and "Youth and Religion." There is a name and subject index (pp. 645-72).

87.   Smith, James Ward, and A. Leland Jamison. **Religion in American Life.** Princeton University Press, 1961- . 4v.
Contents: v. 1, *The Shaping of American Religion* (1961); v. 2, *Religious Perspectives in American Culture* (1961); v. 3, *Religious Thought and Economic Society: The European Background* (apparently never published); v. 4, *Critical Bibliography of Religion in America*, by Nelson R. Burr (2v. 1961). Volume 4 is often cited separately. It is a very comprehensive bibliography, in classified order, with running commentary, tables of contents, and an author index, but no subject index. Burr has more recently produced a much smaller work, *Religion in American Life* (Appleton-Century-Crofts, 1971), which is a classified, briefly-annotated bibliography for graduate and advanced undergraduate students. Martin Marty has written a brief bibliographical essay on "Religion Today and Tomorrow," *American Libraries* 5 (February 1974):69-72.

88. **The Study of Judaism: Bibliographical Essays,** by Richard Bavier and others. KTAV, 1972. 229p.

In reviewing this work, Charles Berlin, of the Harvard College Library, commented as follows: "This collection fills a long-felt need for an authoritative and functional bibliography of Judaism for students and scholars"(*Library Journal* 97 [Oct. 15, 1972]:3303).

BIBLIOGRAPHIES (CURRENT AND RETROSPECTIVE)

89. **Arab Islamic Bibliography: The Middle East Library Committee Guide, Based on Giuseppe Gabrieli's Manuale di bibliografia musulmana,** ed. by Diana Grimwood and others. Humanities, 1977. 292p.

This classified, partially-annotated bibliography has an index of authors and titles of anonymous works. Coverage includes institutions, scientific expeditions, publishing, archives, and libraries, as well as reference books, periodicals, and manuscripts. A highly specialized aspect is covered by Don Wismer in *The Islamic Jesus: An Annotated Bibliography of Sources in English and French* (Garland, 1977), which is concerned with perceptions of Jesus by Islamic writers.

90. Barrow, John Graves. **A Bibliography of Bibliographies of Religion.** Edwards, 1955. 489p.

The basic arrangement is by subject, subarranged by dates of publication. Barrow gives evaluations and locations of many items. There is an author, title, and subject index.

91. Berkowitz, Morris I., and J. Edmund Johnson. **Social Scientific Studies of Religion: A Bibliography.** University of Pittsburgh Press, 1967. 258p.

This selective bibliography of some 6,000 items in English represents both American and European scholarship. The classification scheme shows the relation of religion to society and culture. There are no annotations. An author index provides access which complements the subject arrangement. A more recent work with a somewhat comparable approach is *Sociologia de la religion y teologia: Estudio bibliografico/Sociology of Religion and Theology: A Bibliography* (Madrid, 1975). *Church-State Relations: An Annotated Bibliography*, by Albert J. Menendez (Garland, 1976), is confined to full-length books in English, with emphasis on North America and Europe. *Western Mysticism: A Guide to the Basic Works*, compiled by Mary Ann Bowman (ALA, 1978), annotates some 500 religious and secular titles in English, including works on Judaism and Eastern Orthodoxy.

92. **Bibliographie bouddhique,** 1928/29- . Librairie d'Amérique et d'Orient.

Each volume covers one year, but the publication is irregular and often late. It is a classified, annotated bibliography that covers books and articles in 200 periodicals. The period before 1928 is covered in Shinsho Hanayama's *Bibliography on Buddhism* (Hokuseido Press, 1961), which contains over 15,000 numbered entries, arranged alphabetically by author with a subject index.

93. **A Bibliography of the Catholic Church, Representing Holdings of American Libraries Reported to the National Union Catalog in the Library of Congress.** Mansell, 1970. 572p.

Taken from volumes 99-100 of the *National Union Catalog, Pre-1956 Imprints*, this work includes 16,000 main and added entries, with all organizational and form headings. Most of the other major churches and some of the smaller ones have also published bibliographies. The most extensive is E. C. Starr's *A Baptist Bibliography* (American Baptist Historical Society, 1947-76, 25v.). Other recent examples include *Shaker Literature: A Bibliography*, by Mary L. Richmond (University Press of New England, 1976, 2v.), and *A Guide to the Holiness Movement*, by C. E. Jones (Scarecrow, 1974), the first in a series of bibliographies sponsored by the American Theological Library Association. More than 10,000 items with locations in 200 libraries will be found in Flake Chad's *A Mormon Bibliography, 1830-1930* (University of Utah Press, 1978).

94. Case, Shirley Jackson, ed. **A Bibliographical Guide to the History of Christianity.** University of Chicago Press, 1931; repr. Peter Smith, 1951. 265p.

A selective, classified bibliography of books and journal articles, with an author and subject index. Unfortunately, there is no recent comprehensive bibliography of church history, though specialized aspects and periods are covered in such works as *Vatican II: A Bibliography*, by Charles Dollen (Scarecrow, 1969), and *Medieval Monasticism: A Select Bibliography*, by Giles Constable (University of Toronto Press, 1976).

95. Hebrew Union College—Jewish Institute of Religion. Library. **Dictionary Catalog of the Klau Library, Cincinnati.** G. K. Hall, 1964. 32v.

Photographic reproduction of nearly one-half million cards, including entries for periodical articles.

95a. Holland, Barron, comp. **Popular Hinduism and Hindu Mythology: An Annotated Bibliography.** Greenwood, 1979. 424p.

This classified, annotated bibliography includes 3,500 books, essays, periodical articles and dissertations. Author and subject indexes are provided.

96. **International Bibliography of the History of Religions. Bibliographie internationale de l'histoire des religions . . . ,** 1952- . Brill, 1954- .

Subsidized by Unesco and published under the auspices of the International Council for Philosophy and Humanistic Studies by the International Association for the History of Religions. Classified annual lists of books and journal articles. Author indexes since 1958-59. Book reviews noted. No annotations. About 2,000 items per year. Five-year cumulations. Slow in appearing.

97. McCabe, James Patrick. **Critical Guide to Catholic Reference Books.** Libraries Unlimited, 1971. 287p.

A classified, annotated bibliography of some 900 titles, with an author, subject, and title index that refers to item numbers rather than to page numbers. Emphasis is on works available in the United States.

98. New York (City). Union Theological Seminary. Library. **The Shelf List of the Union Theological Seminary Library in New York City; in Classification Order.**

G. K. Hall, 1960. 10v. **Alphabetical Arrangement of the Main Entries from the "Shelf List"** . . . . G. K. Hall, 1960 (1965). 10v.
The Union Theological Seminary Library has one of the foremost collections of religious literature in the United States. These sets provide author and subject access to more than 350,000 items. Subject searching by means of the shelf list will be facilitated by knowledge of the special classification scheme adopted by the Library: *Classification of the Library of Union Theological Seminary* . . . , prep. by Julia Pettee. Rev. and enl. ed. With additions and corrections 1939-December 1966, ed. by Ruth C. Eisenhart (Union Theological Seminary, 1967).

98a. **Religious Books and Serials in Print, 1978/79.** Bowker, 1978. 1259p.
The works of many specialized publishers not included in *Books in Print* will be found here. A "Subject Area Directory" (which lists LC subject headings under 48 major topics) and a "Sacred Works Index" (which covers Bibles, etc., published in the U.S.) offer valuable supplementary access to that provided by the subject, author, and title sections.

99. Turner, Harold W. **Bibliography of New Religious Movements in Primal Societies; Volume I, Black Africa.** G. K. Hall, 1977. 277p.
First in a planned series of four volumes, with others to cover North America, Latin America and the Caribbean, and Asia (including Oceania). Geographically arranged, with a detailed table of contents and an author and source index. Supplements, corrects, and updates *A Comprehensive Bibliography of Modern African Religious Movements*, by R. C. Mitchell and H. W. Turner (Northwestern University Press, 1966).

100. Williams, Ethel L., and Clifton F. Brown, comps. **The Howard University Bibliography of African and Afro-American Religious Studies: With Locations in American Libraries.** Scholarly Resources, 1977. 525p.
A classified bibliography of 13,000 items, including both primary and secondary sources from 230 libraries and archives. Detailed table of contents and general author index. Appendix I lists manuscripts, and appendix II provides an "Autobiographical and Biographical Index." This is a revision and substantial expansion of *Afro-American Religious Studies* (Scarecrow, 1972), by the same compilers.

101. Yoo, Yushin. **Books on Buddhism: An Annotated Subject Guide.** Scarecrow, 1976. 251p.
Classified, annotated bibliography of over 1,300 books in English. Title index, and author, editor, and translator index. A companion volume to Yoo's *Buddhism: A Subject Index to Periodical Articles in English, 1728-1971* (Scarecrow, 1973). Both works are valuabie for undergraduates and general inquirers, but scholars will need other sources like *Bibliographie bouddhique* and Hanayama's *Bibliography on Buddhism* (see item 92).

INDEXES, ABSTRACTS, AND CURRENT AWARENESS SERVICES

102. American Theological Library Association. **Religion Index One: Periodicals; A Subject Index to Periodical Literature Including an Author Index With Abstracts and a Book Review Index,** 1949/52- . The Association.

Formerly entitled *Index to Religious Periodical Literature* (title changed with semi-annual edition, July-December 1977), this index covers major religious and theological journals on an ecumenical and international basis. Published semi-annually with two-year cumulations, each issue or volume is divided into three parts: subject index; author index with abstracts; and book review index. A companion index, entitled *Religion Index Two: Multi-Authored Works*, began (with coverage of 1976 imprints) in 1978. Supplemental coverage may be found in *Christian Periodical Index* (1958-), *Guide to Social Science and Religion in Periodical Literature* (1964-), *Index to Jewish Periodicals* (1963-), and *Theological and Religious Index* (1972-).

103. **The Catholic Periodical and Literature Index**, 1968- . Catholic Library Association.
Annotated author-title-subject bibliography of adult books by Catholics, with a selection of Catholic-interest books by other authors published during or before the calendar year, and a cumulative author and subject index to a selected list of Catholic periodicals. Book reviews are entered under "Book Reviews," then subarranged by author. Absorbed *Catholic Periodical Index* (1930-68) and *The Guide to Catholic Literature (1888-1968)*.

104.   Diehl, Katharine Smith. **Hymns and Tunes: An Index.** Scarecrow, 1966. 1185p.
Coverage includes 78 hymnals used for public worship in the twentieth century, chiefly in English. Prefatory matter includes detailed instructions on use, and an essay on hymns and tunes. Part I deals with the hymns: index 1—first lines and variants, with citations; index II—authors and first lines. Part II deals with the tunes: index III—tune names and variants, with citations; index IV—composers and tune names; index V—melodies, a systematic index. Appendixes include "The Scales," "Piano Keyboard," etc. T. B. McDormand's *The Judson Concordance to Hymns* (Judson Press, 1965) is also very useful. More specialized are *Early English Hymns: An Index*, by Edna D. Parks (Scarecrow, 1972), which covers some 900 hymns written before the time of Isaac Watts (1674-1748), and *Organ Preludes: An Index to Compositions on Hymn Tunes, Chorales Plainsong, Melodies, Gregorian Tunes, and Carols*, by Jean Slater Edson (Scarecrow, 1970; Supplement, 1974), which covers 3,000 tunes by composer (v. I) and tune name (v. II).

105.   France. Centre Nationale de la Recherche Scientifique. **Bulletin signalétique 527: Sciences religieuses**, v. 24, 1970- . Q.
Includes coverage of religion that was formerly part of *Bulletin signalétique 519: Philosophie, sciences religieuses*, and it keeps the same volume numbering.

106.   London. University. School of Oriental and African Studies. Library. **Index Islamicus, 1906-1955: A Catalogue of Articles on Islamic Subjects in Periodicals and Other Collective Publications.** Comp. by J. D. Pearson and Julia F. Ashton. Heffer, 1958. Suppl. 1956-60, 1962. 2nd suppl. 1961-65, 1967. 3rd suppl. 1965-70 (Mansell, 1972). 4th suppl. 1971-75, 1977.
Tries to cover the entire field of Islamic studies, with over 26,000 entries in the main work. Classified arrangement with author index.

107. **Religious and Theological Abstracts**, 1958- . Q. Religious and Theological Abstracts, Inc.

A non-sectarian abstracting service, this covers 150 journals. Abstracts are initialed unless done by editorial staff, and abstractors are listed in each issue. Arrangement is classified into five major categories: Biblical; Theological; Historical; Practical; and Sociological. Abstracts are in English, average around 100 words in length, and give language of original article if other than English. Annual subject and author indexes.

108. **Religious Studies Review**, 1975- . Q. Council on the Study of Religion, Wilfrid Laurier University.

A useful current awareness service that includes book reviews, bibliographies, bibliographic essays, and lists of dissertations recently completed.

DICTIONARIES AND ENCYCLOPEDIAS

109. **Baker's Dictionary of Christian Ethics**, ed. by Carl F. H. Henry. Baker, 1973. 726p.

The concise, readable, signed articles by 250 evangelical scholars contain frequent references to biblical passages and are sometimes critical of more liberal Protestant viewpoints. A different perspective is found in John Macquarrie's *A Dictionary of Christian Ethics* (Westminster, 1967).

110. **A Catholic Dictionary of Theology: A Work Projected with the Approval of the Catholic Hierarchy of England and Wales.** Nelson & Sons, 1962-71. 3v.

Planned as a four-volume set (v. 4 did not appear) to provide a coherent exposition of Roman Catholic theology through well-written, scholarly articles with bibliographies. *A Catholic Dictionary*, ed. by Donald Attwater (3rd ed., Macmillan, 1958), gives briefer definitions in philosophy, theology, canon law, liturgy, etc. It omits biography except for saints in the calendar of the church. *Maryknoll Catholic Dictionary*, compiled by Albert J. Nevins (Dimension Books, 1965), incorporates new concepts from Vatican II and includes some biographical information about deceased American and Canadian Roman Catholics. The *Concise Theological Dictionary*, by Karl Rahner and Herbert Vorgrimler (Herder, 1965), is at a more advanced level than Louis Bouyer's *Dictionary of Theology* (Desclée, 1965).

111. Davies, John Gordon, ed. **The Westminster Dictionary of Worship.** Westminster, 1979. 385p.

Originally published in 1972 (SCM; Macmillan) as *A Dictionary of Liturgy and Worship* and now reprinted under a new title, this excellent ecumenical work concentrates mainly on Christian worship, with some attention to other religions. Signed articles by the 65 contributors contain not only definitions, but historical accounts and, where substantial differences exist, subsections on the viewpoints of the various denominations. Some entries include brief bibliographies. The 43 black-and-white photographs and 27 sketches are particularly useful for illustrating church architecture and ecclesiastical vestments. There is no index, but the cross references, though insufficient in number, are useful. Another valuable source is Gerald Podhradsky's *New Dictionary of the Liturgy* (Alba House, 1967).

112. **A Dictionary of Comparative Religion**, ed. by S. G. F. Brandon. Scribners, 1970. 704p.

Brandon, whose specialties are Judaism and Christianity, is professor of comparative religion, University of Manchester. Sectional editors cover Buddhism, Hinduism, Islam, China, and the Far East. Short, signed articles (with bibliographies) by British scholars cover such topics as beliefs, rituals, important figures, schools, councils, and sacred books. The style is very compact, with many abbreviations. Arrows designate cross references. There is a general index of names and subjects not given separate articles, as well as a synoptic index, which groups under the name of a religion all entries about that religion. A brief explanation of pronunciation of names in non-European languages is given. This work is a good starting point for most religious questions, though Geoffrey Parrinder's *Dictionary of Non-Christian Religions* (Westminster, 1973), Edward Rice's *Eastern Definitions* (Doubleday, 1978), and R. C. Zaehner's *The Concise Encyclopedia of Living Faiths* (Beacon, 1959; repr., 1967) may be easier for the lay person to use. One major segment of this work has been extracted and published separately as *A Dictionary of Buddhism*, edited by T. O. Ling (Scribners, 1972). Although this technique of extracting from a larger work is questionable, there is a dearth of good, current, convenient sources of information on Buddhism. *The Encyclopedia of Buddhism* (Government of Ceylon, 1961-) appears to have foundered near the end of the letter "B," and Christmas Humphreys's *A Popular Dictionary of Buddhism* (2nd ed., Rowman and Littlefield, 1976) is suitable for general readers, but not for scholars.

113. **Encyclopaedia Judaica.** Macmillan, 1972. 16v.

Comprehensive and authoritative treatment of all aspects of Jewish life is given in more than 25,000 articles (mostly signed) by some 1,800 contributors and 300 editors. The index has been placed in v. I to emphasize its importance; this volume also includes transliteration tables, lists of Israeli place names, and Hebrew periodicals and newspapers. It does not entirely supersede older works like *The Jewish Encyclopedia* (Funk & Wagnalls, 1901-06, 12v.), which was designed to interpret Jewish religion and life to a Christian audience, or *The Universal Jewish Encyclopedia* (U.J.E., Inc., 1939-43, 10v.), which was designed to acquaint Jews with their own heritage. Recent shorter general works like *The New Standard Jewish Encyclopedia* (Doubleday, 1970) and *Gateway to Judaism: Encyclopedia Home Reference* (Yoselof, 1972) may occasionally be useful, as may specialized works like Werblowsky's *The Encyclopedia of Jewish Religion* (Holt, 1966). Geoffrey Wigoder's *Dictionary of Judaica* (Amiel, 1974) is specifically designed to complement the *Encyclopaedia Judaica*. It is profusely illustrated with black and white photographs (on the same pages as the articles) and has some colored plates (but not conveniently linked to the text). It also contains lists and tables, a transliteration key, and a basic Hebrew-English vocabulary. *The International Jewish Encyclopedia*, by Ben Isaacson and Deborah Wigoder (Prentice-Hall, 1973), is suitable for young people (junior high and up) and for adults who want simplified information.

114. **Encyclopaedia of Islam.** New ed. Brill; Luzac, 1954- .

The most authoritative work in English, this scholarly encyclopedia has signed articles, with bibliographies, that cover an extremely wide range of topics. It is published first in separate fascicles, which later became parts of bound volumes. The basic arrangement is alphabetical. However, Arabic terms may be used instead of the more familiar English ones (e.g., "masdjid" for "mosque"), but the new edition includes more cross references in English and French. Until the second edition is complete, libraries will need to retain and use the first (1911-38, 4v., plus suppl.) or at least have on the shelves the *Shorter Encyclopaedia of Islam* (Brill; Luzac, 1953; repr., Cornell, 1965). Despite its age, *A Dictionary of Islam . . .* , by Thomas Patrick Hughes (London, 1885; repr., Humanities, 1978), is often helpful to the general public. Useful information can also be found in the *Concise Encyclopedia of Arabic Civilization*, by Stephen and Nandy Ronart (Praeger, 1960-66, 2v.).

115.   **Encyclopaedia of Religion and Ethics**, ed. by A. J. Hastings and others. Scribners, 1910-27; repr. 1961. 13v.
Despite its age, this is still the most comprehensive religious encyclopedia available in English. Long, scholarly articles are frequently subdivided in a systematic fashion. Articles are signed and have bibliographies. The final volume has an analytical index, an index to foreign words, an index to scripture passages, and an index to authors of articles.

116.   **Encyclopédie des sciences ecclésiastiques.** Letouzey, 1907- .
The most extensive work in modern theology, this multi-volume set is divided into the following parts: 1. Vigouroux, F. G., and L. Pirot, *Dictionnaire de la Bible*, 1907-12, 5v. Suppl., 1928- ; 2. Vacant, A., and others, *Dictionnaire de theologie catholique*, 1909-50, 15v. and *Tables générales*, 1951- ; 3. Cabrol, F., and H. Leclerq, *Dictionnaire d'archéologie chretienne de la liturgie*, 1907-53, 15v. in 30; 4. Baudrillart, A., *Dictionnaire d'histoire et de géographie ecclésiastique*, 1912- ; 5. *Dictionnaire de droit canonique*, 1935- .

117.   Ferm, Virgilius Ture Anselm. **An Encyclopedia of Religion.** Philosophical Library, 1945. 844p.
Writen from a Protestant standpoint, this concise encyclopedia has a wide range of articles with bibliographies, many cross references, and entries for variant spellings of terms. It is supplemented in some respects by Ferm's *A Protestant Dictionary* (Philosophical Library, 1951).

118.   Julian, John. **A Dictionary of Hymnology Setting Forth the Origin and History of Christian Hymns of All Ages and Nations.** Scribners, 1907; repr., Dover, 1957. 2v.
Despite the appearance of several newer books, this is still the standard work on the subject. The novice can easily miss some of the wealth of information because of the way in which supplements and revisions were handled. Contents: 1. Dictionary; 2. Cross reference index to first lines; 3. Index of authors, translators, etc.; 4. Appendix A-Z, late articles; 5. Appendix A-Z, additions and corrections to articles in the main part; 6. New spplement; and 7. Index to appendices and supplement. Additional coverage (especially of newer hymns) may sometimes be found in *The Gospel in Hymns: Backgrounds and Interpretations*, by A. E. Bailey (Scribners, 1950), and in *Companion to the Hymnal*, by Fred Gealy (Abingdon, 1970). The latter is based on the 1964 Methodist hymnal.

119.   **Lexikon für Theologie und Kirche.** Begründet von Michael Buchberger 2, völlig neu bearb. Aufl., unter dem Protektorat von Michael Buchberger und Eugen Seiterich;

hrsg. von Josef Höfer und Karl Rahner. Herder, 1957-65. 10v. Suppl. 1966-68. 3v.
The editors were assisted by a group of European (predominantly German) scholars.
Articles are signed and vary greatly in length. Bibliographical citations are given. Topics
relating to theology and the Church are extensively covered. V. 10 is an index. The supplement covers the Second Vatican Council and follows a classified arrangement instead
of the alphabetic arrangement of the main set.

120. Negev, Avraham, ed. **Archaeological Encyclopedia of the Holy Land.** Putnam,
1972. 354p.
Some 20 Israeli and American scholars have prepared concise, unsigned articles on
places in the Holy Land and nearby countries, peoples who inhabited the area, and
related topics. There are nine maps and numerous black and white illustrations, all
placed on the same pages as the articles to which they refer and captioned clearly to
relate to the articles. Cross references are indicated by asterisks. A glossary and a
chronological chart are provided at the end. *The Encyclopedia of Archaeological Ex-
cavations in the Holy Land* (Prentice-Hall, 1975-), projected as a four-volume set, is
alphabetically arranged and contains some photographs in color plus many in black and
white. Two very readable narratives are Jack Finegan's *Light from the Ancient Past:
The Archaeological Background of Judaism and Christianity* (2nd ed., Princeton, 1959)
and his *Archaeology of the New Testament: The Life of Jesus and the Beginning of the
Early Church* (Princeton, 1969). In a more specialized vein, *The Dead Sea Scrolls* (Viking, 1955) and *More Light from the Dead Sea Scrolls* (Viking, 1958) are successful
popularizations by Millar Burrows, who was director of the American Society for
Oriental Research in Jerusalem when the first scrolls were discovered in 1947.

121. Neill, Stephen Charles, Gerald H. Anderson, and John Goodwin, eds. **Concise
Dictionary of the Christian World Mission.** Abingdon, 1971. 682p.
Articles by over 200 contributors cover the period from 1492 to the present. The viewpoint is international, liberal, and ecumenical. Countries, leaders, and subjects are
given concise articles in one alphabet, with many cross references. Leaders still living are
omitted, as are those lacking strong connections with missionary movements. Coverage
of a supplementary nature will be found in *The Encyclopedia of Modern Christian Missions: The Agencies* (Nelson, 1967).

122. **New Catholic Encyclopedia.** McGraw-Hill, 1967. 15v. V. 16, suppl. 1967-74.
1974.
Prepared under an editorial staff from the Catholic University of America, this is not a
revision of *The Catholic Encyclopedia* (1907-22) but a completely new work. Its scope is
indicated by the subtitle, which describes it as "an international work of reference on the
teachings, history, organization and activities of the Catholic Church, and on all institutions, religions, philosophies and scientific and cultural developments affecting the
Catholic Church from its beginning to the present." There are about 17,000 articles by
4,800 contributors. The index (v. 15) contains 300,000 entries. Articles are signed and
have selective bibliographies. Generally well produced and illustrated, *NCE* is a major
special encyclopedia, particularly valuable for its treatment of scholastic philosophy
and theological writers. Quite different in purpose is the 12-volume *Catholic Encyclopedia for School and Home* (McGraw-Hill, 1965), which presents Roman Catholic
teaching on a great variety of topics (both secular and religious) for students. Encyclopedias have been produced on a smaller scale for several other Christian churches.

Examples would include *The Encyclopedia of World Methodism*, by Nolan R. Harmon (Abingdon, 1974, 2v.), the *Lutheran Cyclopedia* (rev. ed. Concordia, 1975), *The Mennonite Encyclopedia* (Mennonite Publishing House, 1955-59, 4v.), the *Seventh-Day Adventist Encyclopedia* (Review & Herald Publishing Association, 1978), and the *Encyclopedia of Southern Baptists* (Broadman, 1958, 2v.). Not exactly an encyclopedia, but conveniently indexed, is *Official Catholic Teachings* (Consortium Books, 1978, 6v.).

123. **Oxford Dictionary of the Christian Church**, ed. by F. L. Cross and E. A. Livingstone. 2nd ed. Oxford, 1974. 1518p.
With over 6,000 entries from 247 contributors, this concise work is especially good for biographies, definitions, theologies, and heresies. Entries are unsigned, but coverage is generally balanced and there are good bibliographies. Asterisks indicate cross references. Supplementary coverage, from a Roman Catholic perspective, will be found in T. C. O'Brien's *Corpus Dictionary of Western Churches* (Corpus Publications, 1970) and a conservative Protestant viewpoint is expressed in *The New International Dictionary of the Christian Church*, ed. by J. D. Douglas (2nd ed., Zondervan, 1978). *The Westminster Dictionary of Church History*, ed. by J. C. Brauer (Westminster, 1971), is also useful. Small libraries and home purchasers may prefer *The Concise Oxford Dictionary of the Christian Church* (Oxford, 1977) to any of the above, but most libraries will need the fuller treatment of the larger works.

124. **Die Religion in Geschichte und Gegenwart. Handwörterbuch für Theologie und Religionwissenschaft.** 3. vollig. neu bearb. Aufl. in Gemeinschaft mit Hans Freihern v. Campenhausen: hrsg. von Kurt Galligan. Mohr, 1957-65. 7v.
This scholarly work has lengthy signed articles and bibliographies. Biographical notes on the more than 3,000 contributors will be found in v. 7, along with an extensive subject index. The viewpoint is German Protestant. Another work of some usefulness is *Evangelisches Kirchen Lexikon*, ed. by Heinz Brunotte and Otto Weber (Vanderhoeck & Ruprecht, 1956-61, 4v.).

125. Richardson, Alan, ed. **A Dictionary of Christian Theology.** Westminster, 1969. 364p.
The editor and 36 contributors have defined about 500 words, phrases, and ideas in the context of theological debate. Articles are signed and vary widely in length. (The longest is 7,500 words.) There are cross references, citations to sources, and separate bibliographies. Despite its title, this book does include some biographies of leading theologians from various periods. It does not duplicate Richardson's *Theological Word Book of the Bible* (SCM Press, 1950). At a more elementary level is *A Christian Dictionary—A Popular Guide to 1600 Names*, by James Kerr and Charles Lutz (Fortress Press, 1969).

126. **Sacramentum Mundi: An Encyclopedia of Theology**, ed. by Karl Rahner and others. Herder, 1968-70. 6v.
A major work of modern Roman Catholic scholarship, this encyclopedia reflects the outlook since Vatican II. The level is somewhat too erudite and technical for the average lay person, but valuable for the priest, minister, or serious student. Topics covered range over the whole spectrum of knowledge and society. Articles have bibliographies. The final volume is a detailed index. A one-volume edition entitled

Encyclopedia of Theology: The Concise Sacramentum Mundi (Crossroad; Seabury, 1975) has also appeared.

127. **Schaff-Herzog Encyclopedia. The New Schaff-Herzog Encyclopedia of Religious Knowledge** . . . . Funk & Wagnalls, 1908-12; repr. Baker, 1949-50. 13v.
Based on the third German edition, this is more than a translation in that some new material was added and some German articles of the Herzog-Hauch *Realenzyklopädie* were condensed. Though Protestant in tone, it describes all religions and religious leaders. There is extensive coverage of theology, sects, denominations, doctrines, and controversies. It was updated and supplemented by the *Twentieth Century Encyclopedia of Religious Knowledge* . . . (Baker Book House, 1955, 2v.), which may either be used with the basic set or independently.

128. Stutley, Margaret, and James Stutley. **Harper's Dictionary of Hinduism: Its Mythology, Folklore, Philosophy, Literature and History.** Harper, 1977. 416p.
Acclaimed by reviewers and included among the "Reference Books of 1977" (*Library Journal* 103 [April 15, 1978]:817), this work is both more current and more scholarly than G. B. Walker's *The Hindu World: An Encyclopedic Survey of Hinduism* (Praeger, 1968, 2v.). The latter may still be used by reference librarians for topics not covered by the Stutleys and will be welcomed by lay persons for its more popular approach.

129. **Theologische Realenzyklopädie.** In Gemeinschaft mit Horst Robert Balz, et al. hrsg. von Gerhard Krause und Gerhard Müller. deGruyter, 1976- .
This important new work contains long, signed scholarly articles with bibliographies and an index in each volume. A general index is planned when the set is completed in 25 volumes.

130. **Twentieth Century Encyclopedia of Catholicism**, ed. by Henri Daniel-Rops. Hawthorn, 1958-68. 150v.
Each volume in this comprehensive set is a monograph by a noted scholar. LC made an entry for the set as a whole, but also produced separate entries (with different call numbers) for the individual volumes. For a list, see *Titles in Series*, by Eleanora A. Baer (2nd ed., Scarecrow, 1964) and the supplements.

131. Woods, Ralph Louis. **The World Treasury of Religious Quotations: Diverse Beliefs, Convictions, Comments, and Opinions from Ancient and Modern Sources.** Hawthorn, 1966. 1106p.
Although predominantly Christian, this book also includes quotations from scientists, philosophers, and leaders of other world religions. The arrangement is alphabetical under 1,500 subject headings. Many cross references are provided at the end of each subject section. There is an author index. It is more comprehensive than Frank S. Mead's *Encyclopedia of Religious Quotations* (Revell, 1965; repr., 1973).

132. **Word Book of Religious Terms**, ed. by Clara A. McCartt. World, 1969. 320p.
Over 25,000 terms most used by churchmen are defined, given syllabication, and accented, with variant spellings and inflected forms. Another useful work is *The Vocabulary of the Church: A Pronunciation Guide*, by Richard White (Macmillan, 1960), which concentrates on proper nouns and words from the Bible.

DIRECTORIES AND ANNUALS

133. **American Jewish Yearbook**, 1899- . Ann. Jewish Publication Society of America.
Contains annual narrative reviews of Jewish affairs in the U.S. and around the world. A special article of considerable length is usually (though not always) placed at the beginning, followed by articles on the U.S., briefer treatments of other countries, obituaries and necrologies, various directories and lists, and a summary Jewish calendar. Each volume contains a detailed name and title index. Cumulative subject indexes to the special articles have also been issued (v. 40 for v. 1-40 and v. 74 for v. 51-73).

134. **Directory of Religious Organizations in the United States of America.** Consortium; McGrath, 1978. 553p.
Over 1,500 religious organizations (many not covered elsewhere) are listed in this new directory.

135. Mead, Frank S. **Handbook of Denominations in the United States.** 6th ed. Abingdon, 1975. 320p.
Information on more than 250 groups includes brief accounts of histories and doctrines and fairly recent information on memberships. It is well indexed and includes an appended list of addresses of headquarters, a glossary of terms, and a bibliography arranged by denomination.

136. **Official Catholic Directory**, 1886- . Ann. Kenedy.
There have been some variations in title over the years. This directory contains large amounts of institutional and statistical information about the Roman Catholic Church in the United States and other countries. Clergy, missions, schools, churches, religious orders, etc., are covered in detail.

137. Melton, J. Gordon. **A Directory of Religious Bodies in the United States.** Garland, 1977. 305p.
Brief directory information is provided for 1,275 religious groups. There are also chapters that discuss problems of gathering information and systems of classification. More detailed directory information for large churches will be found in the *Yearbook of American and Canadian Churches* (see item 140).

138. Piepkorn, Arthur Carl. **Profiles in Belief: The Religious Bodies of the United States and Canada.** Harper, 1977- .
Projected for completion in seven volumes, this set will be more comprehensive than Mead (see item 135). The arrangement is classified, with a detailed table of contents and an index in each volume. Historical information, major beliefs, current statistics, and extensive footnotes are provided. Contents to date: v. 1—*Roman Catholic, Old Catholic, and Eastern Orthodox*, 1977; v. 2—*Protestantism*, 1978; v. 3—*Pentecostalism*, 1978. *The Encyclopedia of American Religions*, by J. Gordon Melton (Consortium; McGrath, 1979. 2v.) contains descriptions of 1,200 American religious bodies, some of them difficult to find elsewhere.

139. **World Christian Handbook**, ed. by H. Wakelin Coxill and Kenneth Grubb. 5th ed. Abingdon, 1968.
First published in 1949, this work has three main parts: articles, statistics, directory. The coverage generally is worldwide and ecumenical. The statistics section also includes non-Christian religions. Edward R. Dayton's *Mission Handbook: North American Protestant Missions Overseas* (11th ed., Missions Advanced Research and Communications Center, 1976) contains supplementary and more recent coverage.

140. **Yearbook of American and Canadian Churches**, 1916- . Ann. National Council of Churches.
There were some changes of title and some irregularity of publication in earlier years. Canadian coverage was substantially increased in 1972. There are four main parts: 1) A Calendar for Church Use; 2) Directories (classified into several categories and alphabetical within each category); 3) Statistical and Historical Section (also classified, then alphabetical); 4) Index. The index supplements the directory section by grouping denominations under generic headings [e.g., "Baptist Bodies (U.S.)"], thus making it easier to locate groups separated in the directory by the strictly alphabetical arrangement. Care has been taken to gather current statistics and to indicate when information is not current.

HISTORIES

141. **Chicago History of American Religion**, ed. by Martin Marty. University of Chicago Press, 1973- .
Titles published to date include: *American Religious Thought*, by W. A. Clebsch (1973); *Dissent in American Religion*, by E. S. Gaustad (1973); *Judaism in America*, by J. L. Blau (1976); and *Religion in the Old South*, by D. G. Mathews (1976). Most libraries classify and catalog these volumes separately, but with a series added entry. Not a part of this series, but a very convenient one-volume history is *Religion in America: An Historical Account of the Development of American Religious Life*, by W. S. Hudson (2nd ed., Scribners, 1973).

142. **Eerdman's Handbook to the History of Christianity**, ed. by Tim Dowley. Eerdmans, 1977. 656p.
A companion volume to *Eerdman's Handbook to the Bible* (1973), this book is divided into eight major sections, covering Christian history from the beginning to the present. Each section also includes biographical sketches (on differently-colored paper). Profusely illustrated, the book has a detailed table of contents and five indexes: people; places; movements and events; Bible references; and pictures. The compilers represent a conservative Protestant viewpoint, but are fair to other opinions. Designed for the laity, this work does not have footnotes, bibliographies, or other scholarly apparatus.

143. Jedin, Hubert, and John Dolan, eds. **Handbook of Church History.** Burns & Oates; Seabury, 1965- .
A major scholarly history, from a Roman Catholic viewpoint, the English version is translated from the third revised German edition (1962-73, 6v.). Extensive bibliographies are featured. Volumes available in English include: v. 1—*From the Apostolic Community to Constantine* (1965); v. 3—*The Church in the Age of*

Feudalism (1969); v. 4 — *From the High Middle Ages to the Eve of the Reformation* (1970).

144.   Latourette, Kenneth Scott. **A History of the Expansion of Christianity.** Harper, 1937-45. 7v.
Though written by a Protestant historian, this major scholarly study of missions from the earliest times to the twentieth century gives balanced and fair treatment to Roman Catholic and Orthodox missions. Each volume has maps, an extensive bibliography, and an index. It is likely to remain the standard work in this field for many years to come. Other significant works by Latourette include *A History of Christianity* (Harper, 1953) and *Christianity in a Revolutionary Age: A History of Christianity in the Nineteenth and Twentieth Centuries* (Harper, 1958-62, 5v.). The former is not a condensation of *A History of the Expansion of Christianity* but a completely new work. The author was Sterling Professor of Missions and Oriental History at Yale University. All of these works contain extensive bibliographies and good indexes.

145.   **The Sacred Books of the East,** ed. by Max Müller. Oxford, 1879-1910; repr. Verry, 1965-66. 50v.
This is a truly massive collection of translated sacred literature. Despite the fact that v. 50 is an index to the series, most libraries (including LC) catalog each volume separately and assign different call numbers. A complete list is given on page 225 of *Guide to Reference Books* (item 11), by Eugene Sheehy (9th ed., ALA, 1976).

ATLASES

146.   Farūqī, Isma'il Rāgi A., ed. **Historical Atlas of the Religions of the World.** Macmillan, 1974. 346p.
Assisted by an international team of scholars, the editor has prepared a work with substantial narrative comment and numerous black and white photographs, as well as maps showing growth or decline in different historical periods. Part I covers "Religions of the Past," Part II, "Ethnic Religions of the Present," and Part III, "Universal Religions of the Present." There is an "Appendix of Chronologies." Access is provided through the table of contents and by subject and proper name indexes.

147.   Freitag, Anton. **The Twentieth Century Atlas of the Christian World: The Expansion of Christianity through the Centuries.** Hawthorn, 1963. 199p.
Originally published in French (1959), the book was revised and updated when translated into English. The basic arangement is by historical periods. Narrative is interspersed with 29 colored maps, 610 black and white photographs and some line drawings. Notes on the photographs are at the end. There is a detailed table of contents. The index refers both to the pages of the text and to the number of the notes that explain the illustrations. This work reflects a Roman Catholic viewpoint.

148.   Gaustad, Edwin S. **Historical Atlas of Religion in America.** Rev. ed. Harper, 1976. 189p.
By maps, charts, tables, and text, this work shows the expansion of denominations in the United States from 1650 to the present. The revised edition has many new and better maps, some new charts, and updated line graphs.

149. Littell, Franklin Hamlin. **The Macmillan Atlas of Christianity.** Cart. by Emanuel Hausman. Macmillan, 1976. 176p.
Arranged by historical periods and done from a Protestant viewpoint, this atlas contains 197 maps and 101 illustrations conveniently interspersed with the narrative. Many items of information can be found through the detailed table of contents. The index uses roman type to refer to map numbers and italic type for page numbers.

BIOGRAPHIES

150. **American Catholic Who's Who,** 1934/35- . NC News Service.
Although intended to be biennial, publication has sometimes been irregular. Each volume has concise biographical articles on well-known Roman Catholics and a list of members of the National Conference of Catholic Bishops.

151. **The Book of Saints: A Dictionary of Persons Canonized or Beatified by the Catholic Church,** comp. by the Benedictine Monks of St. Augustine's Abbey, Ramsgate. 5th ed. Crowell, 1966. 740p.
Revised in the light of modern research and sometimes better than Butler for identification, this work gives saints' names in alphabetical order. When several of the same name occur, the order of the feast days on the liturgical calendar is used to differentiate. Information given (where appropriate) includes: surname or special appellation; rank; liturgical group; religious order; status of cult; feast date; year of death; chief features of career. Concise entries make extensive use of the abbreviations given on page xii.

152. Bowden, Henry Warner. **Dictionary of American Religious Biography.** Greenwood, 1977. 572p.
Bowden includes 425 religious leaders who died before July 1, 1976. Each article gives a brief career synopsis, followed by paragraphs of narrative exposition and critical evaluation, and concludes with short lists of works by and about the person being discussed. A special effort has been made to include dissidents, women, and minorities. Appendices list biographees by denomination and birthplace. There is a brief name and subject index.

153. Butler, Alban. **Lives of the Saints,** ed. by Herbert Thurston and Donald Attwater. Kenedy, 1956. 4v.
This work is a condensation of Thurston's earlier twelve-volume edition (1925-38). Many sketches have been included without change. Some short ones have been omitted, and some sketches of recently canonized saints have been added. The homilies originally included have been omitted. The basic arrangement is by months and the days of each month. Each volume has a detailed table of contents and an index. A "General Index of Names" is given at the end of v. 4. *A Dictionary of Saints*, by Donald Attwater (Kenedy, 1958), gives brief biographical information in an alphabetical arrangement for 2,500 saints and provides index references to the fuller treatment in Butler. A more recent work is D. H. Farmer's *Oxford Dictionary of Saints* (Oxford, 1978).

154. Delaney, John J., and James Edward Tobin. **Dictionary of Catholic Biography.** Doubleday, 1961. 1245p.
Biographies of 13,000 clergy and laity from earliest times to the present are included, with cross references and bibliographies. Appendices: saints as patrons of vocations;

saints as patrons of places; symbols of saints in art; chart correlating papal and secular reigns.

155.   Moyer, Elgin Sylvester, ed. **Who Was Who in Church History.** Rev. ed. Moody Press, 1968; repr. Keats, 1974. 466p.
This Protestant-oriented publication includes 1,700 people from apostolic times to the twentieth century, but excludes those who are still living. There is a chronological index by death date.

156.   **Who's Who in Religion,** 1975/76- . Marquis.
This new publication includes about 16,000 religious leaders now active in the United States: church officials, leading clergy, faculty in seminaries and prominent laypersons.

157.   **Who's Who in World Jewry,** 1955- . Pitman.
The frequency and publisher have varied. There were about 10,000 biographical sketches in the 1972 edition.

158.   Williams, Ethel L. **Biographical Directory of Negro Ministers.** 3rd ed. G. K. Hall, 1975. 584p.
This is the only directory of living black clergy in the United States. Most of the information on the 2,000 ministers covered is not available from any other source. The alphabetical arrangement of the main entries is complemented by a geographical listing. Heavy use is made of abbreviations (listed, pp. xi-xix).

THE BIBLE

Versions and Editions

The books of the Old Testament were written in Hebrew at various times between 1200 and 100 B.C. Final decisions as to which ones should be included in the Jewish canon (list of divinely inspired books) appear to have been made around 100 A.D. A notable translation into Greek, known as the *Septuagint*, was made in the third and second centuries B.C. It included some books not officially accepted as part of the Jewish canon. The books of the New Testament were written in Greek, mainly in the last half of the first century A.D. By the end of the second century, the contents of today's New Testament were fairly clear. The first complete list of the 27 books accepted today appeared in the *Easter Letter* of Athanasius in 367 A.D. A major translation of the Bible into Latin (known as the *Vulgate*) was completed by Jerome in 404 A.D. Articles in general encyclopedias give further details. The article in the 1978 edition of the *Encyclopedia Americana* has a very useful chart (v. 3, pp. 652-53) comparing books included in the Hebrew, Greek, Latin and English versions. Discussion of the various versions and editions will also be found in the chapter on "Bibles and Related Texts" in v. 3 of *The Reader's Adviser* (12th ed., Bowker, 1977). Only a few of the major English versions are given below:

159a. **King James** or **Authorized Version** (1611).
Because of the majestic beauty of its language, this version is still a favorite among Protestants. Numerous editions are in print.

159b. Douay Bible (1582-1610, rev. by Challoner in 1749-50).
Translated from the *Vulgate*, this version has been for Roman Catholics what the *King James* has been for Protestants.

159c. Revised Standard Version (Nelson, 1952).
This translation into modern English by a group of American scholars from many denominations attempts to follow the style of the *King James Version*.

159d. The New English Bible (Oxford/Cambridge, 1970).
The result of more than 20 years of work by a group of British scholars to translate the Bible into clear, modern English, this one differs from the *Revised Standard Version* in that no effort was made to follow the style of the *King James Version*.

159e. The Holy Scriptures According to the Masoretic Text (Jewish Publication Society of America, 1917).
This translation has been kept in print in a variety of bindings. A revised version was begun in 1955.

159f. The New American Bible (Catholic Press, 1971).
Sponsored by the Bishops' Committee of the Confraternity of Christian Doctrine, this is a thoroughly modern translation for American Catholics, including the deutero-canonical books.

159g. The Anchor Bible (Doubleday, 1964-).
An interfaith project, with noted Jewish, Protestant, and Roman Catholic scholars participating, this modern translation (with commentary in each volume) is planned for completion in 43 volumes, of which more than one-half have now appeared.

159h. The Jerusalem Bible (Doubleday, 1966).
Preceded by a French edition (1956) prepared by the Dominicans at L'École Biblique in Jerusalem, the English version is a direct translation from the original languages, with references to the French edition. It won the Thomas More Association Medal for "the most distinguished contribution to Catholic literature in 1966."

159i. The New Scofield Reference Bible (Oxford, 1967).
A complete updating of the 1909 and 1917 editions, this work (based on the *King James Version*) contains subheadings, cross references, book introductions, a concordance, maps, and other study aids. It is widely used by Protestant fundamentalists.

159j. The Living Bible (Holman, 1973).
This popular version is a paraphrase rather than an exact translation.

159k. Good News Bible: The Bible in Today's English Version (American Bible Society, 1976).
The translators have made a great effort to produce a version in clear, simple English. The New Testament appeared first (*Good News for Modern Man*, 1966) and proved very popular, with sales in excess of 45,000,000 copies in the next ten years.

1591. **New International Version** (International Bible Society; distr. Zondervan, 1978). Planned by a group of conservative Protestant scholars to provide a modern alternative to the *Revised Standard Version*, this is a re-translation from the ancient manuscripts. The *New International New Testament* was published in 1973.

N.B.: Various disputed books, commonly known as *The Apocrypha*, are included in several of the versions listed above and have also been published separately.

Reference Works

Bibliographies and Abstracts

160. **International Zeitschriftenschau für Bibelwissenschaft und Grenzgebiete/International Review of Biblical Studies,** 1951/52- . Ann. Verlag Katholisches Bibelwerk.
This annual abstracting service covers biblical scholarship on an international basis. Most abstracts are in German. Titles are in the original languages. The classified arrangement is supplemented by an index of authors of works abstracted. Periodical articles, books, and essays in festschriften are included.

161. Metzger, Bruce Manning. **Index to Periodical Literature on Christ and the Gospels.** Brill, 1966. 602p.
This book is not really an index but a classified bibliography of more than 10,000 items from 160 periodicals, with an author index, but no annotations. Metzger has also compiled *Index to Periodical Literature on the Apostle Paul* (Eerdmans, 1960). Supplementary coverage is given in *A Classified Bibliography of Literature on the Acts of the Apostles,* by A. J. and M. B. Mattill (Eerdmans, 1966). Edward Malatesta's *St. John's Gospel, 1920-1965* (Pontifical Biblical Institute, 1967) is also a classified bibliography of books and periodical articles.

162. **New Testament Abstracts: A Record of Current Periodical Literature,** 1956- . 3/yr. Theological Faculty, Weston College.
Abstracts are given in English, but pertinent articles from Catholic, Protestant, and Jewish periodicals in many languages are included. Each volume contains indexes of scripture texts and authors.

163. **Old Testament Abstracts,** 1978- . 3/yr. Catholic Biblical Association, Catholic University of America.
This new service promises to be a significant contribution in an area not previously covered by its own abstracting service, though coverage has been available from more general sources.

Concordances and Indexes

164. Cruden, Alexander. **Cruden's Complete Concordance to the Old and New Testaments . . . with . . . a Concordance to the Apocrypha.** Zondervan, 1949. 783p.
First published in 1737, this work has long been a classic and is frequently reprinted. It has about 250,000 English entries in alphabetical order. There are appendices of proper names and a concordance to the *Apocrypha*.

165. Ellison, John William. **Nelson's Complete Concordance of the Revised Standard Version of the Bible.** Nelson, 1957. 2157p.
The pioneer in computer-produced concordances, this work includes all of the words of the *Revised Standard Version* except a few non-significant terms. It does not give Hebrew or Creek originals. Another computer-produced concordance (with 734,000 entries, and key words in boldface type) is the *Living Bible Concordance*, edited by Jack Atkeson Speer (Poolsville, MD, Presbyterian Church, 1973).

166. Garland, George Frederick, comp. **Subject Guide to Bible Stories.** Greenwood, 1969. 365p.
Part I is an alphabetical subject index. Part II lists characters from the Bible.

167. Joy, Charles Rhind. **Harper's Topical Concordance.** Rev. ed. Harper, 1962. 628p.
Approximately 25,000 texts are grouped under 2,100 subject headings. Cross references.

168. **Modern Concordance to the New Testament.** Ed. by Michael Darton. Doubleday, 1976. 786p.
Because at least five modern English translations are in common use, this is a *thematic* concordance, rather than a traditional one based simply on words. The alphabetical arrangement of major themes is subdivided by classified groupings of subthemes. Alphabetical Greek and English indexes.

169. **Nelson's Complete Concordance of the New American Bible.** Stephen J. Hartdegan, gen. ed. Nelson, 1977. 1274p.
Excellent concordance produced by computer (like its counterpart for the *Revised Standard Version*). Has 300,000 entries grouped under 18,000 key terms. The key terms are alphabetical, and entries under each term are in order of their occurrence in the Bible. The number of times a particular key word occurs is also provided. A list of non-significant words (which the computer was programmed to omit) is given in the preface. Scholars will be interested in a new concordance to the *Vulgate* entitled *Novae concordiantiae biblorum sacrorum iuxta vulgatum versionem critice editam quas digessit Bonifatius Fischer OSB* (Stuttgart: Fromman-Holzborg, 1977, 5v.).

170. Stevenson, Burton Egbert. **The Home Book of Bible Quotations.** Harper, 1949. 645p.
Arranged in alphabetical order by subjects, with a concordance-type index. Based chiefly on the *King James Version*. Includes the *Apocrypha*.

171. Strong, James. **The Exhaustive Concordance of the Bible** . . . Hunt, 1894. 4v. in 1. [Frequently reprinted].
Most complete concordance. Subtitle: "Showing every word of the text of the common English Version of the canonical books, and every occurrence of each word in regular order; together with a comparative concordance of the Authorized and Revised versions, including the American variations; also brief dictionaries of the Hebrew and Greek words of the original, with references to the English words."

172. Thompson, Newton Wayland, and Raymond Stook. **Complete Concordance to the Bible (Douay Version).** Herder, 1945. 1914p.
First published under title: *Concordance to the Bible (Douay Version)* in 1942.

173. Young, Robert. **Analytical Concordance to the Bible** . . . 22nd American ed., rev. by W. B. Stevenson. Funk & Wagnalls, 1955; repr. Eerdmans, 1973.
The subtitle reads: "About 311,000 references, subdivided under the Hebrew and Greek originals, with the literal meaning and pronunciation of each." Names of people and places are included. The revised edition has a supplement, "Recent Discoveries in Bible Lands," by W. F. Albright, and one entitled "The Canon of Scripture," by R. K. and E. F. Harrison.

Dictionaries and Encyclopedias

174. Bauer, Johannes Baptist, ed. **Sacramentum Verbi: An Encyclopedia of Biblical Theology.** Herder, 1970. 3v.
In-depth treatment of about 200 terms is given in this major work of modern Catholic biblical scholarship. Bibliographies include works in many languages. A more elementary book, written from a Protestant viewpoint, is H. H. Rowley's *Short Dictionary of Bible Themes* (Basic Books, 1968). *A Companion to the Bible*, by J. J. von Allmen (Oxford, 1958), and *A Theological Word Book of the Bible*, edited by Alan Richardson (SCM Press, 1950), are useful for treatment of theological terms, as is *Dictionary of Biblical Theology*, edited by Xavier Leon-Dufour (2nd ed., Seabury, 1973).

175. Botterweck, G. Johannes, and Helmer Ringgren. **Theological Dictionary of the Old Testament.** Tr. by John J. Willis. Eerdmans, 1974- .
Words and phrases are arranged according to their order in Hebrew. (The English edition has transliterations, whereas the original German edition used only Hebrew or Greek script.) Articles are generally lengthy, technical, liberally provided with footnotes and bibliographies, and signed by noted scholars (mainly European). All articles are included in the detailed table of contents in the front of each volume. Abbreviations for books and journals as well as transliteration tables for Hebrew consonants and vowels are found in the front of v. 1. This is a companion set to G. Kittel's *Theological Dictionary of the New Testament* (see item 178).

176. Gehman, Henry Snyder, ed. **The New Westminster Dictionary of the Bible.** Westminster, 1970. 1027p.
Based originally on J. D. Davis's *Dictionary of the Bible* (4th ed., 1924; repr., Baker, 1972), this work evolved in its 1944 and 1970 editions in a much more liberal direction, with major changes in the latest version to incorporate recent scholarship. It includes short biographies, outlines of the books of the Bible, pronunciation of proper names, and descriptions of things and places. Other one-volume works that should be mentioned include *New Bible Dictionary*, by J. D. Douglas (Eerdmans, 1962), *Dictionary of the Bible*, by J. L. McKenzie (Bruce, 1965), and *Harper's Bible Dictionary*, by M. S. and J. L. Miller (8th ed., Harper, 1973). A recently-revised work that should prove very useful is *Harper's Encyclopedia of Bible Life*, by M. S. and J. L. Miller, rev. by B. M. Bennett and D. H. Scott (rev. ed., Harper, 1978).

177. **Interpreter's Dictionary of the Bible**. Abingdon, 1962. 4v. Suppl. 1976.
The lengthy subtitle contains an excellent description: "An illustrated encyclopedia identifying and explaining all proper names and significant terms and subjects in the Holy Scriptures, including the Apocrypha, with attention to archaeological discoveries and researches into the life and faith of ancient times." Many libraries will also need *Young Reader's Dictionary of the Bible* (Abingdon, 1969). A multi-volume set of great repute but now seriously out of date is *Dictionary of the Bible*, edited by J. L. Hastings (Scribners, 1898-1904, 5v.). Hastings also prepared a one-volume independent work of the same title, first published in 1909 and then thoroughly revised and updated by F. C. Grant and H. H. Rowley (Scribners, 1963).

178. Kittel, Gerhard. **Theological Dictionary of the New Testament**. Tr. and ed. by George W. Bromily. Eerdmans, 1964-72. 8v.
This major scholarly work is the result of collaboration by many specialists. Arranged by letters of the Greek alphabet, it defines the Christian meaning of Greek terms. Many articles are of monographic length.

179. **The Zondervan Pictorial Encyclopedia of the Bible**, ed. by Merrill C. Tenney. Zondervan, 1975. 5v.
Of over 7,500 articles from 238 contributors, all but the shortest are signed and have bibliographies. The set contains 32 pages of full-color maps and an index at the end of v. 5. There are 48 full-color plates (some in each volume) and hundreds of black and white illustrations in close proximity to pertinent articles. (The plates are not keyed to the articles.) Though conservative in viewpoint, the authors of articles do state other opinions, and the work as a whole reflects the latest scholarship in such areas as archaeology.

Commentaries

Multi-Volume Sets

180. **Cambridge Bible Commentary on the New English Bible**. Cambridge University Press, 1963- .
This commentary contains the full text of the *New English Bible* (see item 159d.), along with extensive exposition. The New Testament was completed in 17 volumes (1963-67), and the Old Testament is still in progress. Most libraries (including LC) catalog these books separately. For a list, see the publisher's latest catalog. *The Anchor Bible* (see item 159g.) has extensive notes as well as the full text of a new translation. *The Broadman Bible Commentary*, edited by Clifton J. Allen (Broadman, 1969, 12v.), is a major effort, primarily by Southern Baptist scholars. *The Tyndale Commentary*, edited by R. V. G. Tasker and E. J. Young (Eerdmans, 20v.) should also be mentioned. Major sets designed for the layperson include *The Layman's Bible Commentary* (Knox, 1959-64, 25v.) and the *Daily Study Bible Series*, edited by William Barclay (Westminster, 1957-61, 17v.). For the New Testament, *Harper's New Testament Commentaries* (Harper, 1958-74, 5v.) and the *Moffatt New Testament Commentary* (Harper, 1927-50, 17v.) are especially valuable.

181. **International Critical Commentary on the Holy Scriptures,** ed. by S. R. Driver, A. Plummer, and C. A. Briggs. Scribners, 1896-1937; repr., Allenson, 1956- . 40v. in 39.

This set has long been a vital tool for serious theological and biblical study. Each volume was done by a recognized authority. By 1978, Allenson had reprinted most of the original set and had begun to publish some volumes in new editions (see the Allenson catalog for a list of authors and titles). LC catalogs the volumes as separates with no series entry. A major new series, which will eventually replace the *ICC*, is *Hermeneia: A Critical Commentary on the Bible* (Fortress, 1971-). Christian and Jewish scholars in the United States and Europe are collaborating, and each volume is done by an international authority. Many of the titles have been translated from German (consult the Fortress catalog). LC catalogs and classifies separately, but provides a series added entry. The *New International Commentary on the New Testament*, edited by F. F. Bruce (Eerdmans, 1951-), is planned for completion in 17 volumes. The 1978 publisher's catalog listed 14 volumes as available. The *New International Commentary on the Old Testament*, edited by R. K. Harrison (Eerdmans, 1976-), is also in progress.

182. **The Interpreter's Bible . . . .** Abingdon, 1952-57. 12v.

The subtitle of this major commentary describes its nature and scope: "The Holy Scriptures in the King James and Revised Standard versions, with general articles and introduction, exegesis, and exposition for each book of the Bible." Eminent theologians and biblical scholars from virtually all Christian churches contributed. Most of the large Protestant denominations were represented among the consulting editors. V. 1 has general articles on the Bible and Old Testament as well as specific commentary on Genesis and Exodus. Other volumes follow the order of the books of the Bible. A typical page will have both the King James and Revised Standard versions at the top, then a section of exegesis, and finally a section of exposition. V. 7 has general articles on the New Testament plus Matthew and Mark; v. 12 has James to Revelation, more general articles (including one on the Dead Sea scrolls) and indexes. *The Bible in History: A Contemporary Companion to the Bible*, edited by Robert Tamisier (Hastings House, 1968-), attempts to present, for the lay reader, the historical context in which the biblical writings developed.

One-Volume Commentaries

183. Brown, Raymond E., and others. **The Jerome Biblical Commentary.** Prentice-Hall, 1968. 2v. in 1.

Eminent Roman Catholic scholars at American universities have contributed 80 articles on individual books of the Bible, the Pentateuch, Wisdom Literature, O.T. and N.T. criticism, biblical geography, Pauline and Johannine theology, etc. Bibliographies are also provided.

184. Guthrie, Donald, and others. **The New Bible Commentary.** 3rd ed. Eerdmans, 1970. 1310p.

Reflecting conservative Protestant scholarship, this commentary has undergone substantial updating and revision since its first appearance (ed. by F. Davidson) in 1953. There are 12 general articles and commentaries on all 66 books of the Bible.

185. Laymon, Charles M., ed. **The Interpreter's One-Volume Commentary on the Bible.** Abingdon, 1971. 1386p.

Based on the Revised Standard Version and representing a consensus of liberal Protestant scholarship, this book is designed for the laity as well as the clergy. General articles, comments on individual books of the Bible, maps, and photographs are included. There are two indexes (scripture references and subjects).

186. **Peake's Commentary on the Bible,** ed. by M. Black and H. H. Rowley. Rev. ed. Nelson, 1962. 1126p.

This famous one-volume commentary was completely revised and updated by an internationally-renowned team of scholars, whose articles are signed and whose credentials are given. General articles, introductions to the Old and New Testaments, and book-by-book commentaries are made more accessible by an extensive general index and an index to the colored maps.

Handbooks

187. Alexander, David, and Pat Alexander. **Eerdmans Handbook to the Bible.** Eerdmans, 1973. 680p.

About 40 British scholars contributed to this handbook, which is divided into four parts: general information; Old Testament (book by book); New Testament (book by book); terms, people, and places. There is no index.

188. Bruce, Frederick Fyvie. **The English Bible: A History of Translations from the Earliest Versions to the New English Bible.** Oxford, 1970. 262p.

This very readable, but authoritative, book was first published in 1961. Its reference value is enhanced by an explicit table of contents and by a name and title index. An older, but much lengthier, work is *English Versions of the Bible,* by Hugh Pope (rev. and ampl. by Sebastian Bullough; Herder, 1952). Herbert Dennett's *A Guide to Modern Versions of the New Testament* (Moody, 1966) evaluates from a conservative Protestant viewpoint.

189. **The Cambridge History of the Bible.** Cambridge University Press, 1963-70. 3v.

The contents of this vital reference history are as follows: v. 1—*From the Beginnings to Jerome,* edited by P. R. Ackroyd and C. P. Evans (1970); v. 2—*The West, from the Fathers to the Reformation,* edited by G. W. H. Lampe (1969); v. 3—*The West, from the Reformation to the Present Day,* edited by S. L. Greenslade (1963).

190. Child, Heather, and Dorothy Colles. **Christian Symbols Ancient and Modern: A Handbook for Students.** Scribners, 1973. 270p.

Designed both for continuous reading and for reference, this book is topically arranged (e.g., the Cross) with a detailed table of contents and a good index. There are 33 plates and 114 line drawings.

191. Danker, Frederick W. **Multi-Purpose Tools for Bible Study.** 3rd ed. Concordia, 1970. 295p.

The author has included chapters on such study aids as concordances, Hebrew and Greek grammars and lexicons, and Bible dictionaries and commentaries. In addition to chapters that list and describe these tools, Danker has included separate chapters on how best to use them.

192. Deen, Edith. **All of the Women of the Bible**. Harper, 1955. 410p.
This popular work is divided into three parts: studies of women; alphabetical list of named women; chronological list of unnamed women. Other tools for retrieving biographical information include *Who's Who in the Old Testament, Together with the Apocrypha*, by Joan Comay (Holt, 1971), and *Who's Who in the New Testament*, by Ronald Brownrigg (Holt, 1971).

193. Pfeiffer, Charles F., ed. **The Biblical World: A Dictionary of Biblical Archaeology**. Baker, 1966. 612p.
Over 400 readable (but scholarly and accurate) entries range in length from a few lines to several pages. Bibliographies and a list of archaeologists and their projects are also included. This work largely replaces C. E. Wright's *Biblical Archaeology* (Westminster, 1962). Jack Finegan's *Handbook of Biblical Chronology* (Princeton, 1964) includes descriptions of Egyptian, Babylonian, Jewish, and other ancient calendars.

194. Pfeiffer, Charles F., and Howard F. Vos. **The Wycliffe Historical Geography of Bible Lands**. Moody, 1967. 588p.
This valuable book by two conservative Protestant scholars includes the results of historical, archaeological, and geographical research. There are individual chapters on major countries of the ancient Near East, numerous illustrations, maps, and an index. Denis Baly's *Geography of the Bible* (2nd ed., Harper, 1974) is designed to help lay-persons and college students.

195. Rowley, Harold H., and T. W. Manson, eds. **A Companion to the Bible**. 2nd ed. Allenson, 1963. 628p.
This useful handbook has 18 chapters, with bibliographies, maps, and plans. There are four indexes: scripture references; authors; general; and Latin, Greek, and Oriental words. Another work, edited by a noted scholar but planned for the general reader, is William Neil's *The Bible Companion* (Skeffington, 1959). Also intended for the general reader is A. E. Harvey's *The New English Bible, Companion to the New Testament* (Oxford, 1970).

Atlases

196. Aharoni, Jochanan, and Michael Avi-Yonah. **The Macmillan Bible Atlas**. Macmillan, 1968. 184p.
Sound scholarship and skillful cartography are evident in the 262 well-indexed maps on religious, political, military, and economic events of the Old and New Testaments. Appendices give keys to the maps both by books of the Bible and by chronological order.

197. Grollenberg, Lucas H. **Atlas of the Bible**. Tr. and ed. by J. M. H. Reid and H. H. Rowley. Nelson, 1965 (c.1956).
This scholarly work follows the historical development of the Bible from the beginning through New Testament times. It has 37 excellent maps in color and over 400 black and white photographs. There is substantial explanatory matter in the text and the index is unusually thorough.

198. May, Herbert G., ed. **The Oxford Bible Atlas.** 2nd ed. Oxford, 1974. 144p.
This useful atlas is divided into four parts: historical introduction; maps; essay on biblical archaeology; and a gazetteer. It contains 89 black and white photographs and 26 colored maps. The gazetteer is little more than an index to the maps. There have been both textual updating and other improvements since the first edition in 1962. It is less comprehensive than *The Macmillan Bible Atlas*, Grollenberg's *Atlas of the Bible*, or Negenman's *New Atlas of the Bible*, but generally better than the popular *Rand McNally Bible Atlas*, edited by E. G. H. Kraeling (2nd ed., Rand McNally, 1962).

199. Negenman, Jan H. **New Atlas of the Bible.** Ed. by H. Rowley. Doubleday, 1969. 208p.
This is a new work, rather than a revision of Grollenberg. The text (which traces the Bible from its beginnings through the New Testament) is more prominent than are the 34 maps (21 in color). Of the 200 maps and pictures, many are in full color and were taken in Lebanon, Jordan, and Israel, with the advice of Grollenberg. The index (pp. 201-208) appears somewhat skimpy.

200. Wright, George Ernest, and Floyd V. Filson, eds. **Westminster Historical Atlas to the Bible.** Intro. by William Foxwell Albright. Rev. ed. Westminster, 1956. 130p.
In this authoritative work, the arrangement is plainly set forth in the detailed table of contents. Three indexes: 1. Index to the Text; 2. Index to Maps, Including a Topographical Concordance to the Bible; 3. Index of Arabic Names Identified with Biblical Places in Syria and Palestine. There are 18 colored plates, containing 33 maps and 88 black and white illustrations (mainly photographs).

MYTHOLOGY AND FOLKLORE

201. **Abstracts of Folklore Studies,** 1963-1975. American Folklore Society.
Carried over 1,000 abstracts per year. International coverage was of all areas of folklore, though English-language periodicals were preponderant. Detailed indexes in individual issues cumulated annually in the fourth issue. It also included the annual bibliography formerly carried (1954-1963) in *Journal of American Folklore.*

202. **American Folklore Films and Videotapes: An Index,** comp. by William Ferris and Judith Peiser. Center for Southern Folklore, 1976. 338p.
Over 1,800 films and videotapes are included in this pioneer effort, for which supplements are planned. The work is divided into five main parts: subject index, film annotations, videotape annotations, special collections, and an appendix of distributors' listings and distributors' addresses.

203. Briggs, Katharine M. **A Dictionary of British Folk-Tales.** Indiana University Press, 1970-71. 2v. in 4.
Issued in two parts. Part A (Folk Narratives) contains full tales, and summaries as well as citations to original sources and classification by type or motif. Five main categories: fables, fairy tales, jocular tales, novelle, and nursery tales. Within these categories, arrangement is alphabetical by title. Part B (Folk Legend) is also classified: black dogs, bogies, devils, dragons, etc. Within each category, stories are arranged alphabetically by title. V. 1 of part B also includes a "Tale-type Index" and an "Index to Story Titles in Part B."

204. Briggs, Katharine M. **An Encyclopedia of Fairies: Hobgoblins, Brownies, Bogies and Other Supernatural Creatures.** Pantheon, 1976. 481p.
Compiled by a noted British authority, this book includes both general articles (e.g., "Dress and Appearance of Fairies") and entries for individual supernatural creatures. Pronunciations are indicated for unusual names. Citations to sources are given, and cross references are provided. There are 21 black and white plates and 35 text figures (all listed in the front). The alphabetical main section is followed by a bibliography and an index of types and motifs. Cited in "Reference Books of 1977" (*Library Journal* 103 [April 15, 1978]:817).

205. Bulfinch, Thomas. **Bulfinch's Mythology: The Age of Fable; The Age of Chivalry; Legends of Charlemagne.** Crowell, 1970. 957p.
The original nineteenth century text has been retained, but it is enhanced by 50 photographs of famous art works and a new appendix describing archaeological finds made at about 60 sites mentioned in the myths and legends. The dictionary-index, retained from the original, is good for quick reference. Another popular work is E. C. Brewer's *Dictionary of Phrase and Fable* (9th ed., Harper & Row, 1965). Charles Gayley's *The Classic Myths in English Literature and Art* (Ginn, 1939) was based originally on Bulfinch's *The Age of Fable.*

206. Diehl, Katharine Smith. **Religions, Mythologies, Folklores: An Annotated Bibliography.** 2nd ed. Scarecrow, 1962. 573p.
Includes over 2,300 numbered items in a classified arrangement with author-title (but *not* subject) index. *American Folklore: A Bibliography, 1950-1974,* by Cathleen C. and John T. Flanagan (Scarecrow, 1977), updates some parts of Diehl. It is classified, briefly annotated, and has an author index. Merle E. Simmons's *Folklore Bibliography for 1973* (Indiana University, 1975), and the later volumes are also confined mainly to the United States. These classified, annotated compilations are essentially continuations of those done by Simmons for the *Southern Folklore Quarterly,* 1964-72. Broader, but more selective, coverage will be found in Elsie B. Ziegler's *Folklore: An Annotated Bibliography and Index to Single Editions* (Faxon, 1973). Margaret N. Coughlan's *Folklore from Africa to the United States* (GPO, 1976) is a highly selective list of 190 titles at LC and shows the origins of African tales and their influence.

207. Frazer, Sir James George. **The Golden Bough: A Study in Magic and Religion.** 3rd ed. St. Martin's, 1955. 13v.
Volumes 1-12 of the third edition were published between 1911 and 1915. They have been kept in print but not revised. Contents: v. 1, 2—*Magic Art and the Evolution of Kings*; v. 3—*Taboo and the Perils of the Soul*; v. 4—*The Dying God*; v. 5, 6—*Adonis, Attis, Osiris: Studies in the History of Oriental Religion*; v. 7, 8—*Spirits of the Corn and of the Wild*; v. 9—*Scapegoat*; v. 10, 11—*Balder the Beautiful: Fire Festivals of Europe, and Doctrine of the External Soul*; v. 12—*Bibliography and General Index*; v. 13—*Aftermath.* Supplement, 1936. Theodor H. Gaster edited a one-volume condensation entitled *The New Golden Bough* (New American Library, 1975).

208. **Funk and Wagnall's Standard Dictionary of Folklore, Mythology and Legend,** ed. by Maria Leach and Jerome Fried. Funk & Wagnalls, 1949-50. 2v.
In addition to authoritative survey articles (signed with bibliographies) on regions and major topics, this work has shorter articles on gods, heroes, tales, motifs, customs, beliefs, songs, dances, proverbs, games, etc. Arrangement is alphabetical.

209.   Hamilton, Edith. **Mythology.** Little, Brown, 1942; repr., New American Library, 1971. 497p.

Includes both classical and Norse myths. Comparisons of original and later versions. Family charts, pages 457-73. Illustrations by Steele Savage. A somewhat more subjective treatment is given by Robert Graves in *The Greek Myths* (Penguin Books, 1955) and *The White Goddess: A Historical Grammar of Poetic Myth* (rev. ed., Vintage Press, 1958).

210.   Haywood, Charles. **A Bibliography of North American Folklore and Folksong.** 2nd ed. rev. Dover, 1961; repr., Peter Smith. 2v.

About 40,000 items are included in this extensive classified bibliography, which covers printed music and recordings as well as books and articles. There are some descriptive and evaluative annotations. Some reviewers consider the close classification and detailed tables of contents of great value. The reference librarian is likely to be grateful for the very full index in v. 2 and for the index supplement of composers, arrangers, and performers. Coverage of an aspect neglected until recently will be found in *Afro-American Folk Culture: An Annotated Bibliography of Materials from North, Central and South America and the West Indies*, by John F. Szwed and Roger D. Abrahams (Institute for the Study of Human Issues, 1978. 2v.).

211.   Grimal, Pierre, ed. **Larousse World Mythology.** Tr. by P. Beardsworth, Putnam, 1965. 560p.

Articles by specialists cover mythologies of various countries from prehistory to the present. Material is presented in essay form. There are 40 pages of colored plates and 600 black and white illustrations, but no maps. Index. More scholarly than *New Larousse Encyclopedia of Mythology* (Hamlyn, 1968).

212.   **The Mythology of All Races . . .** , ed. by Louis Herbert Gray and George Foote Moore. Marshall Jones, 1916-32; repr., Cooper Square, 1964. 13v.

Contents: v. 1—*Greek and Roman*; v. 2—*Eddic*; v. 3—*Celtic and Slavic*; v. 4—*Finno-Uqric and Siberian*; v. 5—*Semitic*; v. 6—*Indian and Iranian*; v. 7—*Armenian and African*; v. 8—*Chinese and Japanese*; v. 9—*Oceanic*; v. 10—*North American*; v. 11—*Latin American*; v. 12—*Egyptian*; v. 13—*Index*. The illustrations and the access provided by the index combine to make this set an extremely valuable reference work.

213.   Thompson, Stith. **Motif-Index of Folk Literature** . . . . Rev. ed. Indiana University Press, 1955-58. 6v.

Subtitle: "A classification of narrative elements in folktales, ballads, myths, fables, medieval romances, exempla, fabliaux, jest-books and local legends." A rather intricate decimal classification scheme is used for v. 1-5, with v. 6 serving as an alphabetical index.

214.   Tripp, Edward. **Crowell's Handbook of Classical Mythology.** Crowell, 1970. 631p.

Alphabetical arrangement. Articles vary in length from brief notes to 20 pages and cover both characters and events. The text is interestingly written, designed for the educated layman rather than the specialist. There is a pronouncing index in the back. There are 5 maps of the classical world as well as genealogical charts. Brief entries and some black and white sketches are provided in *Who's Who in Greek and Roman Mythology*, by David Kravitz (Potter, 1976; distr., Crown).

PERIODICALS:
Selected Titles by Category of Use
(Prepared with the assistance of Glenn R. Wittig)

Selection

Primary Reviews

215. **Jewish Bookland**, 1946- . 7/yr. National Jewish Welfare Board.
Although recommended for its reviews of Jewish books, this periodical is, unfortunately, not indexed in the standard sources and is not widely available in libraries.

216. **New Review of Books and Religion**, 1968- . Mo. (except July, Aug.). Seabury.
Indexed: *Rel.Ind.:One*. The present title is the result of a merger in 1976 of *New Book Review* with *Review of Books and Religion*. Each issue contains a few critical reviews of moderate length, numerous shorter reviews, and brief annotations. Special features include "Focus on Resources" (books for Bible study) and "Most in Demand" (books selling most heavily at a particular bookstore).

217. **Religious Studies Review**, 1975- . Q. Council on the Study of Religion.
Indexed: *New Test. Abstr.*; *Rel.Ind.:One*. Subtitle: "A quarterly review of publications in the field of religion and related disciplines." A vital tool for the selection of religious materials.

218. **Theologische Literaturzeitung**, 1876- . Mo. Evangelische Verlagsanstalt GmbH.
Indexed: *Rel.Ind.:One*; *Bull.Sign.:Sci.Rel.*; *New Test. Abstr.* A very important reviewing journal published in East Berlin.

Broad Review Coverage

219. **America; National Catholic Weekly Review**, 1909- . Wk. America Press.
Indexed: *RG*; *Abr.RG*; *Bk.Rev.Dig.*; *Cath.Ind.*; *Bk.Rev.Ind.*; *Film Lit. Ind.*; *Hist.Abstr.*; *Med.Rev.Dig.*; *Multi Med.Rev.Ind.* Published by the Jesuits of the United States and Canada, it presents a liberal viewpoint and is useful for its reviews of books, films, music, and plays.

220. **Archiv für Reformationsgeschichte/Archive for Reformation History**, 1904- .
S-Ann. Guertersloher Verlagshans Gerd Mohn.
Indexed: *Rel.Ind.:One*; *Rel. & Theol.Abstr.* Sponsored by the American Society for Reformation Research and the Verein für Reformations Geschichte, this is an international periodical (with articles in English and German) devoted to reporting the results of Reformation research. The supplement entitled *Literaturbericht/Literature Review* is particularly valuable for selection purposes.

221. **Christian Century; An Ecumenical Weekly,** 1908- . Wk. Christian Century Foundation.
Indexed: *Bk.Rev.Dig.; RG; Rel.Ind.:One; Bk.Rev.Ind.; Film Lit.Ind.; New Test. Abstr.; Rel. & Theol.Abstr.* Presents a liberal Protestant viewpoint on religion, social problems, political issues, the arts, etc. Useful for its book reviews.

222. **Christianity Today,** 1956- . Fortnightly. Christianity Today, Inc.
Indexed: *Christ.Per.Ind.; Rel.Ind.:One; Rel. & Theol.Abstr.; Film Lit.Ind.; New Test.Abstr.; RG.* Presents a conservative Protestant viewpoint on religious and social issues. Useful for its book reviews.

223. **Commentary; Journal of Significant Thought and Opinion on Contemporary Issues,** 1945- . Mo. American Jewish Committee.
Indexed: *A.B.C.Pol.Sci.; Amer.Hist. & Life; Bk.Rev.Dig.; Hist.Abstr.; Hum.Ind.; Ind.Jew.Per.; P.A.I.S.; RG; Bk.Rev.Ind.; Film Lit.Ind.; Multi Med.Rev.Ind.; SSCI; Soc.Abstr.* No longer "New Left" in viewpoint, this periodical contains book reviews as well as articles on a wide range of contemporary issues.

224. **Commonweal,** 1924- . Fortnightly. Commonweal Publishing Co., Inc.
Indexed: *Bk.Rev.Dig.; Cath.Ind.; RG; Bk.Rev.Ind.; Film Lit.Ind.; Multi Med.Rev.Ind.* Reflecting a liberal Catholic viewpoint, this periodical has numerous reviews of books, films, and plays.

225. **Journal of Theological Studies,** 1899- . S-Ann. Oxford University Press.
Indexed: *Br.Hum.Ind.; New Test.Abstr.; Rel.Ind.:One; Rel. & Theol.Abstr.* Wittig notes that this journal is "especially good for biblical works."

226. **Religious Education,** 1906- . Fortnightly. Religious Education Association.
Indexed: *Cath.Ind.; Educ.Ind.; Psych.Abstr.; Rel. & Theol.Abstr.; Bull.Sign.:Phil.* Subtitle: "A platform for the free discussion of ideas in the field of religion and their bearing on education." Each issue includes abstracts of doctoral dissertations and book reviews.

227. **Spectrum,** 1968- . 3/yr. Association of Christian Teachers.
Indexed: *Br.Ed.Ind.; Multi Med.Rev.Ind.; Bk.Rev.Ind.; Theol.Abstr. & Bibliog.Serv.; Ed.Ind.; Rel.Ind.:One.* Subtitle: "A magazine for Christians in education." Strong emphasis on reviews of books and other media.

Reference

Bibliographical

228. **Archives de sciences sociales des religions,** 1956- . S-Ann. Centre Nationale de la Recherche Scientifique.
Indexed: *Rel.Ind.:One.* The "Bulletin bibliographicus" covers periodicals and books with abstracts in the general field of sociology of religion.

229. **Catholic Historical Review,** 1915- . Q. American Catholic Historical Association.
Indexed: *Amer.Hist. & Life; Cath.Ind.; Hist.Abstr.; Hum.Ind.; Rel. & Theol.Abstr.; Bull.Sign.:Sci.Rel.* Attention should be paid to the "Periodical Literature" section, although it gives only listings without annotations.

230. **Ecumenical Review,** 1948- . Q. World Council of Churches.
Indexed: *Hum.Ind.; Rel.Ind.:One; Bk.Rev.Ind.; Bull.Sign.:Sci.Rel.; New Test.Abstr.* Of particular importance is the section entitled "Selective Bibliography of Significant Current Ecumenical Books and Pamphlets." Other reference features include "Ecumenical Chronicle" and "Ecumenical Diary."

231. **Elenchus bibliographicus biblicus,** v.49, 1968- . Ann. Biblical Institute Press.
Begun as a separate publication with v. 49, this annual bibliography of biblical studies was formerly included in *Biblica.*

232. **Ephemerides theologicae Lovanienses,** 1924- . Q. Universite Catholique de Louvain.
Indexed: *Rel. & Theol.Abstr.; Canon Law Abstr.; New Test.Abstr.; Rel.Ind.:One; Bull.Sign.:Sci.Rel.* Articles in English, French and German. Particular attention is directed to the section devoted to theological bibliography and entitled "Elenchus bibliographicus."

233. **International Review of Mission,** 1912- . Q. World Council of Churches.
Indexed: *Br.Hum.Ind.; Rel.Ind.:One; Rel. & Theol.Abstr.* The reference librarian will find "Bibliography on World Mission and Evangelism" especially useful.

234. **Review of Religious Research,** 1959/60- . 3/yr. Religious Research Association.
Indexed: *Rel.Ind.:One; Rel. & Theol.Abstr.; Sociol.Abstr.; SSCI.* Bibliographical features include book reviews, reports of research in progress, and abstracts of church planning studies, journal articles, and dissertations.

235. **Revue biblique,** 1892- . Q. École Biblique et Archéologique de Jerusalem.
Indexed: *Rel.Ind.:One; Rel. & Theol.Abstr.* The reference librarian should be alert for the "Bulletins," which contain various topical surveys.

236. **Revue de Qumran,** 1958- . S-Ann. F. J. Gabalda et Cie.
Indexed: *Rel.Ind.:One; Rel. & Theol.Abstr.* Articles in English, French, German, Italian, Latin, and Spanish. The "Bibliographie" covers both books and periodicals.

237. **Revue des sciences philosophiques et theologiques,** 1907- . Q. Librairie Philosophique, Vrin.
Indexed: *Rel.Ind.:One.* The "Bulletins" contain survey articles of recent periodical literature (Christology, patrology, ecclesiology, history of doctrines, etc.).

238. **Revue d'histoire ecclésiastique,** 1906- . Q. Université Catholique de Louvain.
Indexed: *Rel. & Theol.Abstr.; Rel.Ind.:One.* Each issue includes a major bibliography (classified, with name index) on some aspect of church history as well as numerous book reviews.

239. **Theologische Rundshau,** 1928- . 4/yr. Verlag J. C. B. Mohr.
Indexed: *Rel.Ind.:One; Rel. & Theol.Abstr.* This journal consists entirely of state-of-the-art papers on a broad range of topics (Bible, Qumran, Reformation history, hymnology, etc.).

Documentary

240. **Council on the Study of Religion Bulletin,** 1970- . 5/yr. Council on the Study of Religion.
Indexed: *Rel.Ind.:One.* Features of reference value include "The Societies," "Regional News," "Directory Officers" (of the constituent societies), "Announcements," and "Annual Meeting" information.

241. **Journal of Church and State,** 1959- . 3/yr. Baylor University.
Indexed: *Rel.Ind.:One; Rel. & Theol.Abstr.* Features of special reference value include "Notes on Church-State Affairs" and "Recent Doctoral Dissertations in Church and State" (arranged by country).

242. **Journal of Ecumenical Studies,** 1964- . 3/yr. Duquesne University Press.
Indexed: *Rel.Ind.:One; Rel. & Theol.Abstr.* Valuable reference features include "Ecumenical Abstracts" and "Ecumenical Events."

7 ACCESSING INFORMATION IN THE VISUAL ARTS

MAJOR DIVISIONS OF THE FIELD

The term "art" is derived from the Latin word "ars," which means skill or ability. At the time of the Italian Renaissance, the craft guilds were known as "arti," and the word "arte" denoted craftsmanship, skill, mastery of form, or inventiveness. The phrase "visual arts" serves to differentiate a group of arts that are non-verbal in character and that communicate by means of symbols and the juxtaposition of formal elements. This communication takes place through the creation of emotional moods and through expansion of the range of aesthetic experience. "Beauty," as such, is not an integral part of art, but more a matter of subjective judgment. Nevertheless, certain concepts of harmony, balance, and contrast have become a part of our way of thinking about art as a result of Greek speculation about the nature of beauty. "Style" normally refers to the whole body of work produced at a given time in history; however, there may be regional and national styles as well as one basic style for a period. In modern times, attention has even been given to the "styles" of individual artists. "Iconography" is the use of symbols by artists to express universal ideas; the Gothic style of architecture, for example, symbolized man's reaching out toward God.

The visual arts may be divided into four main groups: 1) pictorial arts; 2) plastic arts; 3) building arts; 4) minor arts.

The pictorial arts employ flat, two-dimensional, surfaces. The term is most frequently applied to painting, but it can also include drawing, graphic arts, photography (including motion pictures), and mosaics. Painting may be done with oil, tempera, water color, or other media. Drawing is usually with pencil, pen and ink, wash, crayon, pastel, or charcoal. The graphic arts are produced by the printing process, with three basic methods employed: 1) intaglio, in which the design is hollowed out of a flat surface (as in engravings and etchings) and the ink is gathered in the hollows for transmission to the paper; 2) cameo, or relief, in which the design is on a raised surface (as in woodcuts, mezzotint, aquatint, or drypoint) and only the raised surface is inked; 3) planographic, in which a completely flat surface is used and the design created by using substances that will either attract or repel ink. This process is often known as lithography because the flat surface was frequently made of stone. The pictorial arts employ one or more of three basic forms: 1) murals, in which the pictures are on the walls of buildings, either painted directly on the walls or painted on canvases and permanently attached to the walls; 2) panels, which are generally painted on canvas or wood and are sometimes known as easel paintings; 3) pages, which may be illuminated manuscripts or produced as a result of the printing process. The basic problems with which the pictorial artist must cope include surface, design, movement, space, and form. These are commonly solved by use of line, color, values (light and dark), and perspective.

In the plastic arts (of which sculpture is the outstanding example), ideas are expressed by means of three-dimensional objects. The materials used include stone, metal, wood, clay, plaster, or synthetics (such as plastic). The techniques used — which are determined by the materials — might include carving, casting, modeling, or welding. The finished product may be free-standing or bas-relief (part of a wall or surface). In sculpture, the human figure has traditionally provided the most common subject matter, although the twentieth century has seen increased use of abstractions.

In the building arts (architecture), spaces are enclosed in such a way as to meet certain practical needs (as in homes, factories, schools, or office buildings) and to make some kind of symbolic statement of basic values. These values may be utilitarian and the symbolic statement very pedestrian, or they may be related to the highest aspirations of the human spirit. Factories and gasoline stations are frequently examples of the former, and Gothic cathedrals are often cited as examples of the latter. Architects design buildings of three basic types: 1) trabeated, in which a lintel (or beam) is supported by two posts; 2) arcuated, in which arches are created capable of supporting rounded vaults and domes; 3) cantilevered, in which only one post is required to support a lintel. The materials used in construction will determine which type is used. Wood is useful for trabeated construction, but brick and stone can be better adapted to the requirements of arcuated construction. Large-scale cantilevered construction became possible only with the advent of structural steel and reinforced concrete.

The minor arts are a special group, often classified on the basis of materials used: ceramics, glass, metals, textiles, ivory, precious gems, woods, reeds, synthetics, etc. Ordinarily, they follow the same styles as the major art forms. The end products may be useful everyday objects like coins, baskets, utensils, furniture, clothing, weapons, and harness; or they may be ornamental items like jewelry, stained-glass windows, and much interior decoration.

A good general history and information on how to locate articles on more specific topics will be found in "Art," by Eugene Johnson [*Encyclopedia Americana* (1978 ed.), v. 1, pp. 382-89]. The articles entitled "Art, Philosophy of" and "Arts, Classification of the" in *The Encyclopaedia Britannica: Macropaedia* (15th ed., 1974, v. 2, pp. 40-56, 81-85) and related articles are at a slightly more advanced level, but they are still intended for the general reader. More technical and detailed information may be found in "Art," by Giulio Carlo Argan [*Encyclopedia of World Art* (McGraw-Hill, 1959), v. 1, cols. 764-810] and "Esthetics," by Ugo Spirito and others [*Encyclopedia of World Art* (McGraw-Hill, 1959), v. 5, cols. 28-75]. Articles on more specific topics will be found in great abundance in this encyclopedia. E. Louis Lucas, a noted authority on art bibliography, wrote the article on "Art Literature" for the *Encyclopedia of Library and Information Science* (v. 1, pp. 621-26).

Some students may wish to pursue the topic further. Most of the encyclopedia articles have bibliographies. Rudolf Arnheim's *Art and Visual Perception* (rev. ed., University of California Press, 1974) deals with the psychology of art. Joseph H. Krause adopts a comparative approach in *The Nature of Art* (Prentice-Hall, 1969), which is designed for the layperson rather than the specialist. Bernard S. Myers's *How to Look at Art* (Watts, 1966) is profusely illustrated with small black-and-white photographs, and his *Understanding the Arts* (rev. ed., Holt, 1963) is sometimes used as a text for undergraduate courses in art appreciation. Another such text of considerable usefulness is Joshua C. Taylor's *Learning to Look* (University of Chicago Press, 1957).

ART LIBRARIANSHIP

Unlike philosophy and religion, where the conventional techniques of librarianship will generally cover most situations, the visual arts pose several distinct problems for librarians. As a result, a specialized branch of the discipline has developed over the years. Lester Asheim's chapter on "Art" in *The Humanities and the Library* (pp. 100-150) is still an excellent starting point for the student interested in everything from art research to the care of paintings and slides.

Another excellent work is *Guide to Basic Information Sources in the Visual Arts*, by Gerd Muehsam (Jeffrey Norton; ABC-Clio, 1978). In chapter 2, "How to Research a Work of Art," the author deals with several of the distinctive types of publications: *catalogues raisonnés; oeuvre* catalogs; museum publications; exhibition catalogs; and the *corpus*. The *catalogue raisonné* is defined and described as follows (p. 12):

> a systematic, descriptive, and critical listing or catalog of all known, or documented, authentic works by a particular artist — or of all his known works in one medium. Each entry aims at providing all ascertainable data on the work in question: (1) title, date, and signature if any, as well as size and medium; (2) present location or owner and provenance (previous recorded owners and history of the work); (3) description, comments, analysis, or literary documentation; (4) bibliographical references to books and

periodicals; (5) listings of exhibitions and reproductions. Usually there is also an illustration. The entries are numbered consecutively. These catalog numbers are often referred to in the scholarly literature about the artist and permanently identify a particular work.

The *oeuvre* catalog is similar but may omit bibliographical documentation and provenance. Museum catalogs are defined as catalogs of a museum's permanent collection. Exhibition catalogs, on the other hand, may include works from many museums and private owners, brought together for a particular exhibition. They are first-rate sources of information, but bibliographical control was extremely difficult before the appearance of the *Worldwide Art Catalogue Bulletin* (1963/64-). The *corpus* attempts to do for an entire category of art what the *catalogue raisonné* does for an individual artist. Because of their scope, international collaboration on these is often necessary.

Art libraries and their collections are beginning to be covered in the literature. A basic source of information is Wolfgang Freitag's "Art Libraries and Collections" [*Encyclopedia of Library and Information Science* (Dekker, 1968), v. 1, pp. 571-621]. William B. Walker's paper, "Art Libraries: International and Interdisciplinary," was first presented at the 1977 IFLA Conference in Brussels. It was later published in *Art Libraries Journal* 3 (Spring 1978):9-20 and reprinted in *Special Libraries* 69 (December 1978):475-81. Judith A. Hoffberg and Stanley W. Hess have prepared for the Art Libraries Society of North America (ARLIS/NA) a *Directory of Art Libraries and Visual Resource Collections in North America* (distr., ABC-Clio, 1978).

Art librarianship as a whole is covered in Philip Pacey's *Art Library Manual* (Bowker, 1977) and Antje Lemke's *Art and Museum Librarianship: A Syllabus and Bibliography* (University of Syracuse School of Information Studies, 1974). Various aspects of art librarianship are discussed in "Music and Fine Arts in the General Library," edited by Guy A. Marco and Wolfgang Freitag [*Library Trends* 23 (January 1975):321-546].

Reference work is discussed in Gerd Muehsam's *Guide to Basic Information Sources in the Visual Arts* (Jeffrey Norton; ABC-Clio, 1978) and in such articles as John Larsen's "The Use of Art Reference Sources in Museum Libraries" [*Special Libraries* 62 (November 1971): 481-86] and D. Toyne's "Requests at the Falmouth School of Art" [*ARLIS Newsletter*, no. 24 (September 1975):7-9]. Bernard Goldman's *Reading and Writing in the Arts: A Handbook* (Wayne State, 1972) is designed for students who must prepare term papers in art history and thus can be a time-saver to the busy reference librarian in instructing art students. A more recent work of similar nature is *Art Research Methods and Resources: A Guide to Finding Art Information*, by Lois S. Jones (Kendall/Hunt, 1978).

Classification has been covered by Peter F. Broxis in *Organising the Arts* (Archon, 1968) and "Library Classification Systems and the Visual Arts," edited by David J. Patten (ARLIS/NA, 1978?).

ARLIS/NA has also published *Standards for Staffing Art Libraries* (1977).

Picture files have received substantial attention, particularly from the Special Libraries Association. Renata Shaw's *Picture Searching: Tools and Techniques* (SLA, 1973) is one of a series of bibliographies issued by SLA. *Picture Sources 3*, edited by Ann Novotny and Rosemary Eakins (SLA, 1975), covers collections of prints and photographs in the United States and Canada. Another guide to picture sources is *The Picture Researcher's Handbook*, by Hilary Evans, Mary Evans, and Andra Nelki (Scribners, 1975). Finally, one must mention *The Picture Reference File*, by Harold H. Hart (Hart, 1976-77. 2v.).

Slide collections are covered with great thoroughness in *Slide Libraries: A Guide to Academic Institutions and Museums*, 2nd ed., by Betty Jo Irvine (Libraries Unlimited, 1979). Irvine has also published "Slide Classification: A Historical Survey" [*College and Research Libraries* 32 (January 1971):23-30]. Juan Freudenthal has discussed the use of slides in "The Slide as a Communication Tool: A State-of-the-Art Survey" [*School Media Quarterly* 2 (Winter 1974):109-115]. The Eastman Kodak Co. has issued a free pamphlet, *How to Teach with Slides*, and the College Art Association has published a *Slide Buyer's Guide*.

MAJOR ART ORGANIZATIONS, PUBLISHERS, AND SPECIAL COLLECTIONS

At the international level, much impetus has come from various projects aided by Unesco. For example, since 1949, Unesco and its national commissions have worked with art publishers throughout the world to establish a central archives service of art reproductions. In this undertaking, Unesco has had the assistance of the International Council of Museums. Other organizations that have been active in recent years include the Artists' International Association, International Association of Art Critics, and the International Union of Architects.

Within the United States, the variety of national, regional, and state organizations is too great for more than a sampling at the national level. The American Federation of Arts (41 East 65th Street, New York, NY 10021) was founded in 1909 to broaden public art appreciation, especially in those areas of the country not served by large museums, and to promote international exchanges of art. Its membership includes 500 art institutions and 3,000 individuals. The program of activities ranges from circulating exhibitions to preparation of curricula on visual education. The Federation gives editorial advice and assistance in the publication of the *American Art Directory, Sources of Films on Art*, and *Who's Who in American Art*.

The National Art Education Association (1916 Association Drive, Reston, VA 22091), an affiliate of the National Education Association, was founded in 1947 to promote study of the problems of teaching art as well as to encourage research and experimentation. Its membership includes approximately 8,000 art teachers, supervisors, and students. Regular publications include *Art Education* and *Studies in Art Education.*

Other national organizations that should be mentioned are the American Art Association, the American Association of Museums, and the College Art Association. Of special interest to librarians is the Art Libraries Society, with headquarters in Coventry, England, which publishes *Art Libraries Journal* (1976-), and its more recent American counterpart, Art Libraries Society/North America (c/o J. A. Hoffberg, Brand Library, Glendale, CA 91201), which has published *ARLIS/NA Newsletter* since November 1972, and which is active in the development of machine-readable data bases, some of which may be accessed through Lockheed. The Visual Resources Group of the Mid America College Art Association encourages research and promotes communication through such publications as *MACAA Slide and Photograph Newsletter* and *Visual Resource Guides.* Further details about activities and publications may be found in "Slide and Photograph Collection: The Shoe Box Days Are Over," by Susan R. Hoover [*American Libraries* 10 (July/August 1979):440-41]. The American Association of Architectural Bibliographers also has a specialized focus.

Certain publishers have been particularly noted for their fine art books. Harry N. Abrams, of New York, has issued such series as "Pocket Library of Great Art," "Collector's Editions," "Panorama of World Art," and the "Library of Great Painters." The New York Graphic Society and Frederick A. Praeger deserve mention. The famous Swiss firm of Skira was noteworthy for "Great Centuries of Painting," and "Taste of Our Time." The British firm, Phaidon Press, has been publishing distinguished books on individual artists for over 50 years. Thames and Hudson, also of London, is noted for its "World of Art" series. Studio Vista and Penguin Press have produced high quality paperbacks. While not a specialist in art books, Prentice-Hall has produced a noteworthy series entitled "Sources and Documents in the History of Art."

Collections in the fine arts are numerous and are found in public, academic, and special libraries. Examples in public libraries are the Art and Architecture Division of the New York Public Library and Fine Arts Library of the Westminster City Libraries (London). The Avery Architectural Library, of Columbia University, the Fine Arts Library of Harvard University (which now combines holdings from the Fogg Art Museum and the Widener Library), and the Marquand Library of Princeton University (noted for its *Index of Christian Art*) are leading examples of academic libraries. Other notable art libraries in this country include the Frick Art Reference Library in New York; the Dumbarton Oaks Research Library in Washington, D.C.; the Ryerson and Burnham Libraries of the Art Institute of Chicago; the Archives of American

Art in Detroit; and the Henry E. Huntington Library and Art Gallery in San Marino, California. Among the notable libraries of Europe that deserve special mention are: the Victoria and Albert Museum Library, London, and the libraries of the Courtauld Institute of Art and the Warburg Institute, University of London; Rijksbureau voor Kunsthistorische Documentatie, The Hague; Bibliothèque Forney, Paris; Kunstbibliothek, Berlin; Zentralinstitut für Kunstgeschichte, Munich; Akademie der Bildenden Kunst, Vienna; Kunsthistorisches Institut, and Biblioteca Berenson, Florence; Biblioteca dell'Istituto Nazionale de Archeologia e Storia dell'Arte, Rome; and Instituto Amatller de Arte Hispanico, Barcelona. Catalogs of several of these libraries have been published by G. K. Hall and Company.

Additional information may be found in *Subject Collections*, by Lee Ash, *ASLIB Directory, Subject Collections in European Libraries*, by Lewanski, in the Freitag *ELIS* article already mentioned, and in the *Handbook* of the Center for Research Libraries.

8 PRINCIPAL INFORMATION SOURCES IN THE VISUAL ARTS

ARTS IN GENERAL

Introductory Works and Bibliographic Guides

243. **Art and Architecture Information Guide Series,** 1974- . Gale.
Planned as a series of classified, annotated bibliographies. Titles to date: v. 1—*American Painting*, edited by Sidney Starr Keaveney (1974); v. 2—*Color Theory*, edited by Mary L. Buckley and David Baum (1975); v. 3—*American Architects from the Civil War to the First World War*, edited by Lawrence Wodehouse (1976); v. 4—*American Architects from the First World War to the Present*, edited by Lawrence Wodehouse (1977); v. 5—*American Sculpture*, edited by Janis Kay Ekdahl (1977); v. 6—*Art Education*, edited by Clarence Bunch (1978); v. 7—*Pottery and Ceramics*, edited by James Edward Campbell (1978).

244. Chamberlin, Mary W. **Guide to Art Reference Books.** ALA, 1959. 418p.
This is a book of fundamental importance; it organizes and appraises more than 2,500 titles ranging from ready reference to highly specialized works. The arrangement is basically by subject, preceded by general chapters by form (bibliographies, etc.). The annotations are descriptive and often evaluative. The last three chapters describe documents and sources, periodicals, and series of art books. An appendix describes the holdings of the most important special art collections and libraries in the United States and western Europe. *Guide to the Literature of Art History*, by Etta Arntzen and Robert Rainwater (ALA, 1979), is essentially a revision, expansion, and updating of Chamberlin.

245. Ehresmann, Donald L. **Fine Arts: A Bibliographic Guide to Basic Reference Works, Histories, and Handbooks.** 2nd ed. Libraries Unlimited, 1979. 349p.
The second edition of this classified, annotated bibliography now incorporates all relevant titles from Chamberlin (see item 244) and includes 322 pre-1958 titles not noted by Chamberlin in addition to 147 post-1973 volumes. There are both a detailed table of contents and a subject index, allowing access to some 1,675 titles.

246.   Muehsam, Gerd. **Guide to Basic Information Sources in the Visual Arts.** Jeffrey Norton/ABC-Clio, 1977. 266p.
Written in the form of a bibliographic essay, this book introduces the reader to search strategies, specialized types of art reference tools (e.g., museum publications, exhibition catalogs), and sources of information about individual artists and their work. Jack Dove's *Fine Arts* (Bingley, 1966) is now less useful, as is James Humphrey's "Architecture and the Fine Arts," *Library Trends* 15 (January 1967):478-93. Also somewhat dated but occasionally useful is *How to Find Out about the Arts*, by Neville Carrick (Pergamon, 1965). Coverage of American research from the 1930s to the early 1960s will be found in *Art and Archaeology*, by James S. Ackerman and Rhys Carpenter (Prentice-Hall, 1963). Extensive notes and bibliographies are given in *The Sociology of Art and Literature*, edited by Milton C. Albrecht, James H. Barnett, and Mason Griff (Praeger, 1970). Julius Ritter von Schlosser's *La letteratura artistica* (3rd Ital. ed., La Nuova Italia, 1964) is an extensive bibliographical essay on the literature of art from the Middle Ages through the eighteenth century, with special emphasis on Italy. The classified arrangement is supplemented by an index of artists and a general bibliographical index.

247.   Rosenberg, Jakob. **On Quality in Art: Criteria of Excellence, Past and Present.** Princeton University Press, 1967. 264p.
Based on the A. W. Mellon lectures of 1964, this book attempts to clarify for the intelligent layman the criteria of excellence in art. The first part is devoted to critical judgments of the past. The second compares similar works of art, one by a master and one by a pupil or imitator. Comparisons are limited to drawings (which reproduce well). Except for the chapter on the twentieth century, it was highly regarded by reviewers.

248.   Taylor, Joshua C. **Learning to Look: A Handbook for the Visual Arts.** University of Chicago Press, 1957. 152p.
The material in this book was developed over a period of years for use in the art portion of the introductory humanities course at the University of Chicago. The book opens with 32 plates (two in color) and continues with chapters on art analysis, color and perspective, the visual arts, materials and techniques, and the artist and the work of art. The emphasis is on critical appreciation based on first-hand experience with art. The text is supplemented by a chronological table and an index.

Bibliographies (Current and Retrospective)

249.   **Art/Design/Photo**, 1974- . Idea Books.
Competes with *ARTbibliographies MODERN* (see item 252) as the successor to *LOMA: Literature on Modern Art: An Annual Bibliography* (Lund, Humphries, 1971-73). Coverage begins with 1972. (*LOMA* covered 1969-71.)

250.   Art Research Libraries of Ohio. **Union List of Periodicals and Serials in Art Research Libraries,** ed. by Stephen G. Matyi. Ohio State University Libraries, 1974. 646p.
This cooperatively produced work lists the holdings of art serials in twelve Ohio libraries with major research collections.

251. **ARTbibliographies CURRENT TITLES,** 1972- . 6/yr. ABC-Clio.
The tables of contents of approximately 250 art periodicals, annuals, museum bulletins and other serials are reproduced in this useful current awareness service.

252. **ARTbibliographies MODERN,** v. 4, 1973- . S-Ann. ABC-Clio.
Books, periodicals, and exhibition catalogs are indexed and abstracted. Art and design of the nineteenth and twentieth centuries are covered. Entries are in one alphabetical sequence for both names and subjects, with a separate author index and a museum/art gallery index. The publishers regard the 1969-71 volumes of *LOMA: Literature on Modern Art* as v. 1-3 of *ARTbibliographies MODERN*. However, the series leaves 1972 without coverage, and one must turn to *Art/Design/Photo* (see item 249) for 1972. Beginning with the 1974 volume year, a machine-readable file is available for online computer searches through DIALOG (Lockheed Information Systems).

253. **Bibliographic Guide to Art and Architecture,** 1975- . Ann. G. K. Hall.
This bibliography is one of a series of twelve guides that provide annual updating of the dictionary catalogs of the Research Libraries of the New York Public Library. It covers painting, drawing, sculpture, architecture, and the applied arts. More limited in scope and geographic coverage is *The Bibliography of Museum and Art Gallery Publications and Audio-Visual Aids in Great Britain and Ireland* (Chadwyck-Healey; Somerset, 1978- . Biennial), which lists publications from 811 institutions. The main part is arranged alphabetically by institutional names. Author, title, and subject indexes are provided.

254. Canada. National Gallery. Library. **Catalogue of the Library of the National Gallery of Canada.** G. K. Hall, 1973. 8v.
This dictionary catalog is particularly strong for all aspects of Canadian art, but it is also good for art history from the Renaissance to the twentieth century. It includes books, journals, exhibition catalogs, and material from pamphlet and clipping files.

255. **Films on Art: A Source Book.** Comp. and ed. by the Canadian Centre for Films on Art for the American Federation of Arts. Watson-Guptill, 1977. 220p.
Entries for over 450 films currently available in the United States and Canada are arranged alphabetically by title, with information on duration, color, gauge (if other than 16mm), sound (noted only if silent), country of origin, date, producer, credits, and distribution rights. Summaries and indications of possible uses are also given. There are subject, artist, and alphabetical title indexes. The "List of Sources" gives addresses of distributors.

256. Freer Gallery of Art, Washington, D.C. Library. **Dictionary Catalog of the Library.** G. K. Hall, 1967. 6v.
The collection includes about 40,000 books, pamphlets, and periodicals dealing with Oriental, Middle Eastern and nineteenth-century American art.

257. Georgi, Charlotte. **The Arts and the World of Business: A Selected Bibliography.** Scarecrow, 1973. 123p.
This classified, unannotated bibliography (with an author index) covers the management of art museums and related topics.

258. Gordon, Donald E. **Modern Art Exhibitions 1900-1916: Selected Catalogue Documentation.** Prestel-Verlag, 1974. 2v.
Covers 851 exhibitions in 82 cities (15 countries). V. 1 has five parts: introduction; essays on the period; list of catalogs consulted (chronological); illustrations (black and white, chronological); index of artists (alphabetical). V. 2 has two parts: exhibition entries (chronological); index of titles and exhibition groups (alphabetical). A detailed explanation of how to use the set is given in the introduction.

259. Harvard University. Fine Arts Library. **Catalogue of the Harvard University Fine Arts Library, the Fogg Art Museum.** G. K. Hall, 1971-72. 15v.
This set consists of photographic reproductions of some 360,000 cards. The Fogg Art Museum has one of the strongest art libraries in the United States.

260. Lucas, Edna Louise. **Art Books: A Basic Bibliography on the Fine Arts.** New York Graphic Society, 1968. 245p.
Based on an earlier work by Lucas, *The Harvard List of Books on Art*, this book contains 4,000 entries (unannotated) in nine major categories, with a detailed index of authors and artists. It is intended as a selection and reference tool for four-year colleges and students of art history.

261. Mason, Lauris, and Joan Ludman. **Print Reference Sources: A Select Bibliography 18th-20th Centuries.** Kraus-Thomson, 1975. 246p.
Designed to address the difficulty of finding information about printmakers and prints, this book includes about 1,300 printmakers listed alphabetically, with references arranged chronologically. "Included as entries are the following sources of primary and secondary information on printmakers: catalogues raissonés, oeuvre catalogues, museum and dealer publications, and checklists and essays from books and periodicals" (p. vii).

262. New York (City). Metropolitan Museum of Art. **Library Catalog.** G. K. Hall, 1960. 25v. Suppls., 1962- .
This is another photographic reproduction of the dictionary card catalog of one of the greatest art libraries in this country. V. 1-23 cover books and periodicals and v. 24-25 deal with sales catalogs.

263. Rave, Paul Ortwin. **Kunstgeschichte in Festschriften.** Mann, 1962. 314p.
Contents: list of Festschriften indexed; list, arranged by subject, of essays on art included in them; indexes of titles of Festschriften, of authors of art essays, of artists, and of places written about. Another specialized work is *The Literature of Byzantine Art, 1892-1967*, edited by Jelisaveta S. Allen (Mansell, 1973-76, 2v. in 3). V. 1 covers specific places, first by continent, then by country, region, and site. V. 2 covers general history and specific art forms. Entries are usually annotated. There are author and place-name indexes. Islamic art is covered in K. A. C. Creswell's *A Bibliography of the Architecture, Arts and Crafts of Islam* (American University of Cairo Press, 1961).

264. **Répertoire d' art ed d'archéologie; depouillement des periodiques et des catalogues de ventes, bibliographie des ouvrages d'art français et étrangers.** Morance, 1910- . Ann.
Classified, annotated bibliography of books, pamphlets, and periodical articles. Indexes for authors and for artists. Separate section for sales catalogs. The major international work in this field, it is now published with the aid of Unesco, under the

auspices of the International Committee on the History of Art and the Library of Art and Archeology, University of Paris.

265. **RILA: Répertoire international de la littérature de l'art/International Repertory of the Literature of Art**, 1975- . S-Ann. College Art Association of America.
Preceded by a demonstration issue in 1973, *RILA* is the product of extensive international collaboration and is modelled on *RILM: Répertoire international de la littérature musicale* (see item 561). Recent issues include the following description: "RILA publishes abstracts and detailed subject indexes of current books, periodical articles, newspaper articles, Festschriften, congress reports, exhibition catalogues, museum publications and dissertations in the field of post-classical European and post-Columban American art." The classified arrangement is supplemented by an exhibition list (with cross references) and a detailed author-subject index.

266. Victoria and Albert Museum, London. **National Art Library Catalogue.** G. K. Hall, 1973. 10v.
Over 300,000 entries, including over 50,000 exhibition catalogs.

267. **The Worldwide Art Catalogue Bulletin**, 1963/64- . Q. Worldwide Books.
The Worldwide Art Center was established in 1962 to meet the need for up-to-date information on art exhibits around the world. It is supported by major national art bodies. Over 900 art museums and galleries in 30 countries send exhibition catalogs to the Center. *The Worldwide Art Catalogue Bulletin* provides the only central record of new and significant art catalogs. Descriptions and reviews are prepared by art experts. In addition, art catalogs may be purchased through the Center. Most are covered by NPAC, and LC numbers are given when available. Each issue has the following indexes: titles, artists, periods, media, and topics. These are cumulated annually.

Indexes, Abstracts, and Current Awareness Services

268. **Art Index**, 1929- . Wilson. Q. A. cum.
The major indexing tool in this field, *Art Index* includes some 140 American and foreign periodicals and museum bulletins in archaeology, architecture, art history, arts and crafts, city planning, fine arts, graphic arts, industrial design, interior decoration, landscape design, photography, and films. The following methods of indexing are used: 1. ordinary articles are under author and subject; 2. book reviews are in a separate section at the end, under authors *reviewed*, beginning with v. 22 (1973-74); 3. exhibitions are under the sponsoring gallery or museum; 4. illustrations are listed under the article they accompany but not individually; 5. if a reproduction appears without accompanying text, it is listed under the name of the artist. *Art Index* is the easiest to use of the major tools and is considered a vital part of all art reference collections.

269. Chicago. Art Institute. Ryerson Library. **Index to Art Periodicals.** G. K. Hall, 1962. 11v. Suppl., 1975.
Photographic reproduction of library's card file. All entries are by subject, alphabetized within subject by periodical. Material that appears in *Art Index* is *excluded*.

Dictionaries and Encyclopedias

270. Adeline, J. **The Adeline Art Dictionary, Including Terms in Architecture, Heraldry and Archaeology.** Tr. from the French with a supplement of new terms by Hugo G. Beigel. Ungar, 1966. 459p.

About 4,000 terms are defined, with about 2,000 illustrations. Although Adeline is still a standard and fundamental source, even the extensive supplement (pp. 423-59) is now somewhat dated. For coverage of art movements, styles, groups, and techniques since the Second World War, it is useful to consult John A. Walker's *Glossary of Art, Architecture and Design since 1945* (2nd ed., Shoe String/Linnet, 1977). Although lacking illustrations, Walker does include, for all entries, citations to sources of further information. In the second edition, the number of entries has been increased from 278 to 521, and coverage of terms from the mid-1970s has been expanded. The index includes names of artists and critics, titles of exhibitions, and subjects.

271. **Britannica Encyclopedia of American Art.** Britannica Educational Corp.; distr., Simon & Schuster, 1973. 669p.

The first encyclopedia devoted to American art, this work not only covers architecture, painting and sculpture, but photography, landscape architecture, crafts, and industrial design as well. There are numerous illustrations, many in color. Articles vary in length from a paragraph to several pages and cover artists, periods, and movements. Reviewers have noted some serious omissions (e.g., American Indian art). The lack of an index is only partially remedied by such features as cross references and a guide to entries by arts. Other features include a bibliography, a glossary, and a guide to museums and public collections.

272. **Dizionario enciclopedico Bolaffi dei pittori e degli incisori italiana.** G. Bolaffi, 1972- . [To be in 10v.].

Covers Italian art and artists from the eleventh to the twentieth centuries. Some 12,000 entries, including biography, critical analysis, authentication, market valuation, and notable art sales. Profusely illustrated, including some color plates.

273. **Encyclopedia of World Art.** McGraw-Hill, 1959-1968; repr. 1972. 15v.

High on any list of vital works. Published simultaneously in Italian and English. English edition has: 1. more cross references; 2. more extensive article on art of the Americas; 3. some 300 separate, short biographies to give quicker access to information about notable people mentioned in longer, monographic articles. Specialists from many parts of the world have assisted with the editorial work or have contributed signed articles, often of considerable length, with extensive bibliographies. Covers the entire field of art in all countries and periods. A major work of high quality. Plates (many in color) make up about one-half of each volume. V. 15 (index) has about 20,000 main entries and is very thorough. *A Pictorial Encyclopedia of the Oriental Arts* (Crown, 1969, 7v.) is compiled from the Oriental section of the *Encyclopedia of World Art*. *The Praeger Encyclopedia of Art* (Praeger, 1971, 5v.) contains about 4,000 articles (mostly signed) and over 5,000 illustrations, including 1,700 in color. A one-volume abridgement has been published as the *Phaidon Encyclopedia of Art and Artists* (Phaidon; Dutton, 1978).

274. Greenhill, Eleanor A. **Dictionary of Art.** Dell, 1974. 560p.
"Designed for the layman or the begining student, this is an index to artists, artistic processes and techniques as well as to ztyles and movements. A compact, fact-filled paperback, it is notably successful" (William J. Dane, *ARBA 1975*, p. 438). Another popular work is Raymond Charmet's *Concise Encyclopedia of Modern Art* (Larousse, 1965; repr., Collins, 1972; distr., Follett, 1974). Julia Ehresmann's *The Pocket Dictionary of Art Terms* (rev. ed., New York Graphic Society, 1971) is designed to be carried on museum visits. James Hall's *Dictionary of Subjects and Symbols in Art* (Harper, 1974) is "exceptionally strong in historical material. . . . It also provides numerous references to primary sources" (Bohdan Wynar, *ARBA 1976*, p. 438). Reginald G. Haggar's *A Dictionary of Art Terms* (Hawthorn, 1962) contains approximately 2,000 brief entries and 200 illustrations as well as a glossary of French, German, and Italian terms with English equivalents.

275. Kaltenbach, Gustave Emile. **Dictionary of Pronunciation of Artists' Names, with Their Schools and Dates, for American Readers and Students. . . .** 2nd ed. Art Institute of Chicago, 1938; repr., Gale, 1976. 74p.
This covers about 1,500 artists.

276. **McGraw-Hill Dictionary of Art,** ed. by Bernard S. Myers. McGraw-Hill, 1969. 5v.
Prepared with the aid of some 125 contributors, this work is best for high school and small public libraries. Larger libraries will need the *Encyclopedia of World Art*. Articles are brief, well chosen, often signed, and some have bibliographies. There are about 2,500 illustrations (mostly black and white). Most of the 15,000 entries are biographies of painters, sculptors, architects, and decorative artists from all periods and countries. Also, there are articles on art types and art terms. The cross reference system links art works and schools with individual artists and vice versa. Bernard and Shirley Myers' *Dictionary of 20th Century Art* (McGraw-Hill, 1974) is a selection of 750 entries from the *McGraw-Hill Dictionary of Art*.

277. Mayer, Ralph. **A Dictionary of Art Terms and Techniques.** Crowell, 1969. 447p.
This vital source contains 3,000 short articles, technical in nature, to help the practising artist or serious student. Heavy emphasis is placed on painting technology, materials, and methods. John Quick's *Artists' and Illustrators' Encyclopedia* (2nd ed., McGraw-Hill, 1977) is actually a dictionary of terms that covers methods and materials used in commercial and fine art, photography, graphic arts, and printing.

278. Murray, Peter, and Linda Murray. **A Penguin Dictionary of Art and Artists.** 4th ed. Penguin, 1976; repr., 1978. 493p.
Technical terms, processes, and movements are included as well as short biographies of more than 1,000 artists. Over 1,000 black and white illustrations and over 50 color plates. Bibliographies (classified and alphabetical) include over 3,000 items. Also published under the title *A Dictionary of Art and Artists*.

279. Osborne, Harold. **The Oxford Companion to Art.** Oxford, 1970. 1277p.
A worthy addition to this excellent series of guides for the general reader. Has about 3,000 entries, alphabetically arranged. Painting and sculpture are emphasized, and

some attention is given to architecture and ceramics—but very little to the minor arts. Entries vary in length from a few lines to several pages and are unsigned, but the list of contributors is distinguished. Covers national and regional schools of art, art movements, art concepts, styles, techniques, iconography, names of artists, art historians, and museums. Selective bibliography of general works and specific subjects includes about 3,000 items. Illustrations are small and designed to support the text. Recommended for all types of libraries of medium to large size.

280. **Phaidon Dictionary of Twentieth Century Art.** Phaidon, 1973; repr., Dutton, 1977. 420p.
Has 1,600 entries on painters, sculptors, and graphic artists (but not architects), and 140 entries on ideas, groups, and movements. Articles are brief (sometimes with bibliographies) and authoritative.

281. Schiller, Gertrud. **Iconography of Christian Art.**, Tr. from German by J. Seligman. New York Graphic Society, 1971-72. 2v.
Arranged thematically rather than alphabetically (with an index at the end of v. 2), this work is thoroughly researched, well written and well translated, with a large number of excellent illustrations. The German original is more comprehensive than the English translation.

282. **A Visual Dictionary of Art**, ed. by Ann Hill. New York Graphic Society, 1974. 640p.
With about 4,500 brief entries, this dictionary covers ancient to modern times, with special attention to non-Western art. About 2,000 black and white photographs and 250 color plates enhance its usefulness as a source of illustrations. Artists who are not well known can often be located here. There is an excellent analytical index.

Directories and Annuals

283. **American Art Directory**, 1898- . Tri. Bowker.
Both the frequency and the title of this essential art reference tool have varied in the past. The 1978 edition includes information on 4,467 art museums, libraries, associations, schools, and studios in the United States, Canada, and other countries. The classified arrangement includes: national and regional organizations in the U.S.; museums, libraries and associations in the U.S. by state; corporate art holdings; national organizations in Canada; art organizations in Canada by province; major museums abroad by country; art schools in the U.S. by state; art schools in Canada by province; major art schools abroad by country; state arts councils; directors and supervisors of art education in school systems; art magazines; newspapers carrying art notes and their critics; scholarships and fellowships; open exhibitions; and traveling exhibitions booking agencies. There is a personnel index in addition to the name and subject index at the end. A subject search may involve dozens of undifferentiated page references under broad headings (e.g., PAINTING—AMERICAN).

284. **Fine Arts Market Place**, 1973/74- . Bi. Bowker.
Using a classified arrangement, this work covers art services, suppliers, organizations, dealers, publishers, etc. Entries give name, address, telephone and telex numbers, and descriptions of services or products.

285. Hudson, Kenneth, and Ann Nicholls, comps. **The Directory of World Museums.** Columbia University Press, 1975. 864p.
The most comprehensive publication of its kind, this directory includes over 22,000 museums. The arrangement is by country, then city, then English form of museum name. There is an excellent classified index of specialized collections. The only major usage problem occurs in the United States section, where cities of the same name from different states are interfiled. For the U.S., a breakdown by state and then city would have been preferable. Highly selective coverage is given by Barbara Cooper and Maureen Matheson in *The World Museum Guide: A Selective Guide to 200 of the World's More Interesting Art Museums* (McGraw-Hill, 1974), which is, nonetheless, very useful for its intended purpose of helping travelers who wish to visit important museums. In this connection, the importance of general travel guides such as the *Baedeker* series, *Muirhead's Blue Guides*, and those issued by Nagel, Fodor, and the Tourist Club of Italy should not be overlooked.

286. **International Directory of Arts**, 1952/53- . Tri. Verlag Muller GMBH.
This two-volume set is arranged by subject. Within each category, addresses are given alphabetically by countries and cities. V. 1 contains: museums and institutional galleries; universities, academies and art schools; restorers and experts. V. 2 contains: art and antique dealers, art dealers' galleries; art publishers; antiquarian and art book dealers; artists; and collectors. "Notes for Use of the Work" should be consulted for details of the coding system. Some minor changes occur from edition to edition (e.g., the shift of the chapter on restorers and experts to v. 1 in the 1974-75 edition). Coverage of American restorers will be found in *Directory of Art and Antique Restoration: A Guide to Art and Antique Restorers throughout the United States*, edited by Arthur Porter and Elizabeth Taylor (new ed., the Authors, 1975).

287. McCoy, Garnett. **Archives of American Art: A Directory of Resources.** Bowker, 1972. 163p.
Lists 535 groups of papers held by the Archives of American Art. Basic listing is by title of collection. Information is given about owners, donors, numbers of items, types, dates covered, etc. Collections include personal papers of art dealers, collectors, curators, painters, and sculptors. Another work to consult is *Archives of American Art; Smithsonian Institution: A Checklist of the Collection* (2nd ed., 1977).

288. Millsaps, Daniel. **National Directory of Arts Support By Private Foundations.** . . . Washington International Arts Letter, 1977. 264p.
This is v. 3 in a series dealing with support for the arts. Users must check not only the main part, but also the sections on changes and on new foundations to be sure of having current information. Millsaps has also prepared *The National Directory of Grants in Aid to Individuals in the Arts* (1976).

289. **Museums of the World: A Directory of 17,000 Museums in 148 Countries, Including a Subject Index.** Verlag Dokumentation, 1973; distr., Bowker. 762p.

Includes art and archaeological museums and galleries, along with other types. Only slightly less comprehensive than Hudson (see item 285). The arrangement is by continent, then alphabetically by countries, cities, and museum names. Each entry gives name, address, year founded, director, museum type, and fields of collection.

290. **The Official Museum Directory: United States, Canada.** 1961- . A. American Association of Museums and National Register Publishing Co.

The title and frequency of publication of this vital reference work have varied. The present title was adopted in 1971. Annual publication began in 1978. The 1978-79 edition has approximately 5,400 entries, covering museums of all types. Prefatory material includes information about the American Association of Museums, state museum associations, state arts agencies, etc., and a display advertising section. The heart of the directory is arranged geographically by country (United States, Canada, Puerto Rico), then alphabetically by state or province, and subarranged alphabetically by city. Information provided includes: name, address, and date of founding; director; scope of collections and areas of specialization; facilities; activities; hours and admission prices. There is *no* mention of individual paintings or other museum objects. Supplementary access is provided by: institutions by name alphabetically; directors and department heads; institutions by category; and a classified buyer's guide.

291. Spaeth, Eloise. **American Art Museums: An Introduction to Looking.** 3rd ed. Harper, 1975. 483p.

Arranged alphabetically by state, city, and museum, this guide gives essay-type information on history, collection emphasis, and a few major individual works. Directory information (address, hours of opening, etc.) is given at the beginning of each entry. There are numerous black and white illustrations. A brief bibliography and a detailed name and title index complete this very useful book. Somewhat less well done, but the best of its kind to date, is Suzanne Lord's *American Travelers' Treasury: A Guide to the Nation's Heirlooms* (Morrow, 1977). E. O. Christensen's *A Guide to Art Museums in the United States* (Dodd, Mead, 1968) gives considerable detail about 88 major museums in 59 cities in part I (arranged geographically) and briefer accounts of lesser museums in part II (arranged alphabetically). Christensen has four indexes: museums alphabetically by name of museum; museums alphabetically by name of city; works of art discussed in the text; and museum architects, donors, etc. Among the useful older works are W. Aubrey Cartwright's *Guide to Art Museums in the United States: East Coast — Washington to Miami* (Duell, Sloan and Pearce, 1958) and S. L. Faison's *A Guide to the Art Museums of New England* (Harcourt, Brace, 1958).

292. **The Year's Art,** 1880-1947. 1968/69- . A. Hutchinson; distr., Putnam.

Subtitle of original: "A Concise Epitome of All Matters Relating to the Arts of Painting, Sculpture, Engraving and Architecture and to Schools of Design, Which Have Occurred During the Year. . . ." Subtitle of revised version: "Europe and the U.S.A.: Architecture — Art   Criticism — Design — Museums — Painting   and Sculpture — People — Salesroom." The newer version gives nearly one-half its space to auctions and prices.

Histories

293. **American Art: Painting, Sculpture, Architecture, Decorative Arts, Photography,** by Milton W. Brown and others. Prentice-Hall; Abrams, 1979. 616p.
The history of all of the American arts from the earliest times to the present is covered in this authoritative work. There are 752 illustrations (104 of them in color). Reference features include a bibliography (pp. 590-603) and an index (pp. 604-615).

293a. Arnason, H. H. **History of Modern Art: Painting, Sculpture, Architecture.** Rev. ed. Abrams, 1977. 740p.
Chronologically arranged, this work includes biographical sketches of major artists of the nineteenth and twentieth centuries. Black and white illustrations are on the same page with the text. Color plates are nearby. Werner Hoffmann's *Turning Points in 20th Century Art, 1890-1917* (Braziller, 1969) explores what the author regards as the decline of easel painting in favor of more total expression. *Art since Mid-Century: The New Internationalism* (New York Graphic Society, 1972) includes essays on various movements and leading exponents as well as an appendix with personal statements by artists. *Art Now: From Abstract Expressionism to Surrealism*, by Edward Lucie-Smith (Morrow, 1977), has excellent explanations of terms such as op, kinetic, minimal, conceptual, earth.

294. **The Arts of Mankind.** Gen. eds., Andre Malraux and George Salles. English cons. ed., Sir Herbert Read. Thames & Hudson, 1960- ; Golden Press, later G. Braziller, 1961- . [To be in 40v.].
Each volume in this excellent series, prepared by noted scholars, contains a detailed history of the period covered, with numerous illustrations and maps (many in color). Many volumes contain substantial bibliographies. American and English titles occasionally differ. LC catalogs each title separately, but with a series added entry. For a list of titles, see A. J. Walford's *Guide to Reference Material* [3rd ed., Library Association, 1977, v. 3, p. 308 (see item 12)]. Another useful series is *Ancient Peoples and Places* edited by Glyn Daniels (Praeger, 1956-). *Art of the World* (Crown, 1959-) is a highly regarded series of regional art histories. *Panorama of World Art* (Abrams, 1968-72, 18v.) and *The Taste of Our Time* (Skira, 1954-) are series issued by noted publishers of art books. *Sources and Documents in the History of Art* (Prentice-Hall, 1965-) is edited by H. W. Janson; LC classifies and catalogs these Prentice-Hall titles separately but makes a series added entry. Each volume in *Columbia University Studies in Art History and Archaeology*, edited by Rudolf Wittkower (Random House, 1964-65?, 5v.?), typically includes photographs, chapter notes, a bibliography, and an index. More comprehensive coverage will be found in *Yale Publications in the History of Art* (Yale, 1939-), which LC catalogs separately, but with a series added entry, and in the *Unesco World Art Series* (New York Graphic Society, 1954-64, 22v.) for which LC uses "United Nations Educational, Scientific and Cultural Organization" as the main entry and makes a series added entry.

295. Bazin, Germain. **A History of Art: From Prehistoric Times to the Present.** Houghton, Mifflin, 1959. 574p.
An authoritative work, written by the Chief Curator of the Louvre. One British reviewer thought it less balanced than E. H. J. Gombrich's *The Story of Art* (13th ed., Phaidon, 1978), but other critics tended to regard it more highly. Gombrich's book is

considered especially attractive for the beginner, but it has been criticized by some reviewers for omission of certain United States and continental European artists.

296. Bussagli, Mario, and Calembus Sivara Mamurti. **5,000 Years of the Art of India.** Tr. by Anna Maria Brainerd. Abrams, 1971. 335p.
Despite differences of approach by the two authors and some unevenness in the quality of the nearly 400 color illustrations, this book is generally recommended. Another recommended title (with an index and a brief bibliography) is *The Art of India*, by C. Sivaramamurti (Abrams, 1977).

297. Clapp, Jane. **Art Censorship: A Chronology of Proscribed and Prescripted Art.** Scarecrow, 1972. 582p.
Painting, sculpture, graphic arts, decorative arts, and architecture are included, but not photography. The basic arrangement is chronological, and brief information about each incident is given. The index leads to the chronology (by date rather than page number) and includes: artists' names, titles of works of art, and various subjects (e.g., geographic locations, art forms, themes) as well as reasons for censorship (e.g., blasphemy, heresy, obscenity, etc.). The few illustrations are generally of unexciting quality. There is an extensive bibliography.

298. Gardner, Helen. **Art through the Ages.** 6th ed. Harcourt, 1975. 959p.
Intended for high school and college students as well as general readers, this long-established standard work has many illustrations, bibliographies at the ends of chapters, a glossary, and an index.

299. Grabar, Oleg. **The Formation of Islamic Art.** Yale University Press, 1973. 233p.
This valuable study concentrates on the seventh to the ninth centuries. A scholarly work, with an excellent critical bibliography, it also includes 131 black and white illustrations. More specialized geographically, but more comprehensive in period covered, is Arthur Upham Pope's *A Survey of Persian Art from Prehistoric Times to the Present* (Oxford, 1938-39, 6v.; index, 1958).

300. Grousset, René. **Chinese Art and Culture.** Tr. by Haakon Chevalier. Orion Press, 1959. 331p.
Writen by a noted scholar in the field, this work is now a bit out of date in some details, but still an excellent (if not easy) overview. There are 64 plates (16 in color) of high quality. Its reference value is enhanced by bibliographical footnotes, a chronology of Chinese dynasties, and a detailed index. For a near neighbor, *Japan: Art and Civilization*, by Louis-Frederic, pseud. (Abrams, 1971), covers the period from prehistoric times to 1868 and includes photographs, line drawings, an ancient calendar, tables of emperors, a glossary, and an index.

301. Hare, Richard. **The Art and Artists of Russia.** New York Graphic Society, 1965. 294p.
Covering the period from early Byzantine to the twentieth century, this history has excellent color plates, a bibliography, and an index. Some reviewers dispute Hare's critical judgments on the later periods, and others point out that his scope tends to be limited to the urban art of Kiev, Novgorod, St. Petersburg, and Moscow. *A History of*

Russian Art, by C. G. E. Bunt (Studio, 1946), covers all phases of art from the pre-Christian period to the time of publication and is generally regarded as authoritative and factual. The illustrations (about 200) are well selected and of good quality.

302. Hartt, Frederick. **Art: A History of Painting, Sculpture, Architecture.** Abrams, 1976. 2v.
This comprehensive history by a noted authority has many features of great value for reference and selection purposes. "The well written and readable text is enhanced by 1,271 clear illustrations (157 in color) and 34 maps. There are six time-line charts that relate important historical and cultural events to the arts of the period. Each volume has a glossary, bibliography, and detailed index (a combined index to the two volumes would improve their reference convenience). This will be one of those tools that reference librarians will respect more and more as the years go by" (Charles A. Bunge, "Current Reference Books," *Wilson Library Bulletin*, November 1976, p. 268).

303. Hartt, Frederick. **History of Italian Renaissance Art: Painting, Sculpture, Architecture.** Abrams, 1969; repr., Prentice-Hall, 1975. 636p.
This is the first single volume in English to treat the painting, sculpture, and architecture of the period. The author includes at least a small reproduction of each of the more than 800 works of art he discusses. There are three main sections: Late Middle Ages; Quattrocento; Cinquecento. Each is subdivided by place or form. The book is well written and edited, with such reference features as a glossary, chronological chart, and an index to artists' works and subjects. There are 80 color prints and 731 in black and white. For each, the date, medium, size, and location of the original are given.

304. Hauser, Arnold. **The Social History of Art.** Tr. by Stanley Godman. Knopf, 1951, 2v.; repr., Vintage, 1958-60, 4v.
A major work by a noted German scholar, reflecting more than 30 years of study, this art history concentrates on the manner in which social forces shaped the development of painting, architecture, sculpture, folk arts, literature, theatre, and music. There is an excellent subject index.

305. Janson, Horst Woldemar, and Dora Jane Janson. **History of Art: A Survey of the Major Visual Arts from the Dawn of History to the Present Day.** Rev. and enl. Prentice-Hall, 1969. 616p.
Generally regarded as a solid and comprehensive overview from a traditional Western approach, this work is more advanced than Gombrich and good as a text. It is well illustrated, but one reviewer thought the black and white plates better than the color. Other reference features include a good index and bibliography. Another work by the Jansons, which contains numerous reproductions of paintings of historical significance, is *Key Monuments of the History of Art: A Visual Survey* (Prentice-Hall/Abrams, 1959).

306. Larkin, Oliver Waterman. **Art and Life in America.** Rev. ed. Holt, 1960. 559p.
This standard history (first published in 1949) covers architecture, painting, and sculpture, with some attention to the minor arts. It is copiously illustrated, with 489 black and white photographs (usually on the page where mentioned in the text) and 30 color plates (following p. 143). Bibliographical notes and a name and title index enhance its reference value. Other useful titles include *American Art*, by Samuel M.

Green (Ronald, 1966), and *A History of American Art*, by Daniel M. Mendelowitz (2nd ed., Holt, 1970). More specialized is *North American Indian Arts*, by A. H. Whiteford (Golden Press, 1970).

307. New York (City) Museum of Modern Art. **Masters of Modern Art**, ed. by Alfred H. Barr, Jr. Rev. ed. Doubleday, 1958. 239p.
Includes nearly 300 black and white illustrations and about 75 color plates based on the works in the Museum's permanent collection. Reviewers were generally enthusiastic about the illustrations (both selection and quality) and the accompanying commentary.

308. **The Oxford History of English Art**, ed. by T. S. R. Boase. Oxford, 1949- .
Titles in this major series that have appeared to date are: v. 2 — *English Art: 871-1100*, by D. T. Rice; v. 3 — *English Art: 1100-1216*, by T. S. R. Boase; v. 4 — *English Art: 1216-1307*, by Peter Brieger; v. 9 — *English Art: 1714-1800, by Joseph Burke*. Eleven volumes are planned.

309. **The Pelican History of Art**. Gen. ed., Nikolaus Pevsner. Penguin Boooks, 1953- .
Planned to cover world art and architecture in 50 volumes, this series is highly regarded for both text and illustrations. It was considered vital by over sixty percent of the art librarians surveyed by Larsen. LC catalogs each title separately but with a series added entry. For a list, see A. J. Walford's *Guide to Reference Material* or Eugene Sheehy's *Guide to Reference Books* (9th ed., ALA, 1976, p. 382).

310. **Propyläen Kunstgeschichte.** Propyläen Verlag, 1924-33. 26v.
Volumes in the main set and its supplements cover art history for all countries and periods from the earliest times to the twentieth century. Chamberlin (*Guide to Art Reference Books*, p. 72) notes: "The strength of this series lies not in the text but in the lavish illustrations — some in color — which form a unique body of visual material. At end of each volume is found a list of plates and for each artist represented, his dates of birth, death, and activity as well as his working place and medium."

311. Reinach, Salomon. **Apollo: An Illustrated Manual of the History of Art throughout the Ages.** Tr. by Florence Simmonds. Rev. ed. Scribners, 1935. 378p.
This handbook, first published in 1904, contains many small illustrations, a bibliography at the end of each chapter, a general bibliography, and an index.

312. Robb, David Methany, and Jessie J. Garrison. **Art in the Western World.** 4th ed. Harper, 1963. 782p.
This standard history has long been regarded as an excellent introduction to all phases of art: architecture, sculpture, painting, and the minor arts. Other features include a chronological and topical concordance, a glossary, a bibliography, a chronological table, an index to illustrations (over 650), and a general index. It was considered "vital" or "recommended" by nearly one-third of the art librarians surveyed by Larsen. Another useful work is *Studies in Art, Architecture and Design*, by Nikolaus Pevsner (Walker, 1968), which includes nearly 800 black and white illustrations.

313. Venturi, A. **Storia dell'arte italiana.** Hoepli, 1901-1940; repr., Kraus, 1967. 11v. in 25 pts.

Regarded by many critics as the most authoritative and comprehensive history of Italian art, this work was formerly difficult to use because there was no combined index for all 11 volumes, although each part had its own indexes of places and artists. Happily, this deficiency has now been remedied by Jacqueline Sisson's *Index to A. Venturi's Storia dell'arte italiana* (Kraus, 1975, 2v.).

314. Willett, Frank. **African Art: An Introduction.** Praeger, 1971. 288p.

Hailed by reviewers as the best introduction to African art yet available, this book sets that art in its wider social and historical context. Reference features include an index and an excellent bibliography as well as illustrations (188 black and white, 61 color), which are of good quality, well chosen and titled, and carefully documented.

315. Wölfflin, Heinrich. **Principles of Art History: The Problem of the Development of Style in Later Art.** Tr. by M. D. Hottinger. G. Bell, 1932; repr., Peter Smith, 1950. 237p.

Long established as a classic in the field, this work appears in an English translation from the seventh German edition of 1929.

Biographies

316. Bénézit, Emmanuel. **Dictionnaire critique et documentaire des peintres, sculpteurs, dessinateurs et graveurs de tous les pays.** New ed. Grund; distr., Wittenborn, 1976. 10v.

Long a vital source of biographical information, especially for relatively minor figures, Bénézit was rated next to *Art Index* as the second most vital source by art librarians. Coverage includes artists from the earliest times to the present. Entries vary in length, but usually include a list of chief works and the museums where these were owned at the time of compilation. Reproductions of symbols and signatures are given with artists' names, and reproductions of signatures used by anonymous artists will be found at the end of each key letter of the alphabet.

317. Bryan, Michael. **Bryan's Dictionary of Painters and Engravers.** New (4th) ed. rev. and enl. by G. C. Williamson. Bell, 1903-1905; repr., Kennikat, 1971. 5v.

Consisting of some 20,000 entries, this is still the largest such effort in English. Longer articles are signed by specialists and usually include lists of chief works and locations. Unfortunately, it is much less current than Bénézit (see item 316) or Thieme and Becker (see item 331). Some monograms are with the articles and others appear on pages 421-25 of v. 5. Nearly one-half of the art librarians in Larsen's 1971 survey still rated this a vital reference work.

318. Caplan, H. H. **The Classified Directory of Artists' Signatures, Symbols and Monograms.** Gale, 1976. 738p.

Over 6,000 artists' signatures, symbols, and monograms are included. The first section is alphabetical, with concise information about each artist and reproductions of signatures and monograms used. The other sections arrange illegible signatures, monograms, and symbols so that one can identify an artist's name and then turn to the first part for more information. Though less comprehensive than Goldstein's *Monogramm Lexikon* (see item 324), this work is more accessible to those not fluent in German.

319. Cederholm, Theresa Dickason. **Afro-American Artists: A Bio-bibliographical Directory**. Boston Public Library, 1973. 348p.
Approximately 2,000 black artists in such fields as painting, sculpture, and graphics are included. Reviewing the book for *RQ* (Winter 1973, p. 169), Norman Lederer wrote: "The present work is of outstanding value and quality for its comprehensive listing and annotation of virtually every black artist past and present, including exhaustive information dealing with the artists' media, titles of known works, places where exhibits have been held, locations where works are permanently represented, artists' affiliations, awards and grants." Biographical data and personal statements by the artists about their work are included in *Black Artists on Art*, by Samella S. Lewis and Ruth G. Waddy (rev. ed., Contemporary Crafts; distr., Ward Ritchie, 1976- , 2v.).

320. **Contemporary Artists**, ed. by Colin Naylor and Genesis P-Orridge. St. Martin's, 1977. 1077p.
Some 1,300 internationally-known artists have been included. A typical entry covers biographical information (including awards and honors), individual shows, selected group shows, collections owning some of the artist's work, publications (both by and about), and an interpretive statement (which may or may not contain a direct quotation from the artist). Articles are signed, though the credentials of authors and advisors are not given. There are numerous black and white reproductions.

321. Cummings, Paul. **A Dictionary of Contemporary American Artists**. 3rd ed. St. Martin's, 1977. 545p.
The new edition includes 872 artists, chosen on the basis of representation in museums and collections. Entries are concise and concentrate on professional activities. Each entry has a short bibliography, with citations only by surnames, leading to full citations in the bibliography at the back of the book (pp. 511-45). There are about 100 black and white illustrations of varying size and quality (many do, however, show the artist's most recent style). Pronunciations of less common names are given in the "Index of Artists and Pronunciation Guide" (pp. 8-18). Interpretation of individual entries will require frequent reference to the "Key to Museums and Institutions and Their Schools" (pp. 19-42). Another useful feature is the list of addresses of "Galleries Representing the Artists in This Book" (pp. 43-53), although one could wish for more consistency in the inclusion of zip codes and foreign postal zone codes.

322. Dawdy, Doris O. **Artists of the American West: A Biographical Dictionary**. Swallow, 1974. 275p.
Over 1,300 artists and illustrators are included. Many entries are very brief, with little more given than birth and death dates and places where the artists lived. Some 300 biographies are more extensive, noting museums or other collections that contain the artists' works. Another work, with similar coverage, is *The Illustrated Biographical Encyclopedia of Artists of the American West*, by Peggy and Harold Samuels (Doubleday, 1976).

323. Fielding, Mantle. **Dictionary of American Painters, Sculptors and Engravers**. With an addendum containing corrections and additional material on the original entries, comp. by James F. Carr. Carr, 1965. 529p.

This is the best edition of a standard older work, which covers some 800 artists and was still rated as vital by 75 percent of the art librarians surveyed by Larsen in 1971. Carr painstakingly corrected the entries in the 1926 edition and put the new information into an addendum (pp. 435-529). Both parts must be consulted for accuracy and completeness. The 1974 edition (Modern Books and Crafts) is a reprint of the 1926 edition *without* Carr's corrections. The only new element is a 31-page supplement, compiled by Genevieve C. Doran, which lists very briefly some 2,500 additional artists of the seventeenth, eighteenth, and nineteenth centuries.

324. Goldstein, Franz. **Monogramm Lexikon: Internationales Verzeichnis der Monogramme bildenden Künstler seit 1850.** Walter deGruyter, 1964. 931p.
"About 20,000 monograms from all countries, with small but clear reproductions (p. 1-810). Supplementary lists of figures and signs, of anonymous artists, and of Cyrillic characters. Name index, p. 835-931" [A. J. Walford, *Guide to Reference Material*, v. III: *Generalities, Languages, the Arts and Literature* (3rd ed., London: Library Association, 1970), p. 368]. Suggested by art museum librarians as a vital addition to the Larsen list.

325. Harris, Ann Sutherland, and Linda Nochelin. **Women Artists: 1550-1950.** Los Angeles Co. Museum of Art and Alfred A. Knopf; distr., Random House, 1976. 368p.
This unusually excellent exhibition catalog has scholarly essays on each of the 84 artists covered, including contributions from 15 specialists. The two compilers have prepared historical essays—Harris to 1780 and Nochelin since the French Revolution. Another valuable contribution is *Women Artists: Recognition and Reappraisal from the Early Middle Ages to the Twentieth Century*, by Karen Petersen and J. J. Wilson (New York University, 1976). Less successful is *Women Artists in America: Eighteenth Century to the Present*, by J. L. Collins (the Author, 1973), which gives no criteria, omits some notable artists, and includes some of lesser stature.

326. Havlice, Patricia Pate. **Index to Artistic Biography.** Scarecrow, 1973. 2v.
International in coverage, this set includes some 70,000 artists whose biographies appeared in 64 reference works published between 1902 and 1970. Dates, nationality, media, pseudonyms, variant name spellings, and coding to the 64 works indexed are given.

327. **The Index of Twentieth Century Artists.** V. 1-4, No. 7, Oct. 1933-April 1937. College Art Association, 1933-37; Arno, 1970. 4v. in 1.
These biographical articles on 120 American artists, which first appeared in the monthly issues, include information about honors, awards, exhibitions, and bibliographical citations. The reprint includes an index.

328. **International Who's Who in Art and Antiques.** 2nd ed. Melrose, 1976. 525p.
This work contains about 4,000 biographies of collectors, sculptors, painters, dealers, educators, gallery and museum directors, etc., and covers over 50 countries. Narrower in national scope is Colin S. Macdonald's *Dictionary of Canadian Artists* (Canadian Paperbacks, 1967-74), which gives biographical information in brief essays that cite sources. Somewhat broader subject coverage is given in *Creative Canada: A Biographical Dictionary of Twentieth-Century Creative and Performing Artists* (University of Toronto Press, 1971-72, 2v.). A major Soviet biographical dictionary is

Khudozhniki Narodov SSSR: Bibliograficheskii Slovar (Izd. "Iskusstvo," 1970- , 6v.), which contains entries for 20,000 painters, sculptors, architects, graphic and decorative artists, and theater and movie designers for all periods from the distant past to the present.

329. Mallett, Daniel Trowbridge. **Mallett's Index of Artists, Including Painters, Sculptors, Illustrators, Engravers and Etchers of the Past and Present.** Bowker, 1935. Suppl. 1940. Repr., Gale, 1976. 2v.
Gives brief biographical information and refers to 22 general and over 1,000 specialized sources. Makes heavy use of symbols. Valuable for minor artists, despite some inaccuracies. Regarded as vital by over one-half the art librarians in the Larsen survey. Geraldine Wernersbach's *Index to Twentieth-Century American Painters Presently Listed in National or Local Publications* (thesis, Kent State University, 1959) is a specialized supplement to Mallett, with references to sources of biographical data on 8,500 painters.

330. New York Historical Society. **Dictionary of Artists in America, 1564-1860**, by George C. Croce and David H. Wallace. Yale, 1957. 759p.
Biographical information and citations to further sources are given for some 11,000 painters, draftsmen, sculptors, engravers, lithographers, etc. This title was among the top ten vital works in the Larsen survey.

331. Thieme, Ulrich, and Felix Becker. **Allgemeines Lexikon der Bildenden Kunstler von der Antike bis zur Gegenwart.** Seemann, 1907-50; repr., 1970-71. 37v.
This is the most comprehensive and authoritative biographical directory in any language. It includes nearly 50,000 artists (mostly painters and engravers, but sculptors and architects as well). About 400 German and foreign experts contributed articles. The longer ones are signed. Locations of art works are often given, and bibliographies are frequently included. The set includes a few living persons, but mostly, these are reserved for Vollmer's supplement on twentieth century artists (see item 333). Austrian artists will also be found in Rudolf Schmidt's *Österreichisches Künstlerlexikón: Von den Aufängen bis zur Gegenwart* (Tusch, 1974- , 6v.).

332. Vasari, Giorgio. **Lives of the Most Eminent Painters, Sculptors and Architects.** Tr. by Gaston du C. De Vere. Macmillan, 1912-1915; repr., AMS Press, 1976. 10v.
First published in 1550, this is the classic source for biographies of Italian Renaissance artists. De Vere's translation is the most reliable in English and includes over 500 illustrations.

333. Vollmer, Hans. **Allgemeines Lexikon der Bildenden Kunstler des XX Jahrhunderts.** Seemann, 1953-62; repr., 1970-71. 6v.
This continuation of Thieme and Becker (see item 331) includes some overlap from the nineteenth century. In all of the approximately 6,000 entries, Vollmer gives brief biographical notes, lists of works, and bibliographical references.

334. **Who's Who in American Art,** 1936/37- . Bi. Bowker.
The 1978 edition gives biographical data on 10,000 living painters, sculptors, illustrators, craftsmen, engravers, museum executives and art patrons. The basic arrangement is alphabetical, supplemented by a geographic index, a professional classifications

index, and a necrology. The geographic index has a separate section for Canadian and other foreign artists.

335. **Who's Who in Art: Biographies of Leading Men and Women in the World of Art Today—Artists, Designers, Craftsmen, Critics, Writers, Teachers, Collectors and Curators, with an Appendix of Signatures.** Art Trade Press, 1927- . Bi.
Sometimes irregular in the past, this work usually contains about 4,000 short biographies, with British artists predominating. Appendices typically include: monograms and signatures; obituaries; abbreviations.

336. Women's History Research Center. **Female Artists, Past and Present: A Directory and Bibliography of Women in the Visual Arts and Related Fields.** 2nd ed. The Center, 1974. 158p. Suppl. 1975. 66p.
This mimeographed publication is highly recommended both for its coverage and for its citations to other sources of information in a field of increasing interest and importance.

337. Young, William. **A Dictionary of America's Artists, Sculptors and Engravers: From the Beginnings through the Turn of the Twentieth Century.** W. Young, 1968. 515p.
With brief entries for some 15,000 artists, this work is very useful for identification of those who are obscure, but less so for details on people reasonably well known. There are no bibliographies or citations to sources. Occasionally, one might question the thoroughness of the research (e.g., details for Agnes Dean Abbat and Agnes-Dean Abbatt are so similar—identical birth and death dates, etc.—that variants of one name might be suspected).

Art Reproductions

Note: Other sources are given under **Painting Reproductions.**

338. Bartran, Margaret. **A Guide to Color Reproductions.** 2nd ed. Scarecrow, 1971. 625p.
Intended primarily as a handbook for retail print dealers but useful to art librarians as well, this book covers the range of art reproductions available in the United States at the beginning of 1969. Intended as a quick first step that would lead to publishers' catalogs for more detailed information, it is limited to color reproductions commercially available in sheet form. The first part is alphabetical by artist (subarranged alphabetically by title) and gives information on size of reproduction, source for ordering, and price. The second part, an index of titles, refers back to the first part. Over 12,000 reproductions are listed.

339. Clapp, Jane. **Art in Life.** Scarecrow, 1959. 504p. Suppl. 1965. 379p.
This index (by author, title, and subject) of reproductions of paintings and graphic arts in *Life* also includes selected photographs of architecture, sculpture, decorative arts, and portraits of artists as well as historical and literary personages.

340. Clapp, Jane. **Art Reproductions.** Scarecrow, 1961. 350p.
Consisting of a list of reproductions available from 95 museums in U.S. and Canada, this work is arranged by medium (e.g., painting) and then by scale. The index includes names of artists, of individuals portrayed, and a few subjects.

341. Greer, Roger C. **Illustration Index.** 3rd ed. Scarecrow, 1973. 164p.
The second edition (comp. by Lucille E. Vance and Esther M. Tracy) covered the period from 1950 through June 1963. The third edition covers *only* the period from July 1963

through December 1971; thus, it is a companion volume rather than a replacement. As in the second edition, the type of illustration is indicated if it is not a photograph. Greer, like his predecessors, has *excluded* furniture, nature subjects, portraits, and paintings (unless the paintings portray historical events or have information of a general nature). The arrangement is alphabetical by subject, and the books and periodicals indexed are listed at the end of the preface.

342.   Havlice, Patricia Pate. **Art in Time.** Scarecrow, 1970. 350p.
All of the photographs and art reproductions in the art section of *Time* from 1923 to 1969 are indexed in a single alphabet, with artist/title and selective (rather than comprehensive) subject entries. There are some cross references (for artists known by more than one name). Because *Time* is not covered in *Art Index* or *Illustration Index*, this book fills a need, especially in school and public libraries.

343.   Hewlett-Woodmere Public Library. **Index to Art Reproductions in Books.** Scarecrow, 1974. 372p.
Reproductions of paintings, sculpture, graphic art, photography, stage design, and architecture in 65 art books from 1956 through 1971 are included in this index, which is divided into two parts: name index; title index. Full information about each reproduction (book, page, size, color or black and white) is given in the name index. The title index gives the artists' names after the titles and thus refers the user back to the name index.

344.   New York Graphic Society. **Fine Arts Reproductions of Old and Modern Masters: A Comprehensive Illustrated Catalog of Art through the Ages.** The Society, 1978. 598p.
Combining the features of a sales catalog and a reference work, successive editions have included increasing numbers of color reproductions from the Society's inventory. The basic arrangement is by period, then by country or region. However, there are some departures, and the best procedure is to consult the table of contents. Other reference features include a classified subject index, a name index, and short biographies of selected artists. With each full-color reproduction, the following information is given: artist, title, date, location of original, size of reproduction, framing size, and price of reproduction.

345.   New York Historical Society. **Catalogue of American Portraits in the New York Historical Society.** Yale University Press, 1974. 2v.
This vital reference tool for art librarians, replacing a 1941 edition, contains 2,420 entries and 939 illustrations, with brief biographical information on each artist and a few details about each picture (acquisition record, occasion, bibliography). Other reference features include a substantial general bibliography and an index.

346.   Parry, Pamela Jeffcott, comp. **Contemporary Art and Artists: An Index to Reproductions.** Greenwood, 1978.
Broader in coverage than Monro (see items 411, 412), this index includes all media except architecture. Some 60 books from the 1940s to the mid-1970s have been included. There is relatively little overlap with Clapp's *Art Reproductions* (see item 340) and Havlice's *World Painting Index* (see item 410). The basic arrangement by artists' names is supplemented by a title and subject index.

347.   Pierson, William Harvey, and Martha Davidson, eds. **Arts of the United States: A Pictorial Survey.** McGraw-Hill, 1960; repr., University of Georgia Press, 1975. 452p.
The editors surveyed American art and selected 4,000 examples to be made into color slides for the use of schools, museums, and libraries. The book is arranged by subject. Each section is introduced by an essay and followed by small black-and-white reproductions of the slides. There is an index of artists, titles, and subjects. For information on what the New York State Library has done to make this collection available to public library users, see "Slides of the Arts of the United States," by Jack B. Spear [*The Bookmark* 29 (November 1969):77-79]. For a critical analysis of the quality of art slides available from museums and commercial sources, see Patricia Sloane's "Color Slides for Teaching Art History" [*Art Journal* 31 (Spring 1972):276-80].

348.   Special Libraries Association. Picture Division. **Picture Sources 3: Collections of Prints and Photographs in the U.S. and Canada,** ed. by Ann Novotny and Rosemary Eakins. 3rd ed. SLA, 1975. 387p.
The new edition is the result of collaborative efforts by members of SLA and the American Society of Picture Professionals. Some 10,000 questionnaires were mailed and 1,084 collections are given numbered entries. Information about each collection typically includes: address, person in charge; size; subjects; dates covered; and conditions of access and use. The basic arrangement is by subject, with division into commercial and noncommercial sources where applicable. Of particular interest is the section on "Fine, Graphic and Applied Arts" (pp. 166-205). Additional access is provided by: a numerical list of sources; an alphabetical list of sources and major collections; a geographical list of sources; and a subject index.

349.   University Prints, Cambridge, MA. **The University Prints: Fine Art Reproductions for Students . . . Complete Catalogue.** University Prints, 1931- . 1972 ed. 278p.
Subtitle: "Listing by period, school and artist all 7,000 basic fine arts subjects—architecture, painting, sculpture—available both as slides and as prints. All prints a uniform 5 ½" x 8" in black and white . . . 275 in color. Available loose leaf or custom bound." Useful for college-level teaching. Selected and frequently revised by specialists.

Handbooks

350.   **Arts and Crafts Market,** 1978- . Ann. Writer's Digest Books.
This publication continues, in part, *Artist's and Photographer's Market.* It covers nearly 4,500 places for sale of art works and crafts. Following an opening section of general advice to freelance artists (covering such topics as business records, methods of shipping, and copyright), the main (directory) portion is divided into broad subject areas such as advertising and public relations, competitions and exhibitions, fine art publishers and distributors, etc. This is followed by a section devoted to practical advice on topics like agents, art colonies, and so forth. A glossary and an index complete the work. The other part of *Artist's and Photographer's Market* is continued in *Photographer's Market,* 1978- (Writer's Digest Books), which follows a similar pattern.

351.   Chamberlain, Betty. **The Artist's Guide to His Market.** Watson-Guptill, 1970. 128p.
Written by the founder of the Art Information Center (New York), this handbook gives advice on exhibiting, galleries, pricing, selling, commissions, contracts, publicity, and artists' groups. Unfortunately, it is limited to New York.

352.   Holden, Donald. **Art Career Guide: A Guidance Handbook for Art Students, Teachers, Vocational Counselors, and Job Hunters.** 3rd ed. Watson-Guptill, 1973. 303p.
Reviewing this book for *ARBA 1974* (p. 209), Shirley Miller wrote: "An important manual for prospective artists and those who attempt to guide them. The book covers all the significant career steps, starting with the initial decision to become an artist. It explores high school preparation and the selection of an art school, assesses the vocational aspects of each major art field, and assists the job seeker with practical advice on writing résumés, organizing job hunts, planning portfolios, and participating in job interviews. At the back of the book there is a directory of degree-granting schools as well as a list of professional organizations and guidance agencies."

353.   Massey, Robert. **Formulas for Painters.** Watson-Guptill, 1967. 224p.
This practical book contains over 200 recipes for sizes, grounds, media, glazes, varnishes, fixatives, and adhesives. Cross references, a bibliography, and an index enhance its reference uses. A. P. Laurie's *The Painter's Methods and Materials* (Lippincott, 1926; repr., Dover, 1967) may occasionally still be useful.

354.   Mayer, Ralph. **The Artist's Handbook of Materials and Techniques.** 3rd ed. Viking, 1970. 750p.
This title was suggested by art librarians in the Larsen survey for addition to the basic list of vital works. Less practical, but occasionally of value will be H. L. Cooke's *Painting Techniques of the Masters* (rev. ed., Watson-Guptill, 1972), which was published in cooperation with the National Gallery of Art and reproduces major paintings from the fifteenth to the twentieth centuries in high quality color, accompanied by informative comments on technique, with sketches to illustrate particular points. Historical coverage will also be found in A. P. Laurie's *Greek and Roman Methods of Painting* (Cambridge, 1910; repr., Longwood, 1978) and in Laurie's *The Materials of the Painter's Craft in Europe and Egypt* (Foulis, 1910; repr., Longwood, 1978).

355.   Snyder, John. **Commercial Artist's Handbook.** Watson-Guptill, 1973. 264p.
Drawing a distinction between fine art, illustration, and commercial art, Snyder confines his efforts to meeting the need for information on tools and techniques of commercial art. His handbook is actually a dictionary, illustrated with numerous black and white sketches. An alphabetical list of articles (with page numbers) in the front enables the user to tell at a glance whether the topic has been given a main entry. Subdivisions and cross references enable one to pursue more minute or related subjects. The advice is practical. Common difficulties and ways to surmount them are frequently noted. Snyder's work was included in "Reference Books of 1973" (*Library Journal*, April 15, 1974, p. 1097).

Art Sales

356.   **Art at Auction: The Year at Sotheby's and Parke Bernet,** 1967- . Ann. Sotheby Parke Bernet.
Arranged in chapters on various topics, this annual has a good table of contents and is profusely illustrated, often in color. Each item sold has a picture, description, sale price, and date of sale. There are two indexes: a general index and an index of books, manuscripts, and miniatures. Prior to 1967, the title varied.

357. **Art Prices Current**, 1907- . Ann. Dawson.
This work is arranged by medium. Part A includes paintings, drawings, and miniatures, while part B covers engravings and prints. Each part is arranged chronologically by sales, with items within that part numbered consecutively. Artist, title, size, purchaser, price, and sometimes condition are given. There are indexes of artists, engravers, and collectors. The publisher has varied in the past.

358. Bérard, Michèle. **Encyclopedia of Modern Art Auction Prices.** Arco, 1971. 417p.
Painters from the Impressionist period to the present whose works brought over $2,000 in sales from 1961 to 1969 are included.

359. **Christie's Review of the Season**, 1960- . Ann. Hutchinson/Macmillan.
Like *Art at Auction* (see item 356), this is a yearly record of sales by a major art dealer. It is noteworthy for the illustrations, many being of art works that have been in private hands and thus not accessible for public viewing. The title and publisher have varied in the past. The work has had the present title since 1972 and been handled by Macmillan only since 1978. (For several years it was carried by Abrams.)

360. **International Auction Records**, 1961/62- . Ann. Editions Publisol.
Formerly entitled *International Yearbook of Sales*, this publication has five parts: engravings, drawings, watercolors, paintings, sculpture. Within each, arrangement is alphabetical by artists. Size and price are given, and there are some illustrations. There is a calendar index.

361. Lancour, Harold. **American Art Auction Catalogues, 1785-1942: A Union List.** New York Public Library, 1944. 377p.
This union checklist of more than 7,000 catalogs of auction sales of art objects locates copies in 21 libraries and includes a list of auction houses and an index of owners. Another valuable resource is the *Library Catalog* of the Metropolitan Museum of Art (see item 262) because v. 24-25 cover sales catalogs.

362. Lugt, Fritz. **Répertoire des catalogues de ventes publiques.** Nijhof, 1938-64. 3v.
A chronological list of catalogs of art sales, this set gives the following information for each entry: date and place of sale, provenance, contents, number of items and pages, auctioneers, and locations of copies in libraries. Its reference value is increased by an index of names of collections sold. The following periods are covered: v. 1, to 1825; v. 2, 1826-1860; v. 3, 1861-1900. The Bibliothèque Forney's *Catalogue des catalogues de ventes d'art/Catalog of the Catalogs of Sales of Art* (G. K. Hall, 1972) is especially rich in twentieth century art and can be used as a continuation of Lugt. In 1974, the Bibliothèque Forney began publishing *Index alphabetique des auteurs.*

Periodicals

363. **AIA Journal**, 1900- . Mo. American Institute of Architects.
Indexed: *Arch.Ind., Art Ind., Avery Ind.Arch.Per.* A professional journal with a wide range of articles and technical information for the practising architect and the student. Reference features include news of architectural events and a calendar of activities. Several books are reviewed in each issue.

364. **American Artist**, 1937- . Mo. Billboard Publications.
Indexed: *RG, Abr.RG, Art Ind., PAIS, ARTbibliog., Bk.Rev.Ind.* Primarily for art students and amateurs. Articles on technique by well-known practitioners and occasional articles on famous artists from the standpoint of elementary appreciation. Includes notices of art exhibitions and reviews of art books.

365. **American Journal of Archaeology**, 1885- . Q. Archaeological Institute of America.
Indexed: *Art Ind., Hum.Ind., A&HCI, Bk.Rev.Dig., Curr.Cont., SSCI.* The close relationship between art and archaeology is exemplified in the copious illustrations in this scholarly journal of art objects excavated from archaeological sites. The issues examined focused heavily on the world of classical antiquity. Archaeological notes, book reviews, and lists of books received appear in every issue. A list of recently completed dissertations is published annually.

366. **Apollo: The Magazine of the Arts**, 1925- . Mo. Apollo Publications.
Indexed: *A&HCI, Bk.Rev.Ind., Br.Hum.Ind., ARTbibliog., Bull.signal.:art.* Features include articles on the history of art, book reviews, and news of auctions and other sales. Planned for collectors, it is frustrating for the librarian to use because the table of contents occurs somewhere past the middle of each issue. A handsomely illustrated (both color and black and white) section of advertising in the front covers forthcoming sales from Christie's, Sotheby's, etc.

367. **Archaeology**, 1948- . Bi-mo. Archaeological Institute of America.
Indexed: *Art Ind., A&HCI, Hum.Ind., SSCI.* Some handsome color reproductions and numerous black and white photographs illustrate the articles dealing with archaeological discoveries in many parts of the world. Notices of exhibitions, book reviews, and lists of books received are regular features.

368. **Architectural Record**, 1891- . Mo. Semi-mo. (May, Aug., Oct.). McGraw-Hill.
Indexed: *AS&T Ind., A&HCI, Arch.Ind., Art Ind., Eng.Ind., RG, CIJE, Bull.signal:soc.* Well illustrated. Vast amounts of technical information for architects and engineers. The emphasis on homes also makes it of more general interest. Reference features include news and product reports and a calendar. Most issues have a section on "office literature," with brief annotations about technical pamphlets.

369. **Art and Artists**, 1966- . Mo. Hansom Books.
Indexed: *Art Ind.* Articles on art, architecture, and artists from various parts of the world, illustrated by numerous black and white photographs, are the mainstay of this British journal. Reviews of exhibitions also appear regularly.

370. **Art Bulletin**, 1917- . Q. College Art Association of America.
Indexed: *Art Ind., Bk.Rev.Dig., Bull.signal.:art, A&HCI.* Long, scholarly articles on all fields of art history, often illustrated with black and white photographs. Lengthy, signed book reviews and lists of books received. Index to v. 1-21 (1917-1948) was published in 1950. Major journal for art historians in the United States. Available on microform.

371. **Art in America**, 1913- . Bi-mo. Whitney Communications.
Indexed: *A&HCI, Art Ind., RG, ARTbibliog., Bk.Rev.Ind., Film Lit.Ind.* One of the

best, perhaps the best, of the general art periodicals. Each issue has many excellent plates (both color and black and white). Coverage includes: painting, sculpture, architecture, design, and photography. Other features include art news and reviews of books and exhibitions.

372.   **Art International: The Art Spectrum**, 1956- . 10/yr. International Art Publications. Foundation.
Indexed: *A&HCI, Art Ind., ARTbibliog., Film Lit.Ind.* An important periodical covering international developments in contemporary art. For the professional artist. Some book reviews and articles on artists and exhibitions (with both color and black and white illustrations).

373.   **Artforum**, 1962- . Mo. (except July, Aug.). California Artforum, Inc.
Indexed: *Art Ind., RILA, A&HCI.* Illustrated articles on art and architecture and reviews of exhibitions and books are characteristic of this periodical.

374.   **ARTnews**, 1902- . Mo. (Sept.-May). Q. (June-Aug.). ARTnews.
Indexed: *A&HCI, ARTbibliog., RG, Bull.signal.:art.* Aimed at professional artists but also of interest to collectors and gallery visitors. Very strong on contemporary art broadly interpreted, especially new developments in the United States. Reviews of books and current exhibitions.

375.   **Arts Magazine**, 1926- . Mo. (Sept.-June). Art Digest Co.
Indexed: *Art Ind., ARTbibliog., RILA, RG, A&HCI.* Short articles, with color and black and white photographs, cover a wide range of contemporary topics, while longer historical articles are heavily footnoted. Reviews of exhibitions appear regularly.

376.   **Bollettino d'arte**, 1907- . S-Ann. Ministero delle Pubblica Instruzione.
Indexed: *Art Ind.* An official publication of the Italian Ministry of Public Instruction, this journal is an essential tool for study of Italian art and architecture, with emphasis on the classical period. It contains lengthy, scholarly articles and book reviews. The illustrations are well printed.

377.   **Bulletin monumental**, 1834- . Q. Société Française d'Archéologie.
Indexed: *Art Ind.* Articles are profusely illustrated with black and white photographs. The "Chroniques" section calls attention to articles and sections of books on art and architecture. The "Bibliographie" section consists of book reviews. The first issue each year lists French buildings that were designated as historic monuments during the preceding year.

378.   **Burlington Magazine**, 1903- . Mo. Burlington Magazine Publications.
Indexed: *A&HCI, Art Ind., Br.Hum.Ind., IBZ, ARTbibliog., Bk.Rev.Ind., Bull.signal.:art.* This research periodical covers art of all periods and countries. Both the lengthy articles and short notices are carefully researched and written by scholars attached to universities and museums. Most are illustrated with black and white photographs. Obituaries, reviews of exhibitions, calendar information, and museum acquisitions are noted. Book reviews are lengthy and critical. An extensive section of advertising in the front covers forthcoming sales of such firms as Sotheby's, copiously illustrated with black and white photographs, and occasionally with handsome color plates. The table of contents is found near the middle of most issues.

379. **The Connoisseur,** 1901- . Mo. National Magazine Co.
Indexed: *A&HCI, ARTbibliog., Art Ind., Br.Hum.Ind., Bk.Rev.Ind., Bull.signal.:art.*
For the art collector, this journal has articles on painting and sculpture. Information on pottery, silverware, furniture, and sales is also given. It is well printed and illustrated with numerous color plates. Other features include good book reviews and a section on art news called "The Connoisseur in America."

380. **Design: For Arts in Education,** 1899- . 6/yr. Saturday Evening Post.
Indexed: *RG.* This is a magazine of creative art for teachers. Art is very broadly interpreted. In the sample examined, articles (usually illustrated) ranged all the way from visual literacy to handicrafts. Also available on microform.

381. **Gazette des beaux arts,** 1859- . 10/yr. Imprimeries Reunies.
Indexed: *A&HCI, Art Ind., ARTbibliog., Bull.signal.:art.* This periodical covers all aspects and periods in a scholarly manner, but with special emphasis on French art. In recent years, it has had a good many articles in English. Included with the periodical is a supplement, "La chronique des arts," which gives news of museum activities, collections, and exhibitions, as well as short reviews of books.

382. **Graphis,** 1944- . Bi-mo. Graphis Press.
Indexed: *Art Ind., A&HCI.* Subtitled "International Journal of Graphic Art and Applied Art," this periodical is copiously illustrated (color, black and white) and includes reviews of books and exhibitions.

383. **L'Oeil; revue d'art,** 1955- . 10/yr. L'Oeil.
Indexed: *A&HCI, Art Ind., ARTbibliog., Bull.signal.:soc.* Designed for collectors, this journal covers art of many different periods. It is superbly illustrated.

384. **Print, America's Graphic Design Magazine,** 1939- . Bi-mo. RC Publications, Inc.
Indexed: *Art Ind.* Articles are profusely illustrated (both color and black and white). Departments (which do not appear in every issue) include "New Developments in Print/TV/Film," "Aids and Information for Designers," "Books in Brief," and "Art Services Market Place."

385. **Progressive Architecture,** 1920- . Mo. Penton/IPC Reinhold.
Indexed: *Arch.Ind., Art Ind., AS&T Ind., Eng.Ind., Bull.signal.:soc., CIJE, Avery Ind.Arch.Per.* One of the best general periodicals in the field, *Progressive Architecture* has international coverage, with emphasis on modern work. Regular features include architectural news, a calendar of events, and information on products and literature.

386. **Studio International,** 1893- . 6/yr. Punch Publications.
Indexed: *Art Ind., Br.Hum.Ind., IBZ, ARTbibliog., Bk.Rev.Ind., Film Lit.Ind.* With international coverage, but especially strong on moden British art, this periodical for collectors is well illustrated. Reviews of books and exhibitions are included.

387. **Zeitschrift fuer Kunstgeschichte,** 1932- . 5/yr. Deutscher Kunstverlag.
Indexed: *Art Ind.* In a typical year, 4 or 5 issues appear (one may be a double number), and the last is a special bibliography issue, devoted to art publications in the preceding year. Long scholarly articles (illustrated with numerous black and white photographs) and lengthy signed book reviews are characteristic of this periodical.

PAINTING

Introductions

388.   Barr, Alfred Hamilton. **What Is Modern Painting?** 9th ed. rev. Museum of Modern Art; distr., Doubleday, 1966; repr., 1975. 48p.
The author of this small book has tried to help persons looking at modern art for the first time. Illustrations (black and white) are numerous and closely related to the text. *What Is a Picture?*, by George Boas and Harold Holmes Wrenn (Schocken, 1966), is the result of collaboration between a philosophy professor and a practising artist. Mary Ann Campbell's *Paintings: How to Look at Great Art* (Watts, 1970) is designed for children in grades five through eight.

389.   Kulturmann, Udo. **The New Painting.** Tr. by Gerald Onn. Praeger, 1970. 207p.
This book provides international coverage of painting since about 1950 and is considered by some reviewers to be the best available guide. It is arranged by subjects or formal themes. Illustrations were regarded as well chosen and reproduced, except for some of the color plates.

Dictionaries and Encyclopedias

390.   Berckalaers, Ferdinand Louis. **A Dictionary of Abstract Painting, with a History of Abstract Painting,** by Michel Seuphor (pseud.). Tudor, 1957. 304p.
Translated from the French, this useful reference tool includes history, chronology, a dictionary (with short biographies of 500 abstract artists), and a bibliography. There are many small illustrations in color.

391.   Champlin, John Denison, Jr. **Cyclopedia of Painters and Paintings.** Scribners, 1887; repr., Kennikat, 1969. 4v.
A product of the late nineteenth century, this alphabetical encyclopedia includes biographies of painters, descriptions of paintings, and reproductions of monograms and signatures of many painters. There are relatively few plates and outline drawings. More recent sources are better for pictures. The entries have brief citations to sources, which are fully listed in v. 1. Bernard S. Myers's *Encyclopedia of Painting: Painters and Painting in the World from Prehistoric Times to the Present Day* (Crown, 1955) covers painters, movements, styles, techniques, etc., in an arrangement that is alphabetical (except for some Oriental painters—country and period) and has about 1,000 illustrations, some in color. *Everyman's Dictionary of Pictorial Art*, by William Gaunt (Dutton, 1962, 2v.), provides brief information on all parts of the world from the earliest times to the present. In addition to short biographies of 1,200 painters and 1,000 illustrations, it contains definitions of terms, information on galleries, and some descriptions of famous paintings.

392.   Daniel, Howard. **Encyclopaedia of Themes and Subjects in Painting.** Abrams, 1971. 252p.
European painting from the Renaissance through the middle of the nineteenth century is included. The arrangement is alphabetical, with about 400 subjects and about 300 illustrations (over 30 in color). A list of illustrations and detailed information about the originals may be found in the back. Unfortunately, the book lacks an overall index.

393. **Dictionary of Modern Painting,** ed. by Carlton Lake and Robert Maillard. 3rd ed. rev. Tudor, 1964. 416p.
Translated from the French, but with some additional entries, this work includes art movements, artists, places, and schools of painting for the period from the Impressionists to World War II.

394. Foskett, Daphne. **A Dictionary of British Miniature Painters.** Praeger, 1972, 2v.
Volume 1 gives brief information on 4,500 artists from 1520 to 1910 and includes 100 color reproductions. V. II consists entirely of plates (black and white), with 967 reproductions. The set is very expensive, but it is likely to remain the definitive work for many years to come. It is much more comprehensive than Basil Long's *British Miniaturists, 1520-1860,* which had been the standard work on the subject after its appearance in 1929.

395. Taubes, Frederic. **The Painter's Dictionary of Materials and Methods.** Watson-Guptill, 1971. 253p.
This work concentrates on technical advice needed when painting and emphasizes purchase of materials now commercially available, in contrast to some older works that contained detailed information on preparation by hand. There are numerous sketches of equipment.

Catalogs

396. Boston Museum of Fine Arts. **American Paintings in the Museum of Fine Arts, Boston.** New York Graphic Society, 1969. 2v.
Each entry gives description, measurement, provenance, a brief biography of the artist, full bibliographical references, and exhibitions in which the painting has been displayed. This scholarly, attractive catalog of over 1,000 American paintings and more than 600 illustrations (many in color) is cited merely as an example of the many catalogs already published or in process of being published by such institutions as the Louvre, the Tate Gallery, the Frick Gallery, the National Gallery, and the Cleveland Museum of Art. Library catalogs should be checked for local availability.

397. Delteil, Loÿs. **Le peintre-graveur illustré; The Graphic Works of Nineteenth and Twentieth Century Artists, an Illustrated Catalog.** Collectors Editions, 1969-70. 32v.
This is a facsimile reprint, with additional material, of the 1906-1930 editions. V. 32 is an appendix and glossary prepared under the supervision of Herman J. Wechsler. Of the earlier printing, Mary W. Chamberlin (*Guide to Art Reference Books,* p. 211) wrote: "For each artist there is a short biography, a portrait, and a catalog of his works. Brief descriptions of the works and identification of their various states are given; sales and prices and provenance are also indicated. Each work is illustrated."

398. Hofstede de Groot, Cornelius. **A Catalogue Raisonné of the Works of the Most Eminent Dutch Painters of the Seventeenth Century; Based on the Work of John Smith.** Tr. and ed. by Edward G. Hawke. Macmillan, 1907-27. 8v.

Concentrates on major painters and covers each in great detail. For each painting, the following types of information are given: condition, location, size, signature, sale date, and price. Index of collections and collectors in v. 1. Indexes of painters and engravers in v. 2-8. No monograms or illustrations.

399. Hollstein, Friedrich Wilhelm Heinrich. **Dutch and Flemish Etchings, Engravings and Woodcuts, ca 1450-1700.** M. Hertzberger, 1949- .
Planned as a series of 25 volumes with 10,000 illustrations and a concluding index, this work is arranged alphabetically by artists' names. In reviewing v. 1 (*Burlington Magazine*, March 1951, p. 98), A. E. Popham wrote: "Not only are the original engravings, etchings and woodcuts by each artist catalogued in detail with references to previous catalogues and almost completely illustrated, but a list is also given of the copies of engravings though these are not reproduced. Drawings made by an artist for or in connection with each engraving are recorded and the sales through which impressions passed with the prices in florins are given. The reproductions of engravings catalogued are noted, a piece of information which is of value to collectors and printrooms. . . . " Hollstein's *German Engravings, Etchings and Woodcuts, ca 1400-1700* (M. Hertzberger, 1954-68, 8v.) is also arranged alphabetically by artists' names and includes brief biographical information as well as some 8,000 illustrations.

400. United Nations Educational, Scientific and Cultural Organization. **An Illustrated Inventory of Famous Dismembered Works of Art: European Painting.** Unipub, 1974. 233p.
Illustrations and descriptions are included in this inventory, which provides such information as the name of the artist, identification of the work, reasons for dismemberment, disposition of fragments, efforts at restoration, ownership, exhibitions, bibliography, and iconography.

Histories

401. **The Great Centuries of Painting.** Skira, 1952- .
The quality of the color reproductions is especially good, and some painters are covered here that might be difficult to locate elsewhere. LC catalogs each title separately, but provides a series added entry. A list of titles is given by A. J. Walford in *Guide to Reference Material* (3rd ed., Library Association, 1977) v. 3, p. 376. Matthew Baigell's *A History of American Painting* (Praeger, 1971), part of the Praeger World of Art series, includes notes and a bibliography.

402. Haftman, Werner. **Painting in the Twentieth Century.** 2nd English ed. Praeger, 1965. 2v.
A history of painting in the twentieth century. V. I has the subtitle: "An Analysis of the Artists and Their Work," while v. II is subtitled: "A Pictorial Survey." Some 50 of the 1,011 illustrations are in color. The 1965 edition was substantially revised and won wide acclaim from reviewers as an excellent and comprehensive work.

403. Marle, Raimond van. **The Development of the Italian Schools of Painting . . . .** Nijhoff, 1923-38; repr., Hacker, 1971. 19v.
Scholarly approach with numerous footnotes and chapter bibliographies. Each volume has indexes of artists, iconography, and places. The final volume is a general index to the whole set.

404.   Siren, Oswald. **Chinese Painting: Leading Masters and Principles.** Ronald Press, 1956-58. 7v.

This vital reference history covers the period from the earliest times to the end of the Ch'ing dynasty in 1912. There are lists of works by Chinese painters and over 800 plates. Bibliographies include works in both Oriental and Western languages. James Cahill is editor of a projected new series entitled *A History of Later Chinese Painting, 1279-1950* (Weatherhill, 1976-). Two volumes have been published: v. 1 — *Hills beyond a River: Chinese Painting of the Yuan Dynasty, 1279-1368*, 1976; v. 2 — *Parting at the Shore: Chinese Painting of the Early and Middle Ming Dynasty, 1368-1580*, 1978.

Biographies

405.   Canaday, John. **The Lives of the Painters.** Norton, 1969. 4v.

Covers four centuries (through the nineteenth), with biographies of 450 European and American painters. V. 1-3 are text, and v. 4 contains plates (both color and black and white) of artists' works.

406.   Harper, J. Russell. **Early Painters and Engravers in Canada.** University of Toronto Press, 1970. 376p.

Restricted to artists born before 1867 or active before 1900, this work includes both Canadians and foreigners working in Canada. Articles include biographies, records of exhibitions, and collections where works are housed. Thorough and comprehensive.

407.   **Kindlers Malerei Lexikon,** ed. by Germain Bazin and others. Kindler Verlag, 1964-71. 6v.

Includes bibliographies, 1,000 artists' signatures, 1,200 color reproductions, and 3,000 black-and-white illustrations. V. 1-5 contain biographies of artists and reproductions of their works. V. 6 contains a section devoted to subjects (terms, movements, etc.) and three indexes: artists' names; places; reproductions. The quality of the reproductions is excellent.

408.   Snodgrass, Jeanne O. **American Indian Painters: A Biographical Directory.** Museum of the American Indian, Heye Foundation, 1968. 269p.

Biographical information concerning 1,187 living and deceased painters is included. Both Indian and English names are given if available. Many abbreviations are used, and one must often refer to the list of abbreviations in the back. An index of artists by tribe and a bibliography enhance the usefulness of this biographical dictionary.

Reproductions

409.   Brooke, Milton, and Henry J. DuBester. **Guide to Color Prints.** Scarecrow, 1953. 257p.

Covers 5,000 reproductions of works by 1,000 painters. Information concerning several additional sources of reproductions may be found in "Pictures: Reproductions of Art," by Sydney Starr Keaveney [*Wilson Library Bulletin* 46 (February 1972):494-95].

410.   Havlice, Patricia Pate. **World Painting Index.** Scarecrow, 1977. 2v.

Intended to supplement and update the two works by Monro and Monro (see items 411 and 412), this index covers reproductions of paintings in 1,167 books and catalogs (both United States and foreign) from 1940 to 1975. V. 1 is alphabetically arranged by artists' names and gives full information on where reproductions may be found. Note that a 27-page list of paintings by unknown artists is found between the bibliography at the beginning of v. 1 and the main alphabetical sequence by artists' names. V. 2 is arranged alphabetically by titles, thus referring the user to v. 1, where complete information is found. A very critical review of this work appeared in *Library Journal* (February 1, 1978, p. 353). Reviews in *ARBA 1978* (p. 421) and *Wilson Library Bulletin* (May 1978, p. 727) were more favorable.

411. Monro, Isabel Stevenson, and Kate M. Monro. **Index to Reproductions of American Paintings: A Guide to Pictures Occurring in More Than Eight Hundred Books.** Wilson, 1948. 731p. Suppl., 1964. 480p.
The main work lists paintings of artists in the United States in 520 books and 300 catalogs of exhibitions. Paintings are entered: 1) under the name of the artist, followed by dates, title of the picture, and an abbreviated entry for the book in which the reproduction is found; 2) under titles; and 3) in some cases, under subjects. Locations of pictures in permanent collections are also included when available. The supplement has 400 books and catalogs (1948-61). Regarded as vital by more than one-half of the art librarians in the Larsen survey, this index is supplemented and updated, but *not* superseded, by Havlice's *World Painting Index* (see item 410).

412. Monro, Isabel Stevenson, and Kate M. Monro. **Index to Reproductions of European Paintings: A Guide to Pictures in More Than Three Hundred Books.** Wilson, 1956. 668p.
Reproductions in 328 books are entered: 1) under the name of the artist, followed by dates if available, by the title of the picture, and by an abbreviated entry for the book where a reproduction is found; 2) under titles; and 3) in some cases, under subjects. Whenever permanent locations could be obtained, this information is recorded by symbols. More than one-half of the art librarians surveyed in the Larsen study regarded this work as vital. Supplemented and updated, but not superseded, by Havlice's *World Painting Index* (see item 410).

413. Smith, Lyn Wall, and Nancy Dustin Wall Moure. **Index to Reproductions of American Paintings Appearing in More Than 400 Books, Mostly Published since 1960.** Scarecrow, 1977. 983p.
Intended to update Monro and Monro (see item 411), this index covers many very specialized books and catalogs. Its reference usefulness is thus greater in libraries with large art collections. The major part is arranged by artists' names. The second, much smaller, part is by broad subjects. There is no title index.

414. United Nations Educational, Scientific and Cultural Organization. **Catalogue of Reproductions of Paintings prior to 1860.** 9th ed. rev. Unipub, 1971. 451p.
First published in 1950 and formerly entitled *Catalogue of Colour Reproductions of Paintings prior to 1860*. The title and the preface are in English, French, and Spanish. Selections are made on the basis of fidelity of color reproduction, significance of the artist, and importance of the painting. Entries are arranged alphabetically by artist (when known) and then by date. If the artist is unknown, the entries are under the country and then by date. (This is sometimes done when the artist's name is known, but country

identification appears more useful. For example, "Country Scene," by Cha Po-Chu, is entered under "China — Sung Dynasty [South] — 1127-1267." However, this artist is noted by name in the index, with a reference to the page on which the entry appears.) Each entry is accompanied by a small black and white reproduction. Other details are similar to those given for the next title.

415. United Nations Educational, Scientific and Cultural Organization. **Catalogue of Reproductions of Paintings — 1860 to 1973.** 10th ed. rev. Unipub, 1974. 343p.
First published in 1949 and formerly entitled *Catalogue of Colour Reproductions of Paintings.* Color reproductions from books and periodicals are not included unless these can be purchased separately. The basic arrangement is alphabetical by artist and then chronological by date of painting. Each entry gives the following information: 1) [for the original painting] name of painter, places and dates of birth and death, title of painting, date when known, mediuim, size (height by width in centimeters and inches), collection of the original; 2) [for the reproduction] process used in printing (as described by the publisher), size, Unesco archives number, printer, publisher, price. Items are numbered consecutively, but the index of artists at the back refers to page numbers. There is also a list of publishers' names and addresses, and a page of instructions for ordering reproductions.

ARCHITECTURE

Introductions

416. Giedion, Siegfried. **Space, Time and Architecture: The Growth of a New Tradition.** 5th ed. rev. and enl. Harvard, 1967. 897p.
Reflections, by one of the leaders of the twentieth century, on architectural history, city planning, and man's perception of space. Reference features include 531 black and white illustrations (listed in the front) and a name index. Another of his works worth considering is *Architecture, You and Me: The Diary of a Development* (Harvard, 1958). A rather different approach is found in T. F. Hamlin's *Architecture, an Art for All Men* (Columbia University Press, 1947). *The Spaces in Between,* by N. A. Owings (Houghton, 1973), is a combined autobiography and history of Skidmore, Owings and Merrill. A good book for beginners is S. E. Rasmussen's *Experiencing Architecture* (MIT, 1962).

417. Sullivan, Louis Henry. **Kindergarten Chats and Other Writings.** Wittenborn, Schultz, 1947. 252p.
Reflections by one of America's leading architects of the late nineteenth and early twentieth centuries. Originally published serially in *Interstate Architect and Builder* (1901-1902) and revised by Sullivan in 1918. The revolutionary ideas of R. Buckminster Fuller may be sampled in *Nine Chains to the Moon* (Lippincott, 1938; repr., Cape, 1973) or in such books about him as Robert Marks's *The Dymaxion World of Buckminster Fuller* (Reinhold, 1960).

418. Wright, Frank Lloyd. **Frank Lloyd Wright on Architecture: Selected Writings 1894-1940,** ed. by Frederick Gutheim. Duell, Sloane and Pearce, 1941. 275p.
A good selection from the writings of one of America's foremost architects in the twentieth century. Another selection of interest is *In the Cause of Architecture: Wright's*

Historic Essays for Architectural Record 1908-1952, ed. by Frederick Gutheim (McGraw-Hill, 1975). Some personal reflections late in life are contained in Wright's *A Testament* (Bramhall House, 1957).

Reference Works

419.   **American Architects Directory.** 3rd ed. Bowker, 1970. 1126p.
Published under the sponsorship of the American Institute of Architects, this work features condensed biographical sketches (of both members and non-members who responded to questionnaires) in the main section. Supplemental information on the American Institute of Architects, a geographical index, and articles on such topics as choosing an architect are also included. Coverage of architectural firms is provided in *ProFile: The Official AIA Directory of Architectural Firms*, edited by Henry W. Schirmer (Archimedia, Gale, 1978). The geographical arrangement is complemented by alphabetical indexes of firms and principal architects.

420.   American Association of Architectural Bibliographers. **Papers,** 1965- . Ann. University Press of Virginia.
These volumes consist of bibliographies on specific topics (often historical), rather than annual coverage of current publications.

421.   Briggs, Martin Shaw. **Everyman's Concise Encyclopedia of Architecture.** Dutton, 1960. 372p.
This convenient dictionary has about 2,000 short entries (definitions, biographies, architectural history). Illustrations are small but clear. Cross references are generally good. Complementary coverage (including Scottish architectural terms) will be found in *English Architecture: An Illustrated Glossary*, by James Curl (David & Charles, 1977).

422.   Columbia University. Avery Architectural Library. **Avery Index to Architectural Periodicals.** 2nd ed. G. K. Hall, 1973. 15v. 1st suppl. 1975. 2nd suppl. 1977.
The main set contains the entire original index of 1963 plus seven supplements through December 1972. In addition to architecture, it includes decorative arts, sculpture (including medieval), city planning, and archaeology. This work is especially good for information on individual architects. It is the most comprehensive index in architecture, with over 360,000 entries. However, it does not include periodicals in non-Western alphabets.

423.   Columbia University. Libraries. Avery Architectural Library. **Avery Obituary Index of Architects and Artists.** G. K. Hall, 1963. 338p.
This photographic reproduction of 13,000 cards draws on obituaries in newspapers (especially the *New York Times*) as well as in periodicals in the Avery collection.

424.   Columbia University. Libraries. Avery Architectural Library. **Catalog. . . .** 2nd ed. enl. G. K. Hall, 1968. 19v. 1st suppl. 1973 (4v.). 2nd suppl. 1975 (4v.). 3rd suppl. 1977)3v.).
The Avery Architectural Library has one of the most outstanding architectural collections in the United States. These photographic reproductions of cards in the catalog

include not only the Avery Collection but all Columbia University Libraries books on architecture.

425. DAA: Dictionary of Architectural Abbreviations, Signs and Symbols, ed. by David D. Dolon. Odyssey, 1965. 595p.
The basic arrangement is a classified one: abbreviations for use in text; abbreviations for associations and societies; abbreviations for unions; abbreviations for degrees; letter symbols; abbreviations for use on drawings; graphic symbols; reinforcing bar designations; color code for residential wiring; abbreviations for use on maps, etc. Within each, there is usually an introduction and then a two-fold division: alphabetically by abbreviation and alphabetically by name. There is no general index, but scrutiny of the table of contents and introductory material should readily lead to the information needed.

426. Harris, Cyril M., ed. **Dictionary of Architecture and Construction.** McGraw-Hill, 1975. 553p.
Working with more than 50 contributing editors, Harris, who is a specialist in electrical engineering as well as architecture, has produced a dictionary useful to engineers, contractors, and planners as well as to architects. Technical standards and materials changes of the late 1960s and early 1970s have been incorporated. There are numerous black and white illustrations and many cross references. The reviewer in *Choice* (November 1975, p. 1142) called it "the most comprehensive one-volume compilation of architectural and construction terms in 70 years," and it was included among "Reference Books of 1975" (*Library Journal*, April 15, 1976, p. 967). It is much more current and complete than Henry Saylor's *Dictionary of Architecture* (Wiley, 1952; repr., 1963). It does not replace *A Dictionary of Architecture and Building*, by Russell Sturgis (Macmillan, 1902; repr., Gale, 1966, 3v.), because of the value of Sturgis for historical purposes. More than 5,000 historical terms (both Eastern and Western) from ancient times to the present are covered by Harris in *Historic Architecture Sourcebook* (McGraw-Hill, 1977), which has numerous cross references and more than 2,000 line drawings.

427. Hatje, Gerd, ed. **Encyclopaedia of Modern Architecture.** Thames and Hudson, 1963. 336p.
Articles, except for very brief ones, are signed and many include bibliographies. It covers architects, schools, styles, associations, countries, construction terms, and materials that, since the mid-nineteenth century, have contributed to modern architecture. *A Short Dictionary of Architecture*, by Dora Ware (3rd ed., Allen & Unwin, 1953; repr., 1961), and *The Architecture Book*, by Norval White (Knopf, 1976), are both small dictionaries that cover commonly-used architectural terms.

428. Pevsner, Nikolaus, John Fleming, and Hugh Honour. **A Dictionary of Architecture.** Rev. and enl. ed. Overlook Press, 1976. 554p.
Definitions of architectural terms, biographical sketches of leading architects of all periods, and articles on trends and movements are included in this greatly expanded version of the *Penguin Dictionary of Architecture* (rev. ed., 1972). An international team of scholars collaborated with the editors. Articles frequently contain bibliographies. There are numerous cross references. The book is profusely illustrated with black and white photographs and line drawings.

429. Roos, Frank J. **Bibliography of Early American Architecture: Writings on Architecture Constructed before 1860 in the Eastern and Central United States.** 2nd ed. Univerity of Illinois Press, 1968. 389p.

The compiler lists 4,377 books and articles in a classified arrangement (basically geographical). A few, brief annotations are given. There are sections on individual architects and on bibliographies. The name index usually refers to item numbers, with references to page numbers in italics. Another specialized bibliography is Anatole Senkevitch's *Soviet Architecture, 1917-1962: A Bibliographical Guide to Source Material* (University of Virginia Press, 1974), which also has a classified arrangement for its 1,187 books and periodical articles, with a name and title index. More general coverage is provided by D. L. Smith's *How to Find Out in Architecture and Building* (Pergamon, 1967) and *Guide to Architectural Information*, by Margaret Phillips (Design Data Center, 1971).

430. **Who's Who in Architecture: From 1400 to the Present Day**, ed. by J. M. Richards. Holt, 1977. 368p.
This very useful biographical dictionary includes 600 architects, engineers, town planners, and landscape architects. Many articles have bibliographies, and there is a classified bibliography at the end. More limited in scope are *Biographical Dictionary of American Architects (Deceased)*, by Henry F. and Elsie Rathburn Withey (Hennessey & Ingalls, 1970), and *A Short Dictionary of British Architects*, by Dora Ware (Allen & Unwin, 1967).

Histories

431. Fletcher, Sir Banister Flight. **A History of Architecture on the Comparative Method.** 18th ed. rev. J. C. Palmes. Scribners, 1975. 1390p.
This famous work has long been regarded as a contemporary classic. When Sir Banister Fletcher died in 1953, he left a trust fund to the Royal Institute of British Architects and the University of London for revising and keeping his history up to date. Substantial changes, by competent scholars, have been made in recent editions. However, the basic comparative plan of earlier editions has been retained. Part I covers "Ancient Architecture and the Western Succession." Part II deals with "Architecture in the East." Each architectural style receives consideration under five headings: influences, architectural character, examples, comparative analysis, and reference books. The work is profusely illustrated with photographs (black and white) and line drawings. Other reference features include a glossary of architectural terms and a detailed analytical index. *Mont-Saint Michel and Chartres*, by Henry Adams (Franklin Library, 1978), is less systematic but ranks as a classic in both architecture and literature. T. F. Hamlin's *Architecture through the Ages* (rev. ed., Putnam, 1953) is an excellent survey from a social point of view. Nikolaus Pevsner's *An Outline of European Architecture* (8th ed. rev., Penguin, 1974) is excellent in coverage, is profusely illustrated, and has such reference features as an index and bibliography. F. M. Simpson's *History of Architectural Development* (new ed., McKay, 1964-66, 4v.) covers the period through the Renaissance.

432. Nervi, Pier Luigi, ed. **History of World Architecture Series.** Abrams, 1971- .
This valuable series covers many parts of the world in unusual depth and detail. Unfortunately, LC and most other libraries classify and catalog each volume separately, without a series aded entry. Titles that have appeared to date are:

> *Ancient Architecture: Mesopotamia, Egypt, Crete, Greece*, by Hans Muller, Seton Lloyd, and Roland Martin (1974);

Baroque Architecture, by Christian Norberg-Schulz (1971);

Byzantine Architecture, by Cyril Mango (1976);

Gothic Architecture, by Louis Grodecki (1977);

Islamic Architecture, by John D. Hoag (1977);

Late Baroque and Rococo Architecture, by Christian Norberg-Schulz (1974);

Oriental Architecture, by Mario Bussagli (1974);

Pre-Columbian Architecture of Mesoamerica, by Paul Gendrop and Doris Heyden (1976);

Primitive Architecture, by Enrico Guidono (1978);

Renaissance Architecture, by Peter Murray (1976);

Roman Architecture, by J. B. Ward-Perkins (1977);

Romanesque Architecture, by Hans Erich Kubach (1975).

SCULPTURE

433. Chase, George Henry, and Chandler Rathfon Post. **A History of Sculpture.** Harper, 1925; repr., Greenwood, 1971. 582p.

Long regarded as the standard history, this book has chapter bibliographies and indexes of sculptors, monuments, and places. Germain Bazin's *The History of World Sculpture* (New York Graphic Society, 1969) has a good text, but the 1,024 color illustrations are uneven in quality. *Masterpieces of European Sculpture* (Abrams, 1959) covers the period from the sixth century B.C. to the middle of the twentieth century. *African Art: Sculpture*, by Pierre Meauze (World, 1968), concentrates on black African art south of the Sahara. It provides a good introduction for the beginner, and both the color plates and the black and white photographs are beautifully done.

434. Clapp, Jane. **Sculpture Index.** Scarecrow, 1970-71. 2v. in 3.

Contents: v. 1 — *Sculpture of Europe and the Contemporary Middle East*; v. 2 (2 parts) — *Sculpture of the Americas, the Orient, Africa, Pacific Area and the Classical World*. The compiler has indexed pictures of works of sculpture in more than 900 publications. Listings are dictionary style, under the names of artists, titles, and subjects. Main entries (with source citations) are under artists, or under titles if anonymous. Limitations and inclusions are not clearly defined, but the set is essential for most art and general reference collections despite these defects.

435. Craven, Wayne. **Sculpture in America from the Colonial Period to the Present.** Crowell, 1968. 722p.

Favorably received by most critics as a solid contribution to the field, it treats both the social background and the works of individual sculptors. Commended for its documentation, bibliography, and index, this is the fullest account since *The History of American Sculpture*, by Lorado Taft (1903). Robert Bishop's *American Folk Sculpture* (Dutton, 1974) is the first comprehensive survey of its field and contains approximately 800 illustrations (over 100 in color).

436. Ekdahl, Janis. **American Sculpture: A Guide to Information Sources.** Gale, 1977. 260p.

Although mentioned previously as part of Gale's Art and Architecture Information Guide Series, this book is singled out for special mention here because of the dearth of bibliographic coverage of American sculpture. There are sections on general research tools, history and aesthetics, and individual sculptors. An appendix lists institutions with extensive collections of American sculpture. There are author, title, and subject indexes. Although much of the information can be found elsewhere, this book is valuable for the convenience of its focus. There are also some items not readily traceable in other sources, like the *Index of American Sculpture*, which is not published but was established in 1964 by Wayne Craven and is maintained by the Department of Art History, University of Delaware.

437. Gunnis, Rupert. **Dictionary of British Sculptors, 1660-1851.** New rev. ed. Murrays Book Sales, 1968. 515p.
Scholarly, thorough, and more complete than any other source, this standard work has over 1,700 biographies and bibliographical citations of sources. There are indexes of names and places.

438. Lami, Stanislas. **Dictionnaire des sculpteurs de l'école française.** Champion, 1898-1921; repr., Kraus, 1970. 8v.
The period covered is from the Middle Ages through the nineteenth century. Information given includes a short biography, a list of works, and a bibliography. Lami included foreigners who worked in France until they died, but he did not include anyone still alive in 1914.

439. **New Dictionary of Modern Sculpture,** ed. by Robert Maillard. Tr. by Bettina Wadia. Tudor, 1971. 328p.
The most recent edition included nearly 200 more artists (for a total of 500-600) and took greater account of new uses of materials (e.g., metal and resins) than did the old. Articles are signed with initials of contributors, give brief biographical information about the sculptor, and concentrate on professional accomplishments (leading works, exhibitions, etc.). Illustrations (black and white) are both numerous and good.

440. Pope-Hennessy, John. **An Introduction to Italian Sculpture.** 2nd ed. Phaidon, 1970-72. 3v.
Contents: v. I—*Italian Gothic Sculpture*; v. II—*Italian Renaissance Sculpture*; v. III—*Italian High Renaissance and Baroque Sculpture*. The typical pattern for each volume includes: introductory chapters on leading sculptors and trends; plates; notes on sculptors and plates; index of places; index of sculptors. The plates, conveniently related to the text, even when not directly beside it, are handsome black and white photographs remarkable for their clarity and detail.

441. Rich, Jack C. **The Material and Methods of Sculpture.** Oxford, 1947. 416p.
Rich's book has long remained a standard source. It covers techniques for a wide range of media and contains a bibliography, a glossary, and tables. It has an excellent detailed index. Another work to be considered is *Zorach Explains Sculpture*, by William Zorach (Tudor, 1961). First published in 1947 by the American Artists Group, it has a chapter on technique that is unusually good for the beginner.

442. Schaefer-Simmern, Henry. **Sculpture in Europe Today.** University of California Press, 1955. 33p.

The focus is on 128 full-page plates, illustrating the work of 60 leading sculptors of the mid-twentieth century. The introduction on trends is brief, but good.

MINOR ARTS

Bibliographies and Indexes

443. Ehresmann, Donald L. **Applied and Decorative Arts: A Bibliographic Guide to Basic Reference Works, Histories, and Handbooks.** Libraries Unlimited, 1977. 232p.

This classified, annotated bibliography includes some 1,240 items in western European languages from 1875 to 1975. The detailed table of contents is supplemented by author and subject indexes.

444. Franklin, Linda Campbell. **Antiques and Collectibles: A Bibliography of Works in English, 16th Century to 1976.** Scarecrow, 1978. 1091p.

This classified, unannotated bibliography contains 10,783 entries for books, pamphlets, exhibition catalogs, and some English trade catalogs. Locations are given selectively for works published before 1925.

445. Hiler, Hilaire, and Meyer Hiler. **Bibliography of Costume: A Dictionary Catalog of about Eight Thousand Books and Periodicals.** Wilson, 1939; repr., Blom, 1967. 911p.

This annotated bibliography of 8,400 books and periodical articles has become a kind of reference classic, still heavily used for older material.

446. Monro, Isabel Stevenson, and Dorothy E. Cook. **Costume Index: A Subject Index to Plates and to Illustrated Texts.** Wilson, 1937. 338p. Suppl. 1957. 210p.

Excellent, detailed indexing of more than 900 works is provided by this standard work, which is approachable by places, types of persons, and kinds of costumes.

Dictionaries and Encyclopedias

447. American Fabrics Magazine. **AF Encyclopedia of Textiles.** 2nd ed. Prentice-Hall, 1972. 636p.

This expertly-edited encyclopedia uses a classified arrangement: textile fibers; history and origins; textile design; textiles in the Americas; manufacturing processes; fabric finishing; specialty uses of textiles; textile definitions. Each of these (except the last, which is an alphabetical glossary) is subdivided into short chapters (e.g., man-made fibers, cotton, wool), which are profusely illustrated by line drawings and black and white photographs. The history section includes a chronology, the origins of fabric names, and a short chapter on inventors and their inventions. Alphabetical access is provided by the analytical index (pp. 604-636).

448. Aronson, Joseph. **The Encyclopedia of Furniture.** 3rd ed. Crown, 1965. 484p.

First published in 1938; the latest edition of this standard work includes 1,400 photographs and many line drawings.

449. Bradley, John William. **A Dictionary of Miniaturists, Illuminators, Calligraphers, and Copyists, with References to Their Works, and Notices of Their Patrons, from the Establishment of Christianity to the Eighteenth Century.** Quaritch, 1887-89; repr., Franklin, 1973. 3v.
The name of each artist and the century are given and a designation as miniaturist, illuminator, calligrapher, or copyist. A summary follows of what is known about the artist's work, usually with sources of further information.

450. Boger, Louise Ade, and H. Batterson Boger. **The Dictionary of Antiques and the Decorative Arts: A Book of Reference for Glass, Furniture, Ceramics, Silver, Periods, Styles, Technical Terms, etc.** Scribners, 1967. 662p.
Illustrated with color plates, line drawings, and black and white photographs, the dictionary section has numerous cross references and is supplemented by a classified list of subjects and terms. There is a short bibliography. The supplement (pp. 567-662) contains nearly 700 entries.

451. Boger, Louise Ade. **The Dictionary of World Pottery and Porcelain.** Scribners, 1971. 533p.
Persons, places, manufacturers, trends, etc., are subjects of short articles in one alphabetical sequence, illustrated with numerous line drawings and generously provided with cross references. There are 57 beautiful illustrations in color and 562 small black and white photographs, with extensive notes. Coverage ranges from the primitive world to our own time. Short bibliography.

452. Comstock, Helen, ed. **The Concise Encyclopedia of American Antiques.** Hawthorn, 1958. 2v.
Articles are essay type on broad topics. Some have glossaries and bibliographies; all are illustrated with good, clear, black and white photographs. The complete table of contents and index are repeated in both volumes. Chinese and Japanese art objects (bronzes, jades, porcelains, cloisonné, textiles, and glass) are covered (with emphasis on the last one hundred years) in *Oriental Antiques and Collectibles: A Guide*, by Arthur and Grace Chu (Crown, 1973).

453. Coysh, Arthur Wilfred. **The Antique Buyer's Dictionary of Names.** Praeger, 1970. 278p.
Divided into 17 categories, this work gives information on 1,700 European and American artists, craftsmen, designers, and firms. It often includes museum locations. Each section has a bibliography.

454. Evans, Paul Frederic. **Art Pottery of the United States: An Encyclopedia of Producers and Their Marks.** Scribners, 1974. 353p.
After a general history, the main section is arranged alphabetically by potters' names, illustrated with black and white photographs and line drawings. Most entries have bibliographic references. There are eight pages of color plates. Four appendices cover: geographical listing of potteries (by state); birth and death dates; exhibitions; and a bibliography of reference works.

455. Fleming, John, and Hugh Honour. **Dictionary of the Decorative Arts.** Harper, 1977. 896p.
Published in Britain as *The Penguin Dictionary of the Decorative Arts* and planned as a companion volume to the *Penguin Dictionary of Architecture* (see item 428), this work

has 4,000 entries and about 1,000 illustrations. The scope is limited to Europe (from the Middle Ages) and North America (from the colonial period). Factories, definitions, biographies, materials, and processes are among the many topics included. Entries are well done, and most have bibliographies. In an otherwise highly favorable review, Jacqueline Sisson noted some North American omissions, most regrettably Indian arts and crafts (*ARBA 1978*, pp. 426-27).

456. Fournier, Robert. **Illustrated Dictionary of Practical Pottery**. Van Nostrand, 1974. 256p.
"Some 1,000 entries provide definitions of terms, descriptions and instructions for processes and techniques, formulas and recipes for materials, information on equipment, and other practical information. Illustrations and charts are plentiful" — Charles Bunge, *Wilson Library Bulletin* 49 (September 1974):93.

457. Hollister, Paul, Jr. **The Encyclopedia of Glass Paper Weights**. Potter; distr., Crown, 1969. 312p.
Covering the entire history from ancient Egypt to the present, this convenient book has many illustrations, a glossary of terms, a bibliography, and a list of museums with paperweight collections.

458. Linton, George E. **The Modern Textile and Apparel Dictionary**. 4th ed. Textile Book Service, 1973. 716p.
More than 16,000 entries provide definitions and explanations for products and processes connected with all aspects of the textile industry. Briefer entries (but occasionally more specific historical information) will be found in *Fairchild's Dictionary of Textiles*, edited by Elizabeth Wingate (6th ed., Fairchild, 1979), which is a revision and updating of Louis Harmuth's **Dictionary of Textiles** (2nd ed., Fairchild, 1920). The 1979 edition has been extensively revised, especially in areas of new technology. Some 1,000 new definitions have been added to the 13,000 in the 1967 edition.

459. Macquoid, Percy. **The Dictionary of English Furniture: From the Middle Ages to the Late Georgian Period**. Rev. and enl. ed. by Ralph Edwards. Country Life, 1954. 3v.
This well-illustrated dictionary provides comprehensive coverage of terms, techniques, periods, styles, cabinet makers, etc. Ralph Edwards prepared a one-volume condensation entitled *The Shorter Dictionary of English Furniture: From the Middle Ages to the Late Georgian Period* (Country Life, 1964).

460. Mason, Anita. **An Illustrated Dictionary of Jewellery**. Illus. by Diane Packer. Harper, 1974. 389p.
Well-illustrated with black and white drawings, this dictionary gives comprehensive coverage to all aspects of jewelry, including some biographies of noted jewelers. Liberal use of cross references makes information easy to find.

461. Newman, Harold. **An Illustrated Dictionary of Glass**. Thames and Hudson, 1977. 351p.
Illustrated with 17 beautiful color plates and over 600 black and white photographs, this dictionary contains more than 2,400 entries that cover definitions, materials, processes, and biographical information on major glassmakers, decorators, and designers from

classical times to the present. Illustrations are conveniently close to the text, and there are numerous cross references.

462. Osborne, Harold, ed. **The Oxford Companion to the Decorative Arts.** Oxford, 1975. 865p.
Similar in plan and arrangement to the other volumes in the Oxford "companion" series, this well-researched work covers such areas as costume, jewelry, and furniture. The emphasis is on Britain, Western Europe, and the United States, with less information about the decorative arts in other parts of the world.

463. Phipps, Frances. **The Collector's Complete Dictionary of American Antiques.** Doubleday, 1974. 640p.
Although this is a dictionary, one must remember that the basic arrangement is a classified one, so the alphabetical arrangement of terms and definitions occurs only within the twelve sections on broad topics like rooms, crafts, woods, class, etc. There is no general index.

464. **The Practical Encyclopedia of Crafts**, comp. by Maria Di Valentin. Sterling, 1970. 544p.
This handy book covers a wide range of crafts (clay, fabrics, metal, glass, etc.) and includes almost 1,200 illustrations (about 40 in color) as well as a good index.

465. Rainwater, Dorothy T. **Encyclopedia of American Silver Manufacturers.** Crown, 1975. 222p.
More than 2,200 marks from approximately 1,400 manufacturers are included in this revision of a 1966 work entitled *American Silver Manufacturers*. Other useful features include a list of trade names and a revised bibliography.

466. Ramsey, L. G. G., ed. **The Complete Color Encyclopedia of Antiques.** Rev. ed. Hawthorn, 1975. 704p.
In this useful overview of all kinds of antiques, much of the information from the 1962 edition is reprinted, but there have been both deletions and additions. Most noteworthy among the latter are 500 color photographs.

467. Savage, George. **Dictionary of Antiques.** 2nd ed. Mayflower, 1978. 534p.
Prepared in order to help collectors and dealers to recognize and date the specimens they examine, this work features short articles on persons, objects, and trends—in one alphabet, illustrated in many cases with black and white photographs (occasionally, color plates), and provided with cross references. There is an appendix of marks and a selected bibliography.

468. Savage, George, and Harold Newman. **An Illustrated Dictionary of Ceramics.** Van Nostrand, 1974. 319p.
This work "concentrates on historical and aesthetic information, defining some 3,000 terms relating to wares, materials, processes, styles, patterns, and shapes throughout history. There is a list of principal European factories and their marks"—Charles Bunge, *Wilson Library Bulletin* 49 (September 1974):93.

469. Stafford, Maureen, and Dora Ware. **An Illustrated Dictionary of Ornament.** St. Martin's, 1975. 246p.
This useful work contains nearly 1,000 definitions and more than 2,000 illustrations. The time period is from antiquity through the nineteenth century. The line drawings by Stafford are particularly noteworthy.

Directories and Annuals

470. **Contemporary Crafts Market Place,** 1975/76- . Biennial. Bowker.
This carefully edited directory has separate sections for: shops and galleries; organizations; courses; AV; suppliers; packers and shippers; calendar information; and periodicals and reference books. The first three sections are arranged by state and then by name. AV materials are by distributor. Suppliers are arranged alphabetically under types of supplies.

471. Porter, Arthur, and Elizabeth Taylor, eds. **Directory of Art and Antique Restoration.** New ed. The Authors, 1975. 251p.
Subtitle: "A Guide to Art and Antique Restorers throughout the United States."

Histories

472. Bishop, Robert Charles. **Centuries and Styles of the American Chair, 1640-1970.** Dutton, 1972. 516p.
This is the most comprehensive book to date, with nearly 1,000 black and white photographs, arranged by period and style. The detailed index includes furniture makers, chair types, and chair parts.

473. Boucher, Francois Leon Louis. **20,000 Years of Fashion: The History of Costume and Personal Adornment.** Abrams, 1967. 441p.
Translated from the French, this scholarly history covers all aspects except armor, with excellent illustrations. Reference features include maps, chronological tables, a glossary, and bibliographies.

474. Comstock, Helen. **American Furniture: Seventeenth, Eighteenth and Nineteenth Century Styles.** Viking, 1966 (c.1962). 336p.
Chapters on the major periods (1. Jacobean — William and Mary: 1640-1720; 2. Queen Anne: 1720-1755; 3. Chippendale: 1755-1790; 4. Classical Period: 1790-1830; 5. Early Victorian: 1830-1870) are illustrated with 665 black and white photographs (with excellent clarity of detail) and 8 color plates. Each chapter has a summary chart at the end. Additional sources of information are given in the notes and selected bibliography. There is a name and subject index, covering both text and illustrations.

475. Davenport, Millia. **The Book of Costume.** New ed. Crown, 1976. 958p.
Historical coverage from the early days to the end of the United States Civil War, is provided, with about 3,000 illustrations (some in color). Locations of the originals are usually given. Costume in Britain from the Roman period to the Victorian is covered in Marian Sichel's *Costume Reference* (Plays, Inc., 1977-78, 6v.).

476.   Fales, Dean A., Jr. **American Painted Furniture, 1660-1880.** Dutton, 1972. 299p.

Chapters deal with various historical styles: 1. Early Colonial; 2. Late Colonial; 3. Federal; 4. American Empire; 5. Nineteenth Century; 6. Cultural Patterns; and 7. Victorian. There are 511 photographs (many in color). Additional sources of information are given in the notes and the bibliography. There are a brief name and subject index and an index of owners.

477.   Honey, William Boyer. **European Ceramic Art from the End of the Middle Ages to about 1815.** Faber, 1949-52. 2v.

Contents: v. 1—*A Dictionary of Factories, Artists, Technical Terms, etc.*; v. 2—*Illustrated Historical Survey.* V. 1 is copiously illustrated with line drawings and has a special "Index to Marks" (pp. 683-788). V. 2 has several plates in color and many plates in black and white (many of the latter have small photographs on one page). There are lists of plates and an index of plates. The compiler was keeper of the Department of Ceramics, Victoria and Albert Museum, London. A second edition of v. 2 was published in 1963.

478.   Hope, Thomas. **Costumes of the Greeks and Romans.** Dover, 1962.

This Dover reprint of a famous nineteenth century work (originally published under the title *Costume of the Ancients*) contains 300 plates.

479.   Macquoid, Percy. **A History of English Furniture.** . . . Putnam, 1904-09; repr., Dover, 1972. 4v.

Contents: v. 1—*The Age of Walnut*; v. 2—*The Age of Mahogany*; v. 3—*The Age of Oak*; v. 4—*The Age of Satinwood.* Covers the period from the sixteenth to the early eighteenth centuries and has numerous illustrations of pieces likely to be available to collectors.

480.   Nutting, Wallace. **Furniture Treasury (Mostly of American Origin); All Periods of American Furniture with Some Foreign Examples in America, Also American Hardware and Household Utensils.** Macmillan, 1928-33; repr., 1977. 3v.

This famous history has 5,000 illustrations, with descriptions on the same page. Another major work by Nutting is *Furniture of the Pilgrim Century (of American Origin), 1620-1720, with Maple and Pine to 1800, Including Colonial Utensils and Wrought-Iron Hardware into the Nineteenth Century* (rev. and enl. ed., Old America, 1924; repr., Dover, 1965, 2v.).

481.   Wanscher, Ole. **The Art of Furniture: 5,000 Years of Furniture and Interiors.** Tr. by David Hohnen. Reinhold, 1967. 419p.

Each chapter consists of a brief introduction to the period, followed by a copious array of illustrations (black and white photographs and some line drawings). Short bibliography and an index of names and places.

Biographies

482.   Gere, Charlotte. **American and European Jewelry, 1830-1914.** Crown, 1975. 240p.

For reference purposes, the biographical sketches of some 120 jewelers and many of the illustrations (from private collections and thus not previously available) are most useful.

483.   Stauffer, David McNeely. **American Engravers upon Copper and Steel.** With additional volume by Mantle Fielding. Repr., Franklin, 1964. 3v.
Biographical sketches, a checklist of engravings, and an index to the checklist enable the user to track down information on more than 700 American engravers and their works.

Guides, Handbooks, and Catalogs

484.   Boger, Louise Ade. **The Complete Guide to Furniture Styles.** Enl. ed. Scribners, 1969. 500p.
A history of furniture by a noted writer in the field of antiques. She has also written an illustrated history entitled *Furniture Past and Present* (Doubleday, 1966).

485.   Boston. Museum of Fine Arts. **American Furniture in the Museum of Fine Arts, Boston,** comp. by Richard H. Randall, Jr. Museum of Fine Arts; distr., October House, 1965. 276p.
The classified arrangement by types of furniture (with 218 black and white photographs) is complemented by a general index and an index of former owners. Each item is fully described as to its general appearance, structure, size, history, etc.

486.   Buhler, Kathryn C. **American Silver 1655-1825, in the Museum of Fine Arts, Boston.** Museum of Fine Arts; distr., New York Graphic Society, 1972. 2v.
Prepared by a former curator, this catalog describes 566 pieces, with good photographs. The basic arrangement is by state, then by silversmiths' dates. Bibliographies and an excellent index enhance its reference usefulness. Another major work by the same author is *American Silver, Garvan and Other Collections in the Yale University Art Gallery* (Yale University Press, 1970).

487.   Eichenberg, Fritz. **The Art of the Print: Masterpieces, History, Techniques.** Abrams, 1976. 611p.
A useful handbook that fills a gap.

488.   Fales, Martha Gandy. **Early American Silver.** Rev. and enl. ed. Dutton, 1973. 336p.
This excellent handbook covers the period from 1675 to 1825 and was first published under the title *Early American Silver for the Cautious Collector* (Funk & Wagnalls, 1970). In addition to chapters on American silversmiths and the special features of American silver, it covers the care of old silver. Reference features include a glossary, a chart on the development of silver, and a classified bibliography.

489.   Hornung, Clarence P. **Treasury of American Design.** Abrams, 1972. 2v.
Based on the WPA *Index of American Design* (1935-41) now housed in the National Gallery of Art, this work has a selection of 2,900 illustrations (about 850 in color) from the 17,000 watercolors in the original *Index.* The period covered is from colonial times to the late nineteenth century. The text is divided into six parts by broad topic, and the illustrations are in close proximity to the text. A condensed version was published under the title *Treasury of American Antiques: A Pictorial Survey of Popular Folk Arts and Crafts* (Abrams, 1977).

490.   Kovel, Ralph, and Terry Kovel. **The Kovels' Collector's Guide to American Art Pottery.** Crown, 1974. 368p.

The Kovels have compiled several very valuable guides for collectors, including *The Complete Antiques Price List* (11th ed., Crown, 1978), *Dictionary of Marks—Pottery and Porcelain* (Crown, 1953), and American Country Furniture, 1780-1875 (Crown, 1965). The reviewer in *ARBA 1975* (p. 469) stated: "The first American art pottery was made in Cincinnati, Ohio, during the 1870's and the art pottery movement seems to have ended in the late 1920's. This dictionary provides in-depth information about small and larger companies, their lines, marks, and methods of manufacture of individual craftsmen, types of pottery, etc. There are excellent illustrations throughout the text and, more importantly, well-selected bibliographies that will be of substantial assistance to the serious reader interested in more information on the subject."

491.   Papert, Emma. **Illustrated Guide to American Glass.** Hawthorn, 1972. 289p.

The author traces the history of glassmaking in the United States, including early craftsmen, glassworks, etc. There are separate chapters on such topics as bottles and cut glass. Reference features include a bibliography, a glossary, and an index. The reviewer in *Choice* (February 1973, p. 1576) thought Papert's book did not replace George and Helen McKearin's *Two Hundred Years of American Blown Glass* (Crown, 1950; repr., 1966). Another useful work by McKearin is *American Glass* (Crown, 1941).

492.   Safford, Carleton L., and Robert Bishop. **America's Quilts and Coverlets.** Dutton, 1972. 313p.

Highly recommended even for the smallest public library reference collection, this work is divided into 15 chapters, each devoted to a particular kind of quilt or covering. The illustrations are unusually beautiful, and give full information about each item (maker, date, etc.).

493.   Turner, Noel D. **American Silver Flatware, 1837-1910.** Barnes, 1972.

Descriptive information and useful illustrations as well as historical background make this a valuable source. Other reference features include lists of silversmiths, trademarks, and pattern names.

Marks and Monograms

494.   Chaffers, William. **Marks and Monograms on European and Oriental Pottery and Porcelain.** 15th ed. Reeves, 1965.

The British section was edited by Geoffrey A. Godden; the European and Oriental sections, by Frederick Litchfield. The basic arrangement is by country and place. Facsimile reproductions of marks are provided. A short history is given at the beginning of each section. Although experts have discovered some inaccuracies, it is still very heavily used.

495.   Grimwade, Arthur G. **London Goldsmiths 1697-1837: Their Marks and Their Lives; From the Original Registers at Goldsmith's Hall and Other Sources.** Rowman and Littlefield, 1976. 728p.

The biographical section also serves as an index to approximately 4,000 marks taken from the registers.

496.   Poche, Emanuel. **Porcelain Marks of the World.** Arco, 1974. 255p.
Translated from the Czech and based on the author's experience in the Prague Museum of Arts and Crafts, this useful reference work groups porcelain works by subject.

497.   Wyler, Seymour B. **The Book of Old Silver: English, American, Foreign, with All Available Hallmarks, Including Sheffield Plate Marks.** Crown, 1937. 447p.
The first part of this history and handbook consists of 19 chapters of text. The second (and much larger) part is devoted to hallmarks, arranged by country, with indexes by country and geographical location. There are also a brief bibliography and general index.

9 ACCESSING INFORMATION IN THE PERFORMING ARTS

MAJOR DIVISIONS OF THE FIELD

The term "performing arts" has not become fully standardized in its usage. Generally, however, three elements are considered necessary: the performer, the piece performed, and the audience. As used in this book, the term will include music, the dance, the theater, film, radio, and television.

Music is commonly defined as the art of organizing sounds. Its principal elements are melody (single sounds in succession), harmony (sounds in combination), and rhythm (sounds in a temporal relationship). The two major divisions are vocal music and instrumental music. Vocal music includes songs, operas, oratorios, etc., while instrumental music includes solos, chamber music, and orchestral music. Musical instruments may be classified as stringed (violin, harp, guitar, etc.), woodwind (flute, bassoon, oboe, English horn), brass (trumpet, cornet, bugle, trombone), percussion (drums, chimes, bells, gongs, etc.), keyboard (piano, organ), and other (accordion, concertina, harmonica, bagpipes, etc.). The modern system of musical notation began to be used around 1700.

The librarian responsible for a music collection will need to keep in mind three major elements: 1) the music itself, which will follow somewhat the divisions outlined above; 2) the literature about music, which will divide itself rather more along the conventional lines for all disciplines, but with some special characteristics; 3) the vast array of recordings on discs, tapes, cassettes, etc., which are a part of any modern music library and which pose problems all their own in terms of organization, retrieval, and use.

The dance may be defined as movement of the body to a certain rhythm. There are three major divisions of the field: folk dancing, ballroom dancing, and theater dancing. Folk dancing, which originated in open-air activities, is characterized by great vigor and exuberance of movement. Ballroom dancing had its origin in the European courts of the Renaissance and is an indoor, participant activity. Theater dancing is a spectator activity that may be traced to religious dances in the ancient world and to performances known as "masques" in the courts of Renaissance Europe. Its most characteristic modern form is the ballet. The dance is usually (though not necessarily) accompanied by music.

Theater is the art of presenting a performance to an audience. In modern usage, the term is normally restricted to live performances of plays. A distinction is sometimes drawn between theater and drama; theater is restricted in meaning to those matters having to do with public performance, while drama includes the literary basis for performance (i.e., the texts of plays). Frequently, the texts of plays are classed with literature. Libraries with subject departments often put plays in a literature department and other works about the theater in a performing arts department. Topics closely related to theatrical performance are acting, costume, makeup, directing, and the architecture of theaters.

Films may conveniently be divided into feature-length (an hour or more) and shorts. Many feature-length films are fictional, often based on books of some popularity. Others, known as documentaries, are prepared for informational purposes. A blending of these forms may result in stories that are essentially colorful travelogues. Two other forms are animated cartoons and puppet features. Short subjects are often filmed by independent producers and sold to distributors of feature-length films to complete an entertainment package. However, they are also widely used by schools, universities, churches, clubs, businesses, etc., for informational and educational purposes. Indeed, films of this latter kind will probably constitute the bulk of those included in most library film collections. Radio depends solely upon sound for its effects. Television bears many similarities to film, but it can also include "live" coverage of events, as can radio.

Coverage of these four areas is reasonably good in the major general encyclopedias. The pivotal article on music in *The Encyclopaedia Britannica: Macropaedia* (15th ed., 1974) is entitled "Music, Art of" (v. 12, pp. 662-69) and is followed by articles on more specialized aspects, such as "Music, East Asian," "Music, Recording of," "Music, Theatrical," "Music, Western," "Musical Composition," "Musical Criticism," and "Musical Instruments." The key dance article in the *Britannica* is "Dance, Art of" (v. 5, pp. 451-57), which is followed by related articles like "Dance, Western" and "Dance and Theatre, East Asian." One must not overlook the article on "Ballet" (v. 2, pp. 645-54). "Theatre, Art of" (v. 18, pp. 212-18) and "Theatre, Western" (v. 18, pp. 218-36) give the *Britannica* overview and are followed by articles like "Theatre and Stages" and "Theatrical Production." The *Britannica* puts information about film into two key articles — "Motion Pictures, Art of" (v. 12, pp. 497-511) and "Motion Pictures, History of" (v. 12, pp. 511-39).

Lester Asheim's chapter on "Music" in *The Humanities and the Library* (pp. 151-98) is still a good introduction to the organization and use of a music collection. It is supplemented and updated by "Music Libraries and Collections," edited by Guy A. Marco [*Encyclopedia of Library and Information Science* (Dekker, 1976), v. 18, pp. 328-493]. "Music Libraries," by Clara Steuerman [*Special Libraries* 69 (November 1978):425-28] was first presented as a paper at the 1977 IFLA Conference in Brussels. Music in the general library is covered in "Music and Fine Arts in the General Library," edited by

Guy A. Marco and Wolfgant Freitag [*Library Trends* 23 (January 1975):3212-546]. Other works covering music librarianship as a whole include Carol Bradley's *Reader in Music Librarianship* (Microcard Editions Books, 1973) and Brian Redfern's *Organizing Music in Libraries* (Linnet, 1978-79, 2v.). Classic older works include *Music Libraries*, by Lionel McColvin (Deutsch, 1965), which was revised and updated by Jack Dove; and E. T. Bryant's *Music Librarianship: A Practical Guide* (Hafner, 1959). (The latter is reported to be under revision, but publication of a new edition could not be verified.)

Cataloging has received considerable attention from music librarians. The *Code internationale de catalogage de la musique*, prepared by the International Cataloging Code Commission of the International Association of Music Libraries, has been appearing in parts since 1957 (C. F. Peters). Perhaps the best source for most purposes is the *Anglo-American Cataloging Rules* (2nd ed., ALA, 1978), which has chapters on "Music" (pp. 125-43) and "Sound Recordings" (pp. 144-63). *Class M*, issued by the Subject Cataloging Division of the Library of Congress (LC, 1963), is a vital tool, as are *Music Subject Headings Used on Printed Cards of the Library of Congress* (LC, 1952) and *Music Subject Headings* of the Reference Department of the New York Public Library (2nd ed., G. K. Hall, 1966).

Recordings have received substantial attention in recent years. The International Association of Music Libraries sponsored *Phonograph Record Libraries: Their Organization and Use*, edited by Henry F. J. Currall (Archon, 1970). Derek Langride dealt with collecting and classifying jazz records in *Your Jazz Collection* (Archon, 1970). The classic work is still *Preservation and Storage of Sound Recordings*, by Andrew G. Pickett and Meyer M. Lemcoe (LC, 1959), but time has rendered some parts obsolete. More recent is Jay E. Daily's *Cataloging Phonorecordings: Problems and Possibilities* (Dekker, 1975). Barbara K. Gaeddert has prepared *The Classification and Cataloging of Sound Recordings: An Annotated Bibliography* (Music Library Association, 1977), and Judith Kaufmann has written *Recordings of Non-Western Music: Subject and Entry Access* (MLA, 1977). Other aids that may be useful include Julian Hodgson's *Music Titles in Translation: A Checklist of Musical Compositions* (Bingley, 1976) and D. W. Krummel's *Guide for Dating Early Published Music: A Manual of Bibliographical Practices* (Joseph Boonin, 1974).

The organization and use of film collections also requires some variation from conventional library practice. Books to consider include *Film Library Techniques: Principles of Administration*, by Helen P. Harrison (Hastings, 1973) and *The Film User's Handbook: A Basic Manual for Managing Library Film Services*, by George Rehrauer (Bowker, 1975).

MAJOR ORGANIZATIONS, PUBLISHERS,
INFORMATION CENTERS, AND SPECIAL COLLECTIONS

The number of national and international organizations in the field of music is so great that attention can be given here only to a small number of those most significant to the librarian. The International Association of Music Libraries has branches in most of the developed countries (United States branch: Northwestern University Music Library, Evanston, IL 60201). It currently sponsors the *International Inventory of Musical Sources/Répertoire international des sources musicales* (RISM). Since 1954, it has published *Fontes Artis Musicae*. The International Music Council (1 rue Miollis, Paris F 750 15, France), one of the first non-governmental organizations established under Unesco sponsorship, studies the development of music through the world and produces numerous books and recordings. The International Musicological Society (Case Postale Box 56, CH-4001 Basel, Switzerland), founded in 1927 to promote research, has published *Acta Musicologica* since 1928. The Music Library Association (343 S. Main St., Room 205, Ann Arbor, MI 48108) supports a wide range of activities, including publication of *Music Cataloging Bulletin* (1970-) and *Notes* (1943-). The Association for Recorded Sound Collections (c/o James Wright, Fine Arts Library, University of New Mexico, Albuquerque, NM 87131), was founded in 1966 and includes in its membership people in the broadcasting and recording industries as well as librarians. Its principal publications are *ARSC Journal* (three per year) and *ARSC Bulletin* (irregular). The Music Educators' National Conference (1902 Association Dr., Reston, VA 22091) was founded in 1907 and now has over 60,000 members. It supports a wide range of publications, including *Music Educators' Journal* (monthly) and *Journal of Research in Music Education* (quarterly). The American Musicological Society (University of Pennsylvania, 201 S. 34th St., Philadelphia, PA 19104) promotes research in various fields of music. Its publications include the *Journal of the American Musicological Society* (three per year) and lists of masters theses and doctoral dissertations. The American Guild of Organists (630 Fifth Ave., New York, NY 10020), one of the oldest and largest of the specialized groups, publishes *Music/AGO-RCCO* (monthly).

By contrast with music, the number of organizations devoted to the dance is comparatively small; those that do exist seem to be largely concentrated in two areas—ballet and the teaching of dancing. The North American Ballet Association (c/o Henry Holth, Dallas Ballet, 3739 Gilbert, Dallas, TX 75219) consists of professional ballet companies, whereas the Ballet Theatre Foundation (888 Seventh Ave., New York, NY 10019) appeals to a broad public for support and publishes *American Ballet Theatre Newsletter* (three to four per year). The National Association for Regional Ballet (1860 Broadway, New York, NY 10023) promotes festivals and other educational activities in the United States and Canada. The Imperial Society of Teachers of Dancing (70 Gloucester Place, London W.1, England) has a branch in the United States (c/o Geoffrey Fells, 4601 N. Park Ave., Chevy Chase, MD 20015) and publishes *Imperial Dance Letter* (bimonthly). The Dance Educators of America (Box 470, Caldwell, NJ 07006) and the Dance Masters of America (723 W. Smith St., Orlando, FL 32804) both consist of dance teachers, and both have regional groups to supplement national activities.

The International Federation for Theatre Research (Department of French, University of Lancaster, Lancaster, England) disseminates scholarly information through *Theatre Research International* (triennial). The American Society for Theatre Research (Department of English, Queen's College, Flushing, NY 11367) issues a *Newsletter* (semi-annual) and *Theatre Survey* (semi-annual). The International Theatre Institute, established in 1948 by Unesco, has a branch in the United States (1860 Broadway, New York, NY 10023); it publishes *Theatre Notes* (ten per year) and *International Theatre Information* (quarterly). The American Theatre Association (1029 Vermont Ave., NW, Washington, DC 20005) is concerned with all phases of the educational theater. Its divisions include American Community Theatre Association; Army Theatre Arts Association; National Association of Schools of Theatre; Children's Theatre Association; Secondary School Theatre Association; University and College Theatre Association; and University Resident Theatre Association. Publications include: *Theatre News* (nine per year); *Placement Service Bulletin* (monthly) and *Directory* (annual). The Theatre Library Association (111 Amsterdam Ave., Room 513, New York, NY 10023) includes actors, booksellers, writers, and researchers in its membership; it issues *Broadside* (quarterly) and *Performing Arts Resources* (annual).

The University Film Association (c/o Dr. Peter J. Bukalski, Department of Cinema and Photography, Southern Illinois University, Carbondale, IL 62901) publishes *UFA Digest* (five to six per year) and *Journal* (quarterly). The American Federation of Film Societies (Three Washington Square Village, New York, NY 10012) includes teachers, librarians, and students; it publishes *Film Society Bulletin* (monthly) and *Film Critic* (monthly). The American Film Institute (John F. Kennedy Center for the Performing Arts, Washington, DC 20566) supports a wide range of archival, research, and production activities. Publications include *American Film* (monthly) and *Guide to College Film Courses* (biennial). The Federation of Motion Picture Councils (142 N. Tucker, Memphis, TN 38104) includes 33 state and local groups that review or endorse films; it publishes *News Reel* (monthly) as well as *Motion Picture Ratings Preview Reports*. The International Federation of Film Archives (74 Galerie Ravenstein, Brussels B-1000, Belgium) publishes books (in English, French, and German) on the preservation of film. The Educational Film Library Association (43 W. 61st St., New York, NY 10023) evaluates books and films through *EFLA Evaluations* (ten per year), *Sightlines* (quarterly), and *EFLA Bulletin* (quarterly). The Film Library Information Council (Box 348, Radio City Station, New York, NY 10019) gathers and disseminates information about actual library performance of films and other nonprint media. It publishes *Film Library Quarterly*.

Music publishing often occurs outside the normal trade channels. One of the best-known firms is Breitkopf and Härtel (Postbox 74, Walkmuhlstrasse 52, Wiesbaden, West Germany), which has published serious and classical music since about 1750. C. F. Peters (U.S. office: 373 Park Ave. South, New York, NY) was founded in Leipzig in 1800. The famous British firm of Novello & Co., Ltd. (Borough Green, Sevenoaks, Kent, England) was founded in 1811. A major American firm is G. Schirmer (609 Fifth Ave., New York, NY 10017), founded in 1861. In 1883, the Theodore Presser Co. (Presser Place, Bryn Mawr, PA 19010) was founded. Further information about publishers of serious and educational music may be obtained from the Music Publishers' Association of the United States (810 Seventh Ave., New York, NY 10019), while information about publishers of popular music is available from National Music Publishers' Association (110 E. 59th St., New York, NY 10022).

The American Music Center (250 W. 57th St., Suite 626-7, New York, NY 10019) was appointed official U.S. Information Center on Music in 1962 by the National Music Council. The American Composers' Alliance (170 W. 74th St., New York, NY 10023) specializes in manuscripts and published music of contemporary American composers.

The Committee on Research in Dance (Department of Dance Education, New York University, 35 W. 4th St., Room 675D, New York, NY 10003) serves as a clearinghouse for research information about the dance.

The International Theatre Studies Center (University of Kansas, Lawrence, KS 66044) publishes the results of its research in various professional journals and issues the following semi-annual publications: *Theatre Documentation, Afro-Asian Theatre Bulletin,* and *Latin-American Theatre Review.* The Wisconsin Center for Theatre Research (University of Wisconsin, 1166 Van Hise Hall, 1220 Linden Dr., Madison, WI 53706) concentrates on the performing arts in America. The Institute of Outdoor Drama (University of North Carolina, Chapel Hill, NC 27514) provides advisory and consultation services, research, and bibliographical work.

The most outstanding music collection in the United States is in the Library of Congress, which benefits from copyright deposit. The Music Division, established in 1897, has issued numerous catalogs, several of which are listed elsewhere in this book. Another notable collection is found in the Music Division of the Research Library of the Performing Arts in Lincoln Center (part of the New York Public Library). Music from the twelfth to the eighteenth centuries is a specialty of the Isham Memorial Library of Harvard University, while primary sources in early opera scores and librettos are a special strength of the University of California Music Library in Berkeley. The Center for Research Libraries has several microform collections of research materials. In Europe, the Austrian National Library (Vienna), the Royal Library of Belgium (Brussels), the State Library of the Czech Socialist Republic (Prague), the Bibliothèque Nationale (Paris), the Deutsche Staatsbibliothek (Berlin), the British Museum (British Library) (London), the

Biblioteca Nazionale Centrale (Florence), and the Vatican Library (Rome) have outstanding collections.

The Dance Collection in the Research Library of the Performing Arts (New York Public Library) includes photographs, scores, programs, prints, posters, and playbills as well as instruction manuals and other literature on the dance. The Archives of Dance, Music and Theatre (University of Florida Libraries) contains about 20,000 similar memorabilia relating to the performing arts in the twentieth century.

The Theater Arts Library (University of California at Los Angeles) has screenplays and pictures in addition to the general collection of English and foreign language books on the film. The Harvard Theatre Collection (Houghton Library) has rare letters, account books, diaries, drawings, promptbooks, and playbills from the United States, Britain, and Europe. Similar materials relating to British and American theater from 1875 to 1935 (especially the Chicago Little Theatre Movement 1912-1917) are found in the Department of Rare Books and Special Collections, University of Michigan. The Theatre Collection in the Research Library of the Performing Arts (New York Public Library) is one of the most notable anywhere. Bibliographic access is provided through its published catalog. The Free Library of Philadelphia has over 1,200,000 items relating to the theater, early circuses, and minstrel and vaudeville shows.

The Library of Congress has several notable film collections, including those received on copyright deposit. The Dell Publishing Company has about 3,500,000 pictures dealing with movie and TV personalities.

These represent but a small sampling of the collections in the United States and Europe that contain specialized information about the performing arts. The previously mentioned works by Young, Ash, and Lewanski (see item 13) should be consulted for more details.

10 PRINCIPAL INFORMATION SOURCES IN THE PERFORMING ARTS

GENERAL AND MISCELLANEOUS

498. **Chicorel Index to the Spoken Arts on Discs, Tapes and Cassettes.** Chicorel, 1973-74. 3v.

Approximately 2,000 albums are indexed in this set, which provides some 23,000 entries. Main entries are under album titles, with added entries under titles of works, authors, performers, editors, directors, etc. Main and added entries are in one alphabet. There are also lists of authors, editors, performers, etc. Subject access is provided through "Subject Indicators with Album Title References." More selective coverage, with evaluative comments, is provided in *Spoken Records*, by Helen Pauline Roach (3rd ed., Scarecrow, 1970), which include speeches, documentaries, authors' readings, and other readings from English and American literature, plays, and children's records. A more recent work (also very selective) is Homer E. Salley's *Selected Sound Recordings of American, British and European Literature in English* (University of Toledo Technological Media Center, 1976), which is arranged by subject areas and then by authors, with an index of authors, performers, and titles of individual works.

499. **Guide to the Performing Arts,** 1957-1968. Ann. Scarecrow, 1960-1972.

Begun as a supplement to *Guide to the Musical Arts* (1953-56), which it superseded, *Guide to the Performing Arts* also incorporated *Guide to Dance Periodicals* and indexed articles in over 50 periodicals, mainly in English. In the years 1957-1965, it had a separate section on "Television Arts," which was incorporated in the main work starting with coverage for 1966. Volumes for the years 1957-1967 were compiled by S. Yancey Belknap; the volume for 1968 (published in 1972) was compiled by Louis Rachow and Katherine Hartley.

500. International Federation of Library Associations. Section for Theatrical Libraries and Museums. **Performing Arts Libraries and Museums of the World/Bibliothèques et musées des arts du spectacle dans le monde.** 2nd ed. Centre Nationale de la Recherche Scientifique, 1967. 801p.

Compiled from questionnaires, this useful international directory is arranged alphabetically by countries (using the French names) and then by cities. The following types of information are given: name and address; hours and admission procedures; assistance to readers; history and nature of the holdings; other activities. The text for each entry is given twice (French, then English). *Performing Arts Resources, 1974-* (Theatre Library Association) complements and partially updates this directory (which now must be used with caution because of its age). These annual volumes are "designed to gather and disseminate scholarly articles dealing with (a) the location of resource materials relating to the theatre, film, television and radio and (b) a description, listing, or evaluation of the contents of such collections, whether public or private" (v. 4, 1978, p. vi). More restricted in scope, but still a vital reference work, is *A Preliminary Directory of Sound Recordings Collections in the United States and Canada*, prepared by the Program Committee of the Association for Recorded Sound Collections (New York Public Library, 1967). Based on questionnaires and unpublished directories, it is arranged alphabetically by states (with Canada listed separately) and then alphabetically by collections. A useful state-of-the-art survey is found in "Trends in Archival and Reference Collections of Recorded Sound," edited by Gordon Stevenson [*Library Trends* 21 (July 1972):3-155].

501. Mapp, Edward. **Directory of Blacks in the Performing Arts.** Scarecrow, 1978. 428p.

Biographical and career data are provided for 850 black performers (both living and dead) in such fields as film, television, night clubs, theater, opera, ballet, jazz, and classical music. The alphabetical arrangement by surnames is supplemented by a classified index, which includes such occupational categories as actors, broadcasters, dancers, pianists, etc. A directory of organizations and a bibliography are also included.

502. **The National Directory for the Performing Arts and Civic Centers**, 1973- . Ann. Handel.

Arranged by state and then by city, this vital directory includes permanent performing arts organizations, civic centers, and performing arts facilities in the United States. *International Directory of the Performing Arts*, 1968/69- [Ann.] (Billboard) was formerly (1968/69-1973) entitled *Musical America: Directory Issue.*

503. Schoolcraft, Ralph Newman, ed. **Performing Arts Books in Print: An Annotated Bibliography.** Drama Book Specialists, 1973. 761p.

This classified annotated bibliography has four main divisions: Books on Theatre and Drama; Books on Motion Pictures, Television, and Radio; Books on the Mass Media; and the Popular Arts. Detailed table of contents indicates subdivisions. The scope and limitations are carefully explained in the introduction. It is supplemented by an author and editor index, a title index, and a list of publishers. A revision and updating of *Theatre Books in Print* (2nd ed., 1966), it is supplemented and updated by a quarterly publication entitled *Annotated Bibliography of New Publications in the Performing Arts*. The care that Schoolcraft took with annotations makes the work more reliable than *Chicorel Bibliography to the Performing Arts* (Chicorel, 1972), which arranges some 9,000 entries under 35 main headings and 300 subheadings; reviewers have noted in *Chicorel* some strange omissions and inclusions, as well as the lack of an author index. Marion K. Whalon's *Performing Arts Research; A Guide to Information Sources* (Gale, 1976) is a classified annotated bibliography divided into seven main parts: guides; dictionaries, encyclopedias, and handbooks; directories; play indexes and finding lists; sources of reviews for plays and motion pictures; bibliographies; indexes and abstracts; and illustrative and audio visual sources.

504. Sharp, Harold S., and Marjorie Z. Sharp, comps. **Index to Characters in the Performing Arts.** Scarecrow, 1966-73. 6v.

Contents: part I—*Non-musical Plays: An Alphabetical Listing of 30,000 Characters*, 1966. 2v.; part II—*Operas and Musical Productions*, 1969. 2v.; part III—*Ballets*, 1972; part IV—*Radio and Television*, 1973. The basic pattern in each part is to have two sections: 1. an alphabetical listing of characters, with cross references tying characters in each production together; and 2. an alphabetical list of citation symbols, with full title, type of production, number of acts, author or composer, name of theater, and place and date of first performance.

505.Sutton, Roberta Briggs. **Speech Index; An Index to 259 Collections of World Famous Orations and Speeches for Various Occasions.** 4th ed. Scarecrow, 1966. 947p. Suppls. 1966-70 (1972) and 1971-75 (1977).
The fourth edition includes material from the three preceding volumes plus new items. Coverage begins with 1935. The work follows a dictionary-type arrangement, with entries for each oration under author, subject, and type of speech.

506. Toole-Stott, Raymond, comp. **Circus and Allied Arts: A World Bibliography, 1500-1970.** Harpur, 1958-71. 4v.
Over 13,000 numbered items (mostly with library locations and call numbers) are included in this classified, annotated bibliography, based on the British Library, LC, the Bibliothèque Nationale, and the compiler's personal collection. The main index (author/subject/title) is at the end of v. 3; there is a similar index to v. 4. Each volume has several black and white plates (mainly reproductions of title pages). Appendices at the end of v. 3 include a circus who's who, a directory of circus collections, a bibliography of hocus pocus books, etc. Appendices at the end of v. 4 include addenda and corrections and a list of items in v. 1-3 that are held by The University of Amsterdam Library. Robert Gill, compiler of *Magic As a Performing Art: A Bibliography of Conjuring* (Bowker, 1977), a librarian and a practising magician, has selected more than 1,000 books in English (originals and translations) from 1935 to 1975 on the basis of usefulness to magicians. Entries are arranged by author and all items are annotated. There are subject, title, and name indexes.

507. **Who's Who in Show Business: The International Directory of the Entertainment World**, 1950- . Bi. Who's Who in Show Business.
International coverage of personalities in the performing and creative arts is provided. For many artists, it gives portraits, credits, and where they or their representatives can be reached. It follows a classified arrangement by entertainment categories, with a name index, and has a detailed table of contents. A history of all aspects of show business in the first one-half of the twentieth century is provided in *Show Biz: From Vaude to Video*, by Abel Green and J. Laurie (Holt, 1951; repr., Kennikat, 1972, 2v.).

MUSIC

Introductory Works and Bibliographic Guides

508. Bayne, Pauline, ed. **A Basic Music Library: Essential Scores and Books.** ALA, 1978. 182p.
Compiled by the Subcommittee on a Basic Music Collection of the Music Library Association, this work includes a series of selective lists of scores for study and performance in such areas as chamber and orchestral music, songs for solo voice and piano, and operas and oratorios. Music reference books, books for home reading and study, and music periodicals are also included. About 250 books are given evaluative coverage

in *Music*, by E. T. Bryant (Philosophical Library, 1965). Another well-written survey is *Musicalia: Sources of Information in Music* (2nd ed., Pergaman, 1969), by J. H. Davies, BBC music librarian. The Public Libraries Commission of the International Association of Music Libraries has prepared a classified, annotated bibliography of some 500 titles in English, French, and German entitled *International Basic List of Literature on Music* (Bibliotheek en Lectuur Centrum, 1975).

509.   Bernstein, Leonard. **Young People's Concerts.** Drawings by Isadore Seltzer. Rev. and enl. ed. Simon and Schuster, 1970. 233p.
In this book, which is based on his television series, Bernstein discusses various aspects of music such as: what is melody? what does music mean? what is classical music? He gives examples that can be played on the piano. Planned for ages 12-18, this book has much to offer the adult listener as well. Another book for lay readers is Aaron Copland's *What to Listen for in Music* (rev. ed., McGraw-Hill, 1957).

510.   Duckles, Vincent. **Music Reference and Research Materials.** 3rd ed. Free Press, 1974. 526p.
An excellent guide for teachers and students of musicology and for reference librarians, this standard work contains annotated entries and bibliographical information. The basic arrangement is by form: dictionaries, encyclopedias, catalogs, histories, etc. Reviews are cited for some titles. There is an author index. *Introduction to Music Research*, by Ruth Watanabe (Prentice-Hall, 1967) offers valuable assistance to graduate students with its discussion of the use of libraries, preparation of research papers, and music reference books and periodicals. More specialized in focus is *Organ Literature: A Comprehensive Survey*, by Corliss Richard Arnold (Scarecrow, 1973), which has two major sections: a historical survey of organ literature, noting major composers, basic forms, and information about organs; and a "biographical catalog," which contains a brief biography of each composer plus a list of published works. A bibliography of organ anthologies and an appendix on J. S. Bach are also provided. Another specialized guide is *Music and Dance Research of Southwestern United States Indians* (Information Coordinators, 1977). The first part is a bibliographic essay on dance and music research in the Southwest. The middle portion covers musical archives and other special collections, and the third part is a bibliography of items cited in the first.

511.   Haggin, Bernard H. **The New Listener's Companion and Record Guide.** 5th ed. Horizon Press, 1978. 456p.
The first part is devoted to music appreciation, covering such topics as form, major periods, and works of selected individual composers. The second part is an annotated discography. There is an index of musical procedures, forms and terms as well as a general index and an index of performers. Another work of music appreciation (with records to accompany the book) is *Music: A Design for Listening*, by Homer Ulrich (3rd ed., Harcourt, 1970). Historical background as well as introductory information will be found in *Our Musical Heritage*, by Curt Sachs (2nd ed., Prentice-Hall, 1955; repr., Greenwood, 1978). *The New Music Lover's Handbook*, by Elie Siegmeister (Harvey House, 1973) is weak on classical music, but generally good otherwise.

Bibliographies

Bibliographies of Music Literature

512.   Basart, Ann Phillips. **Serial Music; A Classified Bibliography of Writings on Twelve-tone and Electronic Music.** University of California Press, 1961; repr., Greenwood, 1976. 151p.
This classified, usually annotated, bibliography contains 823 items and is divided into four parts: twelve-tone music; electronic music; Viennese School; other composers. Access is facilitated by numerous cross references and by an author and analytical subject index.

513.   Blum, Fred. **Music Monographs in Series.** Scarecrow, 1964. 197p.
Blum's bibliography of numbered monograph series in the field of music current since 1945 lists more than 250 series from 30 countries, arranged alphabetically by title of series or issuing organization. Entries for each volume give author, title, and date. A list of publishers and their agents is included as well as an alphabetical list of series and issuing organizations. There is an index of names. Information for the period from 1966 to date may be found for some musical series through use of the subject index to *Books in Series in the United States, 1966-1975* (Bowker, 1977) and its supplement (1978).

514.   Carl Gregor, Duke of Mecklenburg. **International Jazz Bibliography: Jazz Books from 1919 to 1968.** P. H. Heitz, 1969. 198p. Suppl. 1970. Universal Edition, 1971. Suppl. 1971/72/73. Universal Edition, 1975.
The main work includes 250 monographic discographies and 300 discographies published as appendices in books. Periodical articles are omitted in this international bibliography of literature about jazz.

515.   Chase, Gilbert. **A Guide to the Music of Latin America.** 2nd ed. Pan American Union, 1962; repr., AMS Press, 1972. 411p.
A vital reference tool, this classified, annotated bibliography has introductory comments for each country. The country subheadings vary somewhat but usually include: introduction; general and miscellaneous; biography and criticism; national anthem; folk and primitive music. A new edition may be forthcoming.

516.   **Chicorel Bibliography to Books on Music and Musicians.** Chicorel, 1974.
Part of the Chicorel Index Series (v. 10), this work contains about 10,000 entries arranged by subject, without annotations. Reviewers have noted the inclusion of minor works, omission of some major works, and inclusion of some titles (especially reprints) announced but never published. (See reviews in: *ARBA 1976*, p. 470; *RQ*, Spring 1975, p. 255; *Choice*, March 1975, p. 44; *Reference Services Review*, January 1975, p. 20; and *Wilson Library Bulletin*, October 1974, p. 182.)

517.   Gooch, Bryan N. S., and David Thatcher. **Musical Settings of Late Victorian and Modern British Literature: A Catalogue.** Garland, 1976. 1112p.
Over 7,000 settings are listed alphabetically under authors and then titles of the literary works. Full bibliographical information is given about the literary works and their musical settings. Gooch and Thatcher have also compiled *Musical Settings of Early and Mid-Victorian Literature* (Garland, 1979).

518. Horn, David. **The Literature of American Music in Books and Folk Music Collections: A Fully-Annotated Bibliography.** Scarecrow, 1977. 556p.
About 1,400 books covering all types of music and all historical periods are included. The basic arrangement is by subject. Annotations are critical as well as descriptive.

519. Kennington, Donald. **The Literature of Jazz: A Critical Guide.** ALA, 1971. 158p.
First published in 1970 by the Library Association of Great Britain, this useful guide has chapters on: general background; histories; biographies; analysis; theory and criticism; periodical literature; organizations. An appendix deals with jazz on film. Good coverage of books in English is provided, but there is much poorer coverage of foreign languages.

520. Marco, Guy A., and Sharon Paugh Ferris. **Information on Music: A Handbook of Reference Sources in European Languages.** Libraries Unlimited, 1975- . (In progress).
Planned for completion in eight volumes, this very useful comprehensive set follows a classified arrangement. Entries are annotated and references are made to entry numbers in Duckles, Chase, Jackson, *ARBA*, Winchell (1967), and Sheehy (for volumes since 1976). There are cumulative (for v. 1, 2) author/title and subject indexes at the end of v. 2. Contents: v. 1—*Basic and Universal Sources* (1975); v. 2—*The Americas* (1977).

521. Meggett, Joan M. **Music Periodical Literature: An Annotated Bibliography of Indexes and Bibliographies.** Scarecrow, 1978. 126p.
Reviewers have noted that this work may be confusing because dissimilar things are sometimes brought together in the same section. "The most useful feature is a subject index directing the user to sources not obvious to the novice, such as *Index to Legal Periodicals* for music copyright law" (Beth Macleod, *Library Journal*, May 15, 1978, pp. 1050-51).

522. New York (City) Public Library. Reference Department. **Dictionary Catalog of the Music Collection.** G. K. Hall, 1965. 33v. Suppl. I, 1966. 811p. Suppl. II, 1973. 10v. Suppl. III, 1976. 559p.
The main set and the supplements together contain over 700,000 entries. Special strengths include folk songs, full scores of operas, American music, vocal music, programs, record catalogs, and manuscripts. Materials cataloged after September 1974 now appear in *Bibliographic Guide to Music*, 1975- (G. K. Hall). Another major resource is the Boston Public Library's *Dictionary Catalog of the Music Collection* (G. K. Hall, 1972, 20v.).

523. **Repertoire internationale des sources musicales/International Inventory of Musical Sources.** Henle; Novello, 1960- .
In this joint effort by the International Musicological Society and the International Association of Music Libraries, an attempt is made to list all bibliographies of music, writings about music, and textbooks on music published by 1800, with locations. Over 1,000 libraries in 30 countries are taking part. LC cataloged this set under the English title *International Inventory of Musical Sources.* It is commonly referred to as RISM. For a more detailed description, see Sheehy, p. 414 (item 11 herein) or Walford, v. 3, p. 401 (item 12 herein). At least for the foreseeable future, the following work will still be useful: Library of Congress Music Division's *Catalogue of Early Books on Music (Before 1800)* (1913, 312p.).

524. Weichlein, William J. **A Checklist of American Music Periodicals 1850-1900.**
Information Coordinators, 1970. 103p. (Detroit Studies in Music Bibliography, 16).
Periodicals which published *only* music are excluded from this list of 309 titles, arranged
alphabetically, with a chronological register. Full bibliographic information is given
plus *at least one* library location. Some of the titles are not in the *Union List of Serials*.
This work is useful for interlibrary loan as well as reference. LC catalogs and classifies
Detroit Studies in Music Bibliography as separates.

Bibliographies of Music

General

525. **American Music before 1865 in Print and on Records: A Biblio-Discography.**
Institute for Studies in American Music, Brooklyn College, City University of New
York, 1976. 113p.
In her review for *ARBA 1977* (p. 463), Olga Buth gave the following description: "The
purpose of this work is three-fold — it is a classified and annotated bibliography of
pre-1865 American music believed by the Institute to be in print and available for purchase in 1976; it is a discography listing phonorecords issued on 33-1/3 rpm discs up to
1976; and it provides an index that thoroughly cross-references the bibliography in a
simple, uncomplex manner." Several publications from the Institute (directed by the
distinguished musicologist, H. Wiley Hitchcock) have received high praise from
reviewers. This one was included among "Reference Books of 1977," *Library Journal*,
April 15, 1978, p. 818.

526. Aronowsky, Salomon. **Performing Times of Orchestral Works.** Benn, 1959.
802p.
Includes some 15,000 pieces, with entries under composers. Information given includes
name of work, English translation and opus number (if any), instruments taking part,
movements and time for each, and total performing time. *Orchestral Music: A Source
Book*, by D. Daniels (Scarecrow, 1972), provides similar information for about 2,500
works that are often performed. *The Standard Musical Repertoire, with Accurate
Timings*, by William Reddick (Doubleday, 1947; repr., 1969), is especially useful for
radio program directors. It follows a classified arrangement and includes overtures, orchestral works, songs, and choral numbers.

527. **British Union Catalogue of Early Music Printed before the Year 1801: A Record
of the Holdings of Over One Hundred Libraries throughout the British Isles,** ed. by
Edith B. Schnapper. Butterworth, 1957. 2v.
In this scholarly catalog, items are listed generally by composers or anonymous titles.
Periodicals are grouped under "Periodical Publications," and there is an extensive index
of first words and song titles. Another useful source of information on early music is
Catalogue of Music in the Huntington Library before 1801 (Henry E. Huntington
Library, 1949), which includes music published in periodicals (omitting manuscripts,
song texts and opera librettos). Entries are under composers (or titles for anonymous
works), and there is an index of composers and editors.

528. De Lerma, Dominique-René. **Black Concert and Recital Music, a Provisional List.** Afro-American Musical Opportunities Association, 1975- . (In progress).
One of several useful publications on black music, this was compiled by a professor on the faculty of the Music Department, Morgan State University, Baltimore, MD.

529. Eagon, Angelo. **Catalog of Published Concert Music by American Composers.** 2nd ed. Scarecrow, 1969. 348p. Suppls. 1971, 1974.
The main work covered music in print as of June 1968, and the second supplement carried this down to November 1973. Reviewers praised the care and accuracy shown by the compiler in this difficult undertaking.

530. Fuld, James M. **The Book of World-Famous Music, Classical, Popular and Folk.** New rev. ed. Crown, 1971. 688p.
The arrangement is alphabetical by English form of titles, and the compiler gives opening bars, biographical notes, and references. There is an index of personal names.

531. Heyer, Anna Harriet. **Historical Sets, Collected Editions, and Monuments of Music; A Guide to Their Contents.** 3rd ed. ALA, 1979.
First published in 1957, this work covers about 900 major anthologies of music. The compiler attempts comprehensive coverage of nineteenth- and twentieth-century sets. The main part is alphabetical by composer and gives major editions, indicating contents and providing complete bibliographical information. The index includes entries for composers, titles, and form or medium. More selective coverage is given in *A Handbook of Music Literature in Sets and Series*, by Sydney Robinson Charles (Free Press, 1972).

532. Jarman, Lynne. **Canadian Music: A Selected Checklist, 1950-73/La musique canadienne: Une liste selective, 1950-73.** University of Toronto Press, 1976.
Over 400 entries, classified by Dewey, with an index, have been included. The subtitle reads: "A selective listing of Canadian music from *Fontis artis musicae, 1954-73*, based on the catalogue entries of *Canadiana.*" Another source of information is *Canadian Music Scores and Recordings*, by G. Creelman and others (Ralph Packard Bell Library, Mount Allison University, 1976). Current information can be found by checking *Canadiana*, the Canadian national bibliography, which follows a classified arrangement. Information on British music may be found in *British Catalogue of Music* (Council of the National Bibliography, 1957-), which is published quarterly, with annual cumulations.

533. Limbacher, James L., ed. and comp. **Film Music: From Violins to Video.** Scarecrow, 1974. 835p.
Part one is a collection of short articles by noted critics. Part two consists of three lists: alphabetical by title; chronological and then by title; alphabetical by composer. A decade of selective international coverage is provided in the International Music Centre's *Music in Film and Television: An International Selective Catalogue, 1964-1974* (Unesco, 1975).

534. Sonneck, Oscar. **A Bibliography of Early Secular American Music (18th Century).** Rev. and enl. ed. by William Treat Upton. Library of Congress, 1945; repr., Da Capo, 1964. 616p.

This standard, authoritative reference source lists works by title with complete bibliographical information, including first lines. It also contains a list of articles and essays relating to music, and a list of composers and their works. Locations are indicated, making it vital for interlibrary loan as well as reference. Coverage from 1801 to 1825 is provided in another authoritative work, which has also become a classic—Richard J. Wolfe's *Secular Music in America, 1801-1825* (New York Public Library, 1964, 3v.), which covers about 10,000 titles and editions published in the United States. The basic arrangement is alphabetical by composers (or by titles for anonymous works). A useful bonus is the inclusion of short biographical sketches of minor composers. There are indexes of titles, first lines, publishers, etc., as well as a general index. Locations of copies are given. This scholarly work is useful to musicologists, historians, and reference and interlibrary loan librarians. Less vital, but worth noting, are Priscilla Heard's *American Music, 1698-1800: An Annotated Bibliography* (Baylor; distr., Rand McNally, 1976), which is mainly a chronological rearrangement of music entries from Charles Evans's *American Bibliography*; and Donald L. Hixon's *Music in Early America: A Bibliography of Music in Evans* (Scarecrow, 1970).

535. U.S. Library of Congress. **Music, Books on Music, and Sound Recordings,** 1973- . S-Ann. Ann. & quin. cum.
Formerly entitled *Library of Congress Catalog: Music and Phonorecords* (1953-1972), the present title is both a continuation and an expansion. Whereas the old set contained only entries from LC printed cards, the new one includes seven other libraries whose collections supplement those in LC. The gap in the old set has been remedied in admirable fashion by Elizabeth H. Olmstead's *Music Library Association Catalog of Cards for Printed Music, 1953-1972: A Supplement to the Library of Congress Catalogs* (Rowman & Littlefield, 1974, 2v.), which contains approximately 30,000 entries missing from the LC catalogs. The Music Library Association and the Library of Congress cooperated closely in this major undertaking. For publications prior to 1953, one should consult the U.S. Copyright Office's *Catalog of Copyright Entries* (3rd series, Part 5, *Music*, 1947- ; and Part 3, *Musical Compositions*, 1906-1946).

Vocal Music

536. **Bibliografia della musica italiana vocale profana pubblicata dal 1500 al 1700,** by Emil Vogel, Alfred Einstein, Francois Lesure, and Claudia Sartori. Minkoff, 1977- . (In progress).
This major bibliography of secular Italian vocal music is a revision of Vogel's *Bibliothek der gedruckten weltlichen Vocalmusik Italiens*, published in 1892. The new edition includes indexes of musicians, poets, singers, etc.

537. British Broadcasting Corporation. Central Music Library. **Song Catalogue.** BBC, 1966. 4v.
Contents: v. 1-2, *Composers A-Z*; v. 3-4, *Titles A-Z*. Basically devoted to solo songs with keyboard accompaniment, this also includes unaccompanied songs and duets; duets with piano; recitations with piano; songs with instrumental obligati; popular song annuals; and folk, national and patriotic songs.

538. Carman, Judith E., William K. Gaeddart, and Rita M. Resh. **Art-song in the United States, 1801-1976.** National Association of Teachers of Singing, 1976. 308p.

This annotated bibliography also contains a special section by Gordon Myers on the art-song in the United States from 1759 to 1810.

539.   Espina, Noni. **Repertoire for the Solo Voice.** Scarecrow, 1977. 2v.
The subtitle of this extensive (9,726 songs and operatic arias) bibliography is: "A fully-annotated guide to works for the solo voice published in modern editions and covering material from the 13th century to the present." The arrangement is primarily geographical, with some departure (by type of voice) in the opera section. For a more complete description and evaluation of some weaknesses, see the review by John Druesedow in *ARBA 1978* (pp. 455-56). Espina is more extensive in coverage than *The Singer's Repertoire*, by Berton Coffin (Scarecrow, 1960-62, 5v.), which arranges some 8,000 songs by voice type (v. 1-4), with program notes (v. 5). *Word-by-Word Translations of Songs and Arias* (Scarecrow, 1966-72, 2v.) is intended as a companion set to Coffin. V. 1 covers French and German titles and v. 2, Italian.

540.   May, James D. **Avante-Garde Choral Music: An Annotated, Selected Bibliography.** Scarecrow, 1977. 258p.
Reviewing this work for *ARBA 1978* (pp. 457-58), Carol Bradley described it as "a well-annotated bibliography of avant-garde choral music readily available in the United States, for non-professional singers—i.e., high school, college and church choirs." The basic arrangement is by title, with supplementary access through media and composer indexes. William Tortolano's *Original Music for Men's Voices: A Selected Bibliography* (Scarecrow, 1973) is arranged by periods, then alphabetically by composers. There are indexes of authors/sources and titles/first lines. Another work in the field of choral music is Evelyn Davidson White's *Selected Bibliography of Choral Music by Black Composers* (Compiler, 1975).

541.   Nardone, Thomas R., James H. Nye, and Mark Resnick. **Choral Music in Print.** Musicdata, 1974. 2v. Suppl. 1976.
Contents: v. 1—*Sacred Choral Music*; v. 2—*Secular Choral Music*. Entries from several hundred catalogs of music publishers were put into machine-readable form to produce these volumes. Main entries are under composers, if known; otherwise, they are under titles. There are numerous cross references, but generally, very little editing was done. Thus, the same composer or work may appear in more than one place. Still, it is a tremendously convenient source. Compiled in the same fashion, Nardone's *Classical Vocal Music in Print* (Musicdata, 1976) exhibits similar errors and inconsistencies, but is also an extremely useful tool. Composers and titles are in one alphabetical sequence, with cross references. It should be noted that the term "classical" has been very broadly interpreted. Both titles are part of the publisher's Music in Print series.

542.   Stecheson, Anthony, and Ann Stecheson, comps. **The Stecheson Classified Song Directory.** Music Industry Press, 1961. 503p.
Arranged under some 400 catchwords and composers, this work gives titles, publishers, and sometimes dates, of about 100,000 popular songs; it also includes a list of publishers with addresses, but does not have a title index. James L. Limbacher's *The Song List: A Guide to Contemporary Music from Classical Sources* (Pierian, 1973) is in two parts—1) titles and 2) composers.

543. U.S. Library of Congress. Music Division. **Catalogue of Opera Librettos Printed before 1800.** Washington, DC, 1914; repr., Johnson, 1968. 2v.
Paged continuously, this set contains about 6,000 entries arranged alphabetically under title, accompanied by historical, descriptive, and bibliographical notes. Contents: 1) Title Catalog; 2) Author List, Composer List and Aria Index. LC's Music Division also published *Dramatic Music: A Catalogue of Full Scores* (GPO, 1908; repr., 1969), which is arranged alphabetically by composer.

Instrumental Music

544. Altmann, Wilhelm. **Orchester-Literatur-Katalog.** . . . Leukart, 1926-36; repr., Sändig, 1972. 2v.
Orchestral works from 1850 to 1935 are included, with performance times and details of orchestration.

545. American Society of Composers, Authors and Publishers. **ASCAP Symphonic Catalog.** 3rd ed. Bowker, 1977. 511p.
Symphonic literature controlled by ASCAP is listed alphabetically by composers and arrangers. Information is given about instrumentation, duration, and publisher. For symphonies controlled by a rival organization, see the entry under Broadcast Music, Inc. (item 548).

546. British Broadcasting Corporation. Central Music Library. **Chamber Music Catalogue; Chamber Music, Violin and Keyboard, Cello and Keyboard. Various.** BBC, 1965. Various paging.
The first volume published in a series of catalogs listing both printed and manuscript material from the BBC's vast collection, this work is divided into four parts, as indicated in the subtitle, and arranged by composers in four columns: selection; arranger; publisher and date; location. There is a short bibliography. Another comprehensive listing of chamber music (from 1841 to 1944) is Wilhelm Altmann's *Kammermusik-Katalog* (6th ed., Hofmeister, 1945; repr., 1967). Altmann also provided an analytical guide to string quartets in *Handbuch fur Streichquartettspieler* (2nd ed., Heinrichshofen's Verlag, 1972-74, 4v.).

547. British Broadcasting Corporation. Central Music Library. **Piano and Organ Catalogue.** BBC, 1965. 2v.
This very comprehensive work (48,000 items) has sections for piano solos, duets, trios, works for two or more pianos, selected works for left hand and right hand only, organ solos, and selected organ works other than solos.

548. Broadcast Music, Inc. **BMI Symphonic Catalog.** Rev. ed. BM I, 1971. 375p.
Works controlled by BMI are listed alphabetically by composers. Information is given on instrumentation, duration, and publisher. For works controlled by a rival organization, see the entry under American Society of Composers, Authors and Publishers (item 545).

549. Brown, Howard Mayer. **Instrumental Music Printed before 1600: A Bibliography.** Harvard, 1965. 559p.
This excellent, scholarly work follows a chronological arrangement of published music from the 1480s through 1599 and has five indexes: 1. List of Libraries and Their

Holdings; 2. Volumes Described, Arranged by Types of Notation; 3. Volumes Described, Arranged by Performing Medium; 4. Names; 5. First Lines and Titles.

550. Daniels, David. **Orchestral Music: A Source Book.** Scarecrow, 1972. 301p.
Designed to aid in planning programs and organizing rehearsals, this covers the standard repertoire (over 2,500 works) for American orchestras. Gives instrumentation, duration, and publisher. A valuable older work is *Catalogue of Music for the Small Orchestra*, by Cecilia D. Saltonstall and H. C. Smith (Music Library Association, 1947).

551. Farish, Margaret K. **String Music in Print.** 2nd ed. Bowker, 1973. 464p.
The compiler has tried to cover all music for stringed instruments published in the United States.

552. Hinson, Maurice. **Guide to the Pianist's Repertoire,** ed. by Irwin Freundlich. Indiana University Press, 1973. 831p.
In reviewing this work for *ARBA 1974* (pp. 378-79), Dennis North described it as "the most extensive work of its kind for piano presently available." The compiler included 1,166 composers from 47 countries. Many entries are annotated. There is also a general bibliography of books, articles, and dissertations. North mentioned many typographical, spelling, and factual errors and concluded that it does not fully replace *Music for the Piano*, by James Friskin and Irwin Freundlich (Rinehart, 1954; repr., Dover, 1973). *Concert Piano Repertoire: A Manual of Solo Literature for Artists and Performers*, by Albert Faurot (Scarecrow, 1974), follows the same format as Friskin and Freundlich. *Team Piano Repertoire: A Manual of Music for Players at One or More Pianos*, by Frederic M. Chang and Albert Faurot (Scarecrow, 1976), complements Faurot's *Concert Piano Repertoire*. Descriptive information and level of difficulty are given.

553. Nardone, Thomas R., ed. **Organ Music in Print.** Musicdata, 1975. 262p.
Another valuable addition to the Music in Print series, this work includes over 12,000 compositions from 350 publishers. Forms of entry were taken from publishers' catalogs with minimal editing, but there is liberal provision of cross references. The arrangement is alphabetical, with composers and titles of compositions in one sequence.

Indexes, Abstracts, and Current Awareness Services

554. Blom, Eric. **A General Index to Modern Musical Literature in the English Language, Including Periodicals, for the Years of 1915-26.** Curwen, 1927; repr., Da Capo, 1970. 159p.
Author entries for whole books and subject entries for parts of books are in one alphabet. A noted music periodical has benefitted from two retrospective indexes: Herbert Goodkind's *Cumulative Index 1915 through 1959 to "The Musical Quarterly"* (Goodkind Indexes, 1960) and Hazel Gertrude Kinscella's *Americana Index to "The Musical Quarterly," 1915-1957* (Music Educators' National Conference, 1959). Still another major journal is covered by Wayne D. Shirley's *Modern Music: An Analytic Index* (AMS Press, 1976). Good evaluative criticism of published music can also be located through *Music and Letters: Index to Vols. I-XL, 1920-1959* (Oxford, 1962).

555. Cushing, Helen Grant, comp. **Children's Song Index.** Wilson, 1936; repr., Scholarly Press, 1977. 798p.
This valuable older index, recently reprinted, covers more than 22,000 songs in 189 collections. Main entries, with full information, are under titles, with cross references from alternate titles, different titles in different collections, translated titles, original titles in certain languages (e.g., Russian), first lines, and sometimes first lines of choruses. Also, there are added entries under composers, authors, and subjects.

556. de Charms, Désirée, and Paul F. Breed. **Songs in Collections: An Index.** Information Service, 1966. 588p.
This vital reference tool indexes over 9,000 songs in over 400 collections, with heavy emphasis on art songs and operatic arias. Separate sections are provided for composed songs, anonymous and folk songs, carols, and sea chanties. There is an index to all titles and first lines — and an author index. Sears's *Song Index* (see item 568) is supplemented and updated by this valuable work. Another title worth noting is *Index to Song Collections at the Hewlett-Woodmere Public Library* (The Library, 1974).

557. Drone, Jeannette M. **Index to Opera, Operetta and Musical Comedy Synopses in Collections and Periodicals.** Scarecrow, 1978. 171p.
Plot summaries of more than 1,600 works in 74 books and periodicals have been indexed. The main part is arranged by title and there is a composer index. It is designed to supplement, rather than duplicate, *Opera Plots . . .* , by Waldemar Rieck (New York Public Library, 1927).

558. Gerboth, Walter. **An Index to Musical Festschriften and Similar Publications.** W. W. Norton, 1969. 188p.
"Lists about 3,000 articles from nearly 600 volumes under broad areas and eras, with an appended author and subject index" (Frances Neel Cheney, *Wilson Library Bulletin*, May 1970, p. 973). Includes biocritical and bibliographical sources on music and musicians from a wide range of books and journals, chiefly foreign and often hard to locate. More specialized is *An Index of Gregorian Chant*, by John Rennie Bryden and David G. Hughes (Harvard, 1969, 2v.). Arthur Wenk's *Analyses of Twentieth-Century Music, 1940-1970* (Music Library Association, 1975) is an index of critical articles on works of more than 150 twentieth-century composers found in periodicals, festschriften, and dissertations.

559. Havlice, Patricia P. **Popular Song Index.** Scarecrow, 1975. 933p.
The compiler has indexed 301 song collections, mainly American, published between 1940 and 1972. Many are anthologies of folk songs. Main entries are under titles, with cross references from actual first lines and first lines of choruses (all in one alphabet). There is also an index of composers and lyricists. Coverage is complementary to *Songs in Collections*, by de Charms and Breed (see item 556), which emphasizes art songs and operatic arias.

560. Hodgson, Julian. **Music Titles in Translation: A Checklist of Musical Compositions.** Linnet, 1976. 370p.
About 7,000 compositions are listed alphabetically in their original languages and in variant English translations. Another source of variant title information is *Popular*

Titles and Subtitles of Musical Compositions (2nd ed., Scarecrow, 1975). In his review for *ARBA 1975* (p. 469), Guy Marco noted that this is often the quickest source; but he pointed out some problems created for the user by the arrangement of the composer index and by the inconsistent choices of original languages versus English translations. The reviewer in *Choice* (November 1975, p. 1139) thought that other sources (like the *Oxford Companion to Music*) could answer most reference questions about titles.

561.   International Repertory of Music Literature (organization). **RILM: Abstracts of Music Literature.** International RILM Center, Queen's College, 1967- . Q.
RILM (Répertoire internationale de la littérature musicale) abstracts and indexes periodical articles, reviews, books, dissertations, etc., in the field of musicology. It is a cooperative project of the International Musicological Society and the International Association of Music Libraries. The arrangement is classified, with nine main divisions: Reference and Research Materials; Collected Writings; Historical Musicology; Ethnomusicology; Instruments and Voice; Performance Practice and Notation; Theory and Analysis; Pedagogy; Music and Other Disciplines. The fourth issue of each volume is a cumulative author/subject index.

562.   Krohn, Ernest Christopher. **The History of Music: An Index to the Literature Available in a Selected Group of Publications.** Baton Music Co., 1958. 463p.
This index to material on the history of music appearing in some 40 periodicals, mainly German and English, is arranged by broad period divisions, further subdivided by such headings as General Studies, Composers, and the various musical forms. Book reviews are included. Indexes by authors and composers are provided.

563.   Leigh, Robert. **Index to Song Books: A Title Index to Over 11,000 Copies of 6,800 Songs in 111 Books Published between 1933 and 1962.** Compiler, 1964; repr., Da Capo, 1973. 237p.
Leigh's coverage includes American and foreign folk songs, popular songs, children's songs, carols, hymns, operatic arias, etc.; it is limited to sources that have both words and music. Cross references are given for alternate titles and famous lines, but there are no entries for authors or composers. Leigh's work serves as a partial continuation of Sears's *Song Index* (see item 568) and has more coverage of popular songs than de Charms and Breed (see item 556).

564.   Lewine, Richard, and Alfred E. Simon. **Songs of the American Theater.** Dodd, Mead, 1973. 820p.
An expansion and updating of the authors' *Encyclopedia of Theatre Music* (Randon House, 1961), this work includes 12,000 titles. In the first part, the songs are arranged alphabetically by titles, while in the second part, the arrangement is a chronological listing of productions. There is an index of composers and lyricists. The reviewer in *Choice* (October 1973, p. 1168) commented: "Among similar books, Julius Mattfield's *Variety Music Cavalcade* (2nd ed., 1962) and Nat Shapiro's *Popular Music: An Annotated Index of American Popular Songs* (5v., 1964-69) give fuller information about a more selective number of titles" (see item 565). Allen Woll's *Songs from Hollywood Musical Comedies, 1927 to the Present: A Dictionary* (Garland, 1976) includes only American musicals and foreign films of musicals that appeared on Broadway. A brief historical section is followed by an alphabetical list of song titles, with references to numbered entries in the next section for the movies in which they appeared. Finally,

there is a chronological list of shows and an index of composers and lyricists. Some reviewers have noted that the amount of information about each movie in the numbered main section is disappointingly brief: title, year, director, song writers, and stars. Full listings of all songs and casts would have improved this generally useful work.

565. Mattfield, Julius. **Variety Music Cavalcade, 1620-1969: A Chronology of Vocal and Instrumental Music Popular in the U.S.** 3rd ed. Prentice-Hall, 1971. 766p.
In this essential reference work, popular music is listed chronologically, with brief accounts of various events occurring each year. Coverage includes hymns, secular and sacred songs, choral compositions, and instrumental and orchestral works. Only the musical items are indexed. Valuable coverage for a substantial portion of the twentieth century is also provided by Nat Shapiro's *Popular Music: An Annotated Index of American Popular Songs* (Adrian Press, 1964-). The coverage of the six volumes that have appeard to date is: v. 1, 1950-59; v. 2, 1940-49; v. 3, 1960-64; v. 4, 1930-39; v. 5, 1920-29; v. 6, 1965-69. Songs are arranged by year, then alphabetically by title. The compiler gives author, composer, publisher, and first or best-selling record, indicating performer and record company. John H. Chipman's *Index to Top-Hit Tunes, 1900-1950* (Humphries, 1962) contains 3,000 titles of American popular songs that have sold at least 100,000 copies of sheet music or records. Songs are listed by title, alphabetically, and also chronologically. Composer, publisher and date are given. Chipman also indicates if a song was featured in a film or musical.

566. **The Music Index: The Key to Current Music Periodical Literature**, 1949- . Information Service. Mo. Ann. cum.
This vital reference tool indexes, by author and subject, about 180 periodicals representing various aspects of the music field, ranging from musicology to the retailing of music. It gives complete indexing for musical periodicals, and indexes articles pertinent to music in some more general ones. All first performances and obituaries are indexed. Music reviews appear under composer, title, and medium. Information on illustrations may be found in *Guide to the Musical Arts: An Analytical Index of Articles and Illustrations, 1953-56* (Scarecrow, 1957), which otherwise largely duplicates *The Music Index.*

567. **Popular Music Periodicals Index**, 1973- . Ann. Scarecrow.
Edited by Dean Tudor and Andrew Armitage, this annual index attempts to do for popular music what *Music Index* has been doing for serious music. There is a substantial amount of overlap with *MI* in titles covered, but the indexing methods differ. *PMPI* gives more attention to personalities mentioned in the articles.

568. Sears, Minnie. **Song Index.** Wilson, 1926. 650p. Suppl. 1934. Repr., Shoestring, 1966. 2v. in 1.
This important index is still widely used in public, college, and school libraries as well as in music libraries. The main work and supplement together contain over 19,000 songs in 281 collections. Titles, first lines, authors' names, and composers' names are given in one alphabet. More recent song indexes (items 556, 559, 563) were planned to supplement and update, but not duplicate, the coverage by Sears.

Dictionaries and Encyclopedias

Dictionaries

569.   Apel, Willi. **Harvard Dictionary of Music.** 2nd ed. Harvard, 1969; repr., 1977. 935p.

Reviewers and reference librarians alike hail this dictionary as the best work of its kind available, despite reservations about the cutting necessary to keep it in one volume and make room for new topics like Africa and iconography. It omits biographies, and some entries (e.g., periodicals) were not thoroughly updated. It is a necessity for every library, because one reviewer estimates that it will answer 80 percent of the reference questions in music. Larger libraries will want to retain the 1944 edition because of the number of monographic articles that have been drastically shortened. Willi Apel and Ralph T. Daniel used this work as the basis for compiling the *Harvard Brief Dictionary of Music* (Harvard, 1960), which consists of short articles for the non-specialist. Don Michael Randal has also used the *Harvard Dictionary of Music* for compiling the *Harvard Concise Dictionary of Music* (Harvard, 1978), which is more comprehensive than the *Harvard Brief Dictionary of Music*. Unlike either of its predecessors, *Concise* contains about 2,000 biographies. The reviewer in *Library Journal* (October 1, 1978, p. 1969) compared it favorably to *The New College Encyclopedia of Music*, by J. A. Westrup and F. L. Harrison (W. W. Norton, 1976). *Harper's Dictionary of Music*, by Christine Ammer (Harper, 1972), includes musical terms, entries in music history, and biographies of composers.

570.   Baker, Theodore A. **Dictionary of Musical Terms, Containing Upwards of 9000 English, French, German, Italian, Latin and Greek Words and Phrases . . . with a Supplement Containing an English-Italian Vocabulary for Composers.** Schirmer, 1923; repr., AMS, 1977. 257p.

Words and phrases are carefully defined, with accents of foreign words marked. Rules are given for pronunciation of Italian, German, and French terms. There have been many reprintings and some revisions since it was first published in 1895. The 1923 version describes itself as "Twenty-first edition, thoroughly revised and augmented by an appendix of 700 additional words and phrases." A more recent publication (with fewer languages) is the English-German/German-English translating dictionary by Horst Leuchtmann entitled *Wörterbuch Musik: Dictionary of Terms in Music* (Verlag Dokumentation, 1977).

571.   Blom, Eric, comp. **Everyman's Dictionary of Music.** 5th ed. Rev. by Jack Westrup. St. Martin's, 1972. 793p.

Noted for its concise treatment of terms and biographical information, this work contains over 10,000 entries, with numerous cross references. More specialized, but a standard work for the period 1100-1500, is *A Dictionary of Middle English Musical Terms*, by Henry Holland Carter (Indiana University Press, 1961). James B. Coover's *Music Lexicography: Including a Study of Lacunae in Music Lexicography and a Bibliography of Music Dictionaries* (3rd ed., Carlisle books, 1971) began in 1952 as a bibliography of music dictionaries; later, it was expanded to include a substantial essay portion and greater bibliographical coverage. It was considered by one reviewer to be the most comprehensive and authoritative work in this field.

572. Marcuse, Sibyl. **Musical Instruments: A Comprehensive Dictionary.** Corr. ed. W. W. Norton, 1975. 608p.

This standard work includes a bibliography of sources consulted (pp. 603-608) and is regarded by reference librarians as a much more vital search tool than Rowland Wright's *Dictionnaire des instruments de musique: étude de lexicologie* (Battley, 1941), which "traces the names for musical instruments employed in French literature from the earliest times to the end of the nineteenth century" [Vincent Duckles, "Music Literature, Music and Sound Recordings," *Library Trends* 15 (January 1967):499].

573. Riemann, Hugo. **Musik-Lexikon,** ed. by Wilibald Gurlitt. Schott, 1959-67. 3v. Suppl. 1972-75. 2v.

Originally a student's pocket dictionary in 1882, this standard work was expanded substantially over the years. In the main set, v. 1 and 2 are biographical and v. 3 deals with musical terms. The two volumes of the supplement are biographical and include living musicians as well as updated biographical information for musicians included in the basic set. Articles are well supplied with bibliographical references.

574. Vinton, John. **Dictionary of Contemporary Music.** Dutton, 1974. 834p.

This outstanding dictionary, which adheres to high editorial standards comparable to those of the *Harvard Dictionary of Music*, includes subject articles on such topics as musical elements, compositional techniques, movements and countries, as well as biographical sketches of nearly 1,000 composers, with lists of principal works and bibliographies. It was included in "Reference Books of 1974" (*Library Journal*, April 15, 1975, p. 734). *The Language of Twentieth-Century Music: A Dictionary of Terms*, by Robert Fink and Robert Ricci (Schirmer, 1975), has brief definitions and is not of the same calibre as the works by Vinton and Apel. *Jazz Talk*, by Robert S. Gold (Bobbs-Merrill, 1975), deals with a specialized aspect of contemporary music with great care and thoroughness, as indicated by Guy A. Marco's comments in *ARBA 1976* (p. 490): "Building on his earlier *Jazz Lexicon* (Knopf, 1964; Duckles no. 287), Gold has prepared an excellent historical dictionary of about a thousand terms and expressions." *New Music Vocabulary: A Guide to Notational Signs for Contemporary Music*, by Howard Risatti (University of Illinois, 1975), is a pioneer effort but already partly outdated by actions toward standardization taken at the 1974 International Conference on New Musical Notation (according to John D. White in *ARBA 1976*, pp. 478-79).

Sources of Longer Descriptive Articles

General

575. **Enciclopedia della musica.** Ricordi, 1972-74. 6v.

This vital reference source has over 15,000 signed articles by more than 200 contributors, both Italian and foreign, and is illustrated by more than 300 black and white photographs and 48 color plates. It includes catalogs of works of Bach, Beethoven, Brahms, Chopin, Debussy, Donizetti, Handel, Haydn, Liszt, Mozart, Palestrina, Schubert, and Vivaldi in appendixes.

576. **Encyclopédie de la musique,** ed. by François Michel. Fasquelle, 1958-61. 3v.

This very important reference work opens with essays and a chronological table. The encyclopedia portion follows, beginning on page 239 of v. 1. There are many short biographies and definitions of terms. Longer articles on major topics are signed. Another major French encyclopedia is *Larousse de la musique*, edited by Norbert Defourcq (Larousse, 1957. 2v.), which is well illustrated, covers European composers especially well, includes opera plots, and features signed articles by some 150 contributors.

577.   Grove, Sir George. **The New Grove Dictionary of Music and Musicians**, ed. by Stanley Sadie. 6th ed. Grove's Dictionaries of Music, Inc., 1979. 20v.
This distinguished reference work has been updated and greatly expanded to provide fuller international coverage. By far the most comprehensive musical encyclopedia in English, it now rivals *Die Musik in Geschichte und Gegenwart* (see item 579), with some 22,500 articles, 7,500 cross references, 3,000 illustrations, and 16,500 biographies of composers, performers, instrument makers, writers, publishers, and others associated with music, instruments, places, and musical forms. Extensive bibliographies and an index of non-Western terms and instruments are also provided.

578.   Lloyd, Norman. **The Golden Encyclopedia of Music.** Golden Press, 1968.
An informal work for high school readers or adult laypersons, this convenient small encyclopedia has excellent illustrations (especially of musical instruments) and a good index, but it is weak in biographies. There are no bibliographies, cross references, or geographical articles. A more specialized work is Frank Leaza's *The Golden Encyclopedia of Music Theory and Arranging* (Two Worlds, 1975).

579.   **Die Musik in Geschichte und Gegenwart.** Barenreiter, 1949-1968. 14v. Suppl., v. 15, 1973- . (In progress).
A scholarly, comprehensive work, international in scope — with long, signed articles by specialists, including extensive bibliographical notes — this has been for many years the best encyclopedia of music. Profusely illustrated, it is indispensable for music reference and research. An index and supplement are now in preparation. V. 15 (suppl.) covers Aachen to Dyson.

580.   Scholes, Percy Alfred. **The Oxford Companion to Music**, ed. by John Owen Ward. 10th ed. 1970; repr., 1977. 1189p.
The new editor was a colleague of Scholes, who died in 1958. The tenth edition, pruned and updated (90 new articles), represented an improvement over the ninth edition of 1955. Arrangement is alphabetical by topic, with no index or bibliographies. Authoritative, accurate, and well-written, it is a very useful reference source. Another useful one-volume work is Martin Cooper's *The Concise Encyclopedia of Music and Musicians* (4th ed., Hutchinson, 1978), which includes short articles and technical terms, foreign words, musical instruments, and the lives of both well-known and obscure composers. Less highly esteemed by librarians, but often recommended for home use, is *The Milton Cross New Encyclopedia of the Great Composers and Their Music* (Doubleday, 1969, 2v.).

581.   Thompson, Oscar. **International Cyclopedia of Music and Musicians**, ed. by Bruce Bohle. 10th ed. Dodd, Mead, 1975. 2511p.
Most articles are short, but there are some lengthy signed monographs in the single alphabet both on important composers and on special subjects like history of music, music criticism, folk music, opera, etc. Each biographical article is followed by a calendar of the composer's life and a classified list of his works. Strong in biographies, this work has many contemporary names.

582.   Westrup, J. A., and F. L. Harrison. **The New College Encyclopedia of Music.**
Rev. ed., by Conrad Wilson. W. W. Norton, 1976. 608p.
A revision of the *Collins Encyclopedia of Music* (1959), this volume contains 6,000
entries for composers, musical instruments, terms, performers, etc. Articles are frequently illustrated and short bibliographies are often provided. Reviewers have noted
the omission of some major contemporary American musicians.

Specialized

583.   Ayre, Leslie. **The Gilbert and Sullivan Companion.** Dodd, Mead, 1972. 485p.
Favorably received on both sides of the Atlantic, this book first describes the famous
partnership; it then moves on to a series of alphabetical entries on artists, plot summaries, entry and full text for each song, and explanations of obscure references. Song
texts are found under names of operettas. It does not provide complete libretti.
Crowell's *Handbook of Gilbert and Sullivan*, by Frank Ledlie Moore (Crowell, 1962),
arranges the 14 comic operas chronologically, with casts, settings, songs, choruses, and
plot synopses. Appendices cover: biographies of Gilbert, Sullivan, and D'Oyly Carte;
chronology of the lives of Gilbert and Sullivan; roles in the operas; first and famous
lines; themes and texts of famous musical numbers. There is a bibliography, but no
index. An abridged reprint (168p.) was published by Schocken in 1975.

584.   Cobbett, Walter Willson. **Cyclopedic Survey of Chamber Music.** Oxford,
1929-30. 2v. 2nd ed., 1963. 3v.
The first two volumes are reissues of the 1929-30 edition, with a few minor changes in
the text and insertion of symbols in the margins to indicate further references in v. 3.
There are signed articles on subjects concerned with chamber music: topics, persons,
instruments, organizations, etc. Biographies and lists of composers' works are included.
V. 3 contains a selective survey since 1929, a bibliography, and additions and corrections to the 1929-30 volumes. An index of composers is provided.

585.   The Diagram Group. **Musical Instruments of the World: An Illustrated Encyclopedia.** Paddington; Two Continents, 1976. 320p.
Dennis North, reviewing this useful reference book for *ARBA 1977* (pp. 464-65), commented as follows: "Perhaps a better subtitle for this excellent work would be 'A Visual
Encyclopedia.' The illustrations *are* the work, and in this it surpasses all its rivals since
the sixteenth century in coverage and extent. . . . These drawings, more than 4,000 of
them, picture instruments of every type: ancient and modern, ethnic and folk, primitive
and electronic, popular and classical." The basic arrangement is by types: vibrating air
instruments, self-vibrating instruments, vibrating membrane instruments, vibrating
string instruments, and mechanical electronic instruments. There are also sections by
geographical areas, time periods, and instrumental ensembles. A general name and subject index is provided. Another good source is *A Survey of Musical Instruments*, by
Sybil Marcuse (Harper, 1975). The reviewer in *ARBA 1976* (p. 486) wrote that it provided "a wealth of historical and technical information about all important instruments.
The coverage is international and each individual instrument is described in terms of
historical background, important technical changes in design, etc." A more specialized
work is *Encyclopedia of Automatic Musical Instruments*, by Q. David Bowers (Vestal,
1972), which covers cylinder and disc music boxes, player and coin-operated pianos,
orchestrions, calliopes, etc. It includes a glossary and provides many illustrations.

Another excellent specialized source is William Henley's *Universal Dictionary of Violin and Bow Makers* (Amati, 1973).

586. Ewen, David. **New Complete Book of the American Musical Theater.** Holt, 1970. 800p.
Ewen's valuable guide to publications of the American musical theater — with plot, production history, stars, songs, composers, librettists, and lyricists (illustrated with photographs) — is arranged alphabetically by composer, with lists of shows and songs and a full index. *The Book of European Light Opera* (Holt, 1962) is a popularized treatment of a related field.

587. Feather, Leonard G. **The Encyclopedia of Jazz.** Rev. ed. Horizon, 1960. 527p.
The main work contains biographical sketches of more than 2,000 jazzmen, with a guide to their recordings; history of jazz on records; recommended jazz records; bibliography and discography. Companion volumes are *The Encyclopedia of Jazz in the Sixties* (Horizon, 1966) and *The Encyclopedia of Jazz in the Seventies* (Horizon, 1976). Another source that should not be overlooked is *The Illustrated Encyclopedia of Jazz*, by Brian Case and Stan Britt (Harmony Books, 1978).

588. Gentry, Linnell. **A History and Encyclopedia of Country, Western, and Gospel Music.** McQuiddy Press, 1961; repr., Scholarly Press, 1972. 380p.
This vital reference work begins with an anthology of periodical articles since 1904, continues with a listing of shows since 1924, and concludes with a biographical section. Another major source of information is Erwin Stambler's *Encyclopedia of Folk, Country and Western Music* (see item 591).

589. Green, Stanley. **Encyclopedia of the Musical Theatre.** Dodd, Mead, 1976. 488p.
In reviewing this concise, useful book for *ARBA 1977* (p. 478), Koert C. Loomis, described it thus: "For over 200 musicals, then, Green lists background, plot summary, cast, credits, best-known songs, dates of both the London and New York openings, theatres in which they opened, and number of performances. If appropriate, any films based on the musicals are listed. . . . In addition to musicals themselves, Green provides brief professional biographies of actors and actresses, composers, lyricists, librettists, directors, choreographers, and producers (over 600 people in all). . . . Finally, the entries contain brief descriptions of over 1,000 songs from musicals. . . ."

590. Kinkle, Roger D. **The Complete Encyclopedia of Popular Music and Jazz, 1900-1950.** Arlington, 1974. 4v.
Widely and favorably reviewed, this important set covers popular music events chronologically in v. 1, biographies in v. 2 and 3 (with representative discographies), and a major discography from the 1920s to the 1940s in v. 4. There are indexes to personal names, song titles, and musicals.

591. Stambler, Irwin, and Grelun Landon. **Encyclopedia of Folk, Country and Western Music.** St. Martin's, 1969. 396p.
Most of the 500 alphabetically arranged entries are devoted to biographies, but there are also definitions of terms, descriptions of instruments, special events, etc. Appended are a list of awards, a discography of the most popular long playing albums, and a bibliography. There are some photographs. The cross references are adequate. Unlike Stambler's work, *The Country Music Encyclopedia*, by Melvin Shestack (Crowell, 1974)

is limited in coverage to the top stars. The style is informal, and entries for some stars are longer than in Stambler's more factual book.

592. Stambler, Irwin. **Encyclopedia of Pop, Rock and Soul.** St. Martin's, 1975; repr., 1977. 609p.

This book updates and supplements, but does not supersede, Stambler's *Encyclopedia of Popular Music* (St. Martin's, 1965). Several reviewers consider it to be the best, most comprehensive of the various such books now available. The paperback reprint contains some minor updating of the hardcover edition. There are approximately 500 entries on such topics as performers, groups, producers, terms, instruments, and musical styles. Appendices include lists of awards like RIAA Gold Records and Oscar and Grammy winners. *The Illustrated Encyclopedia of Rock*, by Nick Logan and Bob Woffinden (Crown, 1977), concentrates most heavily on individual performers and groups, but also includes producers, executives, etc. American reviewers have occasionally questioned some of the choices of the British editors, but they have noted its usefulness for locating information on obscure groups. There are cross references and an index. A larger number of brief entries on stars and groups (with selective discographies) will be found in Norm N. Nite's *Rock On: The Illustrated Encyclopedia of Rock and Roll*, of which two volumes have appeared: *The Solid Gold Years* (Crowell, 1974) and *The Modern Years to the Present* (Crowell, 1978). Lillian Roxon's *Rock Encyclopedia* (2nd ed., Grosset, 1974) is a highly personal evaluation of individuals and groups, with definitions of terms, and record listings. For an overview of this area, see "State of the Art Survey of Reference Sources in Pop, Rock and Jazz," by David D. Ginsberg [*Reference Services Review* 6 (July/September 1978):5-16].

593. Stieger, Franz. **Opernlexikon/Opera Catalogue/Lexique des operas/Dizionario operistico.** . . .mit e. Einf. von Franz Grasberger. Schneider, 1975- . 4v.

This major operatic dictionary has introductions in German, English, French, and Italian. Bibliographic references are included. Contents: v. 1—*Titelkatalog*; v. 2—*Komponisten*; v. 3—*Librettisten*; v. 4—*Nachtrage. Crowell's Handbook of World Opera*, by Frank Ledlie Moore (Crowell; repr., Greenwood, 1974) provides brief information on individual operas, operatic characters, famous numbers, and performers as well as a chronology of major operas and a glossary. There are indexes of singers by voice ranges. David Ewen's *The New Encyclopedia of the Opera* (Hill and Wang, 1971) places stories, characters, biographies, opera houses, etc. in one alphabetical sequence. *The Concise Oxford Dictionary of Opera*, edited by Harold Rosenthal and John Warrak (2nd ed., Oxford, 1979), is an excellent first source for brief treatment of operas, composers, performers and operatic terms.

Specific Musical Compositions

Thematic Dictionaries

594. Barlow, Harold A., and Sam Morgenstern. **Dictionary of Musical Themes.** Crown, 1975; repr., Benn, 1978. 642p.

This vital work is often called the "Bartlett" of musical themes. It contains some 10,000 themes of instrumental music arranged by composers and titles, with a notation index arranged alphabetically by the first notes of the themes and an index of titles. One must know how to read music and transpose themes to the key of C in order to use the notation index. *The Directory of Tunes and Musical Themes*, a new book by Denys Parsons (see item 597), is easier for the layperson to use. *Concerto Themes*, by Raymond Murdock Burrows and Bessie Carroll Redmond (Simon and Schuster, 1951), is arranged alphabetically by composer, with an index of concerto titles, keys, and solo instruments. There is no thematic index. It contains more concertos than Barlow's *Dictionary of Musical Themes. Symphony Themes*, also by Burrows and Redmond (Simon and Schuster, 1942), includes the major themes of 100 great symphonies, with a list of recommended recordings and a chart of performance times. It has lists of instruments, a bibliography, and an index by keys and by titles of symphonies.

595. Barlow, Harold A., and Sam Morgenstern. **A Dictionary of Opera and Song Themes, Including Cantatas, Oratorios, Lieder, and Art Songs.** Rev. ed. Crown, 1976. 547p.
Originally published under title *A Dictionary of Vocal Themes* (1950), this is a companion volume to *Dictionary of Musical Themes*. It includes themes from operas, oratorios, cantatas, art songs, and miscellaneous vocal works. There is a notation index and an index to songs and first lines.

596. Brook, Barry S. **Thematic Catalogues in Music: An Annotated Bibliography.** Pendragon Press, 1972.
The most comprehensive treatment of the subject to date is provided by this work, published under the sponsorship of the Music Library Association and RILM/Abstracts of Music Literature. It supersedes the Music Library Association's *Checklist of Thematic Catalogues* (1954) and the *Queens College Supplement* (1966).

597. Parsons, Denys. **The Directory of Tunes and Musical Themes.** Spencer Brown, 1975. 288p.
This work is easier for the layperson to use than Barlow's *Dictionary of Musical Themes* (see item 594), because the ability to read music is not required. For a detailed description of this significant new index and comparisons with Barlow and Morgenstern, see "Breaking the Sound Barrier with a Hummingbird's Index to Musical Themes," by Harry C. Bauer [*RQ* 18 (Winter 1978):156-59].

Plots

598. Kobbé, Gustave. **The Complete Opera Book,** ed. and rev. by the Earl of Harewood. 9th ed. Putnam, 1976. 1694p.
This standard work discusses development of the opera and includes the stories of more than 200 operas. Brief notes on composers and musical motifs are also given. It includes older works still being produced and modern works not yet popular but thought likely to become so. It is the most complete general guide available. Other books worth noting include *Opera Themes and Plots*, by Rudolf Fellner (Simon and Schuster, 1958), *Operas and Musical Comedies*, by Joseph McSpadden (enl. ed., Crowell, 1954), and *The Victor Book of Overtures, Tone Poems and Other Orchestral Works* (Simon and Schuster, 1950). Plot summaries will also be found in *A Thousand and One Nights of Opera*, by Frederick Martens (Appleton, 1926; repr., Da Capo, 1978), *A Companion to the Opera*, by Robin May (Hippocrene, 1977) and *The Encyclopedia of Opera*, edited by Leslie Orrey (Scribner, 1975).

Program Notes

599. Tovey, Donald F. **Essays in Musical Analysis.** Oxford, 1935-39; repr., 1972. 6v. Contents: v. I — *Symphonies*; v. II — *Symphonies, Variations and Orchestral Polyphony*; v. III — *Concertos*; v. IV — *Illustrative Music*; v. V — *Vocal Music*; v. VI — *Supplementary Essays, Glossary, and Index*. This standard older work is still the most useful source. Other works that may aid in the search for the "program notes" type of information include *The Complete book of Twentieth Century Music*, by David Ewen (2nd ed., Prentice-Hall, 1959), *The Victor Book of Symphonies*, by Charles O'Connell (Simon and Schuster, 1948), *The Victor Book of Concertos*, by Abraham Veinus (Simon and Schuster, 1948), and *Index to Symphonic Program Notes in Books*, by Anna Tipton Voorhees (Kent State University School of Library Science, 1970).

Directories and Annuals

600. Benton, Rita, ed. **Directory of Music Research Libraries, Including Contributors to the International Inventory of Musical Sources (RISM).** University of Iowa, 1967- .
Part I covers music research libraries in the United States and Canada and was issued in 1967. Part II, issued in 1970, covers 13 European countries (784 libraries). Part III (1972) covers spain, France, Italy and Portugal. For each library are given address, type and size of collection, and lending code service. Indexes are arranged by country and, within that, alphabetically. Indexes include entries by present and former names of libraries, parent institutions, donors, etc. This is intended to be used with *Répertoire Internationale des Sources Musicales (RISM)/International Inventory of Musical Sources* (see item 523). *Music in British Libraries: A Directory of Resources*, by Maureen Long (2nd ed., Library Association, 1974), provides additional coverage for the United Kingdom. A more specialized source that should not be overlooked is *International Directory of Musical Instruments Collections*, edited by Jean Jenkins (Frits Knuf, 1977).

601. **British Music Yearbook**, 1973- . Bowker.
Formerly entitled *The Music Yearbook*, this annual publication covers concert, opera, radio, and television performances, with information on débuts, first nights, and foreign artists. There are reports on jazz, rock, blues, new recordings, and musicals. Directories of performers, associations, concert and rehearsal halls, music publishers, critics, festivals, and competitions are also included. *The International Music Guide* (Barnes, 1976-) is less complete. *Hinrichsen's Musical Yearbook* has not appeared since 1961.

602. Brody, Elaine, and Claire Brook. **Music Guides to Europe.** Dodd, Mead, 1975- .
Although neither the publisher nor LC lists these guides as a series, it seems more appropriate in this context to assign a series title because all six of the books are planned to follow a standard pattern, with information on such topics as "Opera Houses and concert Halls," "Libraries and Museums," "Conservatories and Schools," "Musical Landmarks," "Musical Organizations," and "Business of Music." Information about festivals, competitions, and periodicals is also included. Titles published to date are:

The Music Guide to Austria and Germany (1975); *The Music Guide to Great Britain* (1975); *The Music Guide to Belgium, Luxembourg, Holland and Switzerland* (1977); *The Music Guide to Italy* (1978).

603.　**Directory of Music Faculties in Colleges and Universities, U.S. and Canada.** College Music Society, 1967/68- .

The title varies. From 1967-68 to 1970-72, it was *Directory of Music Faculties in American Colleges and Universities*. It consists of three parts: 1. Directory of Departments of Music; 2. Directory of Areas of Interest; 3. National Alphabetical Listing. Because it is computer produced, the data bank can be used for searches, address labels, etc. Another source to be considered is the *Directory* of the National Association of Schools of Music (NASM, 1976).

604.　Pavlakis, Christopher. **The American Music Handbook.** Free Press, 1974. 836p.

Coverage includes organizations, instrumental ensembles, vocal ensembles, music and the stage, performers, composers, music festivals, contests and awards, music and education, radio and television, music industries, periodicals, and concert managers.

605.　Phillips, Don. **Directory of Music Librarians in the United States and Canada.** Music Library Association, 1976. 46p.

This preliminary edition includes about 600 music librarians.

606.　Sandberg, Larry, and Dick Weissman. **Folk Music Sourcebook.** Knopf, 1976. 260p.

This directory covers North American folk music in English and is divided into four main sections: 1. Listening—an annotated listing of records, with addresses of companies; 2. Learning—scholarly and instructional books; 3. Playing—folk instruments, where to buy them and how to care for them; 4. Hanging Out—organizations, serial publications, films and videotapes. A glossary and an excellent index help make this a superb reference work.

607.　**Songwriters Market,** 1979- . Ann. Writer's Digest.

This directory covers popular song buyers and publishers. It also includes information about grants, agencies, festivals, and reference books.

Histories

General

608.　Grout, Donald Jay. **A History of Western Music.** Rev. ed. W. W. Norton, 1973. 818p.

A survey intended as a text for music students or for general readers, it contains a glossary, a bibliography, and a music chronology, as well as numerous illustrations. There is a title, subject, and name index. Less useful than a conventional history, in the judgment of most reviewers and reference librarians, is Paul Eisler's *World Chronology of Music History* (Oceana, 1972-). Projected to run to 8 or 10 volumes, it may have a place in some large, specialized collections. Volumes to date include: v. 1—*3,000 B.C.-1594 A.D.*; v. 2—*1594-1684*; v. 3—*1685-1735*; v. 4—*Name Index* (to v. 1-3).

609.   Lang, Paul Henry. **Music in Western Civilization.** W. W. Norton, 1941; repr., 1969.
This major work, which has been translated into several foreign languages, sets music in its social, political, and cultural context. The author has provided a multilingual, alphabetical bibliography, pp. 1045-1065.

610.   **New Oxford History of Music.** Oxford, 1954- .
This major set is a vital reference tool. Contents to date include: v. 1 — *Ancient and Oriental Music*, edited by Egon Wellesz, 1957; v. 2 — *Early Medieval Music up to 1300*, edited by Dom Anselm Hughes, 1954; v. 3 — *Ars Nova and the Renaissance, 1300-1540*, edited by Dom Anselm Hughes and Gerald Abraham, 1960; v. 4 — *The Age of Humanism, 1540-1630*, edited by Gerald Abraham, 1968; v. 5 — *Opera and Church Music, 1630-1750*, edited by Nigel Fortune and Anthony Lewis, 1975; v. 7 — *The Age of Enlightenment, 1740-1790*, edited by Jack A. Westrup and others, 1973; v. 10 — *The Modern Age, 1890-1960*, edited by Jack A. Westrup and Martin Cooper, 1974. Other titles (including a final volume with chronological tables and an index) are planned.

611.   **The Norton History of Music Series.** W. W. Norton, 1940- .
Written by distinguished music historians, the individual volumes in this series deal with specific periods. Taken as a group, they constitute a history of music from the earliest times to the present: Curt Sachs, *The Rise of Music in the Ancient World: East and West*, 1943; Gustave Reese, *Music in the Middle Ages, 1940*; Gustave Reese, *Music in the Renaissance*, rev. ed., 1959; Manfred F. Bukofzer, *Music in the Baroque Era: From Monteverdi to Bach*, 1947; Alfred Einstein, *Music in the Romantic Era*, 1947; Adolfo Salazar, *Music in Our Time: Trends in Music since the Romantic Era*, 1946; William W. Austin, *Music in the Twentieth Century: From Debussy through Stravinsky*, 1966.

612.   **Prentice-Hall History of Music Series.** Prentice-Hall, 1965-69. 9v.
LC catalogs and classifies these volumes separately. For a list, consult Eleanor A. Baer's *Titles in Series* and its supplements.

613.   Slonimsky, Nicholas. **Music since 1900.** 4th ed. Scribners, 1971. 1595p.
Contents: Tabular views of stylistic trends in music; Descriptive chronology; Letters and documents. David Ewen's *The World of Twentieth Century Music* (Prentice-Hall, 1968) may also be useful.

Special Topics and Countries

614.   Apel, Willi. **The History of Keyboard Music to 1700.** Tr. and rev. by Hans Tischler. Indiana University Press, 1972. 878p.
This standard scholarly work, by the editor of the *Harvard Dictionary of Music*, is arranged by forms and countries. In his review for *ARBA 1974* (p. 372), Guy A. Marco described the work as follows: "There are 871 musical examples, most of them long enough — six to eight measures — to give a good impression of the music. In addition to an index of names, there is a very useful title index — prepared by the translator — which coves all pieces cited in the text. Because composers' names are given for entries in the title index, this index will serve as a valuable identification aid in its own right."

615. Grout, Donald Jay. **A Short History of Opera.** 2nd ed. Columbia, 1965. 852p.
This valuable reference history is divided into five parts, each covering a century from the sixteenth to the twentieth (to 1960). There is a long bibliography (pp. 585-786) arranged by chapters. Appendices cover modern versions or excerpts from operas before 1800 and sources of examples and translations.

616. Howard, John Tasker. **Our American Music: A Comprehensive History from 1620 to the Present.** 4th ed. Crowell, 1965. 944p.
This standard and very detailed history has an extensive bibliography (pp. 769-845). Major composers receive extended treatment. There are numerous illustrations. The index (pp. 847-944) includes titles of compositions if at all distinctive. More specialized in focus are *American Musical Theater: A Chronicle*, by Gerald Bordman (Oxford, 1978); *All the Years of American Popular Music*, by David Ewen (Prentice-Hall, 1977); and Kate H. Mueller's *Twenty-seven Major American Symphony Orchestras: A History and Analysis of Their Repertoires, Seasons 1842-43 through 1969-70* (Indiana University Press, 1973).

617. Humphries, Charles, and William C. Smith. **Music Publishing in the British Isles from the Earliest Times to the Middle of the 19th Century.** 2nd ed. Blackwell, 1970. 392p.
Subtitle: "A dictionary of engravers, printers, publishers and music sellers, with a historical introduction." This standard work is essential for dating. It includes a dictionary section, a general bibliography, an index of firms outside London, and a list of instrument makers and repairers.

618. Kinsky, Georg. **A History of Music in Pictures.** Dent, 1930; repr., Dover, 1951. 363p.
This collection of approximately 1,500 illustrations—portraits, instruments, facsimiles, etc.—forms a valuable pictorial history of music from the earliest times to the present. The pictures are most important and the text is brief: 1. Explanatory note for each picture; 2. Indexes and tables of contents; 3. Introduction and foreword. Three editions (German, French, English) were published in 1930. Detailed coverage may be found in *Musikgeschichte in Bildern*, edited by H. Bessler and M. Schneider (VEB Deutscher Verlag fur Musik, 1961-).

619. Loewenberg, Alfred. **Annals of Opera, 1597-1940.** 2nd ed. Societas Bibliographica, 1955; repr., Scholarly Press, 1971. 2v.
The text is in v. 1 and the indexes are in v. 2. Nearly 4,000 operas are listed, arranged chronologically by date of first performance, then followed by name of composer and title of opera (given in original language), name of town where first performed, (sometimes) name of theater, and history of performances. References to translations, revivals, etc. are also given. There are four indexes: 1. Operas; 2. Composers, with dates of birth and death, giving names of operas by each, with dates; 3. Librettists; 4. General index. More limited in scope, but equally vital, is William H. Seltsam's *Metropolitan Opera Annals: A Chronicle of Artists and Performances* (Wilson, 1947; Suppl., 1957), which is a chronological record of the casts of the operas performed from the first season in 1883-84. It also gives excerpts from press reviews for each season, especially those covering important débuts and first performances. The work is profusely illustrated with photographs of leading singers in typical roles. The index traces all references to artists, performances, reviews, and portraits.

620.   Sachs, Curt. **The History of Musical Instruments.** W. W. Norton, 1940; repr., 1968. 505p.
This scholarly history is divided into four parts: The Primitive and Prehistoric Epoch; Antiquity; The Middle Ages; The Modern Occident. A glossary (pp. 454-67), a bibliography (pp. 469-87), and an index (pp. 489-505) are provided. *Ancient European Musical Instruments*, by Nicholas Bessaraboff (Harvard, 1941; repr., October House, 1964) is an authoritative historical study with excellent illustrations. It includes a useful bibliography of books about musical instruments and catalogs of collections.

621.   Strunk, William Oliver, ed. **Source Readings in Music History.** W. W. Norton, 1965. 5v.
Writings of composers and theorists from ancient times are included, translated into English where necessary. Most are abstracts.

Anthologies

622.   Davison, Archibald Thompson. **Historical Anthology of Music.** Harvard, 1946-50; repr., 1962. 2v.
Contents: v. 1 — *Oriental, Medieval and Renaissance Music*; v. 2 — *Baroque, Rococo and Pre-classical Music*. Davison and Willi Apel have also edited a series of sound recordings entitled *Historical Anthology of Music in Performance* (Pleiades Records, 1969-). *Medieval Music*, by W. Thomas Marrocco and Nicholos Sandon (Oxford, 1979), has two records to accompany the book and is part of the Oxford Anthology of Music.

623.   Haywood, Charles, ed. **Folk Songs of the World.** Day, 1966. 320p.
Recommended by reviewers for reference work and music appreciation classes, this book is well described by its subtitle: "Gathered from more than one hundred countries, selected and edited with commentary on their musical cultures and descriptive notes on each song; in the original languages with English translations, and with chord suggestions for instrumental accompaniment; drawings by Carl Smith."

624.   Lang, Paul Henry, ed. **The Symphony 1800-1900: A Norton Music Anthology.** W. W. Norton, 1969. 873p.
Selections from Beethoven, Berlioz, Brahms, Bruckner, Dvorak, Mendelssohn, Schuman, Tchaikovsky are clearly reproduced in this useful anthology, edited by a professor of musicology at Columbia University. It is recommended for circulation as well as reference. Lang has prepared a companion volume entitled *The Concerto 1800-1900: A Norton Music Anthology* (W. W. Norton, 1969).

625.   Marrocco, William Thomas, and Harold Gleason, eds. **Music in America.** W. W. Norton, 1964. 371p.
The subtitle of this very useful source gives a good description: "An anthology from the landing of the pilgrims to the close of the Civil War, 1620-1865. Compiled and edited, with historical and analytical notes, by Thomas Marrocco and Harold Gleason."

626.   Miller, Philip Lieson. **The Ring of Words: An Anthology of Song Texts.** W. W. Norton, 1973. 518p.
This useful work includes German, French, Italian, Spanish, Russian, Norwegian, and Swedish songs, with English translations and introduction by Miller. More specialized is

The Oxford Book of English Madrigals, edited by Philip Ledger (Oxford, 1979), which includes sixty songs by seventeen composers from the late sixteenth and early seventeenth centuries. The critical commentary by Andrew Parker will aid in verification of texts. A two-record set of 35 of the madrigals sung by Pro Cantione Antiqua has been prepared as an Oxford Recording to accompany the book.

627.   Parrish, Carl. **Masterpieces of Music before 1750.** W. W. Norton, 1951. 235p.
To accompany this anthology, which has become a vital reference tool, Parrish prepared a phonodisc (with historical and analytical notes, with which he was assisted by John F. Ohl), *Masterpieces of Music before 1750: An Anthology of Musical Examples from Gregorian Chant to J. S. Bach* (Haydn Society Records, 1953).

628.   Parrish, Carl. **A Treasury of Early Music.** W. W. Norton, 1958. 331p.
To accompany this book, Parrish edited a phonodisc entitled *A Treasury of Early Music: An Anthology of Masterworks of the Middle Ages, the Renaissance, and the Baroque* (Haydn Society Records, 1964).

629.   Shaw, Martin, Henry Coleman, and T. M. Cartledge, eds. **National Anthems of the World.** 4th ed. Arco, 1976. 477p.
The new edition includes a total of 166 national anthems, with original texts, English translations, and piano accompaniments.

Biographies

630.   American Society of Composers, Authors and Publishers. **The ASCAP Biographical Dictionary of Composers, Authors and Publishers.** 3rd ed. ASCAP, 1966. 845p.
Biographical sketches of composers and lyricists, the majority of whom are writers of popular music, are included, as well as a list of publishers of works of ASCAP members.

631.   Anderson, E. Ruth, comp. **Contemporary American Composers: A Biographical Dictionary.** G. K. Hall, 1976. 513p.
Between 4,000 and 5,000 composers who were born after 1870 and have had at least one work published, recorded, performed or been given an award in the United States are included. Some omissions and inaccuracies have been noted by reviewers (e.g., see *ARBA 1977*, p. 466), but there is general agreement on its usefulness for minor composers. An appendix lists women composers. By contrast, only the most successful are included in Warren Craig's *Sweet and Lowdown: America's Popular Song Writers* (Scarecrow, 1978). The biographical entries include lists of songs by year. Appendices cover comparative rankings, and there are indexes of song titles, productions, and names. A highly reliable source of information on 332 serious composers (1915-1947) is *Composers in America*, by Claire Reis (Macmillan, 1947; repr., Da Capo, 1977).

632.   Baker, Theodore. **Baker's Biographical Dictionary of Musicians.** 6th ed. Completely revised by Nicholas Slonimsky. Schirmer, 1978. 1955p.
This useful, reliable dictionary gives compact biographies (varying from a few lines to several pages) of musicians of all periods and countries, with bibliographies of the musicians' own works and books about them. Pronunciation of foreign names is indicated.

633. Bull, Storm. **Index to Biographies of Contemporary Composers.** Scarecrow, 1964-74. 2v.
Indexes 177 sources containing biographical information on nearly 10,000 composers who are now living, or who were born in 1900 or later, or, if deceased, who died after 1949. An extremely useful shortcut when in doubt about where to turn for contemporary composers.

634. Eitner, Robert. **Biographisch-bibliographisches Quellen-Lexikon der Musiker and Musikgelehrten der christlichen Zeitrechnung bis zur Mitte des 19. Jahrhunderts.** Breitkopf und Hartel, 1900-1904; repr., Akademische Druck und Verlagsanstalt, 1959. 10v. v. 11: *Nachträge und Miscellanea.* Graz, 1960.
Long a major location tool for biographies and music sources from the beginning of the Christian era to the middle of the nineteenth century, this classic work is gradually being superseded by *Répertoire internationale des sources musicales (RISM)* (see item 523).

635. Gilder, Eric, and June G. Port. **The Dictionary of Composers and Their Music: Every Listener's Companion, Arranged Chronologically and Alphabetically.** Paddington, 1978. 406p.
The arrangement of this book makes it complementary in access despite its duplication of information found in many standard sources. The first part is alphabetical, with very brief biographical information about 275 composers and lists of their works. The second part is a chronological survey from 1554 to 1975, giving important musical events and compositions for each year. The third part is a time line that shows which composers were living when. In *The Dictionary of Composers* (Taplinger, 1978), Charles Osborne and 26 specialists have compiled biographies of 175 composers whose works are likely to be performed in concert halls and opera houses. The biographies are interestingly written and well illustrated. However, most of the factual information can be found in other sources. Similar "human interest" writing, accompanied by similar duplication and some errors, tends to characterize the numerous works by David Ewen, like *Composers of Tomorrow's Music* (Dodd, Mead, 1971), *Composers since 1900* (Wilson, 1969), *Great Men of American Popular Song* (Prentice-Hall, 1972), and *Musicians since 1900* (Wilson, 1978). A more specialized popularization (based on a series of radio talks) is *Great Pianists of Our Time*, by Joachim Kaiser (Herder, 1971).

636. Hixon, Don L., and Don Hennessee. **Women in Music: A Bibliography.** Scarecrow, 1975. 358p.
The subtitle is misleading. This work is actually an index to 48 standard sources of biographical information. Richard A. Gray (*ARBA 1976*, p. 479) summed up its value and weakness in these words: "The idea that inspired this volume is good – hitherto there has been no reference source that identified musicians by sex – but its execution is deficient." More limited in scope is *Women Composers: A Handbook*, by Susan Stern (Scarecrow, 1978), which includes about 1,500 women composers from the sixteenth century to the present. Brief biographical information is provided, along with references to other sources.

637. **International Who's Who in Music and Musicians' Directory**, ed. by Adrian Gaster. 8th ed. Melrose; Gale, 1977. 1178p.
Continuing *Who's Who in Music and Musicians' International Directory*, this British publication provides biographical sketches of a large number of living musicians. Lists of publishers, journals, festivals, organizations, etc. are also included.

638. Kutsch, K. J., and Leo Riemans. **A Concise Biographical Dictionary of Singers: From the Beginning of Recorded Sound to the Present.** Chilton, 1969. 487p.
This collection of brief biographies of singers of opera and classical music who made phonograph recordings lists many singers not found in other standard sources and gives at least one recording label per singer.

639. Langwill, Lyndesay G. **An Index of Musical Wind-Instrument Makers.** Heinman, 1975. 272p.
Brief information on about 5,000 instrument makers is given in the alphabetical main section. There are also lists of instrument makers under places of residence and of marks when the place is not known.

640. Lawless, Ray McKinley. **Folksingers and Folksongs in America: A Handbook of Biography, Bibliography, and Discography.** Rev. ed. Duell, 1965; repr., Meredith, 1968. 750p.
Biographical sketches of singers and an annotated bibliography of collections of folk songs are provided as well as checklists of titles and discography, and chapters on instruments, societies, and festivals. There are indexes of names, titles, and subjects.

641. Pulver, Jeffrey. **Biographical Dictionary of Old English Music.** Dutton, 1927; repr., Da Capo, 1973. 537p.
Pulver covered English musicians from about 1200 to the death of Purcell in 1695, citing manuscripts, contemporary publications, and some modern ones. The reprint contains a new introduction as well as a bibliography of the writings of Jeffrey Pulver (by Gilbert Blount).

642. Vodarsky-Shiraeff, Alexandrea. **Russian Composers and Musicians; A Biographical Dictionary.** Wilson, 1940; repr., Greenwood, 1969. 158p.
Composers, performers, teachers, and critics are included, with classified lists of major works. Variant spellings of Russian names are cross-referenced. David Moldon's *A Bibliography of Russian Composers* (Rowman and Littlefield, 1977) begins with a section of general works and then proceeds to the main part, which is arranged alphabetically by composers (subdivided into general studies and specific compositions). Only works in English (books and journals to the early 1970s) are included. These are two indexes (authors, editors, and compilers; and translators and illustrators).

643. **Who's Who in Opera: An International Biographical Directory of Singers, Conductors, Directors, Designers and Administrators, Also Including Profiles of 101 Opera Companies,** ed. by Maria F. Rich. Arno Press, 1976. 684p.
This excellent work provides detailed biographical information on 2,300 artists from 144 opera companies. Criteria for inclusion are carefully defined in the introduction. The compiler served as editor of *Central Opera Service Bulletin* for ten years preceding publication of this book. The profiles of 101 opera companies are given in a separate section. Budgets, repertories, and information on the two seasons preceding compilation are provided. There is also a directory of international agents, with addresses.

644. York, William, comp. and ed. **Who's Who in Rock Music.** Atomic Press, 1978. 260p.
Brief career information on 7,000 individuals in the rock field is provided. The jackets of record albums served as primary information sources. Many minor artists not found elsewhere are included here.

Music Education

645. Boyden, David Dodge. **An Introduction to Music.** 2nd ed. Knopf, 1970. 554p. Written by a former chairman of the Department of Music, University of California at Berkeley, this college textbook is designed to offer the teacher of a beginning course a variety of alternatives. Topics covered include: elements, structure, aesthetics, perform-ance, history, repertory, and suggestions for study and listening. Other useful books for music teachers include James Mursell's *Music Education: Principles and Programs* (Silver, Burdett, 1956), Dominique-René de Lerma's *Black Music in Our Culture: Curricular Ideas on the Subjects, Materials and Problems* (Kent State University Press, 1970), and Peter Dykema and Hannah Cundiff's *School Music Handbook: A Guide for Music Educators* (rev. ed., Birchard, 1955; University Microfilms, 1968). *Teacher Education in Music* (Music Educators' National Conference, 1972) and *Selected Instructional Programs in Music* (MENC, 1977) should not be overlooked.

646. Goodman, A. Harold. **Instrumental Music Guide.** Brigham Young University Press, 1977. 240p.
Intended as a guide for teachers and music directors, this work includes annotated sec-tions for bands and school orchestras, arranged by grade levels and historical periods, noting special features and levels of difficulty. Other sections (mostly unannotated and arranged by levels of difficulty) include: chamber ensembles, college and community orchestras, instrumental solos, studies, and group methods. A bibliography and a sec-tion with brief information about composers and major publishers are also included. Stanley Butler's *Guide to the Best in Contemporary Piano Music* (Scarecrow, 1973, 2v.) is an annotated list from 1950, with grades 1-5 covered in v. 1 and grades 6-8 covered in v. 2.

647. Kagen, Sergius. **Music for the Voice: A Descriptive List of Concert and Teaching Material.** Rev. ed. Indiana University Press, 1968. 780p.
Originally published in 1949, and revised by the author before his death in 1964, this work does not include every song, but represents as many composers as space permits. Information for each title includes: range of song, type of voice, descriptive remarks. References to preferred editions are given. There is no title index, but this book is necessary for any music collection.

648. Music Educators' National Conference. **Selective Music Lists.** Music Educators' National Conference, 1968- .
Various lists are issued from time to time. A selection (with dates) follows: *Vocal Solos, Vocal Ensembles* (1974); *Band Music Guide* (1975); *Woodwind Solo and Study Material Guide* (1975); *Brass Solo and Study Material Guide* (1976); and *Full Orchestra, String Orchestra* (1978).

649. Music Educators' National Conference. Committee on Bibliography of Research Projects Theses. **Bibliography of Research Studies in Music Education, 1932-48.** MENC, 1949. 119p. Suppl. 1949-56. 1957.

The main work has about 1,600 titles and the supplement, 350. This bibliography is continued by "Doctoral Dissertations in Music and Music Education," which appears from time to time in the *Journal of Research in Music Education*. The years covered (with date of publication in parentheses) are as follows: 1957-63 (1964); 1963-67 (1968); 1968-71 (1972); 1972-77 (1978). Dissertations from the 1890s through 1973 may also be located in Rita H. Mead's *Dissertations in American Music: A Classified Bibliography* (Institute for Studies in American Music, Brooklyn College, 1974). Another source for checking is *Doctoral Dissertations in Musicology*. The first (1952) through fifth (1971) editions had various editors and were the result of collaboration between the Music Teacher's National Association and the American Musicological Society. Beginning in 1977, these have been issued as a part of the *International Index of Dissertations and Musicological Works in Progress* (American Musicological Society), which is cumulated from issues of *Acta Musicologica* (see item 665).

Recordings

650. **Annual Index to Popular Music Record Reviews**, 1972- . Ann. Scarecrow.
Edited by Andrew D. Armitage and Dean Tudor, this useful source includes reviews from such diverse periodicals as *Crawdaddy* and *Ethnomusicology*.

651. Bauer, Robert. **The New Catalogue of Historical Records, 1898-1908-09.** 2nd ed. Sedgwick and Jackson, 1947; repr., Greenwood. 494p.
Recordings are listed under performers, with brief entries for composers and titles. More specialized is James Creighton's *Discopaedia of the Violin, 1889-1971* (University of Toronto Press, 1974). Another specialized source is *Medieval and Renaissance Music on Long-Playing Records*, by James B. Coover and Richard Colvig (Information Service, 1974; Suppl. 1962-71, 1973).

652. **The Classical Record Catalogue and Recommended Recordings**, 1953- . Q. The Gramophone.
Selections are made by the editors of a highly-respected British periodical.

653. Cooper, David E. **International Bibliography of Discographies.** Libraries Unlimited, 1975. 272p.
The scope of this useful book is defined by the subtitle: "Classical music and jazz and blues, 1962-1972: A reference book for record collectors, dealers, and libraries."

654. Clough, Francis F., and G. J. Cuming. **The World's Encyclopaedia of Recorded Music.** 2nd ed. Ambassador, 1966; repr., Greenwood, 1970. 890p.
This comprehensive list of recorded music to the date of publication has very detailed information and a convenient arrangement.

655. **Consumers Union Reviews Classical Recordings**, by CU's Musical Consultant and the Editors of Consumer Reports. Bobbs-Merrill, 1973. 376p.
Record reviews from the past 10 years of *Consumer Reports* are included. Reviews are unsigned. The basic arrangement is by composers, with cross references from performers, conductors, and orchestras. There are 358 reviews plus a basic discography of 500 selections.

656.   Gray, Michael H., and Gerald Gibson. **Bibliography of Discographies**, 1977- .
Bowker.
Contents: v. 1—*Classical Music, 1925-1975* (1977). Other volumes planned will cover
jazz (2), popular music (3), ethnic and folk music (4), and general discographies (5).

657.   Halsey, Richard S. **Classical Music Recordings for Home and Library.** ALA,
1976. 340p.
For collection developers and music program planners, this work opens with explanatory information. The major section is occupied with record listings (double asterisked
if the reviews were especially good), followed by chapters on: reviews; buying sound
recordings; classification, cataloging, and care of sound recordings; and equipment and
environments for listening. A glossary of audio terms is included. There are two
indexes: title index to composer; subject, proper name, and composer. A more
specialized work is *Opera Recordings: A Critical Guide*, by Kenn Harris (Drake, 1973).

658.   Jepsen, Jorgen Grunnet, ed. **Jazz Records, 1942-1965 — 1942-1969: A
Discography.** K. E. Knudsen, 1963-1970. 8v. in 11.
This is a major compilation, highly regarded by music librarians. For the preceding
period, consult Brian Rust's *Jazz Records, 1897-1942* (4th ed., Arlington, 1978, 2v.).
Coverage (excluding jazz, blues and dance bands) can be found in *The Complete Entertainment Discography, from the Mid-1890's to 1942*, by Brian Rust and Allen G. Debus
(Arlington, 1973). Rust has also compiled *The American Dance Band Discography,
1917-1942* (Arlington, 1976, 2v.). Michael L. Pitts and Louis H. Harrison have
prepared **Hollywood on Record: The Film Stars Discography** (Scarecrow, 1978).

659.   **Katalog der schallplatten Klassischer Musik**, 1953- . S-Ann. Bielefelder
Verlagsanstalt KG.
This vital German work lists a smaller number of records than Schwann (see item 665),
but it includes many classical records not listed by Schwann. The main entries are under
composers, with complete analytics and selective cross references. New releases are indicated by dots preceding the entries. Artist listings are also included. Other foreign
listings that may occasionally be useful include *Harmonie* (French), *Santandnea*
(Italian) and Celleti's *Il teatro d'opera in disco* (Italian).

660.   Merriam, Alan P. **African Music on LP: An Annotated Discography.** Northwestern University Press, 1970. 200p.
There are 389 numbered main entries, arranged by recording companies. These are
followed by 18 indexes, based on such things as album titles, performing groups,
stylistic characteristics, tribal groupings, song titles, etc. A more recent work is Patricia
Turner's *Afro-American Singers: An Index and Preliminary Discography of Long-
playing Recordings of Opera, Choral Music and Song* (Challenge Productions, 1977).
Black Music, by Dean and N. Tudor (Libraries Unlimited, 1978) annotates 1,300 items
available on LP and stars 220 "first purchase" albums.

661.   Myers, Kurtz, and Richard S. Hill. **Record Ratings: The Music Library Association's Index of Record Reviews.** Crown, 1956. 440p.
This cumulation of "Index of Record Reviews" originally appearing in quarterly issues
of *Notes* lists each release with complete information, and gives references to reviews in
28 reviewing media. It is in two parts: 1. composer and subject; 2. composite releases. A
performer index is included. A new edition is in preparation.

662. Osborne, Jerry. **Popular & Rock Records, 1948-1978.** 2nd ed. O'Sullivan, Woodside, 1978. 252p.

Formerly entitled *The Record Collector's Price Guide* (1976), this new edition includes 30,000 listings of 45 rpms and selected 78s, arranged by performer or group. Prices for "good" to "very good" and "mint" conditions are given. Prefatory material gives advice about collecting. A glossary of terms and a directory of dealers (by states, then surnames) appear at the end. Stewart Goldstein and Alan Jacobson have compiled *Oldies but Goodies: The Rock and Roll Years* (Mason/Chester, 1977). Jerry Osborne's *33 1/3 & 45 Extended Play Record Album Price Guide* (O'Sullivan, Woodside, 1977) includes rock, musical comedy, and movie sound tracks. Two additional price guides were announced for 1979: *Jazz/Big Band Price Guide* and *Rhythm/Blues Price Guide*. David Dalton's *Rock 100* (Grosset, 1977) should not be overlooked. Some historical coverage is found in Jerry Osborne's *55 Years of Recorded Country/Western Music* (O'Sullivan, Woodside, 1976) and *Blues and Gospel Records, 1902-1942*, by John Godrich and Robert M. W. Dixon (Storyville, 1969).

663. **Polart Index to Record Reviews,** 1960- . Ann. Polart.

Reviews published in major periodicals are indexed, without evalutions but with indication of length. Main entries are under composers. *Record and Tape Reviews Index*, 1971- (Scarecrow) tends to overlap "Record Ratings" in *Notes* (see item 684).

664. **Records in Review,** 1955- . Wyeth.

Lengthy, signed reviews from *High Fidelity* (see item 676) are arranged by composers with an index of performers.

665. **Schwann-1,** 1949- . Mo. Schwann.

Nearly 45,000 available recordings on more than 700 record labels, 230 tape labels and 80 quadraphonic labels are included, with prices. The basic arrangement is by composers. This catalog includes classical music, recent popular music, rock, jazz, musical shows, country, opera, ballet and electronic music. Although not attempting to be an encyclopedia, the Schwann Catalog does include dates of composers, of compositions if available, opus numbers, languages used in vocal music. Special care is taken to list contemporary American composers as completely as possible. This basic work is now supplemented by *Schwann-2* (S-Ann.), which covers monaural records, popular releases more than two years old, classical jazz, reissues, international pop and folk on domestic labels, spoken, educational, religious, etc.

Music Periodicals

666. **Acta Musicologica,** 1928- . 2/yr. International Musicological Society.

Indexed: *Mus.Ind., RILM*. Fully documented research papers, often with valuable bibliographies, are staple features of this official publication of the International Musicological Society. Papers are in the languages chosen by their authors.

666a. **American Music Teacher,** 1951- . Bi-mo. Music Teachers National Association.

Indexed: *Educ.Ind., Mus.Ind.* Articles on and reviews of keyboard, vocal, organ, and string music are written to assist teachers. Bibliographies are occasionally included.

667. American Musicological Society. **Journal**, 1948- . 3/yr. The Society. Indexed: *Mus.Ind., RILM.* Scholarly articles, usually with bibliographies, appear regularly in *JAMS*. Other features include extensive book reviews, information on new editions of music and recordings, reports on doctoral dissertations, and abstracts of papers presented at various meetings of the Society.

668. **American Record Guide**, 1934- . Mo. ARG Publishing. Indexed: Mus.Ind., RG. This excellent review medium for recordings and tapes compares new releases with older recordings. On the more popular side is *Record Collecting for All It's Worth*, 1977(?)- . Q. (O'Sullivan, Woodside).

669. **Audio**, 1947- . Mo. North American Publishing Co. Indexed: *Mus.Ind., ASTI, Eng.Ind.* New products, installation, and maintenance are emphasized. Reviews are analytical. Also, there are articles on theory of sound and reviews of records — classical, popular, jazz. More emphasis is placed on equipment than in *Hi-Fi/Stereo Review* and *High Fidelity*.

670. **Billboard**, 1894- . Wk. Billboard Publishing Co. Indexed: *Mus.Ind.* Subtitle: "International Music Record News-weekly." A newspaper that focuses on publishing, recording, and selling music. Information on new albums, tapes, performers, and pop music is provided, along with sections on: country, gospel, and classical music; musical instruments; audio retailing; and "Hits of the World," arranged by country.

671. **Crawdaddy**, 1966- . Bi-wk. Superstar Productions, Inc. Indexed: *Mus.Ind.* Subtitle: "The Magazine of Rock." Illustrated articles on personalities, music, concerts, and "teen-age" songs are featured, with an emphasis on analysis and on social issues. Each number has an interview with a leading musical figure.

672. **Current Musicology**, 1965- . 2/yr. Department of Music, Columbia University. Detailed, scholarly articles, often with lengthy bibliographies, make this periodical a valuable tool for reference librarians and musical researchers. Some coverage is given to collections in music libraries.

673. **Down Beat**, 1934- . Bi-wk. Maher Publications. Indexed: *Mus.Ind.* Devoted to personalities, music, scenes, and recordings of jazz, *Down Beat* also includes reviews of books, concerts, and recordings. Teenagers may prefer rock magazines like *Crawdaddy* or *Rolling Stone*.

674. **Fontes artis musicae**, 1954- . Q. International Association of Music Libraries. Indexed: *Mus.Ind., RILM.* In summing up its first 25 years, the current editor commented (v. 35, no. 1 [1978], p. 2): "In its approximately sixty-five issues, it has chronicled our meetings, inventoried a substantial portion of the world's yearly output of major music publications, evaluated bibliographic monographs, reported on little-known music collections, described national library systems, presented novel schemes for the cataloging, classification, or encoding of music, and honored its distinguished founding editor with a Festschrift."

675. **Gramophone**, 1923- . Mo. General Gramophone Publications.
Indexed: *Mus.Ind.* Long, critical reviews of classical recordings in the United Kingdom are featured along with articles on music and audio equipment.

676. **High Fidelity and Musical America**, 1951- . Mo. Billboard Publishing Co.
Indexed: *Mus.Ind., RG, Abr. RG.* This vital periodical for the informed hi-fi enthusiast features articles on music and musicians; audio and video equipment; reviews of records and tapes; and, in the "Musical America" section, coverage of current music perform- ances, music centers, and performing artists.

677. **JEMF Quarterly**, 1965- . Q. John Edwards Memorial Foundation, Folklore and Mythology Center, University of California, Los Angeles.
Indexed: *Mus.Ind., RILM.* Country, western, country-western, hillbilly, bluegrass, mountain, cowboy, old time, and sacred music are featured. The Foundation also preserves material on race, blues, and gospel.

678. **Journal of Jazz Studies**, 1973- . 2/yr. Transaction Periodicals Consortium.
This is a scholarly, well-researched periodical, well edited, with excellent documentation.

679. **Journal of the Association for Recorded Sound Collections**, 1968(?)- . 3/yr. Association for Recorded Sound Collections.
This is the professional journal of those charged with responsibility for organizing and servicing recorded sound collections.

680. **Music and Letters**, 1920- . Q. Music and Letters, Ltd.
Indexed: *Br.Hum.Ind., Mus.Ind., RILM.* Noted for its international coverage of classical music and musicians, it features long, scholarly articles on styles, outstanding musicians, and subjects of historical importance, in addition to critical reviews of books and new music. The emphasis is British.

681. **Music Educators Journal**, 1914- . Mo. (Sept.-June). Music Educators National Conference.
Indexed: *Educ.Ind., Mus.Ind.* The major periodical in the field, covering grade school through university, this journal features teaching suggestions and developments, research, awards, competitions, etc.

682. **The Musical Quarterly**, 1915- . Q. Schirmer.
Indexed: *Mus.Ind., Hum.Ind., RILM.* This scholarly journal publishes research results in the field of serious music. A section of about 25 pages called "Current Chronicle" covers events in the United States and abroad. In addition to signed, critical book reviews, there is a quarterly booklist—not annotated—that covers international publications. Record reviews report in depth and include bibliographies.

683. **The Musical Times**, 1844- . Mo. Novello & Co.
Indexed: *Br.Hum.Ind., Mus.Ind., RILM.* Planned for students and teachers, it con- tains long articles on music, musicians, concerts, instruments, and education, usually based on original research. News stories are also included along with reviews of books, records, new music, and concerts.

684. **Notes: The Quarterly Journal of the Music Library Association**, 1931- . 2nd Series, 1948- . Q. Music Library Association.
Indexed: *Mus.Ind., RILM, Lib.Lit., LISA, Bk.Rev.Ind., A&HCI.* A typical issue begins with articles on music libraries, publishing, or other topics of interest to librarians and musicians. A major portion of each issue is devoted to reviews of books, music periodicals, and music. A major feature is the index to record reviews, by Kurtz Myers. News and lists of new books, music publishers' catalogs, and music received are other regular features.

685. **Opera News**, 1936- . Mo. Metropolitan Opera Guild.
Indexed: *Mus.Ind., RG, RILM.* During the Metropolitan Opera season, this appears more frequently and deals with the operas to be performed each week — plot, cast, historical notes, photographs of characters, and staging. Monthly issues more likely to have articles on history and personalities, with reports on music centers in the United States and abroad. It is the chief periodical in the U.S. devoted to opera.

686. **Rolling Stone**, 1967- . Bi-wk. Straight Arrow.
Indexed: *Mus.Ind.* A newspaper-format magazine devoted to rock, *Rolling Stone* has articles on the meaning of music for teenagers as well as coverage of current figures. The articles are well illustrated. Record reviews are also featured. This one should be included, along with *Crawdaddy*, if a library serves patrons interested in rock.

687. **Sing Out**, 1950- . Bi-mo. 270 Lafayette St., New York, NY 10012.
Indexed: *Mus.Ind.* All aspects of folk music are covered, including interviews with singers, songwriters, and teachers. There are articles on the guitar, banjo, etc., as well as news and notes. It is attractive to players because each issue has several folk songs, with words, music, and guitar chords.

688. **Stereo Review**, 1958- . Mo. Ziff-Davis Publishing Co.
Indexed: *Mus.Ind., RILM.* Both equipment and recordings are covered. There are well-illustrated general articles on music, advertisements, test reports and reports on new products, general equipment surveys, and a question-and-answer section. A valuable feature is the review section for all types of recordings.

DANCE

Introductory Works and Bibliographic Guides

689. Bowers, Faubion. **Theatre in the East: A Survey of Asian Dance and Drama.** Nelson, 1956; repr., Grove, 1969. 374p.
This well-illustrated book gives the history of the dance and describes folk, traditional, and modern forms in 14 chapters on the following countries: India, Ceylon [Sri Lanka], Burma, Thailand, Cambodia, Laos, Malaya, China, Indonesia, Philippines, Vietnam, Hong Kong, Okinawa, and Japan.

690. DeMille, Agnes. **The Book of the Dance.** Golden Press, 1963. 252p.
Encyclopedic coverage is provided for all periods and many countries. Definitions, types and methods of choreography, brief biographies of performers, and excellent illustrations (many in color) are included, together with lists of major ballets and choreographers and an index.

691. Martin, John Joseph. **Book of the Dance.** Tudor, 1963; repr., 1970. 192p.
After a brief opening treatment of basic dance movements and primitive dances, the main part of the book provides a detailed history of classic ballet and modern dance, especially contemporary American, with excellent illustrations. A name and subject index enhance its reference use.

692. Shaw, Lloyd. **Cowboy Dances; A Collection of Western Square Dances.** Rev. ed. Caxton Printers, 1949. 417p.
This illustrated book provides history, description, directions, and calls, together with a glossary of terms and an appendix of cowboy dance tunes.

Bibliographies (Current and Retrospective)

693. Beaumont, Cyril William, comp. **A Bibliography of Dancing.** Blom, 1963. 228p.
Based on items in the British Library, this bibliography consists of 422 annotated entries arranged alphabetically by author, with a subject index. Bibliographies are included in John Mueller's *Films on Ballet and Modern Dance: Notes and a Directory* (American Dance Guild, 1975).

694. Forrester, Felicitée Sheila. **Ballet in England: A Bibliography and Survey, c. 1700-June 1966.** Library Association, 1968. 224p.
This classified, annotated bibliography of 664 items also has appendices, which include exhibitions and a guide for further study as well as an analytical index of names, titles, and subjects.

695. Leslie, Serge. **A Bibliography of the Dance Collection of Doris Niles and Serge Leslie.** Annotated by Serge Leslie. Edited by Cyril Beaumont. Beaumont, 1966-68. 2v.
The coverage centers on ballet, although folk dancing and social dances are included. The arrangement is alphabetical by author (v. 1, A-K; v. 2, L-Z), and there are about 2,000 entries. Each volume has a subject index.

696. Magriel, Paul David. **A Bibliography of Dancing: A List of Books and Articles on the Dance and Related Subjects.** Wilson, 1936; repr., Blom, 1966. 229p.
About 1,000 items, including folk dances and ballet are included. Locations are given for rare and out-of-print books. There is an author and subject index. Steven E. Winick's *Rhythm: An Annotated Bibliography* (Scarecrow, 1974) suffers from some deficiencies (e.g., omission of certain standard works and a few authors' first names), but is a useful starting point, strong in English-language twentieth-century books, periodicals, and dissertations.

697.   New York (City). Public Library. **Dictionary Catalog of the Dance Collection.**
G. K. Hall, 1974. 10v.
Subtitle: "A list of authors, titles and subjects of multi-media materials in the Dance
Collection of the Performing Arts Research Center of the New York Public Library."
About 225,000 catalog cards have been reproduced, representing books, periodicals,
playbills, letters, films, scrapbooks, tapes, and dance scores. This set is now kept up to
date by *Bibliographic Guide to Dance*, issued annually since 1975 by G. K. Hall. The
latter also includes MARC records.

698.   **Tanzbibliographie. Verzeichnis der in deutscher Sprache veroffentlichen
Schriften und Aufsatze zum Buhnen; Besellschafts, Kinder-, Volks- und Turniertanz
sowie zur Tanzwissenschaft, Tanzmusik und zum Jazz.** Hrsg. von Institut für Volks
Kunstforschung beim Zentralhaus für Kulturarbeit, Leipzig. VEB Bibliographisches
Institut, 1966- .
"A classified bibliography of books and periodical articles in German on theatrical,
social, children's folk and competition dancing as well as on the science of dancing,
dance music and Jazz" [A. J. Walford, *Guide to Reference Material* (3rd ed., Library
Association, 1977), v. 3, p. 461].

699.   United Nations Educational, Scientific and Cultural Organization. **Ten Years of
Films on Ballet and Classical Dance, 1956-1965.** Unesco, 1968. 105p.
The basic arangement is alphabetical, listing 190 films from 23 countries by country and
then by title. Entries give information about production, music, choreography,
costumes, dancers, etc. Three indexes are provided: countries, choreographers, and
composers.

Indexes, Abstracts, and Current Awareness Services

700.   **Guide to Dance Periodicals**, v. 1-10, 1931/35-1961/62. Scarecrow.
Quinquennial coverage was provided for years from 1931-35 through 1946-50 and biennial, after 1951-52. It was irregular and often late in appearance, but the indexing of 19
periodicals by subject and author (with separate index for illustrations) won high praise
for its thoroughness. Compiled by S. Yancey Belknap, it was later incorporated into
Guide to the Performing Arts. The reprint edition of *Dance Index* (Arno, 1970, 7v.)
includes v. 1-7, no. 7/8 (1942-1948) and has a new cumulative index.

701.   Minneapolis Public Library. Music Department. **An Index to Folk Dances and
Singing Games.** ALA, 1936. 202p. Suppl. 1949. 98p.
Together, the two volumes cover 178 books on folk dancing, singing games, classic
dances, tap and clog dances, and some square dances.

Dictionaries and Encyclopedias

702.   Baril, J. **Dictionnaire de la danse.** Editions du Seuil, 1964. 285p.
This useful dictionary has approximately 1,500 entries, including definitions of more
than 200 technical terms and notes on 845 dances and 530 ballets, as well as 450
illustrations.

703. Beaumont, Cyril William, comp. **A French-English Dictionary of Technical Terms Used in Classical Ballet.** Rev. ed. Beaumont, 1939; repr., 1968. 44p.
Some 140 French terms are given, with explanations in English.

704. Chujoy, Anatole, and Phyllis Winifred Manchester. **The Dance Encyclopedia.** Rev. and enl. ed. Simon and Schuster, 1967. 992p.
The revised edition of this standard work (first published in 1949) is nearly doubled in size and contains about 5,000 entries on the dance, especially ballet. About 40 of the longer articles are signed. Brief definitions are given. Entries for individual ballets include synopses, names of choreographers, designers, composers, original casts, and performance dates. Coverage includes virtually everything from biographies to techniques and education. Especially strong for American ballet, it is still a first source to check.

705. **A Dictionary of Modern Ballet,** ed. by Francis Gadan and Robert Maillard. Methuen, 1959. 359p.
Originally published in France, its coverage includes France, Britain, U.S.S.R., U.S.A., Denmark, Sweden, Italy, and Spain. There are about 650 articles on artists, performers, ballets, and institutions of the twentieth century. It does not include definitions of terms.

706. **The Encyclopedia of Dance and Ballet,** ed. by Mary Clarke and David Vaughan. Putnam, 1977. 376p.
Contemporary dance styles as well as classical ballet are included in this concise work, which has initialed articles by over 50 contributors from various countries. Many articles include bibliographical references. There are many cross references, numerous black-and-white photographs, 18 color plates, a glossary and a general bibliography.

707. Grant, Gail. **Technical Manual and Dictionary of Classical Ballet.** 2nd ed. Dover, 1967.
This vital reference tool includes technical terms and their pronunciations, small line drawings, and a brief bibliography.

708. Kersley, Leo, and Janet Sinclair. **A Dictionary of Ballet Terms.** 3rd ed. A. & C. Black, 1973. 112p.
Approximately 500 entries and cross references, illustrated with 127 line drawings, are included in this vital work.

709. Koegler, Horst. **The Concise Oxford Dictionary of Ballet.** Oxford, 1977. 583p.
Some 5,000 entries on all aspects of ballet are contained in this excellent dictionary, which was included among the best reference books of 1977 (*Library Journal*, April 15, 1978, p. 819). It does not replace Chujoy's *Dance Encyclopedia* (see item 704), but it has more coverage than G. B. L. Wilson's *A Dictionary of Ballet* (see item 711). *The Language of Ballet: An Informal Dictionary*, by Thalia Mara (World, 1966; repr., 1972), gives pronunciations and definitions of some terms not readily found elsewhere.

710. Raffé, Walter George, and M. E. Purdon. **Dictionary of the Dance.** Barnes, 1964; repr., 1975. 583p.
Definitions for 2,500 terms are given in this excellent work, which is especially strong on

folk and ethnic dances. There are no biographies. Coverage is international. Geographical and subject indexes and a bibliography are provided.

711.   Wilson, George Buckley Laird. **A Dictionary of Ballet.** 3rd ed. A. & C. Black, 1974. 539p.
Some 2,500 entries deal with such aspects of classical and operatic ballet as technical terms, individual ballets, biographies, companies, etc. The work is illustrated and has good cross references.

Directories and Annuals

712.   **The Ballet Annual: A Record and Year-book of the Ballet.** A. & C. Black, 1947-63. 18v.
Discontinued at end of v. 18 (1963), its coverage was then incorporated into the monthly periodical *Dancing Times.*

713.   **Dance World.** Crown, 1966- . Ann.
Pictorial survey of New York dance season is provided, with personnel of companies, repertoires, etc. There is some coverage outside New York. Biographies are included.

714.   **The Folk Directory,** 1966- . Ann. English Folk Dance and Song Society.
Various song and dance clubs in Britain are covered, as well as books, folk music on cassettes, events, writers, etc.

Histories

715.   Anderson, Jack. **Dance.** Newsweek, 1974. 192p.
Part of the World of Culture series, this book covers dance history from 1581 to 1974. It is well illustrated and has brief biographical information about most of the major performers. A useful chronology is provided at the end.

716.   Brinson, Peter. **Background to European Ballet: A Notebook from Its Archives.** Sijthoff, 1966. 195p.
Part of "European Aspects — Series A: Culture," this is a carefully-researched history. A valuable illustrated history, of somewhat broader scope, is *Ballet: An Illustrated History*, by Mary Clarke and Clement Crisp (Universe books, 1973; repr., 1978).

717.   Cohen, Selma Jeanne, ed. **Dance as a Theatre Art: Source Readings in Dance History from 1581 to the Present.** Dodd, Mead, 1974. 224p.
The compiler has made a judicious selection of important writings on dance, with introductions written for all items. This illustrated reader also has an excellent bibliography. Lincoln Kirstein's *Dance: A Short History of Classic Theatrical Dancing* (Putnam, 1935; repr., Dance Horizons, 1969) is a useful concise history.

718.   Sachs, Curt. **World History of the Dance.** W. W. Norton, 1937; repr., 1973. 469p.
Originally published in German, this is still a vital source of historical information. Less vital, but also useful, is Walter Sorell's *The Dance through the Ages* (Grosset & Dunlap, 1967).

719.   Terry, Walter. **The Dance in America.** Rev. ed. Harper, 1971; repr., 1973. 272p.
The revised edition added chapters on black dance, the regional ballet movement, and new or expanded dance companies. Another important work is *Black Dance in the United States from 1619 to 1970*, by Lynne Fauley Emery (National Press books, 1972). *Jazz Dance: The Story of American Vernacular Dance*, by Marshall and Jean Stearns (Macmillan, 1968), should not be overlooked.

Biographies

720.   McDonough, Don. **The Complete Guide to Modern Dance.** Doubleday, 1976. 534p.
This carefully researched book is divided into five chronological sections and then arranged alphabetically by names of choreographers (over 100 in all). Biographical information is followed by descriptions of major works and lists of all works. A chronology, a bibliography, and an index are also provided. In addition, several works noted in the section on Dictionaries and Encyclopedias are excellent sources of biographical information. Most notable among these are Chujoy's *The Dance Encyclopedia* (item 704), *A Dictionary of Modern Ballet* (item 705), Koegler's *The Concise Oxford Dictionary of Ballet* (item 709), and Wilson's *A Dictionary of Ballet* (item 711).

Ballet Digests

721.   Balanchine, George. **Complete Stories of the Great Ballets.** Rev. and enl. ed. Doubleday, 1977. 838p.
The main part (stories and reviews) is arranged alphabetically by title, followed by sections on history, careers, etc. The book includes an illustrated glossary, an annotated selection of ballet records, and a bibliography. The analytical index is unusually detailed.

722.   Beaumont, Cyril William. **Complete Book of Ballets: A Guide to the Principal Ballets of the Nineteenth and Twentieth Centuries.** Rev. ed. Putnam, 1949; repr., 1956. 1106p.
This vital reference source covers 198 ballets chronologically by birth dates of choreographers. It provides synopses, authors, designers, composers, choreographers, dates, and casts of first productions, and criticism. There is a supplement on Soviet ballet. The index is very detailed.

723.   Brinson, Peter, and Clement Crisp. **The International Book of Ballet.** Stein and Day, 1971.
This well-illustrated reference work includes 115 ballets of 38 choreographers, from 1653 to 1969. It gives synopses, original dancers, and criticism.

724.   Drew, David, ed. **The Decca Book of Ballet.** Muller, 1958. 572p.
After a brief historical introduction, the main section describes 198 ballets and is alphabetical by composer. Other parts deal with dancers and choreographers, and major ballet companies.

725. Lawrence, Robert. **The Victor Book of Ballets and Ballet Music.** Simon and Schuster, 1950. 531p.
Over 70 ballets with musical examples are included. There are three indexes: choreographers, composers, and general index. A selective discography of RCA Victor records is also provided.

726. Terry, Walter. **Ballet Guide: Background, Listings, Credits and Descriptions of More than Five Hundred of the World's Major Ballets.** Dodd, Mead, 1975. 330p.
The synopses of ballets are well done and the other background information is very useful. The only major deficiency is the lack of indexes to composers, choreographers, and performers.

Periodicals

727. **Dance and Dancers,** 1950- . Mo. Hansom Books.
International coverage of ballet and modern dance, including a range of topics from education to reviews of records and recitals, is provided by this well-illustrated periodical.

728. **Dancemagazine,** 1926- . Mo. Danad Publishing Co.
Indexed: *RG, Bk.Rev.Ind., Curr.Biog.* International coverage is provided for all aspects of the subject, including information on such topics as performers, tours, schools, costumes, dance companies, accompanied by excellent photographs. The annual directory is arranged alphabetically by states and then by names of schools, companies, etc.

729. **Dance Perspectives,** 1959-1977. Q. Dance Perspectives Foundation.
Indexed: *Mus.Ind.* This now-defunct journal is still a vital source of critical and historical articles. Each issue was normally devoted to one topic and might include several articles by different authorities or a monograph by one.

730. **Dance Research Journal,** 1969- . 2/yr. Committee on Research on Dance.
V. 1-6 (1969-1974) were entitled *Committee on Dance Research News.*

731. **Square Dancing,** 1948- . Mo. American Square Dance Society.
Designed for teachers, callers, and dancers, this useful magazine includes information on dances and calls, record reviews, news items, etc.

THEATER

Introductory Works and Bibliographic Guides

732. Cheshire, David F. **Theatre: History, Criticism and Reference.** Bingley/Archon, 1967. 131p.
Chapters of this extended bibliographic essay written by a librarian for librarians include: general reference works; histories; dramatic criticism; biographies and autobiographies; theory; current periodicals. There is an extensive author, subject, and

title index. The coverage is international, but from a British viewpoint. More specialized coverage of the British scene is provided in *The Popular School: A Survey and Bibliography of Recent Studies in English Renaissance Drama*, by Terence P. Logan and Denzell S. Smith (University of Nebraska Press, 1975); *English Drama to 1660 (Excluding Shakespeare): A Guide to Information Sources*, by Frederick Link (Gale, 1976); and *English Drama and Theatre, 1800-1900: A Guide to Information Sources*, by L. W. Connolly and J. P. Wearing (Gale, 1978).

733.   Crothers, J. Francis. **The Puppeteer's Library Guide: The Bibliographic Index to the Literature of the World Puppet Theatre.** Scarecrow, 1971- .
Projected as part of a six-volume set, v. 1 (*The Historical Background of Puppetry and Its Related Fields*) was well received by reviewers as an authoritative guide for study and research. The reviewer in *Choice* (March 1972, p. 73) described the book as follows: "It includs a section on already published bibliographies of puppet literature, a general history of puppets of all kinds, a cursory yet informative comment on the development of Punch and Judy drama in over 30 different countries, and a most valuable treatment of international material by country. The second half of the volume is devoted to the organizations, guilds, and periodicals of puppetry throughout the world. The book concludes with an extensive author index and publishers and booksellers addresses. . . . "

734.   Drury, Francis Keese Wynkoop. **Drury's Guide to Best Plays**, ed. by James M. Salem. 3rd ed. Scarecrow, 1978. 421p.
This guide for locating those plays most often used by amateur and educational theater groups is arranged alphabetically by authors. Main entries give publishers, cast breakdowns, settings, plot synopses, current holders of plays, and royalty fees. Indexes provide listings under co-authors, lists of plays most popular among producing groups, lists of play publishers, and lists by number of characters and by subjects. Another useful work is *Guide to Play Selection: A Selective Bibliography for Production and Study of Modern Plays* (3rd ed., National Council of Teachers of English, 1975). Still useful for amateur groups is Gail Plummer's *Dramatists' Guide to Selection of Plays and Musicals* (Brown, 1963).

735.   Howard, Vernon Linwood. **The Complete book of Children's Theater.** Doubleday, 1969.
More than 350 non-royalty plays, skits, and monologues are included. Selections are suitable for home, youth group, and classroom use. The author has also provided suggestions for beginning students on such topics as conveying emotions, conducting rehearsals, and overcoming stage fright.

Bibliographies (Current and Retrospective)

736.   Adelman, Irving, and Rita Dworkin. **Modern Drama: A Checklist of Critical Literature on 20th Century Plays.** Scarecrow, 1967. 370p.
This exceedingly useful guide to sources of criticism and interpretation continues to be a vital source after more than a decade. Another valuable source of more specialized scope is *Children's Theatre and Creative Dramatics: An Annotated Bibliography of Critical Works*, by Rachel Fordyce (G. K. Hall, 1975), which includes more than 2,200 books, theses, dissertations, and periodical articles from around 1900 through 1973.

737. Baker, Blanch (Merritt). **Theatre and Allied Arts: A Guide to Books Dealing with the History, Criticism, and Technic of the Drama and Theatre, and Related Arts and Crafts.** 2nd ed. Wilson, 1952; repr., Blom, 1967. 536p.

This classified annotated bibliography of some 6,000 items (mainly in English and with an American emphasis) published between 1885 and 1945 has author and subject indexes. Coverage includes costume, puppet plays, and the dance, but *not* radio, motion pictures, opera, or television.

738. British Drama League. Library. **The Player's Library: The Catalogue of the Library of the British Drama League.** 2nd ed. Faber, 1950. 1115p. Suppls. 1951, 128p.; 1954, 256p.; 1956, 256p.

Some 14,500 plays are listed under authors, with brief information on number of acts, cast, setting, period, and costume. There is a title index of plays and an author index of books on the theater. It is the most comprehensive bibliography of English plays and books about the drama. A more specialized library collection is described by William R. Dubois in *English and American Stage Productions: An Annotated Checklist of Prompt Books, 1800-1900, from the Nisbet-Snyder Drama Collection, Northern Illinois University Libraries* (G. K. Hall, 1973).

739. Coleman, Arthur, and Gary R. Tyler. **Drama Criticism.** Alan Swallow, 1966-69. 2v.

Contents: v. 1 — *A Checklist of Interpretation since 1940 of English and American Plays* (1966); v. 2 — *A Checklist of Interpretation since 1940 of Classical and Continental Plays* (1969). The basic arrangement is alphabetical by authors, then by titles of plays.

740. Eddeman, Floyd Eugene. **American Drama Criticism: Interpretations, 1890-1977.** 2nd ed. Shoe String, 1979.

The first edition (1967) of this essential reference work was compiled by Helen H. Palmer and Anne Jane Dyson. All playwrights from the earliest period to the present are covered insofar as criticism of their works appeared between 1890 and 1977. The arrangement is alphabetical by playwrights and then by plays. There is an author/title index. Less vital, but useful, is Pat M. Ryan's *American Drama Bibliography: A Checklist of Publications in English* (Fort Wayne Public Library, 1969). Complementary coverage of the American theater before 1915 is provided in Don B. Wilmet's *The American Stage to World War I: A Guide to Information Sources* (Gale, 1978).

741. Greg, Sir Walter Wilson. **A Bibliography of the English Printed Drama to the Restoration.** Bibliographical Society, 1939-1959; repr., 1970. 4v.

Arranged chronologically, Greg's classic work gives locations in European and American libraries. Contents: v. 1 — *Stationers' Records: Plays, to 1616, nos. 1-349* (1939); v. 2 — *Plays, 1617-1689, nos. 350-386; Latin Plays; Last Plays* (1951); v. 3 — *Collections; Appendix; Reference Lists* (1958); v. 4 — *Introduction; Additions; Corrections; Index of Titles* (1959). A work that deals more selectively with early English drama is *The English Morality and Related Drama: A Bibliographical Survey*, by Peter J. Houle (Archon, 1972). An index to all of the characters in all of the plays listed in Greg's bibliography has been prepared by Thomas L. Berger and William C. Bradford, Jr.: *An Index of Characters in English Printed Drama to the Restoration* (Microcard Editions Books, 1975).

742. Hatch, James Vernon. **Black Image on the American Stage: A Bibliography of Plays and Musicals, 1770-1970.** DBS Publications, 1970. 162p.
If a play (one-act, musical, revue, or opera) includes a black character, has black authorship or a black theme, and was produced in America, it is included. The book has a good introduction, author and title indexes, a bibliography, and suggestions for research. Manuscripts have library locations indicated if the plays are available only in this form. A more recent work in which Hatch collaborated with Omanii Abdullah is *Black Playwrights, 1823-1977: An Annotated Bibliography of Plays* (Bowker, 1977).

743. Litto, Fredric M. **American Dissertations on Drama and the Theatre: A Bibliography.** Kent State University Press, 1969. 519p.
Dissertations up through 1965 are listed by an alphanumeric code which appears to create an alphabetical author listing, but actually does *not*. There are finding indexes by author, keyword-in-context, and subject.

744. New York (City). Public Library. The Research Libraries. **Catalog of the Theatre and Drama Collections.** G. K. Hall, 1967- .
This tremendous bibliographical search tool covers more than 120,000 plays (excluding children's and Christmas plays) and works about the theater in the broadest sense. Contents: pt. I — *Drama Collection: Listing by Cultural Origin; Author Listing.* 12v. 1967. First Suppl. 1973; pt. II — *Theatre Collection; Books on the Theatre.* 9v. 1967. First Suppl. 1973; pt. III — *Non-book Collection.* 30v. 1975. A useful auxiliary aid for searching (since NYPL differs from LC) is *Theatre Subject Headings* (G. K. Hall, 1966). Annual updating is now available in *Bibliographic Guide to Theatre Arts*, 1975- (G. K. Hall).

745. Palmer, Helen H. **European Drama Criticism, 1900-1975.** 2nd ed. Shoe String, 1977. 653p.
Includes criticisms of dramatic works by outstanding European playwrights past and present. The emphasis is on English-language materials, and the arrangement is alphabetical by playwrights. There is an index of playwrights, pseudonyms, and play titles. It is a companion to *American Drama Criticism* (see item 740). Leon F. Lyday and George F. Woodward compiled *A Bibliography of Latin American Theater Criticism* (University of Texas, 1976).

746. Salem, James M. **A Guide to Critical Reviews.** 2nd ed. Scarecrow, 1973- .
Contents: I — *American Drama*, 1909-1969; II — *The Musical*, 1909-1974; III — *British and Continental Drama from Ibsen to Pinter* (1st ed.); IV — *The Screenplay from The Jazz Singer to Dr. Strangelove* (1st ed.).

747. Stratman, Carl Joseph. **American Theatrical Periodicals, 1789-1967: A Bibliographical Guide.** Duke University Press, 1970. 133p.
The compiler of this carefully researched and essential bibliography has brought together "for the first time some 685 American theatrical periodicals, published in 122 cities and in 31 states, with locations of issues noted in 137 libraries" (introduction, p. ix). The basic arrangement is chronological, with a name/title index. A table of periodical publication spans is also provided. A detailed explanation of how to use the book is given in the introduction.

748.　Stratman, Carl Joseph. **A Bibliography of British Dramatic Periodicals, 1720-1960.** New York Public Library, 1962. 58p.
This valuable work covers 674 titles in a chronological arangement and gives locations of complete files in American and British libraries. Stratman has also compiled *Bibliography of English Printed Tragedy, 1565-1900* (Southern Illinois University Press, 1966), which is arranged alphabetically by authors and gives locations in libraries. It has an appendix of manuscript locations, a list of anthologies and collections, a chronological table, and a title index. Another title by Stratman worth noting is *Bibliography of Medieval Drama* (2nd ed., Ungar, 1972, 2v.), which is a classified bibliography of the drama of medieval Europe, covering a wide range of topics and furnishing references to reviews of major books.

749.　Stratman, Carl Joseph. **Bibliography of the American Theatre, Excluding New York City.** Loyola University Press, 1965. 397p.
Coverage includes books, periodical articles, theses and dissertations on the American theater (including ballet, opera, and children's theater). It is arranged by state and then by city. Locations for books are indicated. There is an author and subject index.

750.　Stratman, Carl Joseph, and others, eds. **Restoration and Eighteenth Century Theatre Research: A Bibliographical Guide, 1900-1968.** Southern Illinois University Press, 1971. 811p.
Over 6,000 entries are arranged under 780 subject headings in alphabetical order. More than 5,000 of the entries are annotated. The name and subject index (pp. 783-811) consists of three columns per page of very small type.

751.　"Théâtre." In **Bulletin signalétique.** C(19-24): **Sciences humaines;** Section 23: **Littérature et arts du spectacle,** 1961- . Centre National de la Recherche Scientifique.
Bibliographical information and brief descriptive abstracts are given in a classified arrangement.

Indexes, Abstracts, and Current Awareness Services

752.　Breed, Paul F., and Florence M. Sniderman. **Dramatic Criticism Index: A Bibliography of Commentaries on Playwrights from Ibsen to the Avant-Garde.** Gale, 1972. 1022p.
The compilers used about 630 books and over 200 periodicals in preparing this work, which includes some 12,000 entries in English on about 300 playwrights, both American and foreign. The basic arrangement is alphabetical by playwrights, subarranged by titles of plays. There are indexes by play titles and by critics. A list of books indexed is also provided.

753.　**Chicorel Theater Index,** 1970- . Chicorel.
This set of index volumes relating to theater includes books (mostly in print) and periodicals in the English language. Authors, editors and titles (of plays and anthologies) are in one alphabet. There are appended lists of authors, editors, and titles of plays. These volumes are part of the Chicorel Index Series: v. 1 – *Chicorel Theater Index to Plays in Anthologies, Periodicals, Disc and Tapes* (1970); v. 2 – *Chicorel Theater Index to Plays in Anthologies, Periodicals, Discs and Tapes* (1971);

v. 3 — *Chicorel Theater Index to Plays in collections, Anthologies, Periodicals and Discs in England* (1972); v. 8 — *Chicorel Theater Index to Plays in Periodicals* (1973); v. 9 — *Chicorel Theater Index to Plays for Young People, in Periodicals, Anthologies and Collections* (1974); v. 21 — *Chicorel Index to Drama Literature* (1975); v. 25 — *Chicorel Theater Index to Plays in Anthologies and Collections: 1970-1976* (1977). Somewhat broader in scope are v. 7, 7A, and 7B, entitled *Chicorel Index to the Spoken Arts on Discs, Tapes and Cassettes* (1973-74).

754. **Cumulated Dramatic Index, 1909-1949.** G. K. Hall, 1965. 2v.
This useful set cumulates the 41 annual volumes of the *Dramatic Index*, including the three appendices (Author List of Books about the Drama; Title List of Published Play Texts; and Author List of Published Play Texts). Arranged dictionary style, some 300,000 entries provide access to: articles about the drama, the theater, actors and actresses, playwrights, librettists, managers, etc.; reviews; stage and dramatic portraits; scenes from plays and other theatrical illustrations; texts of plays.

755. Firkins, Ina Ten Eyck. **Index to Plays, 1800-1926.** Wilson, 1927; repr., AMS, 1971. 307p. Suppl. 1927-34. 1935. 140p.
This vital index shows where the texts of more than 10,000 plays can be found in collections or other sources. Only plays in English are covered, but this does include translations. There are two parts: 1) author index, with full bibliographical information and, often, number of acts, brief characterization (comedy, tragedy, social, domestic, etc.); 2) title and subject index, referring to the author list.

756. Ireland, Norma (Olin). **Index to Full Length Plays 1944-1964.** Faxon, 1965. 296p.
This is the companion volume to Ruth Thomson's *Index to Full Length Plays* (see item 763). Instead of separate author, subject, and title indexes (as was done by Thomson), all three types are combined in one alphabet.

757. Keller, Dean H. **Index to Plays in Periodicals.** Rev. ed. Scarecrow, 1979.
Keller has indexed well over 5,000 plays. The work is divided into two parts. The main entry is under author and includes full name and dates, title of play, number of acts, brief description, citation, name of translator or adapter, and title in original (if translated). The second part, a title index, refers to the item number of the main entry. Much more limited in coverage is Stan Coryn's *A Selective Index to Theatre Magazine* (Scarecrow, 1964).

758. Logasa, Hannah. **An Index to One-Act Plays.** Faxon, 1924-1966. 6v.
The basic volume of this vital set was issued in 1924, with supplements as follows: 1st suppl., 1924-31; 2nd, 1932-40; 3rd, 1941-48; 4th, 1948-57; 5th, 1956-64. The set provides title, author, and subject indexes to one-act plays both in collections and separately published pamphlets. The third supplement includes radio plays, while the fourth and fifth also include television. Mostly intended for children and young people, it is supplemented and updated by Barbara A. Kreider's *Index to Children's Plays in Collections* (2nd ed., Scarecrow, 1977).

759. Ottemiller, John H. **Ottemiller's Index to Plays in Collections: An Author and Title Index to Plays Appearing in collections Published between 1900 and Early 1975,** by John M. and Billie M. Connor. 6th ed. rev. and enl. Scarecrow, 1976. 523p.
Plays from ancient to modern times are included in this standard work, but it does *not* include children's plays, amateur plays, or one-act plays, unless they appear in one of

the collections indexed. Contents: 1) author index, giving name and date, title of play, date of first production, references from original titles, variant translated titles, joint authors, translators, etc.; 2) list of collections and keys to symbols; 3) title index. A work that supplements Ottemiller and Keller (see item 757), with more emphasis on foreign periodicals, is *The Drama Scholars' Index to Plays and Filmscripts in Selected Anthologies, Series and Periodicals*, by Gordon Samples (Scarecrow, 1974).

760.   Patterson, Charlotta A. **Plays in Periodicals.** G. K. Hall, 1970. 240p.
More than 4,000 plays published in 97 English-language periodicals between 1900 and 1968 are included. For a comprehensive search, one should also consult *Index to Plays in Periodicals*, by Dean H. Keller (see item 757).

761.   **Play Index,** 1949/1952- . Wilson.
V. 1, 1949-52, edited by Dorothy West and Dorothy Peake; v. 2, 1953-60, edited by Estelle Fidell and Dorothy Peake; v. 3, 1961-67, v. 4 and v. 5, 1972-77, edited by Estelle Fidell. Each volume has four parts: 1. main list, arranged by author, title and subject; 2. cast analysis, listing each play under type of cast (male, female, mixed, puppet); 3. list of collections indexed; and 4. directory of publishers.

762.   **Theatre/Drama Abstracts,** 1974- . 3/yr. & cum. Theatre/Drama & Speech Information Center.
Begun in 1974 as *Theatre/Drama and Speech Index*, this publication assumed its present format and coverage in 1975. The classified arrangement is complex, but it is supplemented by indexes.

763.   Thomson, Ruth. **Index to Full Length Plays.** Faxon, 1946-1956. 2v.
Contents: v. 1 — 1895-1925; v. 2 — 1926-1944. Each volume places the main entry under title and gives detailed information on number of acts, characters, etc. There are author and subject indexes. This vital set is supplemented by Norma Ireland's *Index to Full Length Plays 1944-1964* (see item 756).

Dictionaries and Encyclopedias

Dictionaries

764.   Band-Kuzmany, Karin R. M. **Glossary of the Theatre: In English, French, Italian and German.** Elsevier, 1969. 130p.
Slang phrases as well as standard theater terminology are included in this vital dictionary, which is well supplied with cross references and was compiled by an expert in theater history. Another essential source is Kenneth Rae's *An International Vocabulary of Technical Theatre Terms in Eight Languages: American, Dutch, English, French, German, Italian, Spanish, Swedish* (Elsevier, 1959; repr., Theatre Arts, 1968).

765.   Bowman, Walter Parker, and Robert Hamilton Ball. **Theatre Language: A Dictionary of Terms in English of the Drama and Stage, from Medieval to Modern Times.** Theatre Arts Books, 1961. 428p.
About 5,000 concise definitions of technical terms are provided in this essential reference work.

766. Granville, Wilfred. **The Theater Dictionary: British and American Terms in the Drama, Opera and Ballet.** Philosophical Library, 1952; repr., Greenwood, 1970. 227p.
About 3,000 terms are defined in this vital work (the British edition was entitled *A Dictionary of Theatrical Terms*). John Russell Taylor's *The Penguin Dictionary of the Theatre* (rev. ed., Penguin, 1970; repr., 1974) also includes playwrights, actors, theaters, and movements.

767. Hathorn, Richard Yancey. **Crowell's Handbook of Classical Drama.** Crowell, 1967. 350p.
Play summaries and biographical accounts of authors are included, as are concise treatment of places, mythical figures, historical and dramatic terms, and most of the characters in the plays.

768. Philpott, Alexis Robert. **Dictionary of Puppetry.** Plays, Inc., 1969. 128p.
All forms of puppetry, past and present, are included, with information on technical terms, literature, individuals, history, and asociations. Many cross references are provided. Compiled in England, the book has a British emphasis, though the coverage is international. It is designed to aid the reader who knows very little about the subject. The American edition lacks the appendix with the bibliography. Libraries should consider Philpott's *Modern Puppetry* (Plays, Inc., 1967).

769. Vaughn, Jack A. **Drama A to Z: A Handbook.** Ungar, 1979. 224p.
Terms relating to drama are defined simply and concisely. Theater history and stagecraft are excluded. A chronology of theory and criticism is provided at the end.

Encyclopedias

770. **Crowell's Handbook of Contemporary Drama**, by Michael Anderson and others. Crowell, 1971. 505p.
Short articles in one alphabetical sequence provide information on dramatists, outstanding dramatic works, theater companies, and the drama in Europe and the Americas. This vital tool is especially strong on avant-garde artists and movements.

771. **Enciclopedia dello spettacolo.** Maschere, 1954-1962. 9v. Suppl. 1955-1965, Unione Editoriale, 1966.
This valuable set is similar in format and profusion of illustrations to the *Enciclopedia Italiana*. It covers the period from antiquity to the present and includes: theater, opera, ballet, motion pictures, vaudeville, the circus, etc. Information is provided on: performers, authors, composers, directors, designers; types of entertainment; dramatic themes; historical and technical subjects; organizations and companies; and pertinent place-names. The supplement is mainly devoted to biographical sketches of figures not in the basic set. A supplement on the cinema, published in 1963, is now superseded except for the illustrations.

772. Gassner, John, and Edward Quinn, eds. **The Reader's Encyclopedia of World Drama.** Crowell, 1969. 1030p.
The drama of five continents from earliest times to the present is covered, with emphasis on drama as literature: biography and criticism of playwrights, plots of plays,

articles on genres, and historical surveys of national drama. Some articles give references to best editions, translations, and sources of added information. Some pictures of playwrights and scenes from plays are also included in this vital reference work.

773. Gröning, Karl, and Werner Kliess. **The Encyclopedia of World Theater**, tr. by Estella Schmid and adapted and amplified by Martin Esslin. Scribners, 1977. 320p.
Esslin has revised, expanded, and updated *Friedrichs Theaterlixikon*, which was published in Germany in 1969. Coverage is much stronger for Continental Europe than in most English-language encyclopedias. Playwrights, actors, theaters, and terms are covered in concise articles, which often have only one bibliographical reference. Many are illustrated by black and white photographs. An index of play titles provides complementary access.

774. Hartnoll, Phyllis. **The Oxford Companion to the Theatre.** 3rd ed. Oxford, 1967; repr., 1972. 1088p.
International in scope, this standard work covers all periods of history. The emphasis is on popular rather than literary theater, and on actors more than dramatists. Opera and ballet are each treated in single articles; the cinema is omitted. The arrangement is alphabetical, with short articles predominating. Other features include a "Select List of Theatre books" (pp. 1029-1074) and 175 illustrations with notes at the end.

775. **McGraw-Hill Encyclopedia of World Drama.** McGraw-Hill, 1972. 4v.
World coverage is attempted in this essential tool, which includes biographies of 910 dramatists, definitions of terms, and about 60 articles on schools and movements. The listing of works of major playwrights includes date of writing, first performance, and first publication. About 2,000 illustrations are also provided.

776. Matlaw, Myron. **Modern World Drama: An Encyclopedia.** Dutton, 1972. 960p.
Matlaw includes geographical entries (theater in various countries and regions), biographical entries (playwrights of the twentieth century), and technical terms (limited to modern ones describing movements and trends) all in one alphabetical sequence, with many cross references. There are short bibliographies at the end of many entries and a general bibliography. There is a "Character Index" (pp. 859-83) as well as a "General Index" (pp. 887-960).

777. Melchinger, Siegfried. **The Concise Encyclopedia of Modern Drama**, tr. by George Wellwarth and ed. by David Popkin. Horizon, 1964. 288p.
European and American coverage since about 1900 is provided. The work is divided into the following parts: Introduction to the Modern Drama; Documents on Contemporary Playwriting; Glossary of Modern Dramatic Theory; Biographies of Playwrights; Chronology of First Performances; Bibliography. There are 64 pages of production photographs.

778. Sobel, Bernard, ed. **The New Theatre Handbook and Digest of Plays.** 8th ed. Crown, 1959. 749p.
This vital handbook contains about 3,500 alphabetically arranged entries on topics ranging from general subjects to individual plays, actors, playwrights, producers, theaters, etc. There is a short bibliography, but no index.

Directories and Annuals

779. **Best Plays of 1894/99-** . Ann. Dodd, Mead.
A complicated bibliographical situation—created by attempts to provide retrospective coverage of the years 1894 to 1920—should not be allowed to obscure the usefulness of this vital reference work. A typical annual volume contains: digests and criticisms of selected plays; a title list of New York productions; plays produced outside New York; Shakespeare festivals; statistics of runs; lists of actors; prizes and awards; indexes of authors, plays, and casts, producers, directors, and designers. When used in conjunction with O'dell's *Annals of the New York Stage* (see item 799), the reader will have continuous coverage from 1699 to the present. Otis L. Guernsey has compiled an index entitled *Directory of the American Theater, 1894-1971; Index to the Complete Series of Best Plays Theater Yearbooks: Titles, Authors and Composers of Broadway, Off-Broadway, and Off-Off Broadway Shows and Their Sources* (Dodd, Mead, 1971).

780. **"The Stage" Year Book**, 1908- . Ann. Carson and Comerford.
Traditionally a directory of theaters and survey of theatrical events, this publication has broadened its scope in recent years to include television. British coverage, with particular emphasis on London is provided by *Theatre*, 1954/55- (Reinhardt). Research is covered in *The Theatre Annual*, 1942- (Theatre Library Association).

781. **John Willis' Theatre World**, 1944/45- . Ann. Crown.
Productions, openings, closings, casts, obituaries, and biographies are included. It was entitled *Theatre World* v. 1-27 (1944/45-1970/71).

782. **New York Theatre Annual**, 1976/77- . Ann. Gale.
Broadway, Off-Broadway, and Off-Off Broadway productions are covered. Information for each play includes: cast, opening date, closing date, plot summary, and excerpts from reviews. There are fewer illustrations than in *John Willis' Theatre World*.

783. Pride, Leo Bryan, ed. and comp. **International Theatre Directory: A World Directory of the Theatre and Performing Arts**. Simon & Schuster, 1973. 577p.
The basic arrangement is alphabetical by country, then by city and name of theater. In a few countries (e.g., Brazil, Canada, United States), the state or province is given, then the city and theater. Information is very brief, usually no more than a street address and seating capacity. Numerous black and white photographs are provided, as are some introductory comments on each country. There is a table of contents, but no index.

784. Young, William C. **American Theatrical Arts: A Guide to Manuscripts and special Collections in the United States and Canada**. ALA, 1971. 166p.
Collections in 138 institutions are described. Part I is arranged alphabetically by state or province, subarranged by institution and (if necessary) by name of collection. Part II is an analytical index by person and subject.

Histories

General

785.   Berthold, Margot. **A History of World Theater**, tr. by Edith Simmons. Ungar, 1972. 733p.
The author teaches theater history at the University of Munich. "The book includes an extensive index, separate bibliographies for each historical period, and over 400 illustrations" (review by Louis A. Rachow, *Library Journal*, October 15, 1972, p. 3330). Another useful work is *On Stage: A History of the Theatre*, by Vera Mowry Roberts (2nd ed., Harper, 1974).

786.   Brockett, Oscar G. **History of the Theatre**. Allyn and Bacon, 1968. 741p.
The entire period from ancient Egypt to the present is covered. One critic thought it the best one-volume history available, and another said that it superseded Sheldon Cheney's *The Theater* (1929), a judgment that might need revision with the 1972 appearance of a new edition of Cheney's book.

787.   Cheney, Sheldon. **The Theatre: Three Thousand Years of Drama, Acting and Stagecraft**. Rev. and reset illustrated ed. McKay, 1972. 710p.
Originally published in 1929, this work has been substantially updated. The revised edition contains about 60 new illustrations, some changes of text, about 50 pages of new text, and a new bibliography.

788.   Freedley, George, and John A. Reeves. **A History of the Theatre**. 3rd ed. Crown, 1968. 1008p.
Freedley and Reeves cover the entire period from ancient Egypt to the present and deal with all aspects of the theater in this well-illustrated work, which includes a bibliography. Bamber Gascoigne's *World Theatre: An Illustrated History* (Little, Brown, 1968) includes 31 color plates and 290 black and white illustrations. Another iullustrated history is Marion Geisinger's *Plays, Players and Playwrights* (rev. ed., Hart, 1975). Phyllis Hartnoll's *A Concise History of the Theatre* (Abrams, 1968) and *Histoire des spectacles* (Gallimard, 1965) may occasionally prove useful.

789.   Kindermann, Heinz. **Theatergeschichte Europas.** Müller, 1957-1974. 10v.
Contents: v. 1 — *Das Theater der Antike und des Mittelalters* (1957); v. 2 — *Das Theater der Renaissance* (1959); v. 3 — *Das Theater der Barockzeit* (1959); v. 4, 5 — *Von der Aufklärung zur Romantik* (1961/62); v. 6 — *Romantik* (1964); v. 7 — *Realismus* (1965); v. 8-10 — *Naturalismus und Impressionismus* (1968/74). Includes bibliographies.

Special Topics and Countries

790.   Abramson, Doris E. **Negro Playwrights in the American Theatre**, 1925-1959. Columbia, 1969. 335p.
Favorably reviewed as the best, most comprehensive study to its date of publication, this book is an analysis of twenty plays by black writers, with biographical information as well as critical commentary. Lofton Mitchell's *Black Drama: The Story of the American Negro in the Theatre* (Hawthorn, 1967) covers the period from 1820 to 1966 and is valuable for information on theatrical groups and contemporary dramatists.

791. Bentley, Gerald Eades. **The Jacobean and Caroline Stage.** Oxford, 1941-68. 7v.
Contents: v. 1, 2—*Dramatic Companies and Players* (1941); v. 3, 4, 5—*Plays and Playwrights* (1955); v. 6—*Theatres* (1968); v. 7—*Appendices to V. 6 and General Index* (1968). This valuable set covers the period from the death of Shakespeare (1616) to the closing of the theaters in 1642. Entries in v. 3-5 are alphabetical by playwright and give brief biographical information, manuscripts and important editions of plays, and a bibliography about the plays and their performance. The set is a continuation of *The Elizabethan Stage*, by E. K. Chambers (see item 793).

792. Blum, Daniel C. **A Pictorial History of the American Theatre, 1860-1976.** 4th ed. Crown, 1977. 448p.
This work continues to be a major source of pictorial and other information about the American stage (especially New York). There is an excellent index to plays and players. *Century of Innovation*, by Oscar G. Brockett and Robert R. Findlay (Prentice-Hall, 1973), is a useful source for the period since 1870. Another source is *Theatre U.S.A.: 1665 to 1957*, by Bernard Hewitt (McGraw-Hill, 1959).

793. Chambers, Sir Edmund Kerchiver. **The Elizabethan Stage**, Oxford, 1923; repr., 1974. 4v.
Chambers is still the standard work, though parts have been updated in other studies. Topics covered include: the Court and control of the stage; companies and playhouses; staging at Court and in the theaters; plays and authors. At end of v. 4 are listed anonymous works, appendices of original documents, and the indexes (plays, persons, places, subjects). Chambers also wrote a companion work, *William Shakespeare: A Study of Facts and Problems* (Oxford, 1930). These two works have been indexed by Beatrice White in *Index to "The Elizabethan Stage" and "William Shakespeare"* (Oxford, 1934; repr., Blom, 1964).

794. Chambers, Sir Edmund Kerchiver. **The Mediaeval Stage.** Oxford, 1903; repr., 1967. 2v.
Contents: v. 1—*Minstrelsy. Folk Drama*; v. 2—*Religious Drama; The Interlude; Appendices; Subject Index.* This is the most comprehensive and authoritative account of the period from the fall of the Roman Empire to early Tudor England.

795. Genest, John. **Some Account of the English Stage, from the Restoration in 1660 to 1830.** H. E. Carrington, 1832; repr., Franklin, 1965. 10v.
The arrangement is chronological. V. 10 deals with Ireland but also includes additions, corrections, and the index to the set. The earlier period is covered by Alfred Harbage's *Annals of English Drama, 975-1700; An Analytical Record of All Plays, Extant or Lost, Chronologically Arranged and Indexed by Authors, Titles, Dramatic Companies, Etc.*, rev. by S. Schoenbaum (Methuen, 1964; suppls., 1966, 1970).

796. Hughes, Glenn. **A History of the American Theatre, 1700-1950.** French, 1951. 562p.
Good general coverage is provided for the years indicated. More specialized sources include *American Vaudeville: Its Life and Times*, by Gilbert Douglas (Peter Smith, 1940); *The City and the Theatre: New York Playhouses from Bowling Green to Times Square* (J. T. White, 1973); and *Nineteenth-Century American Drama, a Finding Guide*, by Donald L. Hixon and Don A. Hennessee (Scarecrow, 1977).

797. **The London Stage, 1660-1800: A Calendar of Plays, Entertainments and After-pieces, Together with Casts, Box Receipts and Contemporary Comment; Compiled from the Playbills, Newspapers and Theatrical Diaries of the Period.** Southern Illinois University Press, 1960-1968. 5 pts. in 11v.

Each volume covers part of the period. Day by day chronologies of performances are provided. Information about each play includes cast, incidental comments, and supporting references. *The London Stage: A Critical Introduction*, by Emmett L. Avery and others (SIU Press, 1968, 5v.), contains the critical introductions to each of the five parts of *The London Stage*. Intensive coverage of a brief later period is provided by J. P. Wearing in *The London Stage, 1890-1899: A Calendar of Plays and Players* (Scarecrow, 1976, 2v.).

798. Nicoll, Allardyce. **A History of English Drama, 1660-1900.** Cambridge, 1952-59. 6v.

V. 1-5 follow the same general pattern of a historical section followed by appendices covering such topics as lists of theaters, handlists of plays, etc. V. 6 serves as an index to the set, although it is much more than that. Contents: v. 1—*Restoration Drama, 1660-1700*; v. 2—*Early Eighteenth Century Drama, 1700-1750*; v. 3—*Late Eighteenth Century Drama, 1750-1800*; v. 4—*Early Nineteenth Century Drama, 1800-1850*; v. 5—*Late Nineteenth Century Drama, 1850-1900*; v. 6—*A Short-Title Alphabetical Catalogue of Plays Produced or Printed in England from 1600 to 1900*.

799. Odell, George. **Annals of the New York Stage.** Columbia, 1927-49; repr., AMS, 1970. 15v.

Odell chronicles the period from 1699 to 1894. Each volume covers a specified part of the period (v. 1, to 1798; v. 2, 1798 to 1821, etc.), and each is extremely detailed, with many illustrations and an analytical index. Access to the illustrations is facilitated by *Index to the Portraits in Odell's "Annals of the New York Stage"* (American Society for Theatre Research, 1963). Coverage from 1894 to the present is provided by the *Best Plays* series (see item 779).

800. Wickham, Glynne William Gladstone. **Early English Stages, 1300 to 1660.** Columbia, 1959- .

Contents: v. 1—*1300 to 1576* (1959); v. 2—*1576 to 1660*—pt. 1 (1963), pt. 2 (1965). Planned for completion in three volumes, it is expected that v. 3 will cover theater buildings and performances. V. 1 covers outdoor and indoor entertainment and dramatic theory, while v. 2 covers emblems and images. Illustrated.

801. Williams, Raymond. **Drama from Ibsen to Brecht.** Oxford, 1968; repr., Penguin, 1973. 408p.

The 1953 edition was published under the title *Drama from Ibsen to Eliot*. Bibliographical references are included.

802. Young, William C., ed. **Documents of American Theater History.** ALA, 1973; Bowker, 1975- .

Contents: v. 1—*Famous American Playhouses, 1716-1899* (1973); v. 2—*Famous American Playhouses, 1900-1971* (1973); v. 3, 4—*Famous Actors and Actresses of the American Stage* (1975). A seven-volume series was projected. In v. 1, 2 the compiler included excerpts on 199 black and white illustrations and 18 plans. Each volume has the following indexes: theaters arranged alphabetically, theaters arranged geographically, and personal names and theatrical specialties. Reviewers differed widely in their assessments, ranging from highly favorable (*Library Quarterly*, April 1974, p. 167) to withholding judgment (*Booklist*, January 1, 1974, p. 451) to highly critical of many inaccuracies and peculiarities of selection (*ARBA 1974*, pp. 419-20). Reviews of v. 3, 4 appeared to be similarly mixed, ranging from highly favorable (*Choice*, February 1976, p. 1554) to highly unfavorable (*ARBA 1976*, pp. 493-94).

Biographies

803.   Arata, Esther Spring, and Nicholas John Rotoli. **Black American Playwrights, 1800 to the Present: A Bibliography.** Scarecrow, 1976. 295p.
Finding biographical information with this tool is, of course, a two-step process. There are 1,550 entries for 530 playwrights. The main part is alphabetical by playwrights' names and includes listings of plays and citations to sources of criticism. This is followed by a general bibliography and a title index. A similar plan is used in Arata's *More Black American Playwrights: A Bibliography* (Scarecrow, 1978). Regular dictionaries of biography are more useful for most searches, but these volumes will help for many playwrights not easily found elsewhere.

804.   **A Biographical Dictionary of Actors, Actresses, Musicians, Dancers, Managers and Other Stage Personnel in London, 1660-1800,** ed. by Philip H. Highfill, Jr., Kalman A. Burnim, and Edward A. Langhams. Southern Illinois University Press, 1973- .
This vital source, arranged alphabetically by surnames, is to be published in twelve volumes: v.1—*Abaco to Belfille*; v. 2—*Belfort to Byzand*; v. 3—*Gabanel to Cory*; v. 4—*Corye to Dynion*. The preceding period is covered by Frederick Gard Fleay's *A Biographical Chronicle of the English Drama, 1559-1642* (Reeves and Turner, 1891; repr., Franklin, 1973, 2v.), which is arranged alphabetically by authors with appendices at the end of v. 2 on anonymous plays and masques, university plays, and translations.

805.   Kosch, Wilhelm. **Deutsches Theater-Lexikon: biographisches und bibliographisches Handbuch.** Francke, 1951- .
Covers theater and drama in Germany, including movements, actors, playwrights and critics, with lists of works. Contents: v. 1—*A-Hurk* (1953); v. 2—*Hurka-Pallenberg* (1960); v. 3 (in progress).

806.   **Notable Names in the American Theatre.** J. T. White, 1976. 1250p.
This is actually the second edition of Walter Rigdon's *Biographical Encyclopedia and Who's Who of the American Theatre* (Heineman, 1966). The opening sections of this excellent reference work cover New York productions 1900-1974, premieres in America, premieres of American plays abroad, theater group biographies, theater building biographies, awards, biographical bibliography, and necrology. The main part consists of detailed biographies of Americans and others connected with the American theater. Some obscure authors not found in standard reference works may be located in *The National Playwright's Directory*, edited by Phyllis Johnson Kaye (distr., Drama Books Specialists, 1977). Also less than vital, but occasionally useful, is Allan Lewis's *American Plays and Playwrights of the Contemporary Theatre* (rev. ed., Crown, 1970).

807.   Vinson, James, ed. **Contemporary Dramatists.** 2nd ed. St. Martin's, 1977. 1088p.
This essential reference tool has biographies of 300 living dramatists writing in English, with signed critical essays, and bibliographies of their published works. Briefer information is also given for screenwriters, librettists, and radio and TV writers. A necrology of playwrights who have died since the mid-1950s and a title index of plays mentioned in the text enhance the usefulness of this book.

808.   **Who's Who in the Theatre: A Biographical Record of the Contemporary Stage**, 1912- . Pitman; Gale.
Published at irregular intervals, the latest edition (16th) appeared in 1977. Contents typically include playbills in major theater cities, biographies of about 2,000 actors (mainly British and American), major productions and long runs in London and New York, centers for theater research, etc. *Who Was Who in the Theatre, 1912-1976* (Pitman; Gale, 1978, 4v.) is based on the first fifteen editions of *Who's Who in the Theatre* and includes some 4,100 biographies.

Anthologies and Digests of Plays

809.   **Best American Plays**, 1939- . Crown.
The title has varied. For the first series, it was *Twenty Best Plays of the Modern American Theatre.* A supplementary volume, edited by John Gassner and covering the years 1918 to 1958, was published in 1961. Jane E. Bonin's *Prize-Winning American Drama: A Bibliographical and Descriptive Guide* (Scarecrow, 1973) provides descriptive information, plot summaries, and selective references to reviews and evaluations for 78 plays, arranged by theater seasons, from 1917 to 1971. There is an author/title index.

810.   Gassner, John, and Bernard F. Dukore, eds. **A Treasury of the Theatre.** 4th ed. Simon and Schuster, 1970- .
The main part is an anthology of plays arranged by periods, with brief period introductions. There is also a selection of additional plays, grouped topically, with brief introductions to the topical sections. About forty of the world's most famous plays are reproduced in full. Other essential anthologies edited by Gassner include *Best Plays of the Early American Theatre: From the Beginning to 1916* (Crown, 1967; repr., 1974) and *Twenty Best European Plays on the American Stage* (Crown, 1957).

811.   Goldman, Mark, comp. **The Drama: Traditional and Modern.** Allyn and Bacon, 1968. 690p.
Goldman includes introductions to periods and types as well as representative plays with notes. Bibliographical references are also given. This book covers a relatively small selection of landmark plays, with emphasis on the modern period. Another useful source is Van Henry Cartmell's *Plot Outlines of 100 Famous Plays* (Barnes & Noble, 1945; repr., Smith, 1975). In its own area, Abe Laufe's *Broadway's Greatest Musicals* (rev. ed., Funk & Wagnalls, 1977) is also useful. John Lovell's *Digests of Great American Plays: Complete Summaries of More Than 100 Plays from the Beginnings to the Present* (Crowell, 1961) may also be useful. *One-Act Plays for Our Times*, edited by Francis J. Griffith (Popular Library, 1973) has introductions and study aids. Evert Sprinchorn's *20th-Century Plays in Synopsis* (Crowell, 1966) has act-by-act summaries for 133 plays.

812. **One-Act Plays for Stage and Study.** French, 1925. 490p.
This essential work includes contemporary plays by English, Irish, American and other writers.

813. Patterson, Lindsay, comp. **Anthology of the Afro-American in Theatre: A Critical Approach.** Rev. ed. Publishers Agency, 306p.
Another valuable anthology by the same compiler is *Black Theater: A 20th Century Collection of the Work of Its Best Playwrights* (New American Library, 1971), which is regarded as a vital tool by many reference librarians. Also essential because it reprints a number of plays not easily obtainable is James V. Hatch's *Black Theater U.S.A.: Forty-Five Plays by Black Americans, 1847-1974* (Free Press, 1974).

814. Richards, Stanley, comp. **Best Plays of the Sixties.** Doubleday, 1970. 1036p.
This is a valuable anthology, with introductory comments, for an interesting decade in American theater history.

815. Shank, Theodore, Jr., ed. **a Digest of 500 Plays: Plot Outlines and Production Notes.** Crowell-Collier, 1963. 475p.
This useful work follows a classified arrangement (by country and period) with an author and title index.

816. Shipley, Joseph T. **Guide to Great Plays.** Public Affairs Press, 1956. 867p.
For each play chosen, the following information is given: 1. name of author, country, date, etc.; 2. a brief synopsis; 3. important aspects of the play's history; 4. analysis; 5. opinions of critics and reviewers; 6. prominent actors who acted in it. The book is arranged alphabetically by authors.

Reviews

817. **New York Theatre Critics Reviews,** 1940- . 30/yr. New York Theatre Critics Reviews.
Complete Broadway theater reviews are reproduced from the *New York Daily News, New York Post, New York Times, Newsweek, Time, Wall Street Journal, Women's Wear Daily, Christian Science Monitor*, and NBC.

818. **New York Times Theater Reviews, 1920-1970.** New York Times, 1971. 10v.
Reviews are arranged chronologically in v. 1-8. V. 9 has an appendix of theater awards and summaries of productions and runs, by season as well as indexes by titles and production companies. V. 10 is an index of personal names. *New York Times Directory of the Theater* (Arno, 1973) contains an appendix and index to *New York Times Theater Reviews, 1920-1970. On Stage: Selected Theater Reviews from the New York Times, 1920-1970*, edited by Bernard Beckerman and Howard Siegman (Arno, 1973), is a handy one-volume anthology. Updating of the basic set is provided by the biennial publication, *New York Times Theater Reviews*, 1971/72- (Arno).

819. Stanley, William T. **Broadway in the West End: An Index of Reviews of American Theater in London, 1950-1975.** Greenwood, 1978. 206p.
Citations are provided for 3,000 reviews of 339 productions. There are three parts: a bibliography of reviews, arranged alphabetically by playwrights and titles of plays; a chronological listing of shows; and a title index that refers to the authors in part one.

Appendices cover longest-running productions, plays and musicals in London, New York productions, and London theaters.

Production and Direction

820.   Cole, Toby, and Helen Krich Chinoy. **Directors on Directing: A Source Book of the Modern Theater.** 2nd rev. ed. Bobbs-Merrill, 1976. 464p.
This well-illustrated work, which covers history, theory, and practice (including some examples of famous productions), first appeared in 1953 under the title *Directing the Play*. Other books to help the director include *Stage Direction in Transition*, by Hardie Albright (Dickenson, 1972); *Sense of Direction: The Director and His Actors*, by John Fernald (Stein and Day, 1968; repr., University Microfilms, 1978); *Play Directing: Analysis, Communication and Style*, by Francis Hodge (Prentice-Hall, 1971); and *Theatrical Direction: The Basic Techniques*, by David Harold Welker (Allyn and Bacon, 1971).

821.   Farber, Donald C. **From Option to Opening.** 3rd ed. Drama Book Specialists, 1977. 144p.
Topics covered in this vital source include: optioning a property; co-production agreements; the producing company; raising the money; obtaining a theater; cast, crew, and personnel; musicals; rehearsals, run, open, or close; repertories, children's theater, and Off-Off Broadway; vitally important odds and ends. An older work of value to amateurs is *The ABC's of Play Producing: A Handbook for the Nonprofessional*, by Howard Bailey (McKay, 1955), which covers such topics as selection, casting, rehearsing, scenery, and lighting. *Hendrik Baker's Stage Management and Theatrecraft: A Handbook for the Nonprofessional* (2nd ed., Miller, 1971) covers such topics as stage history, scripts, rehearsals, staff, the stage, scenery, properties, lighting, wardrobe, dress rehearsals, first nights, and runs. It also has a glossary of theatrical terms, an index, and suggestions for further reading. Harold Clurman's *On Directing* (Macmillan, 1972; repr., Collier, 1974) covers the process from the selection of a script through the dress rehearsal and acting methods and audience reactions. There are also directors' notes on specific modern plays. A brief name and title index is provided. *Theatre and Stage: An Encyclopaedic Guide to the Performance of All Amateur Dramatic, Operatic and Theatrical Work*, edited by Harold Downs (Pitman, 1951; repr., Greenwood, 1978), deals with techniques (acting, lighting, etc.) and consists of alphabetically arranged articles, with copious illustrations (some in color).

822.   Gassner, John. **Producing the Play, with the New Scene Technician's Handbook,** by Philip Barber. Rev. ed. Holt; Dryden, 1953. 915p.
Gassner's excellent book covers all phases of play production. A work noted for its practicality, especially for amateur groups, is *Play Production for Little Theatres, Schools, and Colleges*, by Milton Smith (Appleton, 1948).

823.   Heffner, Hubert C. **Modern Theatre Practice.** 5th ed. Appleton, 1973. 660p.
This authoritative text covers all phases of the subject; it includes glossaries, an annotated bibliography, and an index. The fifth edition contains an expansion of the scenery section by Tom Rezzuto and a chapter on sound by Kenneth K. Jones.

824. Lounsbury, Warren C. **Theatre: Backstage from A to Z.** University of Washington Press, 1972. 191p.

Lounsbury's vital reference book is intended for those concerned with the technical aspects of production (lighting, scenery, etc.) and is usefully complemented by such books as *Stage Scenery, Machinery and Lighting*, by Richard Stoddard (Gale, 1977), *Theatre Lighting: An Illustrated Glossary*, by Albert F. C. Wehlbury (Drama Book Specialists, 1976), and *Theatrical Set Design: The Basic Techniques*, by David Welker (2nd ed., Allyn and Bacon, 1979).

Periodicals

825. **Drama: The Quarterly Theatre Review**, 1919- . Q. British Drama League.

Indexed: *Br.Hum.Ind., Abstr.Engl.Stud., Hum.Ind., Bk.Rev.Ind.* All aspects of the theater are covered by this vital periodical. Many excellent book reviews are included.

826. **Educational Theatre Journal**, 1949- . Q. American Educational Theatre Association.

Indexed: *Abstr.Engl.Stud., CIJE, Ed.Ind., Hum.Ind., MLA Abstr., Art.Schol.J., MLA Int.Bib.* Planned for teachers and students, this journal provides a survey of contemporary scholarship, reviews of college productions, and bibliographies.

827. **Players Magazine**, 1924- . Bi-mo. National Collegiate Players.

Indexed: *Abstr.Eng.Stud., Hum.Ind., MLA Int.Bib.* Articles are directed at the interests of the college theater community.

828. **Plays and Players**, 1953- . Mo. Hansom.

Indexed: *Hum.Ind.* Articles cover such topics as theater in general, actors, and specific plays. A large part of each issue is devoted to reviews of plays and particular performances in London. Each issue also contains part of the text of a play.

829. **Plays: The Drama Magazine for Young People**, 1941- . Mo. (Oct.-May). Plays, Inc.

Indexed: *RG, Subj.Ind. to Child.Mag.* A typical issue will contain 8-10 plays suitable for elementary, junior, or senior high school performances as well as book reviews.

830. **Revue d'histoire du théâtre**, 1948/49- . Q. Société d'histoire du théâtre.

The first three issues each year contain articles on theater history. The fourth issue is a classified bibliography of 4,000-5,000 items.

831. **Theatre Design and Technology**, 1965- . Q. U.S. Institute for Theatre Technology.

Articles on construction, design, lighting, sound, etc. are included, as well as bibliographies.

832. **Theatre Information Bulletin**, 1944- . Wk. Proscenium Publications.

This weekly processed publication is rather expensive and unlikely to be available except in large research collections. *Theatre Documentation*, 1968-1971, used to be issued semi-annually by the Theatre Library Association, but it ceased publication with v. 4, no. 1, 1971-72.

833. **Tulane Drama Review**, 1955- . Q. Tulane University.
Issues of this periodical typically contain scholarly articles on films and the theater. Reviews of books and plays appear from time to time, but not on a regular basis.

FILM, RADIO, AND TELEVISION

Introductory Works and Bibliographic Guides

834. Artel, Linda, and Susan Wengraf. **Positive Images: A Guide to Non-Sexist Films for Young People.** Booklegger Press, 1976. 168p.
Critical annotations are provided for 400 films, filmstrips, videotapes, slide shows, and sets of photographs. Entries provide information about such matters as length, color or black and white, distributor, date, price, and age level. A subject index and a directory enhance the value of this unique tool for reference and selection purposes.

835. Bukalski, Peter J., comp. **Film Research: A Critical Bibliography with Annotations and Essay.** G. K. Hall, 1972. 215p.
An introductory essay on film research is followed by a classified, annotated bibliography and a separate section on films, distributors and rental agencies.

836. Gottesman, Ronald, and Harry M. Geduld. **Guidebook to Film: An Eleven-in-One Reference.** Holt, 1972. 230p.
A good starting point for a variety of searches. Contents: Books and Periodicals: An Annotated List; Theses and Dissertations; Museums and Archives; Film Schools; Equipment and Supplies; Film Organizations and Services; Festivals and Contests; Awards; Terminology in General Use. Complementary coverage may be found in Joan Cohen's "A Visual Explosion: The Growth of Film Literature," *Choice*, March 1973, pp. 26-40; Michael Stuart Freeman lists and describes briefly over 40 bibliographic guides in "Guide to the Bibliographic Sources on Film Literature," *RQ*, Summer 1974, pp. 308-312; William Jinks provides information on camera techniques, editing, sound, symbolism, and criticism in *The Celluloid Literature: Film in the Humanities* (2nd ed., Glencoe, 1974). Paul Roy Madsen provides analysis and an extensive bibliography in *The Impact of Film: How Ideas Are Communicated through Cinema and Television* (Macmillan, 1973). Frank Manchel's *Film Study: A Resource Guide* (Fairleigh Dickinson University Press, 1973) is an important annotated bibliography of printed materials and films used in the study of motion pictures.

837. Huss, Roy Gerard, and Norman Silverstein. **The Film Experience: Elements of Motion Picture Art.** Harper, 1968. 172p.
Well-written and illustrated, this valuable book supplies examples from all periods of the cinema and from most film-producing countries.

838. Manoogian, Haig P. **The Film-Maker's Art.** Basic Books, 1966. 340p.
Manoogian's book on production for reviewers and film makers provides some blending of theory and technique and has been praised for its lucidity and practicality.

839. Mast, Gerald, and Marshall Cohen, comps. **Film Theory and Criticism: Introductory Readings.** 2nd ed. Oxford, 1979. 877p.
Almost all the major dimensions of film theory are covered in this anthology of articles and essays grouped by broad topics. Photographs and a bibliography enhance its

reference usefulness. Andre Bazin's *What Is Cinema?* (University of California Press, 1967-71, 2v.) also contains bibliographical references. Significant older works on film theory include *Film as Art*, by Rudolf Arnheim (University of California Press, 1957; repr., 1974), *Film Form and The Film Sense*, by S. M. Eisenstein (Meredian, 1957; repr., World, 1967), and *Theory of Film: The Redemption of Physical Reality*, by Siegfried Kracauer (Oxford, 1960; repr., 1965).

840. Rufsvold, Margaret Irene. **Guides to Educational Media: Films, Filmstrips, Multimedia Kits, Programmed Instruction Materials, Recordings on Discs and Tapes, Slides, Transparencies, Videotapes.** 4th ed. ALA, 1977. 159p.
The first and second editions of this essential bibliographic guide were published under the title *Guides to Newer Educational Media*. The present edition annotates 245 educational media catalogs, indexes, and reviewing services. Annotations indicate scope, content, arrangement, and suggested audience. The book is arranged alphabetically by title, with an index by subjects, authors, publishers, etc. James L. Limbacher's *A Reference Guide to Audiovisual Information* (Bowker, 1972) is an annotated bibliography of 400 reference works and 100 periodicals, with a glossary and a subject index.

Bibliographies (Current and Retrospective)

841. **The American Film Institute Catalog of Motion Pictures Produced in the United States.** Bowker, 1971- .
This multi-volume set, when completed, will be the most exhaustive listing of films ever compiled. The project is housed in the Library of Congress and funded by grants from the National Endowment for the Arts, the Ford Foundation, and the Motion Picture Association of America. Part A will cover all films from 1893 to 1910. Parts F1 through F6 will cover feature films from 1911 through 1970. Parts S1 through S6 will cover short films from 1911 through 1970, and parts N1 through N6 will be devoted to newsreels from 1908 through 1970. F2, *Feature Films, 1921-1930*, was published in 1971; F6, *Feature Films, 1961-1970*, was published in 1976. Each part consists of two volumes. The first volume lists films alphabetically by title, assigns to each a unique number, and provides very complete descriptive information, including casts and plot summaries. The second volume provides detailed credit and subject indexes. For an excellent description of the whole project, see "The American Film Institute Cataloging Project," by Phyllis Zucker, in *Performing Arts Resources* (Drama Book Specialists), v. 1, 1974, pp. 147-52. For a detailed description and evaluation of *Feature Films 1961-70*, see the review by Richard M. Buck in *ARBA 1977*, pp. 485-86. Complementary coverage is provided by Denis Gifford in *The British Film Catalogue, 1895-1970: A Guide to Entertainment Films* (David & Charles, 1973) and by W. E. Hurst in *Film Superlist: 20,000 Motion Pictures in the Public Domain* (7 Arts Press, 1973).

842. **Bibliographie internationale du cinéma et de la télévision,** by Jean Mitry. Institut des Hautes Etudes Cinématographiques, 1966- .
Contents: 1. France et pays de langue francaise (4v., 1966-67); 2. Italie (2v., 1967); 3. Espagne, Portugal et pays de langue espagnol et portuguaise (1968).

843. California. University at Los Angeles. Theatre Arts Library. **Motion Pictures: A Catalog of Books, Periodicals, Screen and Production Stills.** G. K. Hall, 1973. 2v.
This valuable catalog makes accessible a rich collection of primary and secondary sources, including personal papers and over 3,000 unpublished scripts of American, British, and foreign films.

844.   McCarty, Clifford. **Published Screenplays: A Checklist.** Kent State University Press, 1971. 127p.
The compiler has attempted comprehensive coverage of published screenplays that have been produced. Other forms (outlines, synopses, novels made into movies) have been excluded. Arrangement is alphabetical by title. Information given includes: production company and date; director; author(s) of screenplay; source (if not original); location of published screenplay.

845.   McCavitt, William E., comp. **Radio and Television: A Selected, Annotated Bibliography.** Scarecrow, 1978. 241p.
A classified arrangement (with a detailed table of contents) provides subject access, and this is supplemented by an author index. There are 1,100 items, mostly annotated, and numerous cross references. The period covered is 1920 to 1976.

846.   Rehrauer, George. **Cinema Booklist.** Scarecrow Press, 1972. 473p. Suppls. 1974, 1977.
Primarily an annotated bibliography, Rehrauer's book and its supplements are designed for the general reader as an aid in locating information and for the librarian as a guide in collection development. Over 1,500 items are included. The arrangement is alphabetical by title. Entries are given consecutive numbers. The basic arrangement is supplemented by lists of: classic film scripts; modern film scripts; film periodicals; study guides. There is an author index and a selective subject index. Lists and indexes refer back to the main part by item number. The reviewer in *ARBA 1977* (p. 483) thought Alan R. Dyment's *The Literature of the Film: A Bibliographical Guide to the Film as Entertainment, 1936-1970* (White Lion; Gale, 1975) was good for selection purposes, but less valuable than Rehrauer.

847.   Schuster, Mel. **Motion Picture Performers: A Bibliography of Magazine and Periodical Articles, 1900-1969.** Scarecrow Press, 1971. 702p. Suppl., 1970-1974. 1976.
This vital book is a time-saver for obscure figures (despite the formidable list of omissions because nothing could be found) and for relatively complete access to sources for better-known ones. The arrangement is alphabetical by performers' surnames. The coverage is limited to English-language publications (primarily American). Schuster has also compiled *Motion Picture Directors: A Bibliography of Magazine and Periodical Articles, 1900-1972* (Scarecrow, 1973), which covers some 2,300 directors, film makers, and animators. The basic arrangement is alphabetical by surnames and then chronological for bibliographical entries. Important minority coverage is provided by Anne Powers in *Blacks in American Movies: A Selected Bibliography* (Scarecrow, 1974).

848.   U.S. Library of Congress. **National Union Catalog: Motion Pictures and Filmstrips,** 1953- . Q. Ann. & 5-yr. cum.
The basic arrangement is by title, with a subject index. There are many cross references, and the bibliographic detail is good. This is a vital source because of its comprehensive coverage. More specialized guides may be useful on particular occasions, e.g., James L. Limbacher's *Feature Films on 8mm and 16mm: A Directory of Feature Films Available for Rental, Sale and Lease in the United States and Canada, with Serials and Directors' Indexes* (5th ed., Bowker, 1977). Selective coverage of another sort is provided by Salvatore J. Parlato's *Superfilms: An International Guide to Award-Winning Educational Films* (Scarecrow, 1976). Specialized subject guides include Helen W. Cyr's *A*

Filmography of the Third World: An Annotated List of 16mm Films (Scarecrow, 1976) and Rosemary R. Kowalski's *Women and Film: A Bibliography* (Scarecrow, 1976). Valuable coverage of the "incunabula" of the film world is provided in Kent Niver's *Motion Pictures from the Library of Congress Paper Print Collection, 1894-1912* (University of California Press, 1967). This classified, annotated bibliography of some 3,000 films provides supplementary access through subject and title indexes.

849. Writers' Program, New York. **The Film Index, a Bibliography.** Wilson, 1941; repr., Arno, 1966. 723p.
Part I of this classified, annotated bibliography deals with "History and Technique," while part II covers "Types of Film." A detailed index includes authors, titles of books and films, names of persons listed in production credits, names of important persons discussed in digests, and titles of classifications.

Indexes, Abstracts, and Current Awareness Services

850. Batty, Linda. **Retrospective Index to Film Periodicals, 1930-1971.** Bowker, 1975. 425p.
This work is divided into three parts: index of reviews of individual films; index of film subjects; and index of book review citations. Reviewers have noted that coverage is very weak before 1950, but reasonably strong after that date. A similar deficiency limits the usfulness for those early years of Stephen E. Bowles's *Index to Critical Film Reviews in British and American Film together with Index to Critical Reviews of Books about Film* (Franklin, 1974-75, 2v.). For reviews of both, see *ARBA 1976*, pp. 509-510.

851. Dimmitt, Richard Bertrand. **An Actor Guide to the Talkies: A Comprehensive Listing of 8,000 Feature-Length Films from January, 1949, until December, 1964.** Scarecrow, 1967-1968. 2v.
Volume I is by film titles, with listings of casts. V. II is a name index to the thousands of actors mentioned in v. I. This basic set is continued and updated by *An Actor Guide to the Talkies, 1965 through 1974*, by Andrew A. Aros (Scarecrow, 1977).

852. Dimmitt, Richard Bertrand. **A Title Guide to the Talkies: A Comprehensive Listing of 16,000 Feature-Length Films from October, 1927, until December, 1963.** Scarecrow, 1965. 2v.
The chief purpose is to help reference librarians meet the needs of patrons who have seen movies and want to read the novels, plays, poems, short stories, or screen stories on which those movies were based. It is continued and updated by Andrew Aros's *A Title Guide to the Talkies, 1964 through 1974* (Scarecrow, 1977). Carol A. Emmens has prepared another kind of convenient supplement to Dimmitt in *Short Stories on Film* (Libraries Unlimited, 1978), which covers movies from 1920 to 1976 that were based on stories by American and well-known foreign authors. Over 1,300 entries are arranged alphabetically by writers and indexed by film titles.

853. Enser, A. G. S. **Filmed Books and Plays: A List of Books and Plays from Which Films Have Been Made, 1928-1974.** Rev. cum. ed. Deutsch, 1975. 549p.
Compiled by a British librarian, this book takes 1928 as its starting point because most films from that time forward have been talking pictures. There are three parts: film title index; author index; change of original title index.

854. **Film Literature Index: A Quarterly Author-Subject Periodical Index to the International Literature of Film**, 1973- . Q. Ann. cum. Filmdex.
Over 150 periodicals dealing primarily with films are indexed completely, and over 100 other periodicals are indexed selectively. Gerald Shields (*ARBA 1977*, p. 489) described it as "not only the most complete on the subject but also the best organized and most user-oriented." *International Index to Film Periodicals*, 1972- (irreg., St. Martins) is a specialized scholarly work prepared by the International Federation of Film Archives. **International Index to Multi-Media Information**, 1970- (Q., Audio-Visual Associates) carried the title *Film Review Index* from 1970 through 1972 and restricted its coverage to 16mm films. It changed to the present title in 1973 and expanded to include other AV formats, more complete bibliographical information, and excerpts from reviews. In 1975, cumulated volumes for 1970-1972 were issued under the new title and with coverage expanded to conform to the new scope.

855. Gerlach, John C., and Lana Gerlach. **The Critical Index: A Bibliography of Articles on Film in English, 1946-1973, Arranged by Names and Topics.** Teachers College Press, 1974. 726p.
This excellent index includes some 5,000 items on all aspects of the film (directors, producers, actors, critics, topics, specific films, etc.). The "names" section is alphabetical, and the "topics" section is hierarchically classified with an alphabetical "dictionary" and instructions in the front. Author and film indexes are provided. Appendices include supplementary bibliographies and a list of magazines not indexed. Another useful tool is *The New Film Index: A Bibliography of Magazine Articles in English, 1930-1970*, by Richard Dyer McCann and Edward S. Perry (Dutton, 1975).

856. **Media Review Digest**, 1970- . Q. Ann. cum. Pierian.
Entitled *Multi-Media Reviews Index* from 1970 through 1972, its title was changed and its coverage expanded in 1973. Citations to approximately 40,000 reviews in about 200 periodicals are provided, together with some excerpts from reviews. Part I is divided into three sections: films and videotapes; filmstrips; miscellaneous media. Each section is arranged alphabetically by title. Part II lists records and tapes in a single alphabet by composer, performer, author, or title (for educational items). Subject indexes (both alphabetical and classified by Dewey) are also provided.

857. Weaver, John T. **Forty Years of Screen Credits, 1929-1969.** Scarecrow, 1970. 2v.
The basic arrangement is alphabetical by surnames of actors and actresses and then chronological, with years and titles of movies each year.

858. Weaver, John T. **Twenty Years of Silents, 1908-1928.** Scarecrow, 1971. 514p.
Part I is entitled "The Players." The heart of this section is "Screen Credits," arranged alphabetically by actor, then chronologically with years and titles of movies each year. A similar plan is followed in part II, "The Directors and Producers." Both parts also have separate sections on "vital statistics." Part III deals with corporations and distributors.

Dictionaries and Encyclopedias

859. Bessy, Maurice, and Jean-Louis Chardans. **Dictionnaire du cinéma et de la télévision.** Jean-Jacques Pauvert, 1965-1971. 4v.
This important set is especially good on the history and technology of the movies, but it

is less consistent on television. It is profusely illustrated with small black and white photographs.

860. Boussinot, Roger. **L'Encyclopédie du cinéma.** Bordas, 1967. 1550p.
International in scope, this valuable reference tool encompasses all aspects in one volume. One alphabetical listing includes individuals, films, techniques, organizations, and countries. There are no bibliographies, and the articles are unsigned.

861. Brown, Les. **The New York Times Encyclopedia of Television.** Times Books; distr., Harper, 1977. 650p.
Considered one of the best reference books of 1977 (*Library Journal*, April 15, 1978, p. 818) this convenient source has short articles on producers, commentators, critics, news correspondents, individual shows, organizations, technical terms, and miscellaneous topics related to TV.

862. Dunning, John. **Tune in Yesterday: The Ultimate Encyclopedia of Old-Time Radio, 1925-1976.** Prentice-Hall, 1976. 703p.
Included in "Reference Books of 1977" (*Library Journal*, April 15, 1978, p. 818), this useful work contains alphabetically arranged articles on radio shows, with the articles varying in length from a short paragraph ("Captain Flagg and Sergeant Quirt") to several pages ("Fibber McGee and Molly"). There is an index of names to complement the basic arrangement by show titles. The plates (black and white photographs) are neither numbered nor indexed.

863. Graham, Peter John. **A Dictionary of the Cinema.** Rev. ed. Barnes, 1968. 175p.
Over 600 short biographies, a brief guide to technical terms, and an index to 7,500 film titles are included in this convenient dictionary.

864. Halliwell, Leslie. **The Filmgoer's Companion.** 6th ed. Avon, 1978. 825p.
Planned for the general public, this convenient reference work has entries for actors, directors, producers, photographers, technical terms, general topics, and outstanding individual films. The expanded edition adds many biographical articles and short articles on new topics. There are many short entries in one alphabet, thus avoiding need for an index. *Halliwell's Film Guide: A Survey of 8,000 English-Language Movies* (Granada, 1977) has about ten times as many films as *The Filmgoer's Companion*, but its scope is restricted to films. Entries in the *Guide* are arranged alphabetically by title and give such information as country of origin, year of release, running time, black and white or color, credits, alternative title, plot synopsis, and cast. Evaluations are given in narrative form and also by means of a rating system (with 4 stars as the best). A very useful feature is the "Alphabetical Index of Alternative Titles," pp. 893-97.

865. **The International Encyclopedia of Film,** ed. by Roger Manvell. Crown, 1972; repr., 1975. 574p.
This vital reference work contains nearly 1,300 entries, a good bibliography, and many illustrations. *The Oxford Companion to Film*, edited by Liz-Ann Bawden (Oxford, 1976) also offers substantial international coverage, but it suffers from subjectivity (see Richard M. Buck's review in *ARBA 1977*, pp. 481-82). Paul Michael's *American Movies Reference Book: The Sound Era* (Prentice-Hall, 1969) has chapters on: history; players (600 actors and actresses in alphabetical order), films (1,010 arranged alphabetically by

title); directors; producers; and awards. It is profusely illustrated and has name indexes of actors, directors, and producers.

866. Sadoul, Georges. **Dictionary of Films**, tr. and ed. by Peter Morris. University of California Press, 1972. 432p.
International, selective coverage is given in this valuable work, which lists about 1,200 films by title and provides the following types of information: country, date, credits, cast, plot, criticism. More specialized is *The Great Science Fiction Pictures*, by James R. Parish and Michael R. Pitts (Scarecrow, 1977), which has a major section by film titles (with many cross references) and provides information on companies, dates, running times, producers, actors, directors, plot summaries, evaluations, and references to other sources. About 300 films are described by Parish and Pitts in *The Great Western Pictures* (Scarecrow, 1976). *Hitchcock's Films*, by Robin Wood (3rd ed., Barnes, 1977), contains a filmography and a bibliography. John Baxter's *Science Fiction in the Cinema* (Barnes, 1970) covers plots, directors, stars, writers, etc.

867. Sampson, Henry T. **Blacks in Black and White: A Source Book on Black Films.** Scarecrow, 1977. 333p.
Sampson covers motion pictures with all-black casts between 1910 and 1950. Historical chapters are followed by sections of film synopses and biographical sketches of leading performers. Appendices include: a list of all-black films to 1950; a list of producers (not complete); and credits. There is also a subject index.

Directories and Annuals

868. **Academy Awards: An Ungar Reference Index**, comp. by Richard Shale. Ungar, 1978. 350p.
Awards are listed by year and category. A brief history of the Academy, biographies of its organizers, and a bibliography give added reference value to this useful book. The Academy has announced a new publication entitled *Annual Index to Motion Picture Credits* (Greenwood, 1979-).

869. **International Motion Picture Almanac**, 1929- . Ann. Quigley.
Contents: index of subjects; index of advertisers; statistics; the great hundred (best of all time); awards and polls; who's who; pictures; corporations; theatre circuits; buying and booking; drive-in theatres; equipment; services; talent and literary agencies; the industry in Great Britain and Ireland; non-theatrical motion pictures; the world market; organizations; the press; codes and censorship. Other publications to be considered are *International Film Guide* (Tantivy, 1963-), *Film Daily Yearbook of Motion Pictures* (1918-1970) and *Film Review Digest* (Kraus-Thomson, 1976-).

870. **International Television Almanac**, 1956- . Ann. Quigley.
This useful directory provides statistical data and reports on people and businesses involved in the television industry. It lists and describes TV stations, TV shows, networks, personnel, distributors, etc. Another useful source is *Television Drama Series Programming: A Comprehensive Chronicle, 1959-1975*, by Larry James Gianakos (Scarecrow, 1978).

871. Limbacher, James L., comp. and ed. **Feature Films on 8mm, 16mm and Videotape.** 6th ed. Bowker, 1979. 447p.
Arranged alphabetically by title, with an index of directors and their films, this work does not give prices. The subtitle is: "A directory of feature films available for rental, sale and lease in the United States and Canada, with a serial section and a director index." Supplements appear quarterly in *Sightlines Magazine.*

872. **Traveling? F.M. Radio Guide,** ed. by Krompotich. And/Or Press, 1977. 122p.
Under each state, FM stations are arranged in two ways: Under names of towns and cities; alphabetically under call letters. Brief program descriptions, place on the radio dial, power, and hours of broadcasting are given.

873. Weber, Olga S., comp. **North American Film and Video Directory: A Guide to Media Collections and Services.** Bowker, 1976.
About 1,300 libraries and media centers are included. Information is provided about collections, loan policies, equipment, facilities, hours of opening, etc.

Histories

874. Bardeche, Maurice, and Robert Brasillach. **The History of Motion Pictures,** tr. and ed. by Iris Barry. W. W. Norton, 1938; repr., Arno, 1970. 412p.
Covering the period from 1895 to 1935, this classic was first published in 1938 as *History of the Film.*

875. Hampton, Benjamin. **A History of the Movies.** Friede, 1931; repr., Arno, 1970. 456p.
Originally published as *History of the American Film Industry from the Beginning to 1931,* this work has long been regarded as a major contribution. *The Movies,* by Richard Griffith and Arthur Meyer (2nd ed., Simon & Schuster, 1970) was described by the reviewer in *Choice* (February 1971, p. 1680) as "the best general *illustrated* survey of U.S. movies." *Hollywood in the Twenties,* by David Robinson (Barnes, 1968), *Hollywood in the Thirties,* by John Baxter (Barnes, 1968), *Hollywood in the Forties,* by Charles Higham (Barnes, 1968), *Hollywood in the Fifties,* by Gordon Gow (Barnes, 1971), and *Hollywood in the Sixties,* by John Baxter (Barnes, 1972) chronicle an important period by decade.

876. Jacobs, Lewis. **The Rise of the American Film: A Critical History.** Columbia University Teachers college Press, 1967; repr., 1974. 631p.
Covers period to 1939. British films are covered by Rachel Low's *History of the British Film* (Bowker, 1973, 4v.).

877. Mapp, Edward. **Blacks in American Films: Today and Yesterday.** Scarecrow, 1971. 278p.
Mapp attempts to analyze the manner in which blacks have been portrayed in American films. The first part of the book surveys blacks in American films from the days of silent movies to 1961. The second part gives a year-by-year account of the decade of the 1960s. Other major works on this subject include Peter Noble's *The Negro in American Films* (Robinson, 1948; repr., Arno, 1970) and Thomas Cripps' *Slow Fade to Black: The Negro in American Film, 1900-1942* (Oxford, 1977).

877a. Mast, Gerald. **A Short History of the Movies.** 2nd ed. Bobbs-Merrill, 1976. 575p.

In reviewing what has now become the standard general history of the cinema, Peter Dart commented: "This book will probably be the most widely adopted text for surveys of film history . . . " [*Journalism Quarterly* 53 (Autumn 1976), 573].

878. Ramsaye, Terry. **A Million and One Nights: A History of the Motion Picture.** Simon & Schuster, 1926; repr., 1964. 868p.

This standard history covers the period to 1925 and has a detailed index. John Stewart provides a more recent perspective in his *Filmarama: V.1, The Formidable Years, 1893-1919* (Scarecrow, 1975) and *Filmarama: V.2, The Flaming Years, 1920-1929* (Scarecrow, 1977).

878a. Rotha, Paul. **The Film Till Now: A Survey of World Cinema**, with an additional section by Richard Griffith. 4th ed. Spring books, 1967. 831p.

Originally published in 1930, this scholarly history has country-by-country surveys, a theoretical section, and an update. Reference features include a glossary, a selective bibliography, and an analytical index.

Biographies

879. **Filmlexikon degli autore e della opere.** Edizioni di Bianco e Nero, 1958-1967. 7v. Suppl. 1958-1971, 1973- .

Over 50,000 entries are contained in this international, illustrated biographical dictionary of actors, authors, directors, writers, producers, cameramen, composers, costume designers, and art directors. *Soviet Cinema: Directors and Films*, by Alexander S. Birkos (Archon, 1976), provides additional coverage for the USSR, though some deficiencies have been noted by reviewers.

880. Sadoul, Georges. **Dictionary of Film Makers.** Tr. and ed. by Peter Morris. University of California Press, 1972. 288p.

This international biographical dictionary of over 1,000 producers, directors, script-writers, cinematographers, art directors, composers, and inventors does *not* include actors or actresses. Stanley Hochman's *American Film Directors: With Filmographies and Index of Critics and Films* (Ungar, 1974) provides access to criticism of the films of 65 important directors, such as Alfred Hitchcock and Stanley Kubrick. Reviewers have noted that J. R. Parish's *Film Directors: A Guide to Their American Films* (Scarecrow, 1974), *Film Directors Guide: Western Europe* (Scarecrow, 1976), and *Hollywood Character Actors* (Arlington, 1978) have deficiencies as reference books but do appeal to film buffs.

881. **Theatre, Film and Television Biographical Master Index.** Gale, 1979. 200p.

This useful addition to Gale's series of biographical master indexes provides more than 70,000 citations to sketches in over 35 biographical sources covering the stage, screen, opera, popular music, radio, and television.

882. Thomson, David. **A Biographical Dictionary of Film.** Secker and Warburg, 1975; Morrow, 1976. 629p.

Praised by reviewers for its literate and witty (if subjective and opinionated) approach, this is a major source of critical evaluation. The English edition has the title *A Bibliographical Dictionary of the Cinema*. Esther Stineman's review of David Ragan's *Who's Who in Hollywood, 1900-1976* (Arlington, 1976) in *ARBA 1978* (pp. 493-94) noted serious deficiencies in arrangement and types of information, but concluded that obscure figures hard to locate elsewhere might be found here. Mark Piel's review of *Who Was Who on the Screen*, by Evelyn Mack Truitt (2nd ed., Bowker, 1977), in *ARBA 1975* (p. 553) noted serious deficiencies in the 1974 edition.

Reviews

883.   Bowles, Stephen E., comp. and ed. **Index to Critical Film Reviews in British and American Film Periodicals Together with Index to Critical Reviews of Books about Film.** Franklin, 1975. 3v. in 2.

Apart from noting skimpy coverage of the 1930s and 1940s, reviewers found this a useful means of access to reviews. A smaller work, but useful for libraries with specialized film collections, is *Film Criticism: An Index to Critics' Anthologies*, by Richard Heinzkill (Scarecrow, 1975).

884.   **The New York Times Directory of the Film.** Arno; Random, 1971. 1243p.

This is a collection of reviews from *The New York Times*. Contents: I. Listings of Awards: The Times "10 Best" — The New York Film Circle Critics Awards — The Academy Awards; II. Reprints of Reviews (by year, and then alphabetically by title); III. Portrait Gallery (2,000 stars, grouped by sex, then by name); IV. Index. The index covers all reviews from 1913 to 1968 and is divided into two parts — Personal Name Index and Corporate Index. The former lists every performer, producer, director, screen writer, etc. and runs to nearly 900 pages; the latter covers producing, participating, and other companies mentioned in the reviews and runs to 70 pages. Both are computer-produced and remarkably detailed. An abridged edition was published by Arno in 1974.

885.   **New York Times Film Reviews, 1913-1968.** Times, 1970. 6v.

The actual newsprint reviews are reproduced in facsimile in v. 1-5. V. 6 contains an appendix and the index. Over 17,000 reviews as well as articles on outstanding films of the year are included. Reviews are arranged chronologically. The appendix includes overlooked reviews, New York Film Critics Circle Awards, Academy Awards, and pictures of 2,000 actors and actresses. The index has 250,000 entries. There are separate sections for movie titles, people, and corporations. A one-volume selection, edited by George Amberg, was published by Arno in 1971. The set is kept up to date by *New York Times Film Reviews, 1969-1970-* .

Periodicals

886.   **Art and Cinema**, 1975- . 3/yr. Visual Resources.

Indexed: *Int.Ind.Mult.Med.Inf.* Brief (150-250 word) reviews of 40 to 50 films and videotapes make up the bulk of most issues. Prices for purchase or rental are given.

887.   **Cahiers du cinéma**, 1951- . Mo. Editions de l'Etoile.

The emphasis is on French film making. Ratings and information about awards are given. Avant-garde in tone, it has been somewhat political in recent years. Reviews of film journals and books are included.

888. **Film Comment**, 1962- . Bi-mo. Film Society of Lincoln Center.
Indexed: *Film Lit.Dig., Hum.Ind., Int.Ind.Film Per., Med.Rev.Dig., RG.* In addition to critical commentary, which relates the films to pressing social issues, this periodical has a good section of book reviews.

889. **Film Culture**, 1955- . Irregular. Jonas Mekas.
Indexed: *Art Ind., Film Lit.Ind., Int.Ind.Film Per., Med.Rev.Dig.* Avant-garde and imaginative, this periodical features interviews with film makers, news of film festivals, and a bibliography of books received.

890. **FLQ: Film Library Quarterly**, 1967- . Q. Film Library Information Council.
Indexed: *Film Lit.Ind., Hum.Ind., Int.Ind.Mult.Med.Inf., LISA, Lib.Lit., Med.Rev.Dig.* Reviews and information on 16mm films for use in public and academic libraries and good book reviews are staples of this useful periodical.

891. **Film Quarterly**, 1945- . Q. University of California Press.
Indexed: *Art Ind., Bk.Rev.Ind., Film Lit.Ind., Hum.Ind., Int.Ind.Mult.Med.Inf., Med.Rev.Dig.* This periodical has a good reputation for scholarly reviews of films and for lengthy articles on historical or biographical topics. Book reviews stress academic titles.

892. **Films and Filming**, 1954- . Mo. Hansom.
Indexed: *Film Lit.Ind., Int.Ind.Film Per.* In addition to articles on topics of current interest, this periodical has excellent reviews of recent films.

893. **Films in Review**, 1950- . Mo. (October-May), Bi-mo. (June-September). National Board of Review of Motion Pictures.
Indexed: *Art Ind., Film Lit.Ind., Int.Ind.Film Per., Med.Rev.Dig.* A typical issue includes reviews of 10 to 15 films and 4 to 5 books, in addition to general articles.

894. **Filmfacts**, 1958- . Bi-mo. American Film Institute.
Indexed: *Int.Ind.Mult.Med.Rev.Inf., Med.Rev.Dig.* This looseleaf service contains reviews of 10 to 15 films in a typical issue, providing full information on credits, plot summaries, and citations of favorable, unfavorable, and mixed reviews, much as *Book Review Digest* does for books.

895. **Sight and Sound**, 1932- . Q. British Film Institute.
Indexed: *Art Ind., Br.Hum.Ind., Film Lit.Ind., Hum.Ind., Int.Ind.Film Per., Int.Ind.Mult.Med.Rev.Inf., Med.Rev.Dig., A&HCI.* Each issue contains a book review section (usually covering 3 to 5 books on film) as well as a film review section (8 to 10 films per issue). News and historical articles are also featured.

896. **Variety**, 1905- . Wk. Variety, Inc.
Indexed: *Film Lit.Ind., Med.Rev.Dig., Mus.Ind.* Published in newspaper format, *Variety* contains articles dealing with films, video, radio, music, stage, and TV film events. There is major emphasis on the business aspect of these activities.

11 ACCESSING INFORMATION IN LANGUAGE AND LITERATURE

MAJOR DIVISIONS OF THE FIELD

Both of the two basic approaches to the division of literature—by language and by form—are usually taken into account in customary divisions of the field. Division of literature on the basis of the language in which it is written may require some refinements and modifications. For example, the volume of literature written in English is so large that further subdivision is desirable. In this case, the term "English literature" is restricted to the literary output of the United Kingdom that appears in English, or even to the literature of England alone. Separate provision is customarily made for American literature, Australian literature, etc. At the other extreme, some of the world's smallest literatures may be grouped together under a parent language.

The two basic forms of literature are prose and poetry. Prose is normally divided into novels, short stories, and essays. Poetry is normally treated as a unit, but it may be further subdivided by type (lyric poems, epic poems, etc.). The drama, as a literary record of what is to be performed on stage, has an independent life of its own and is also considered to be one of the major literary forms. Modern drama is ordinarily in prose, but it may also be in verse or may consist of both poetry and verse.

Another approach to the organization of literature is by historical periods or literary movements, often in combination with the basic schemes described above.

In addition to the general coverage and that of individual languages and literatures available through the *Encyclopedia Americana* and *The Encyclopaedia Britannica: Macropaedia*, the student is referred to the introductory and historical sections of chapter 12, "Principal Information Sources in Language and Literature." Many pertinent comments on reference work will be found in the chapter on "Literature" in Asheim's *The Humanities and the Library* (ALA, 1957).

MAJOR ORGANIZATIONS, INFORMATION CENTERS, AND SPECIAL COLLECTIONS

Languages

The oldest, largest, and best-known of the organizations that promote the study and teaching of languages in this country is the Modern Language Association of America (62 Fifth Avenue, New York, NY 10011). Founded in 1883, it has more than 30,000 members, primarily college and university teachers, and it conducts an immense range of programs and activities. Publications include: *MLA Newsletter* (quarterly); *PMLA* (quarterly); *Job Information List – English* (quarterly); *Job Information List – Foreign Languages* (quarterly); *Directory* (annual); and *MLA International Bibliography* (annual).

The American Council on the Teaching of Foreign Languages (Two Park Avenue, New York, NY 10016) was founded by MLA in 1966, but now exists as a separate entity. Its publications include: *Foreign Language Annals* (6/yr.); and *Series on Foreign Language Education* (annual).

The International Federation of Modern Language Teachers (Seestrasse 247 CH-8038 Zurich, Switzerland) is made up of multilingual and unilingual associations. It corresponds at the international level to the National Federation of Modern Language Teachers Associations (Gannon College, Erie, PA 16501), a federation of national, regional, and state associations in this country that publishes *Modern Language Journal* (6/yr.).

The National Association of Learning Lab Directors (c/o Dale Lally, Department of Modern Languages, University of Louisville, Louisville, KY 40208) conducts workshops and seeks to improve the liaison between manufacturers and users of language lab equipment. It publishes *NALLD Journal* (quarterly).

The American Association of Language Specialists (Suite 9, 1000 Connecticut Avenue, N.W., Washington, DC 20036) is a small group of interpreters, editors, and translators. The International Committee for Breaking the Language Barrier (268 West 12th Street, New York, NY 10014) develops international signs and other aids to facilitate communication and offers consulting services to businesses and governmental agencies.

Literature

The International Comparative Literature Association (c/o Frederick Garber, SUNY, Binghamton, NY 13901) promotes the worldwide study of comparative literature and is preparing to publish a *Dictionary of International Literary Terms* and a *Comparative History of Literatures in European Languages*.

The International Institute for Children's Literature and Reading Research (Fuhrmannsgasse 18a, 1080 Vienna, Austria) promotes and evaluates international research in children's literature. Its publications are *Jugend und Buch* (quarterly) and *Bookbird* (quarterly).

Grants from the National Endowment for the Arts (matched by private gifts) have enabled the Coordinating Council of Literary Magazines (80 Eighth Avenue, Room 1302, New York, NY 10011) to assist "little" magazines in a variety of ways.

The American Comparative Literature Association (Department of Comparative Literature, State University of New York, Binghamton, NY 13901) promotes the study and teaching of comparative literature in American universities, publishes a newsletter, co-sponsors *Yearbook of Comparative and General Literature*, and assists in the publication of two quarterly journals: *Comparative Literature* and *Comparative Literature Studies*.

Regional interests within the United States are served by such groups as the Society for the Study of Southern Literature (c/o Robert L. Phillips, Jr., P.O. Box 2625, Mississippi State, MS 39762) and the Western Literature Association (UMC 32, Utah State University, Logan, UT 84322).

Information Centers in Language and Literature

The identification of information centers as distinct from professional organizations, on the one hand, and from special collections, on the other, is not a clearcut and simple matter. Many (but by no means all) professional organizations conduct programs of research and information dissemination. Many libraries holding special collections do the same. Nevertheless, mention should be made here of a few noteworthy examples.

The first is the Folger Shakespeare Library (201 East Capitol Street, Washington, DC 20003), which has an active research and publication program in British civilization of the Tudor and Stuart periods and theatrical history as these relate to Shakespeare.

The Center for Hellenic Studies (3100 Whitehaven Street, Washington, DC 20003) is an international center associated with Harvard University. It conducts research in such areas as classical Greek literature, philosophy, and history.

The Center for Textual Studies (323 Main Library, Ohio State University, Columbus, OH 43210) conducts research on definitive texts of nineteenth- and twentieth-century authors, including the publication of definitive editions of Hawthorne and Emerson.

Special Collections in Language and Literature

The number of special collections in language and literature is so vast that mentioning names beyond the obvious giants like the Library of Congress, the British Library, the Bibliothèque Nationale, the New York Public Library and Harvard University could easily run to several pages. Once again, the works of Young, Ash and Lewanski (see item 13) are very useful. Searching under fairly specific headings, including the names of individual authors, will often be most fruitful. The *Handbook* of the Center for Research Libraries also devotes considerable space (pp. 50-57) to special collections in European and American literature.

12 PRINCIPAL INFORMATION SOURCES IN LANGUAGE AND LITERATURE

LANGUAGE

Introductory Works and Bibliographic Guides

897. DeBray, Reginald George Arthur. **Guide to the Slavonic Languages.** 2nd ed. Dutton, 1969. 798p.

Each language has a separate section. Information is given on the history, alphabet, pronunciation, morphology, word order, and special characteristics, with brief literary quotations. There is a detailed table of contents but no index.

898. **The Great Languages.** L. R. Palmer, gen. ed. Faber, 1934- .

Each volume covers a major language or group of languages comprehensively and is written by a subject specialist. LC catalogs and classifies each volume separately. Some libraries make a series added entry. For a list of titles published and planned, see item 13, A. J. Walford's *Guide to Reference Material* (3rd ed., Library Association, 1973-77, v. 3, p. 207). Scripts for 1,399 languages may be found in *A Book of a Thousand Tongues* (2nd ed., United Bible Societies, 1972) and passages in 200 native scripts are given in Kenneth Katzner's *The Languages of the World* (Funk and Wagnalls, 1975).

899. Jespersen, Otto. **A Modern English Grammar on Historical Principles.** E. Munksgaard, 1949; Barnes & Noble, 1954. 7v.

Part I of this standard work deals with sounds and spellings. Parts II through V cover syntax, and part VI covers morphology. Actual usage from the time of Chaucer to the present is emphasized, rather than "correct" usage. There are numerous illustrative quotations.

900. Kister, Kenneth F. **Dictionary Buying Guide: A Consumer Guide to General English-Language Wordbooks in Print.** Bowker, 1977. 358p.

General advice on choosing a dictionary, comparative charts, and evaluative profiles of individual titles are features of this excellent guide, which has a detailed table of contents, a directory of dictionary publishers, and a title-author-subject index.

901. Meillet, Antoine, and M. Cohen, eds. **Les Langues du monde.** New ed. Centre Nationale de la Récherche Scientifique, 1952. 1294p.

This is the main reference work in the field, with coverage of some 10,000 languages and dialects. It includes a pocket atlas with 21 maps.

902. Palmer, Leonard R. **Descriptive and Comparative Linguistics: A Critical Introduction.** Crane, Russak, 1972. 430p.
As an introduction and state-of-the-art review, this work has been rated as highly successful.

903. Rice, Frank, and Allene Guss, eds. **Information Sources in Linguistics: A Bibliographical Handbook.** Center for Applied Linguistics, 1965. 42p.
Virtually all areas are covered except individual languages, which are included in *Bibliographie linguistique* (see item 905). Rice has also compiled *Study Aids for Critical Languages* (rev. ed., Center for Applied Linguistics, 1968). Wallace Goldstein's *Teaching English As a Second Language: An Annotated Bibliography* (Garland, 1975) concentrates on publications since 1965.

Bibliographies (Current and Retrospective)

904. Alston, Robin C. **A Bibliography of the English Language from the Invention of Printing to the Year 1800.** E. J. Arnold and Son, 1965- .
To be published in 20 volumes, about one-half of which have appeared to date, this major set will eventually supersede Kennedy (see item 908) for the period before 1800. LC catalogs separately but classifies as a set and provides a series entry. A supplement entitled *Additions and Corrections V. I-X* was published in 1973.

905. **Bibliographie linguistique,** 1939/47- . Ann. Spectrum.
This comprehensive annual bibliography of books, reviews, and articles is international and multilingual in coverage. There are separate sections on individual languages.

906. Brasch, Ila Wales, and Walter Milton Brasch. **A Comprehensive Annotated Bibliography of American Black English.** Louisiana State University Press, 1974. 289p.
Reviewers considered this to be the most comprehensive work of its kind, but they noted that the straight alphabetical arrangement with no subject index was a hindrance to easy access for certain types of research.

907. Brenni, Vito Joseph, comp. **American English: A Bibliography.** University of Pennsylvania Press, 1964. 221p.
Brenni has provided a classified, annotated bibliography of books, articles, and dissertations that is still a vital reference tool.

908. Kennedy, Arthur Garfield. **Bibliography of Writings on the English Language from the Beginning of Printing to the End of 1922.** Cambridge, 1927; repr., Books for Libraries, 1973. 517p.
For many years, this has been the standard work. It is now being superseded for the period before 1800 by R. C. Alston's *A Bibliography of the English Language from the Invention of Printing to the Year 1800* (see item 904).

909. Wawrzyszko, Aleksandra K. **Bibliography of General Linguistics: English and American.** Archon, 1971. 120p.
This classified, annotated bibliography of 344 books and periodicals is especially useful for graduate students.

Indexes, Abstracts, and Current Awareness Services

910.   **LLBA: Language and Language Behavior Abstracts**, 1967- . Q. Sociological Abstracts, Inc.
A collaborative international effort, this abstracting service covers a large number of journals in such areas as linguistics, psychology, and communication sciences. There are indexes to authors, subjects, source publications, and book reviews. A *User's Reference Manual* began publication in looseleaf form in 1977.

911.   **Language-Teaching and Linguistics Abstracts**, 1968- . Q. Cambridge University Press.
Compiled by the English-Teaching Information Centre of the British Council and Centre for Information on Language Teaching and Research, this publication abstracts articles from nearly 400 periodicals and includes notes on new books.

912.   **The Year's Work in Modern Language Studies**, 1930- . Ann. Modern Humanities Research Association.
"A critical annual survey of recent research and publications in the fields of Romance, Germanic and Slavonic languages and literatures"—A. J. Walford , *Guide to Reference Material* (3rd ed., Library Association, 1973-77), v. 3, p. 207.

Dictionaries

913.   Baldinger, Kurt. **Dictionnaire étymologique de l'ancien français.** Les Presses de l'Université Laval, 1971- . (In progress).
Baldinger's historical dictionary covers the period from the middle of the ninth to the middle of the fourteenth century. A bibliographic supplement, edited by Frankwalt Möhran, began publication in 1974.

914.   Bernstein, Theodore, and Jane Wagner. **Bernstein's Reverse Dictionary.** Quadrangle; distr., Harper, 1975. 277p.
"A conventional dictionary lists words alphabetically and gives you their meanings. This unconventional dictionary lists an array of meanings alphabetically and gives you the words" (preface, p. vii). Suppose one is trying to think of the word that means "faster than the speed of sound"; in this dictionary, one can look under "faster than the speed of sound" and find the word "supersonic." One variation from this pattern should be noted. Phobias and manias are grouped together, and terms for groups of creatures are put under "creature terms." A handy tool, this work was included among "Reference Books of 1975" (*Library Journal*, April 15, 1976, p. 969). Another unconventional dictionary is -*Ologies and -Isms: A Thematic Dictionary*, edited by Howard G. Zettler (Gale, 1978), which defines over 3,300 terms ending in "-ology," "-ism," "-ity," "-ic," or "-phobia" that are usually omitted from, or hard to find in, standard dictionaries. One more effort to help locate elusive words is *A Dictionary of Collective Nouns and Group Terms*, compiled by Ivan G. Sparkes (Gale, 1975). Another valuable supplement to conventional dictionaries is *Dictionary of Pronunciation*, by Abraham and Betty Lass (Quadrangle, 1976), which was included in "Reference Books of 1977" (*Library Journal*, April 15, 1978, p. 816). Finally, one should not overlook *The New York Times Manual of Style and Usage*, edited by Lewis Jordan (Quadrangle, 1976).

915. Bliss, Alan Joseph. **A Dictionary of Foreign Words and Phrases in Current English.** Dutton, 1966; repr., Routledge, 1977. 389p.
Over 5,000 entries provide extensive information about sources and original meanings, as well as current definitions and pronunciations. Advice on spelling, transliteration, grammatical handling, etc. is also given, as is a table that shows what was borrowed when. Another work that covers several languages is Jerzy Gluski's *Proverbs: A Comparative Book of English, French, German, Italian, Spanish and Russian Proverbs with a Latin Appendix* (Elsevier, 1971). Another very useful work is C. O. S. Mawson's *Dictionary of Foreign Terms*, revised by Charles Berlitz (2nd ed., Crowell, 1975).

916. Bosworth, Joseph. **An Anglo-Saxon Dictionary**, ed. and enl. by T. Northcote Toller. Oxford, 1898; repr., 1973. 1302p. Suppl. 1921. 768p.
The most comprehensive such source yet available, this scholarly work has many quotations, with citations of manuscripts and printed sources. Addenda and corrections to the supplement were published in 1972.

917. Chantraine, Pierre. **Dictionnaire étymologique de la langue grecque; histoire des mots.** Klincksieck, 1968- . (In progress).
The compiler has relied on standard earlier works except when modern scholarship requires a different interpretation. This dictionary concentrates on the use of words from about 2000 B.C. to modern Greek. Citations to classical authors and inscriptions are provided. Derivations and compounds are listed. References are made to linguistic and philological studies in books and journals.

918. Dalbiac, Lilian. **Dictionary of Quotations (German) with Author and Subject Indexes.** Macmillan, 1906; repr., Ungar, 1958. 485p.
About 3,000 German quotations are arranged in alphabetical order, with English translations. Subject indexes are in both German and English.

919. de Gamez, Tana, ed. **Simon and Schuster's International Dictionary: English/Spanish, Spanish/English.** Simon and Schuster, 1975. 1379p.
Some 200,000 entries here range from scientific and technical terms to regionalisms and colloquialisms. The International Phonetic Alphabet is used to explain English pronunciations. There is a general guide to Spanish pronunciation, but no pronunciations for individual words. Definitions, typography, and layout are good. Portuguese is covered (without translation) in de Holanda's *Novo dicionario da lingua portuguesa* (Rissoli, 1975). Another Spanish translating dictionary is *Diccionario moderno Español-Ingles* (Larousse, 1977).

920. Grimm, Jakob Ludwig Karl, und Wilhelm Grimm. **Deutsches Wörterbuch.** Hrsg. von der Deutschen Akademie der Wissenschaften zu Berlin in Zusammenarbeit mit der Akademie der Wissenschaften zu Gottingen, Neubearbeitungen. Leipzig: Hirzel, 1965- .
A new edition of this pioneer work, which first promoted the idea of a dictionary compiled on historical principles and which influenced both Littré and the *Oxford English Dictionary*.

921. Harbottle, Thomas Benfield. **Dictionary of Quotations (Classical).** 3rd ed. Sonnenschein, 1906; Ungar, 1958. 678p.
Separate sections are provided for Latin and Greek. The arrangement is alphabetical by

first word. Sources are cited and English translations are given. The following indexes are included: authors; subjects, Latin; subjects, Greek; subjects, English.

922. Harbottle, Thomas Benfield, and P. H. Dalbiac. **Dictionary of Quotations (French and Italian).** Macmillan, 1901; repr., Ungar, 1958. 565p.

Under each language, the arrangement is alphabetical by the first word of the quotation. There is an index of authors and subjects. Norbert Guterman's *A Book of French Quotations with English Translations* (Doubleday, 1965) follows a chronological arrangement, with about 2,000 French and English quotations on opposite pages. The following indexes are provided: authors; first lines in French; first lines in English. Another useful tool is *Dictionary of Modern French Idioms*, by Barbara L. Gerber and Gerald H. Storzer (Garland, 1977, 2v.).

923. Hartmann, R. R. K., and F. C. Stork. **Dictionary of Language and Linguistics.** Wiley, 1972. 302p.

The compilers concentrate on technical terms not adequately defined in general dictionaries. Cross references are indicated by arrows. Appendix I is a list of languages with over one million speakers. Appendix II is a classified bibliography (pp. 277-302). Another work of value to scholars is *Encyclopedic Dictionary of the Sciences of Language*, by Oswald Ducrat and Tzvetan Todorov (Johns Hopkins, 1979), which has an index to complement the topical arrangement.

924. Mansion, J. E. **Harrap's New Standard French and English Dictionary**, rev. and ed. by R. P. L. and Margaret Ledésert.

Earlier standards of excellence have been maintained in this new edition, with its large vocabulary, good definitions, and clear indications of pronunciation. Many new terms have been added.

925. **Middle English Dictionary**, ed. by Hans Kurath. University of Michigan Press, 1952- .

The period covered is from 1100 to 1475. This is the most comprehensive work to date and uses quotations assembled for the *Oxford English Dictionary* as well as thousands more that were gathered for this set. It is expected to be published in about 65 parts (of which approximately one-half have appeared) and to run to some 10,000 pages.

926. Murray, Sir James Augustus Henry. **New English Dictionary on Historical Principles; Founded Mainly on the Materials Collected by the Philogical Society.** Oxford, 1888-1933. 10v. and Suppl. New Suppl., ed. by R. W. Burchfield, 1972- . (In progress).

Commonly known as the *Oxford English Dictionary* (OED), this monumental work changed to that title in 1895, and the 1933 reprint bears the new title. Inspired by Grimm (see item 920), the compiler and his associates arranged their definitions according to historical usage at different periods and made liberal use of quotations from those periods. Words in use from 1150 to the present (over 400,000) are included, illustrated by more than 1,800,000 quotations. E. Klein has carried the principle of tracing word history even further in *Klein's Comprehensive Etymological Dictionary of the English Language* (Elsevier, 1965-67, 2v.), with some 45,000 entries traced back before their appearance in English.

927. **Oxford Dictionary of English Proverbs,** rev. by F. P. Wilson. 3rd ed. Oxford, 1970. 930p.

This standard work is a first choice when searching for proverbs in the English language, with emphasis on England but not neglecting other parts of Great Britain. More specialized works exist for particular periods. Bartlett Jere Whiting devoted over 40 years to the compilation of his authoritative *Proverbs, Sentences and Proverbial Phrases: From English Writings Mainly before 1500* (Harvard, 1968). Based on historical principles, it provides key word entries, cross references, a general index, and a separate index for proper nouns. The next period is covered by Morris Palmer Tilley's *A Dictionary of the Proverbs of England in the 16th and 17th Centuries* (Michigan, 1950). Attention has also been given to proverbs in the United States. In an early effort, Archer Taylor and B. J. Whiting confined their attention to a narrow time span. The result was *A Dictionary of American Proverbs and Proverbial Phrases, 1820-1880* (Harvard, 1958; repr., 1967). More recently, Whiting has devoted his efforts to the period before 1820 in *Early American Proverbs and Proverbial Phrases* (Harvard, 1977). German proverbial phrases are listed and defined, with many cross references and bibliographic citations, by Rohrich Lutz in *Lexikon der Sprichwortichen Redensarten* (Herder, 1973, 2v.). More popular treatment is provided by Burton E. Stevenson's *Home Book of Proverbs, Maxims and Familiar Phrases* (Macmillan, 1948), which was reprinted in 1965 as *The Macmillan Book of Proverbs, Maxims and Familiar Phrases.*

928. **The Oxford-Harrap Standard German-English Dictionary,** ed. by Trevor Jones. Oxford, 1977- . (In progress).

This major work (German-English, English-German) is expected to be complete in 8 volumes. Another standard tool is *Langenscheidt's New Muret-Sanders Encyclopedic Dictionary of the English and German Languages* (Langenscheidt, 1974-75, 2v.).

929. **Oxford Latin Dictionary.** Oxford, 1968- . (In progress).

Planning has been underway since 1931 for this standard set, which covers classical Latin from its beginnings to the end of the second century A.D. An effort is made to treat all known words from whatever source – literary or non-literary. Proper names are included if important. Similar in layout and organization to the OED (see item 926), it uses quotations to show usage in chronological order. Notes on etymology are brief. Fascicles are to be published at two-year intervals.

930. Partridge, Eric. **Dictionary of Slang and Unconventional English.** 7th ed. Routledge; Macmillan, 1970. 1528p.

This classic work concentrates on words that have not been readily accepted into standard usage and meanings for ordinary words that differ from the standard ones. A more specialized source is *Dictionary of Afro-American Slang*, by Clarence Major (International Publishers, 1970).

931. Reynolds, Barbara. **The Cambridge Italian Dictionary.** Cambridge, 1962- . (In progress).

Volume 1 covers Italian into English and has about 50,000 entry words. V. 2 will cover English into Italian. Meanwhile, Reynolds has compiled a one-volume work, *The Concise Cambridge Italian Dictionary* (Cambridge, 1975), which uses material from the forthcoming v. 2 of the larger work as well as a condensation of v. 1.

932. Robert, Paul. **Dictionnaire alphabétique et analogique de la langue française: les mots et les associations d'idées.** Paris: Société du nouveau Littré, 1975. 6v. Suppl. 1975. 514p.

This major modern French-language dictionary was compiled on historical principles and published with the approval of the Academie Française. It is a worthy complement and successor to E. Littré's *Dictionnaire de la langue française* (7v., Pauvert, 1956-58), which is still especially good for examples from the ninth to the seventeenth centuries. A revised edition of the abridged, one-volume version, known as *Petit Robert*, was published in 1977.

933. Roget, Peter Mark. **The Original Roget's Thesaurus of English Words and Phrases.** New ed. St. Martin's, 1965; repr., 1978.

The basic arrangement is a classified one, with an alphabetical index. Reviewers have tended to prefer this edition to *Roget's International Thesaurus*, revised by Robert Chapman (4th ed., Crowell, 1977). Some readers, in searching for synonyms, will find it easier to use an alphabetical work, like *Webster's Collegiate Thesaurus* (1976).

934. Wall, C. Edward, and Edward Przebienda, comps. **Words and Phrases Index: A Guide to Antedatings, New Words, New Compounds, and Other Published Scholarship Supplementing the Oxford English Dictionary, Dictionary of American English and Other Major Dictionaries of the English Language.** Pierian Press, 1969- . (In progress).

Over 60,000 citations to words and phrases from *American Notes and Queries, American Speech, Notes and Queries*, etc. are given in this computer-produced work, which serves as a valuable supplement to such classic sets as Sir James A. H. Murray's *Oxford English Dictionary* (see item 926) and its United States counterpart, *Dictionary of American English on Historical Principles*, by Sir William Alexander Craigie and James R. Hulbert (University of Chicago Press, 1938-1944, 4v.).

Histories

935. Baugh, Albert Croll. **A History of the English Language.** 3rd ed. Prentice-Hall, 1978. 438p.

Planned as a text for college students, this book is also useful in language and literature departments for reference work. It includes a chapter on the English language in America, an analytical index, and evaluative chapter bibliographies.

936. Brunot, Ferdinand. **Histoire de la langue française, des origines à nos jours.** New ed. A. Colin, 1966- .

A major scholarly work that is still in progress, this set's volumes cover specific chronological periods. The earlier edition was begun in 1905.

Periodicals

937. **American Speech: A Quarterly of Linguistic Usage**, 1925- . Q. University of Alabama Press.

Indexed: *Abstr.Engl.Stud., Abstr.Folk.Stud., DSH Abstr., Hist.Abstr., Hum.Ind.,*

Lang. Teach. and Ling. Abstr., LLBA, MLA Abstr., MLA Int. Bibliog. Scholarly articles cover both the historical and the contemporary aspects of American speech. A few book reviews and short notices are included.

938. **Anglia: Zeitschrift für englische Philogie**, 1878- . 4/yr. Max Niemeyer Verlag.
Indexed: *Abstr. Engl. Stud., Bull. signal.: hist. sci. lit., Lang. Teach. and Ling. Abstr., MLA Int. Bibliog.* All periods from Old English to the twentieth century are covered, including American language and literature.

939. **Journal of English and Germanic Philology**, 1897- . Q. University of Illinois Press.
Indexed: *Abstr. Engl. Stud., Bk. Rev. Ind., Bull. signal.: sci. lang., Hum. Ind., MLA Abstr., MLA Int. Bibliog., A&HCI.* The coverage includes German, English, and Scandinavian languages and literatures.

940. **Lingua: International Review of General Linguistics**, 1947- . 9/yr. North-Holland Publishing Co.
Indexed: *Bull. signal.: sci. lang., DSH Abstr., IBZ, Lang. Teach. and Ling. Abstr., MLA Abstr., MLA Int. Bibliog.* The text — in English, French, and German — features long critical reviews of major books.

941. **Modern Language Quarterly**, 1940- . Q. University of Washington.
Indexed: *Abstr. Engl., Am. Lit. Abstr., Bull. signal.: hist. sci. lit., Hum. Ind., MLA Abstr., MLA Int. Bibliog., A&HCI.* American, English, Germanic, and Romance languages are covered. There are excellent book reviews.

942. **Modern Language Review**, 1905- . Q. Modern Humanities Research Association.
Indexed: *Abstr. Engl. Stud., Abstr. Folk. Stud., Bk. Rev. Ind., Br. Hum. Ind., Bull. signal.: sci. lit., Hum. Ind., MLA Abstr., MLA Int. Bibliog., A&HCI.* A large proportion of the space is given over to book reviews.

943. **Studies in Philology**, 1906- . 5/yr. University of North Carolina Press.
Indexed: *Hum. Ind., MLA Abstr., MLA Int. Bibliog., A&HCI.* Classical and modern languages and literatures are covered.

GENERAL LITERATURE

Introductory Works and Bibliographic Guides

944. Altick, Richard Daniel. **The Art of Literary Research.** Rev. ed. Norton, 1975. 246p.
Planned by a noted scholar to help graduate students, this book is useful for discussion of such topics as research methodology, textual study, authorship, origins, reputation, and influence. A more specialized guide is *The Medieval Literature of Europe: A Review of Research, Mainly 1930-1960*, edited by John H. Fisher (Modern Language Association, 1966).

945. Haviland, Virginia, ed. **Children's Literature: A Guide to Reference Sources.** Library of Congress, 1966. 341p. 1st suppl., 1972. 316p. 2nd suppl., 1977. 413p.
This classified, annotated bibliography and its supplements—prepared by the staff of the Children's Book Section of the Library of Congress under the direction of Virginia Haviland—covers books, periodicals, articles, and pamphlets of importance for the study of children's literature.

946. **Modern Literature.** Prentice-Hall, 1966-68. 2v.
This valuable set is part of a larger series, The Princeton Studies: Humanistic Scholarship in America. Contents: v. 1—*The Literature of France*, by H. Peyre; v. 2—*Italian, Spanish, German, Russian, and Oriental Literature*, by G. L. Anderson and others.

947. Patterson, Margaret C. **Literary Research Guide.** Gale, 1976. 385p.
This outstanding guide, included in "Reference Books of 1977" (*Library Journal*, April 15, 1978, p. 817), bears the cumbersome but descriptive subtitle: "An evaluative, annotated bibliography of important reference books and periodicals on American and English literature, of the most useful sources for research in other national literatures, and of more than 300 reference books in literature-related subject areas." The classified arrangement facilitates subject searching and is complemented by an excellent index. Other features include brief explanations of Dewey and LC and a glossary of bibliographical terms.

948. Pellowski, Anne. **The World of Children's Literature.** Bowker, 1968. 538p.
Pellowski gives brief summaries of literary trends in 106 countries and lists, with critical annotations, 4,495 books, journals, and articles on children's books and library services. A related book by the same author is *The World of Storytelling* (Bowker, 1977).

949. Seymour-Smith, Martin. **Funk & Wagnalls Guide to Modern World Literature.** Funk & Wagnalls, 1973. 1206p.
The author attempts to survey world literature in the twentieth century, with chapters devoted to individual countries or to regions. Trends, leading writers, and major works are discussed. Reference features include a select bibliography and a detailed index.

Bibliographies (Current and Retrospective)

950. Baldensperger, Fernand, and Werner P. Friederich. **Bibliography of Comparative Literature.** University of North Carolina Press, 1950; repr., Russell, 1960. 705p.
This extensive and authoritative work covers literary influences from ancient to modern times and is arranged in four books: 1 and 3 deal with themes, motifs, genres, international literary relations, etc.; 2 and 4 cover specific literatures, according to country or author exerting influence. There is a detailed table of contents but no index. For current updatings, see the "Annual Bibliography" section of *Yearbook of Comparative and General Literature* (Indiana University, 1952-). John O. McCormick and the faculty of Livingston College, Rutgers University, have compiled an unannotated classified bibliography entitled *A Syllabus of Comparative Literature* (2nd ed., Scarecrow, 1972). Arthur Coleman's *Epic and Romance Criticism* (Watermill, 1973-74, 2v.) is valuable for beginning students of comparative literature because it contains over 20,000 citations to works in English for the period from 1940 to 1973. Another work of value for comparative study is Joseph L. Laurenti's *Bibliografia de la literatura picaresca; desde sus*

orígines hasta el presente/A Bibliography of Picaresque Literature: From Its Origins to the Present (Scarecrow, 1973). More specialized is *Medieval Celtic Literature: A Select Bibliography*, by Rachel Bromwich (University of Toronto Press, 1974).

951. **MLA International Bibliography**, 1921- . Ann. Modern Language Association of America.

From 1921 to 1955, this standard work was entitled *American Bibliography* and was limited to writings by Americans on the literature of various countries. From 1956 to 1962, the coverage varied. Since 1963, it has had its present title and includes writers in other languages. Coverage is still mainly American and European. Research is facilitated by the classified arrangement with an author index. There are no cumulations, but online access to 400,000 entries from 1970 is available through Lockheed's DIALOG system. Answers to many of the questions frequently asked by scholars and prospective authors about the 3,000 journals and series indexed in the *MLA International Bibliography* may be found in the *MLA Directory of Periodicals: A Guide to Journals and Series in Languages and Literatures* (MLA, 1979- ; biennial). More specialized is the *Quarterly Check-List of Literary History* (American Bibliographic Service, 1958-).

952. Pownall, David E. **Articles on Twentieth-Century Literature: An Annotated Bibliography, 1954-1970.** Kraus-Thomson, 1973- . Projected in 7v.

Starting with the "Current Bibliography" section of *Twentieth Century Literature* (which may be consulted for articles published since 1970), Pownall added information from a variety of other sources, covering 370 journals in all, including some 22,000 entries, and arranging items under authors as *subjects*. All entries are numbered and will be cross indexed in v. 7. The bibliography excludes book reviews, review articles, and popular journalism. International coverage is attempted, and the articles on European authors, though much smaller in number than those for English-language writers, are apt to be particularly useful. The annotations are well written.

953. Schwartz, Narda L. **Articles on Women Writers: A Bibliography.** ABC-Clio, 1977. 236p.

Approximately 600 women writers of various countries and periods are included. The criterion for selection was the appearance of at least one article in an English-language publication between 1960 and 1975. There are no cross references or annotations. Another source to check is Barbara A. White's *American Women Writers: An Annotated Bibliography of Criticism* (Garland, 1977).

Indexes, Abstracts, and Current Awareness Services

954. **International Directory of Little Magazines and Small Presses**, 1964- . Ann. Dustbooks.

Planned as an aid to authors, this publication includes editors, addresses, types of material accepted, requirements for manuscripts, rates, royalty arrangements, etc.

955. **MLA Abstracts of Articles in Scholarly Journals**, 1970- . Ann. Modern Language Association of America.

The classified arrangement in three volumes (bound together in the "Library Edition") parallels that of the *MLA International Bibliography,* for which it is a supplement and with which it must be used, because *MLA Abstracts* does not yet have cross references or author indexes and the subject indexes are very brief. Another abstracting service, also international in scope, is *Children's Literature Abstracts*, 1973- (Subsection on Library Work with Children, International Federation of Library Associations), which appears four times a year, follows a classified arrangement, and publishes around 100 abstracts in a typical issue.

Dictionaries and Encyclopedias

956. Beckson, Carl, and Arthur Ganz. **Literary Terms: A Dictionary.** 2nd ed. Farrar, Strauss & Giroux, 1975. 280p.
First published in 1960 under the title *A Reader's Guide to Literary Terms*, this valuable paperback is noted for its clear, concise definitions and is recommended for home purchase as well as for use in public, academic, and school libraries. Libraries with the 1960 edition should keep it as well, because some important terms were omitted in the new one.

957. Benet, William Rose. **The Reader's Encyclopedia.** 2nd ed. Crowell, 1965. 1118p.
Brief articles on writers, scientists, etc. of all periods are featured, together with allusions, literary expressions and terms, literary schools and movements, plots and characters, and descriptions of musical compositions and works of art. The second edition covers world literature, with emphasis on areas of growing interest—e.g., the Orient, Soviet Union, Latin America, and the Near East.

958. **Cassell's Encyclopaedia of World Literature,** ed. by J. Buchanan-Brown. 2nd ed. Cassell; Morrow, 1973. 3v.
First published in 1953, this standard work devotes v. 1 to literary definitions and essays on the literatures of various countries. The two final volumes are given over to biographies. Articles are signed and usually contain bibliographies.

959. **Columbia Dictionary of Modern European Literature,** ed. by Horatio Smith. Columbia, 1947. 899p.
This scholarly work features biographical sketches and critical evaluations (signed) covering major writers of Europe in the twentieth century, as well as survey articles with bibliographies for 31 literatures of Europe. Good balance in coverage and careful editing are evident in the 1,167 articles by 239 specialists.

960. Deutsch, Babette. **Poetry Handbook: A Dictionary of Terms.** 4th ed. Funk & Wagnalls, 1974. 203p.
Useful for both browsing and reference, this book features alphabetized definitions—often subjective, but supported by examples. The emphasis is on classical and French poetry, but recent editions show more interest in German poetry than did the earlier ones. Reviewers noted relatively little change between the third and fourth editions.

961. **Dizionario letterario Bompiani delle opere e dei personaggi di tutti i tempi e di tutti le letterature.** 5th ed. Bompiani, 1947-50. 9v. Suppl. 1964-66. 2v.

Contents: v. 1-7 — literary works, A-Z; v. 8 — dictionary of literary characters; v. 9 — indexes. Bompiani's dictionary lists and describes the works of all times and countries in literature, art, and music. The main emphasis is on literature, but musical works and many famous pictures are described. It is lavishly illustrated, with many colored plates and black and white illustrations. Biographical and critical sketches of 6,000 authors from all periods and countries are provided in a handsomely illustrated set entitled *Dizionario letterario Bompiani degli autori, di tutti i tempi e di tutti le letterature* (Bompiani, 1956-57; repr., 1968-69, 3v.). Authors, literary movements, national literatures, periodicals, etc. for the period from 1870 to 1960 are covered in *Dizionario universelle delle letteratura contemporanea* (Mondadori, 1959-63, 5v.). This set has extensive illustrations; v. 5 contains chronological tables and indexes.

962. **Encyclopedia of Poetry and Poetics**, ed. by Alex Preminger. Enl. ed. Princeton University Press, 1974. 992p.

The 1965 edition included about 1,000 individual entries, ranging from 20 to 20,000 words in length and dealing with history, theory, techniques, and criticism of poetry from the earliest times to the present. Most articles were signed with initials, and most had bibliographies. International in scope, this authoritative work included special articles on poetry of various nationalities and ethnic groups. The 1974 edition simply adds a supplement of new topics (about 85 pages in length).

963. **Encyclopedia of World Literature in the 20th Century**, ed. by Wolfgang Bernard Fleischmann. Ungar, 1967-75. 4v.

V. 1-3 were translated or adapted from *Lexikon der Weltliteratur im 20 Jahrhundert*. V. 4 is a supplement and index. About 1,400 articles cover twentieth century world literature on a global scale. There are survey articles on individual literatures, literary movements, and major genres, a well as articles on individual authors of importance. Some photographs of authors are included. Details of inclusions, omissions, and fine points of arrangement are explained in the introduction. The *Longman Companion to Twentieth Century Literature*, edited by A. C. Ward (2nd ed., Longman, 1975) attempts to be international in coverage but is best for British writers. In addition to biographical articles, it provides definitions of terms, summaries of famous works, and descriptions of fictional characters.

964. Eppelsheimer, Hanns Wilhelm. **Handbuch der Weltliteratur von der Anfängen bis zur Gegenwart**. 3rd rev. and enl. ed. Klosterman, 1960. 808p.

This standard work covers the literature of East Asia, India, ancient Near East, Islam, Greece and Rome, the Middle Ages and Europe (the last group being arranged by century and then by country). Each section has a brief introduction, followed by a bibliography, with biographical sketches of authors, giving editions, translations, criticism, etc.

965. Fowler, Roger, ed. **A Dictionary of Modern Critical Terms**. Routledge, 1973. 208p.

Context and usage are described in signed articles, which furnish vastly more than mere definitions. Some literary background is presupposed. There are suggestions for further reading.

966. Hargreaves-Mawdsley, William N. **Everyman's Dictionary of European Writers**. Dutton, 1968. 561p.

The compiler has included writers of the past and present, both prominent and obscure (the latter if they influenced prominent writers or helped to start a movement).

967.   Holman, Clarence Hugh. **A Handbook to Literature.** 4th ed. Bobbs-Merrill, 1980.
Explanations of terms, concepts, schools and movements are given in this standard work, which has been the best in the field since the first edition appeared in 1936, prepared by W. F. Thrall and Addison Hibbard. Cross references are indicated by small capitals in the text of entries. Special features include "Outline of Literary History, English and American," which covers leading events and works by periods from 55 B.C. to the present, and lists of: National Book Awards for Fiction, Poetry, Arts, and Letters; Nobel Prizes for Literature; and Pulitzer Prices for Fiction, Poetry, and Drama.

968.   **International Literary Market Place,** 1965- . Bowker.
Lists between 1,500 and 2,000 firms, often with the number of titles published in the preceding year, titles in stock, subject specialties, date of founding, foreign representatives, subsidiaries, distributors, and names of bookstores or book clubs owned by these firms. There are indexes to firms, book clubs and advertisers, but NO index to subject specialties.

969.   **Kindlers Literatur Lexikon.** Kindler Verlag, 1965-1972. 7v.
Some 150 literatures of the world are covered, with entries by titles (usually in the original languages). There are many color plates. Each volume has an index, and v. 7 is the index for the set.

970.   Magill, Frank N. **Cyclopedia of Literary Characters.** Harper, 1963. 1280p.
Sometimes appearing under the title *Masterplots Cyclopedia of Literary Characters*, this work has over 16,000 characters from 1,300 novels, dramas, and epics. It is international in coverage, from ancient times to the present. The basic arrangement is alphabetical by title, with information about author, time of action, date of publication, and principal characters. It is supplemented by an author index and an alphabetical character index.

971.   **Penguin Companion to Literature.** McGraw-Hill, 1969-1971. 4v.
Contents: v. 1—*English*, edited by David Daiches; v. 2—*European*, edited by A. Thorlby; v. 3—*American*, edited by M. Bradbury and others; v. 4—*Classical and Byzantine* [edited by D. R. Dudley] *and Oriental and African* [edited by D. M. Lang]. Biographical and bibliographical information about authors is provided. Some volumes have supplementary information, such as guides to entries by language and country as well as lists of general articles. The volume on American literature includes a section on Latin America.

972.   Shaw, Harry. **Dictionary of Literary Terms.** McGraw-Hill, 1972. 402p.
This standard source includes literary terms, references, and allusions drawn from books, periodicals, films, plays, television programs, and speeches. Shaw gives examples and includes phrases (e.g., "Theater of the Absurd") as well as individual words. The book is planned for the beginning student and the general reader.

973.   **World Encyclopedia of Comics,** ed. by Maurice Horn. Chelsea House, 1976. 790p.
More than 1,200 entries, over 700 black and white illustrations, and 64 pages of full-color reproductions are included in this scholarly work, which was cited among "Reference Books of 1976" (*Library Journal*, April 15, 1977, p. 876).

Biographies

974.   Havlice, Patricia P. **Index to Literary Biography.** Scarecrow, 1975. 2v.
This valuable timesaver, which was included among "Reference Books of 1975" (*Library Journal*, April 15, 1976, p. 967), provides access to 68,000 biographies in 50 sources, including 9 of the Kunitz books, 13 foreign-language works, and some popular sources for children's writers. All periods from antiquity to the present are included. Another useful index, despite some problems noted by reviewers (e.g., variant spellings), is *Author Biographies Master Index: A Consolidated Guide to Biographical Information Concerning Authors Living or Dead as It Appears in a Selection of the Principal Biographical Dictionaries Devoted to Authors, Poets, Journalists and Other Literary Figures*, edited by Denis La Beau (Gale, 1978, 2v.).

975.   **The International Authors and Writers Who's Who.** 7th ed. Melrose; Rowman & Littlefield, 1976. 676p.
More international in scope than *The Authors and Writers Who's Who* (which was confined to English-language authors), the present work has about 10,000 short biographies, with selective bibliographies. One reviewer noted some coverage of writers not found in *Contemporary Authors*.

976.   **International Who's Who in Poetry**, ed. by Ernest Kay. 4th ed. Melrose; Rowman & Littlefield, 1974. 880p.
Biographical information on 4,500 living poets from 50 countries will be found in this vital reference work, together with lists of national and international poetry societies, magazines, and publishers interested in poetry, poetry awards and contests, poetry recordings, etc. Special features include a photographic appendix and a list of pseudonyms and pen names of poets included in the current edition.

977.   Magill, Frank N. **Cyclopedia of World Authors.** Rev. ed. 1974. 3v.
Biographies of 1,000 authors from many periods and countries are included. Sketches vary in length from 200 to 1,000 words and provide basic biographical data, principal works, a narrative assessment of significance, and bibliographical references. Entries for authors best known by their pseudonyms are under the pseudonyms, with cross references from their real names in the author index at the end of v. 3.

978.   **Who Was Who among English and European Authors, 1931-1949.** Gale, 1978. 3v.
This composite biographical dictionary contains 23,000 entries. All biographical sketches from *Who's Who among Living Authors of Older Nations* (1931) and the last bio-bibliographical sketches from *Writers and Authors Who's Who* (1934-1949) are included. Both current and retrospective coverage of about 300 Canadian authors can be found in *Canadian Writers; Écrivains canadiens: A Bibliographical Dictionary*, edited by Guy Sylvestre, Brandon Conron, and Carol F. Klinck (new ed., Ryerson, 1966). Articles on French-Canadian writers are in French. A chronological table and an index of those titles mentioned in the articles enhance its reference usefulness.

Anthologies and Digests

979.   Koehmstedt, Carol L. **Plot Summary Index.** Scarecrow, 1973. 312p.
What originally began in a reference department as an index to *Masterplots* was expanded to include some 25 works that provide plot summaries and digests. The first part is a title index (with complete citations), and the second part is an author index (again, with complete citations).

980.   Magill, Frank N., ed. **Magill's Quotations in Context.** Harper, 1966. 2nd series, 1969. 2v.
Although this could be placed with books of quotations, it is really an attempt to go beyond merely identifying sources and to provide background remarks or a summary of the context to clarify meaning. There are about 2,000 quotations in alphabetical arrangement, with keyword and author indexes.

981.   Magill, Frank N., ed. **Masterplots: 2010 Plot Stories and Essay Reviews from the World's Fine Literature.** Rev. ed. Salem Press, 1976. 12v.
Main entries are under titles, with author indexes. This popular series of digests of famous works first began to appear in 1949. Its bibliographical proliferation over the years has been bewildering. The most complete listing readily available is given on pages vii-ix of Koehmstedt (see item 978), and that is no longer up to date. Beginning in 1954, Magill and his associates prepared summaries and appraisals of one hundred new books each year in *Masterplots Annual*, which continued until 1976, when these were cumulated in *Survey of Contemporary Literature* (Salem Press, 1977, 12v.). From 1977 to date, some 200 new books selected from among those which appear in the United States are included each year in *Magill's Literary Annual*. Reference librarians have long been aware of the temptation to use these excellent summaries when school or college assignments actually call for reading the originals. *Thesaurus of Book Digests: Digests of the World's Permanent Writings from the Ancient Classics to Current Literature*, edited by Hiram Haydn and Edmund Fuller (Crown, 1949), is arranged by titles, with indexes of authors and characters. *Reader's Digest of Books*, edited by Helen Rex Keller (Macmillan, 1929), provides synopses of fiction and nonfiction from many countries and periods. *Juniorplots* (Bowker, 1967) and *More Juniorplots*, by John Gillespie (Bowker, 1977), provide plot summaries of books of special interest to those 11-17 years of age.

Theory and Criticism

982.   Frye, Northrop. **Anatomy of Criticism: Four Essays.** Princeton, 1957; repr., 1971. 383p.
Frye's book has been cited by numerous authors as a landmark work in the development of critical theory. Another useful work by Frye is *The Critical Path: An Essay on the Social Context of Literary Criticism* (Indiana, 1971; repr., 1973).

983.   **In Search of Literary Theory**, ed. by Morton W. Bloomfield. Cornell, 1972. 274p.
Essays by major literary critics: M. H. Abrams, E. D. Hirsch, Morton W. Bloomfield, Northrop Frye, Geoffrey Hartman, and Paul de Man. Five of these were originally published in the spring 1970 issue of *Daedalus*.

984. Wellek, René. **Concepts of Criticism**, ed. by Stephen G. Nichols, Jr. Yale, 1963. 403p.

Reflections on this subject by one of the foremost contemporary scholars. Somewhat less vital, but useful, is Wellek's *Discriminations: Further Concepts of Criticism* (Yale, 1970).

985. Wellek, René. **A History of Modern Criticism: 1750-1950.** Yale, 1955- .

A landmark work in this field. Contents: v. 1 — *The Later Eighteenth Century*; v. 2 — *The Romantic Age*; v. 3 — *The Age of Transition*; v. 4 — *The Later Nineteenth Century*; v. 5 — *The Twentieth Century*. Another major work is *English Literary Criticism*, by John W. H. Atkins (Cambridge, 1943; Methuen, 1947-51. 3v.), which covers *The Medieval Phase* (1943), *The Renascence* (1974), and *The 17th and 18th Centuries* (1951).

986. Wellek, René, and Austin Warren. **Theory of Literature.** 3rd ed. Harcourt, 1956; repr., 1977. 374p.

Contents: Definitions and Distinctions; Preliminary Operations; The Extrinsic Approach to the Study of Literature; The Intrinsic Study of Literature; The Academic Situation; Notes; Chapter Bibliographies; Index. Another significant title is *Critical Approaches to Literature*, by David Daiches (Prentice-Hall, 1956; repr., W. W. Norton, 1965).

987. Wimsatt, William Kurtz, and Cleanth Brooks. **Literary Criticism: A Short History.** Knopf, 1957; repr., University of Chicago Press, 1978. 2v.

A survey of critical approaches from antiquity to the twentieth century. Reference features include an analytical index and extensive bibliographies.

Serials

988.**Comparative Literature**, 1949- . Q. University of Oregon.
Indexed: *Abstr.Engl.Stud., Hum.Ind., MLA Abstr., Bk.Rev.Ind., Bull.signal.:hist.sci.lit.* The text is mainly in English, but occasionally in French, German, Italian, or Spanish.

989. **Comparative Literature Studies**, 1963- . Q. University of Illinois.
Indexed: *Abstr.Engl.Stud., Hum.Ind., MLA Abstr., MLA Int.Bibliog.* The text is in English, French, German, Italian, and Spanish.

990. **Contemporary Literature**, 1960- . Q. University of Wisconsin.
Indexed: *Hum.Ind., MLA Abstr., Abstr.Engl.Stud., MLA Int.Bibliog.*

991. **Modern Philology: A Journal Devoted to Research in Medieval and Modern Literature**, 1903/04- . University of Chicago Press.
Indexed: *Abstr.Engl.Stud., Bk.Rev.Dig., Hum.Ind., Bk.Rev.Ind., Bull.signal.:hist.sci.lit.* Literature in English is the prime focus, with secondary emphasis on Romance and Germanic literatures.

992. **PMLA: Publications of the Modern Language Association of America,** 1884/85- . 6/yr. Modern Language Association of America. Indexed: *Abstr.Engl.Stud., Hum.Ind., LLBA, MLA Abstr., MLA Int.Bibliog.* The user will find a wide range of scholarly articles on modern languages and literatures.

993. **Revue de littérature comparée,** 1921- . Q. Marcel Didier. There is a cumulative index every 10 years. The text is in English, French, German, Italian, and Spanish.

994. **World Literature Today,** 1927- . Q. University of Oklahoma Press. Indexed: *Bk.Rev.Dig., Hum.Ind., LLBA, MLA Int.Bibliog.* The purpose of this journal is to keep abreast of foreign literature and interpret it for American readers. It was formerly entitled *Books Abroad.*

995. **Yearbook of Comparative and General Literature,** 1952- . Indiana University. Indexed: *MLA Abstr.* This useful work includes articles, news items, biographical sketches, and the "Annual Bibliography" designed as a supplement to Baldensperger (see item 950).

LITERATURE IN ENGLISH

Introductory Works and Bibliographic Guides

996. Altick, Richard Daniel, and Andrew Wright. **Selective Bibliography for the Study of English and American Literature.** 6th ed. Macmillan, 1979. 180p. Intended primarily for the use of graduate students, this standard guide omits works considered inferior unless coverage would be seriously incomplete. Inclusion generally denotes excellence in the view of the compilers. Evaluative annotations are given only when this is *not* the case. A classified arrangement is followed. Reference features include a glossary, and a name-title-subject index. Reviewers have recommended *Guide to American Literature from Its Beginnings through Walt Whitman* and *Guide to American Literature from Emily Dickinson to the Present*, both by James T. Callow and Robert J. Reilly (Barnes & Noble, 1977) for use by high school students and undergraduates. Jackson R. Bryer's *Sixteen Modern American Authors: A Survey of Research and Criticism* (rev. ed., Duke, 1974) gives greater depth of treatment for the few selected.

997. Bateson, Frederick Wilse, Harrison T. Meserole, and Marilyn R. Mumford. **A Guide to English and American Literature.** 3rd ed. Gordian Press, 1976. 334p. Evaluative comments aid the graduate student. A classified arangement is followed with an index. Previous editions carried the title *A Guide to English Literature.* Other useful works include *A Concise Bibliography for Students of English,* by Arthur G. Kennedy and Donald B. Sands (5th ed., rev. by William E. Colburn; Stanford, 1972) and *Reference Sources in English and American Literature: An Annotated Bibliography,* by Robert C. Schweik (Norton, 1977).

998. Bell, Inglis F., and Jennifer Gallup. **A Reference Guide to English, American and Canadian Literature: An Annotated Checklist of Bibliographical and Other Reference Materials.** University of British Columbia Press, 1971. 139p. Planned for undergraduates who are majoring in English, this book has two parts: a classified, annotated bibliography of standard research tools, and bibliographies of individual authors. There are indexes to authors as contributors and to authors as subjects.

999. Dick, Aliki Lafkidou. **A Student's Guide to British Literature: A Selective Bibliography of 4,128 Titles and Reference Sources from the Anglo-Saxon Period to the Present.** Libraries Unlimited, 1972. 285p.
This useful guide opens with general works, divided by form. There is a period arrangement in the main part, subdivided by authors, followed by an author and subject index. More specialized are *Twentieth Century British Literature: A Bibliography and Reference Guide*, by Ruth Temple and Martin Tucker (Ungar, 1968), and *Anglo-Irish Literature; A Review of Research*, edited by Richard J. Finnerman (Modern Language Association, 1976). James Thompson's *English Studies: A Guide for Librarians to the Sources and Their Organization* (Linnet, 1971) should not be overlooked. For information on literary periodicals, consult *The English Literary Journal to 1900: A Guide to Information Sources*, by Robert B. White, Jr. (Gale, 1977), and *Literary Reviews in British Periodicals, 1821-1826: A Bibliography*, by William S. Ward (Garland, 1977).

1000. Jones, Howard Mumford, and Richard M. Ludwig. **Guide to American Literature and Its Backgrounds since 1890.** 4th ed. Harvard University Press, 1972. 264p.
A guide listing works presenting the intellectual, sociological, and political backgrounds of American literary history, followed by reading lists on various aspects and schools in American literature since 1890. Walter Sutton's *Modern American Criticism* (Prentice-Hall, 1963; repr., Greenwood, 1977) is a review of American scholarship of the preceding 30 years.

1001. Meacham, Mary. **Information Sources in Children's Literature: A Practical Reference Guide for Children's Librarians, Elementary School Teachers, and Students of Children's Literature.** Greenwood, 1978. 256p.
Designed for the person with little or no formal training in library science, this convenient guide provides useful current information on such topics as: building the collection; keeping up to date; science books; indexes and abstracts; special help for special fields (topics ranging from children's magazines to reference books for school libraries); illustrators, authors, awards; using books with children; technical processes. Appendices include: organizing and running the library/media center; criteria for evaluating a children's book; and suggestions for further reading. *The Best in Children's Books*, edited by Zena Sutherland (University of Chicago Press, 1973), contains 1,400 recommended titles reviewed in the *Bulletin of the Center for Children's Books* from 1966 to 1972. A briefer guide by Harriet B. Quimby and Rosemary Weber is entitled *Building a Children's Collection: A Suggested Basic Collection for Academic Libraries and a Suggested Basic Collection of Children's Books* (rev. ed., *Choice*, 1978). *How to Find Out about Children's Literature*, by Alec Ellis (3rd ed., Pergamon, 1973), is directed toward a British audience. Useful supplementary coverage is provided by *A Multimedia approch to Children's Literature: A Selective List of Films, Filmstrips and Recordings Based on Children's books*, edited by Ellin Greene and Madalynne Schoenfeld (2nd ed., ALA, 1977).

Bibliographies (Current and Retrospective)

1002. Abrash, Barbara. **Black African Literature in English since 1952: Works and Criticism.** Johnson, 1967. 92p.
The compiler included citations to general bibliography and criticism, anthologies, individual author bibliographies (works and criticism), a selected list of periodicals, and

an author index. Complementary coverage is provided in *Black American Writers: Bibliographic Essays*, edited by Thomas M. Inge (St. Martin's, 1978, 2v.).

1003. Annals of English Literature, 1475-1950: The Principal Publications of Each Year, Together with an Alphabetical Index of Authors with Their Works. 2nd ed. Oxford, 1961; repr., 1965. 380p.
Chronological bibliography that provides factual underpinning for research in literary history.

1004. Blanck, Jacob Nathanial. **Bibliography of American Literature.** Yale, 1955- .
Contents: v. 1—*Henry Adams to Donn Byrne* (1955); v. 2—*George W. Cable to Timothy Dwight* (1957); v. 3—*Edward Eggleston to Bret Harte* (1959); v. 4—*Nathaniel Hawthorne to Joseph Holt Ingraham* (1963); v. 5—*Washington Irving to Henry Wadsworth Longfellow* (1969); v. 6—*Augustus Baldwin Longstreet to Thomas William Parsons* (1973). This selective bibliography will include about 300 authors from the federal period to 1930. It *excludes* authors without literary interest. Material for each author is arranged chronologically and includes: 1) first editions of books and pamphlets and any other book containing the first appearance of a work; 2) reprints containing textual or other changes; and 3) a selected list of biographical, bibliographical, and critical works. *Locations* are indicated for copies examined. The compiler has excluded periodical and newspaper publications, later editions, translations, and volumes with isolated correspondence. Another work of special value to reference and rare books librarians as well as researchers is *First Printings of American Authors: Contributions toward Descriptive Checklists*, edited by Matthew J. Bruccoli (Gale, 1977-78, 4v.), which contains detailed information on different editions and printings of some 500 authors, supplemented by facsimile reproductions of numerous title pages.

1005. Brown University. Library. **Dictionary Catalog of the Harris Collection of American Poetry and Plays.** G. K. Hall, 1972. 13v.
The significance of this catalog is indicated by the review in *ARBA 1973* (p. 489): "The Harris Collection contains over 150,000 printed books and pamphlets by American, Canadian and Mexican authors. The policy of the collection is all-inclusive on the thesis that every volume of American verse is potentially useful to the scholar. A separate catalog of broadsides will be published. Supplements are planned."

1006. English Association. **The Year's Work in English Studies**, 1919- . Oxford.
This critical, selective survey of studies in English literature appearing in books and articles published in Britain, Europe, and America is arranged by periods and indexed by author and subject. A chapter on American literature has been included since 1954.

1007. Gohdes, Clarence Louis Frank. **Bibliographical Guide to the Study of the Literature of the U.S.A.** 4th ed. Duke University Press, 1976. 173p.
Classified arrangement with short, evaluative annotations. Indexes: subjects; names of authors, editors, and compilers. Gohdes has also compiled *Literature and Theatre of the States and Regions of the U.S.A.: An Historical Bibliography* (Duke, 1967). Another major segment of American literature is covered in Louis D. Rubin's *A Bibliographical Guide to the Study of Southern Literature* (Louisiana State, 1969). Specialized coverage of a related area is provided in *The Literary Journal in America to 1900: A Guide to Information Sources* (Gale, 1975) and *The Literary Journal in*

America, 1900-1950: A Guide to Information Sources (Gale, 1977), both by Edward E. Chielens. The earliest period is also covered in *An Annotated Bibliography of American Literary Periodicals, 1741-1850*, by Jayne K. Kribbs (G. K. Hall, 1977). Current information may be found in *Fourth Directory of Periodicals Publishing Articles on English and American Literature and Language* (Swallow, 1975). Important regional coverage of American literature is provided by Richard W. Etulain's *Western American Literature: A Bibliography of Interpretive Books and Articles* (Dakota Press, 1972).

1008.   Howard-Hill, Trevor Howard. **Index to British Bibliography.** Oxford, 1969- . 3v.
Contents: v. 1 – *Bibliography of British Literary Bibliographies* (1969); v. 2 – *Bibliography of Shakespeare Bibliographies*; v. 3 – *Bibliography of British Bibliography and Textual Criticism.* Appears to complement, rather than supersede, C. S. Northup's *A Register of Bibliographies of the English Language and Literature* (Yale, 1925; repr., Hafner, 1962). Focusing on more restricted periods are Elgin W. Mellown's *A Descriptive Catalogue of the Bibliographies of Twentieth Century British Poets, Novelists and Dramatists* (2nd ed., Whitston, 1978); A. C. Elkins and L. J. Forstner's *The Romantic Movement Bibliography, 1936-1970: A Master Cumulation from ELH, Philological Quarterly, and Modern Language Notes* (Pierian Press, 1973, 7v.); *English Literature, 1660-1800: A Bibliography of Modern Studies* (Princeton, 1950-); and James Edward Tobin's *Eighteenth Century English Literature and Its Cultural Background: A Bibliography* (Fordham, 1939).

1009.   Jacobson, Angeline, comp. **Contemporary Native American Literature: A Selected & Partially Annotated Bibliography.** Scarecrow, 1977. 262p.
Included among the best reference books of 1977 (*Library Journal*, April 15, 1978, p. 819), this bibliography of 2,034 books, periodical articles, and individual poems has a classified arrangement with a title and first line index to individual poems as well as an author index. Another useful source is Jack W. Marken's *The American Indian: Language and Literature* (AHM Pub. Corp., 1978).

1010.   **Literary Writings in America: A Bibliography.** KTO Press, 1977. 8v.
Part of an immense WPA project, this set consists of photographic reproductions of some 250,000 entries out of nearly 750,000 originally gathered. Reviewers have noted some curious inclusions and omissions as well as unevenness in the quality of the reproductions. Despite these deficiencies, it is essential for tracing obscure writers who may not be found at all elsewhere.

1011.   McNamee, Lawrence F. **Dissertations in English and American Literature: Theses Accepted by American, British and German Universities, 1865-1964.** Bowker, 1968. 1124p. Suppl. 1, 1969. Suppl. 2, 1974.
McNamee's computer-produced, classified listing includes sections on English language and linguistics, the teaching of English, comparative literature, and "creative" dissertations as well as the usual sections for periods, types, individual authors, etc. If a dissertation deals with more than one literary figure, the "cross index of authors" will provide access to those items that do not appear under a given literary figure's name in the main body of the work. There is also an index by authors of dissertations. It is confined to dissertations submitted in a single department. Though more limited in coverage, *Dissertations in American Literature, 1891-1966*, by James Woodress (Duke, 1968), is somewhat more attractive and easier to use, despite its lack of a good analytical index. Patsy C. Howard has compiled *Theses in English Literature, 1894-1970* (Pierian, 1973)

and *Theses in American Literature, 1896-1971* (Pierian, 1973). Both contain entries for theses from over 200 universities (mainly United States and Canadian) and include only theses on individual writers. The arrangement is alphabetical by writers and then by authors of theses.

1012. Modern Humanities Research Association. **Annual Bibliography of English Language and Literature**, 1920- . Cambridge University Press.
Books, pamphlets, and articles are covered in a classified arrangement that includes English and American literature and also gives references to reviews. Occasionally, a volume will cover two or three years. The language section is arranged by subject and the literature section, chronologically. There is a name index.

1013. Modern Language Association of America. American Literature Section. **American Literary Manuscripts: A Checklist of Holdings in Academic, Historical, and Public Libraries, Museums, and Authors' Homes in the United States.** 2nd ed. University of Georgia Press, 1977. 387p.
This is a valuable finding tool because so few repositories have been able to publish their own catalogs. One particularly fine example of such a publication is the New York Public Library's *Dictionary Catalog of the Albert A. and Henry W. Berg Collection of English and American Literature* (G. K. Hall, 1970, 5v.), which gives access to 50,000 manuscripts.

1014. New, William H., comp. **Critical Writings on Commonwealth Literatures: A Selective Bibliography to 1970, with a List of Theses and Dissertations.** Pennsylvania State University Press, 1975. 333p.
A noted authority has compiled an excellent bibliography notable for its breadth and thoroughness. Individual Commonwealth countries are treated in greater depth in such works as R. E. Watters's *A Checklist of Canadian Literature and Background Materials, 1628-1960* (see item 1020) or Morris Miller's *Australian Literature from Its Beginnings to 1935: A Descriptive and Bibliographical Survey of Books by Australian Authors in Poetry, Drama, Fiction, Criticism and Anthology, with Subsidiary Entries to 1938* (Sydney University Press, 1940; repr., 1973, 1975, 3v.). A one-volume abridged version by F. T. Macartney (Angus & Robertson, 1956) carried the coverage down to 1950, but it also eliminated much useful detail.

1015. **The New Cambridge Bibliography of English Literature**, ed. by George Watson. Cambridge University Press, 1969-1977. 5v.
Individual NCBEL volumes provide coverage as follows: v. 1, 600-1660; v. 2, 1660-1800; v. 3, 1800-1900; v. 4, 1900-1950; v. 5, index. A revision and substantial expansion of *The Cambridge Bibliography of English Literature*, edited by F. W. Bateson (Cambridge, 1940, 4v.; suppl., 1957). A work of absolutely fundamental importance. Entries are arranged by literary periods and then by form (poetry, drama, etc.). Within these divisions, there are further subdivisions by special topics and individual authors. *The Concise Cambridge Bibliography of English Literature, 600-1950*, edited by George Watson (2nd ed., Cambridge University Press, 1965), follows the same plan as the basic set but is highly selective.

1016. Nilon, Charles H. **Bibliography of Bibliographies in American Literature.** Bowker, 1970. 483p.
There are 6,463 entries arranged by author, genre, literary period, and special categories. The work includes an author index and a detailed subject index, plus

numerous cross references. On occasion, it will still be useful to consult Nathan Van Patten's *An Index to Bibliographies and Bibliographical Contributions Relating to the Work of American and British Authors, 1923-1932* (Stanford University Press, 1934).

1017. Pollard, Alfred William, and G. R. Redgrave. **A Short-Title Catalogue of Books Printed in England, Scotland and Ireland, and of English Books Printed Abroad, 1475-1640.** 2nd ed. rev. and enl. begun by W.A. Jackson and F. S. Ferguson, completed by Katherine F. Panzer. Bibliographical Society, 1976. 2v.

Often cited as STC, this is the most comprehensive record of English books for the period, with about 26,500 editions. Arranged alphabetically by author and other main entries, it gives author, brief title, size, printer, date, reference to *Stationers' Register*, and symbols for libraries (mainly British) that have copies. The compilers tried to record all known copies of very rare items and a representative sampling of libraries with more common titles. Because the original work recorded holdings of only 15 American libraries, William Warner Bishop compiled *A Checklist of American Copies of Short Title Catalogue Books* (2nd ed., University of Michigan Press, 1950; repr., Greenwood, 1968), which records over 26,000 holdings from 120 libraries. P. G. Morrison prepared *Index to Printers, Publishers and Booksellers in A. W. Pollard and G. R. Redgrave, "A Short-Title Catalogue"* (Bibliographical Society of Virginia, 1950). A. F. Allison and V. F. Goldsmith have produced a useful index, *Titles of English Books (and of Foreign Books Printed in England): An Alphabetical Finding-List by Title of Books Published under the Author's Name, Pseudonym or Initials, Volume I, 1475-1640* (Archon, 1976). Books listed in the STC are available on microfilm from University Microfilms. Complementary coverage for the period is provided in Matthias A. Shaaber's *Check-list of Works of British Authors Printed Abroad in Languages Other Than English, to 1641* (Bibliographical Society of America, 1975).

1018. Severs, Jonathan Burke, and Albert E. Hartung, eds. **A Manual of the Writings in Middle English, 1050-1500.** Connecticut Academy of Arts and Sciences; distr., Archon, 1967- .

Five volumes have appeared in this scholarly set, which contains information about critical commentaries and MSS of original works. The authors make heavy use of abbreviations that may not be familiar to librarians. The work has been done by the Middle English Group of the Modern Language Association of America. When completed, it will be an expansion and updating of *A Manual of the Writings in Middle English, 1050-1400*, by John Edwin Wells (Yale, 1916; Suppls. 1-9, 1919-45).

1019. Templeman, William D. **Bibliographies of Studies in Victorian Literature for the Thirteen Years, 1932-1944.** University of Illinois Press, 1945; repr., Johnson, 1971. 450p.

Compiled from annual lists in *Modern Philology*. Cumulations continued by A. Wright in *Bibliographies of Studies in Victorian Literature for the Ten Years, 1945-1954* (University of Illinois Press, 1956; repr., Johnson, 1971) and R. C. Slack in *Bibliographies of Studies in Victorian Literature for the Ten Years, 1955-1964* (University of Illinois Press, 1967). Now continued as "Victorian Bibliography for . . . " in *Victorian Studies* (see item 1158). Supplemental coverage is offered in *Guide to Doctoral Dissertations in Victorian Literature, 1886-1958*, by Richard D. Altick and William R. Matthews (University of Illinois Press, 1960; repr., Greenwood, 1973), which is a classified bibliography of more than 2,000 items, with an author index.

1020. Watters, Reginald Eyre. **A Checklist of Canadian Literature and Background Materials, 1628-1960.** 2nd ed. University of Toronto Press, 1972. 1085p.
Although confined to Canadian literature in English, this is the most comprehensive compilation available. Part I covers fiction, drama, and poetry. Part II deals with background materials. Library locations are given. One segment is given selective in-depth coverage by Sheila Egoff in *The Republic of Childhood: A Critical Guide to Canadian Children's Literature in English* (2nd ed., Oxford, 1975). Less comprehensive than Watters, but very useful, is *English-Canadian Literature to 1900: A Guide to Information Sources*, by R. G. Moyles (Gale, 1976).

1021. Wing, Donald. **Short-Title Catalogue of Books Printed in England, Scotland, Ireland, Wales and British America and of English Books Printed in Other Countries, 1641-1700.** 2nd ed. Modern Language Association, 1972- .
A continuation of the STC by Pollard and Redgrave, this work shows where items are located in many libraries in Britain and the United States. Geographical distribution is attempted but not a census of copies. The location symbols are *not* the same as in the STC or NUC but were devised by Wing. It is supplemented by P. G. Morrison's *Index of Printers, Publishers, and Booksellers in Donald Wing's "Short-Title Catalogue"* (Bibliographical Society of the University of Virginia, 1955). A. F. Allison and V. F. Goldsmith have also produced an index to Wing, *Titles of English Books (and of Foreign Books Printed in England): An Alphabetical Finding-List by Title of Books Published under the Author's Name, Pseudonym or Initials, Volume II, 1641-1700* (Archon, 1977). Books listed in Wing are available on microfilm from University Microfilms.

Indexes, Abstracts, and Current Awareness Services

1022. **Abstracts of English Studies,** 1958- . 10/yr. National Council of Teachers of English.
Abstracts are grouped under journal titles, with monthly and annual subject indexes and an annual author-title index. Some 400 American and foreign periodicals on English, Commonwealth, and American literature and English philology are included.

1023. **Canadian Essay and Literature Index,** 1973- . Ann. University of Toronto Press.
In a typical year, some 75 English-Canadian anthologies and collections, plus more than 50 periodicals not indexed elsewhere, are covered. Authors, titles, and subjects are all in one alphabet. Coverage of literature predominates, including individual poems, plays, and short stories. A separate section indexes book reviews.

1024. **Children's Book Review Index,** 1975- . 3/yr. Ann. cum. Gale.
Each issue covers about 100 authors. Entries include brief biographical notes, excerpts from reviews, and citations of additional reviews and commentary. Each issue contains three indexes: cumulative critic index; cumulative title index; and cumulative author index.

1025. **Children's Literature Review,** 1976- . 2/yr. Gale.
Subtitle: "Excerpts from reviews, criticism, and commentary on books for children and young people." Each semi-annual volume contains information on books by about 50

authors. The arrangement is alphabetical by authors being reviewed; then a general section for evaluations of more than one work and a section (arranged by titles) for authors and citations to reviews not excerpted are also provided. Each volume has cumulative indexes to authors, critics, and titles.

1026.   Combs, Richard E. **Authors: Critical and Biographical References: A Guide to 4,700 Critical and Biographical Passages in Books.** Scarecrow, 1971. 221p.
Using a double-columned page and letter symbols similar to Granger, this work covers 1,400 authors from about 500 books.

1027.   **Comprehensive Index to English-Language Little Magazines 1890-1970, Series One,** ed. by Marion Sader. Kraus-Thomson, 1976. 8v.
The contents of 100 little magazines (primarily literary) are made available through this major index. The editor was formerly in charge of the Marvin Sukov collection of little magazines at the University of Wisconsin. Access is by authors *as subjects.* Subject indexing per se is not attempted. Other sources to be consulted include *Index to Commonwealth Little Magazines* (see item 1031) and *Index to Little Magazines* (see item 1032).

1028.   **Contemporary Literary Criticism,** 1973- . Gale.
These volumes complement the *Contemporary Authors* series by providing extracts of criticism from various reviewing media. Each volume covers about 200 authors. Succeeding volumes provide additional criticism on authors already covered as well as criticism of new authors. Cumulative indexes of authors and critics began to appear in 1975.

1029.   Havlice, Patricia Pate. **Index to American Author Bibliographies.** Scarecrow, 1971. 204p.
"This index duplicates information readily available on standard American authors, especially fiction writers; but it will be particularly valuable in locating bibliographies of minor American authors . . . " — Carolyn A. Hough, *Library Journal,* June 1, 1972, pp. 2075-76.

1030.   Houghton, Walter Edwards, ed. **The Wellesley Index to Victorian Periodicals, 1824-1900.** University of Toronto Press, 1966- .
Providing subject, book review, and author indexing, this set is particularly valuable for contemporary criticism of Victorian authors.

1031.   **Index to Commonwealth Little Magazines,** 1964/65- . Bi. Johnson, v. 1, 2. Whitston, v. 3 to date.
Edited by Stephen H. Goode, this index was formerly somewhat slow in appearing. V. 4 was to cover 1970-71 and was announced for 1973. When it actually appeared in 1975, it covered 1970-73. A more regular pattern was resumed with v. 5 (1974-75), which appeared in 1976.

1032.   **Index to Little Magazines,** 1948- . Swallow Press.
This index is of importance because of the number of major writers who began their careers by having creative works published in little magazines. Over the years, the various editors have tried to concentrate on publications likely to have some permanent

value. For current coverage, one may also wish to check *Access Index to Little Magazines*, 1976- (Gaylord). Retrospective coverage is achieved through *Index to Little Magazines, 1943-1947* (Swallow, 1965), *Index to Little Magazines, 1940-1942* (Johnson, 1966), *Index to American Little Magazines, 1920-1939* (Whitston, 1970), and *Index to American Little Magazines, 1900-1919* (Whitston, 1974).

1033.   Ireland, Norma (Olin). **Index to Fairy Tales, 1949-1972, Including Folklore, Legends and Myths in Collections.** Faxon, 1973. 741p.
The compiler analyzes over 400 collections of fairy tales, folklore, legends, and myths. This volume updates Mary H. Eastman's *Index to Fairy Tales* (Faxon, 1926) and supplements, but with titles and subjects in one alphabet.

1034.   Leary, Lewis Gaston. **Articles on American Literature, 1900-1950.** Duke University Press, 1954. 437p.
Based primarily on bibliographies published in *American Literature* and *PMLA*, this book follows a classified arrangement. The largest section is devoted to individual authors, followed by sections on biography, fiction, etc. It is supplemented, updated, and corrected in *Articles on American Literature, 1950-1967* (Duke, 1970).

1035.   **Reader's Index to the Twentieth-Century Views of Literary Criticism Series, Volumes 1-100.** Prentice-Hall, 1973. 682p.
An important need is met because the individual volumes in this series have lacked indexes.

1036.   **Twentieth Century Literary Criticism,** 1978- . Gale.
Subtitle: "Excerpts from criticism of works of novelists, poets, playwrights, short story writers and other creative writers, 1900-1960." The format is used as for *Contemporary Literary Criticism* (see item 1028), but there are fewer authors per volume, with more intensive coverage. There is some overlap with *A Library of Literary Criticism*, by Ruth Z. Temple and Martin Tucker, and *Modern American Literature*, by Dorothy Nyren Curley (see item 1046n), but both are needed in large reference collections.

Encyclopedias, Dictionaries, and Handbooks

1037.   Cuddon, J. A. **A Dictionary of Literary Terms.** Doubleday, 1977. 745p.
Clear, readable definitions of more than 2,000 literary terms are given in this excellent reference work which was ranked among the best of 1977 (*Library Journal*, April 15, 1978, p. 819). Information about origins, history, and notable examples of usage is also provided. Another useful source is *Current Literary Terms*, edited by A. F. Scott (St. Martin's, 1965; repr., 1978).

1038.   **The Explicator Cyclopedia,** ed. by Charles Child Walcutt and J. Edwin Whitesell. Quadrangle, 1966-68. 3v.
V. 1—*Modern Poetry*; v. 2—*Traditional Poetry: Medieval to Late Victorian*; v. 3—*Prose*. The contents of these volumes were taken from *The Explicator*, v. 1-20 (1942-62), for which the set now represents a cumulation. The arrangement is alphabetical by author of a poem or prose selection and then by title of a poem or prose selection.

1039. Fisher, Margery. **Who's Who in Children's Books: A Treasury of the Familiar Characters of Childhood.** Holt, 1975. 399p.
Information on 1,000 characters in children's books is arranged in alphabetical order, using the first word of each name (e.g., "Great Aunt Dympha" is under "G"). Nursery and fairy tale figures, real historical persons, and many minor characters are excluded. Some British names unfamiliar to American readers are included, and some beloved by American children are omitted. There are about 400 illustrations (16 full-page ones in color). Despite the limitations, it is very useful and was included among "Reference books of 1975" (*Library Journal*, April 15, 1976, p. 969).

1040. Halkett, Samuel, and John Laing. **Dictionary of Anonymous and Pseudonymous English Literature.** New & enl. ed. by James Kennedy, W. A. Smith, and A. F. Johnson. Oliver and Boyd, 1926-62; repr., Haskell House, 1971. 9v.
The basic arrangement is alphabetical by title. V. 6 contains a supplement, and v. 7 has indexes of pseudonyms and real names, plus a second supplement. These volumes contain about 70,000 entries. V. 8 has 9,000 entries and covers 1900-49, while v. 9 has 8,000 entries drawn from the period before 1900 as well as the years 1900-1950. Frank Atkinson's *Dictionary of Literary Pseudonyms* (2nd ed., Linnet, 1977) has about 8,000 names of twentieth-century writers in English.

1041. Hardwick, John Michael Drinkrow. **Literary Atlas and Gazetteer of the British Isles.** Gale, 1973. 216p.
A geographical arrangement is followed for 4,500 deceased writers, supplemented by an author index. Also good for those who wish to travel knowledgeably is *A Literary Tour Guide to England and Scotland*, by Emilie C. Harting (Morrow, 1976).

1042. Hart, James David. **The Oxford Companion to American Literature.** 4th ed. Oxford, 1965. 991p.
Short biographies and bibliographies of American authors and summaries and descriptions of major American novels, stories, essays, poems, and plays are given in alphabetical order, along with information on movements, literary societies, magazines, anthologies, literary prizes, book collectors, printers, etc. It is not as inclusive as Benet or Burke and Howe, but it has longer articles and is more thorough. It is also less inclusive, but more scholarly, than *The Reader's Encyclopedia of American Literature* (Crowell, 1962).

1043. Harvey, Sir Paul. **Oxford Companion to English Literature.** 4th ed. Oxford, 1967; repr., 1974. 961p.
Brief articles on authors, literary works, characters in fiction, drama, etc., and literary allusions. The fourth edition was revised by Dorothy Eagle, who also revised an abridged version entitled *The Concise Oxford Dictionary of English Literature* (2nd ed., Oxford, 1970).

1044. Lanham, Richard A. **A Handlist of Rhetorical Terms: A Guide for Students of English Literature.** University of California Press, 1968. 148p.
Until now, such definitions have been scattered in a variety of sources. Of special interest is a section to help the user move from a definition to the term defined or from an example of use to the rhetorical term that describes it.

1045. Leggett, Glenn, C. David Mead, and William Charvat. **Prentice-Hall Handbook for Writers.** 7th ed. Prentice-Hall, 1978. 468p.
This standard handbook includes a detailed index to the contents and an index to grammatical terms.

1046. Moulton, Charles W. **Library of Literary Criticism of English and American Authors.** Moulton, 1901-05; repr., Smith, 1959. 8v.
This compilation of quoted material covers the period from 680 to 1904. For each author, Moulton gives brief biographical data, then selected quotations from criticisms of that person's work, grouped as 1) personal, 2) individual works, 3) general. Extracts are of some length and have exact references. The set can serve both as an anthology and as an index. *The Critical Temper: A Survey of Modern Criticism on English and American Literature from the Beginnings to the Twentieth Century*, edited by Martin Tucker (Ungar, 1969, 3v.), supplements Moulton by providing extracts from twentieth-century criticism of authors who wrote prior to the twentieth century. Coverage for twentieth-century writers is provided in *A Library of Literary Criticism: Modern British Literature*, compiled by Ruth Z. Temple and Martin Tucker (Ungar, 1966, 3v.; suppl., 1975), *Modern American Literature*, compiled by Dorothy Nyren Curley (4th ed., Ungar, 1969, 3v.), and *Modern Commonwealth Literature*, edited by John H. Ferres and Martin Tucker (Ungar, 1977). Critical appraisals may also be found in Martin Tucker's *Africa in Modern Literature: A Survey of Contemporary Writing in English* (Ungar, 1967).

1047. Ruoff, James E. **Crowell's Handbook of Elizabethan and Stuart Literature.** Crowell, 1975. 468p.
A vast amount of useful information is compressed into 500 alphabetically-arranged entries for authors, literary movements, genres, etc. There are numerous cross references. This essential tool was included among "Reference Books of 1975" (*Library Journal*, April 15, 1976, p. 969).

1048. Story, Norah. **The Oxford Companion to Canadian History and Literature.** Oxford, 1967. 935p. Suppl. 1973. 318p.
Much of what the average reader or student wishes to know about Canadian literature can be found in this excellent addition to the Oxford Companion series and its 1973 supplement. Bibliographies lead the user to sources of further information.

1049. **Webster's New World Companion to English and American Literature,** ed. by Arthur Pollard. World Publishing/Times Mirror, 1973; repr., Popular Library, 1976. 850p.
Over 1,100 entries for authors, literary genres, are included. Mention is made of some 6,000 individual works. An alphabetical arrangement is used, with a 92-page appendix listing works of criticism.

Biographies

1050. **American Writers: A Collection of Literary Biographies,** ed. by Leonard Unger. Scribners, 1974. 4v.
Originally published as the University of Minnesota *Pamphlets on American Writers* (1959-72), these biobibliographical sketches (about 100 in all) have been nominally revised, placed in alphabetical order, and supplied with a cumulative index. The

sketches are important for students because each gives a critical evaluation of a particular writer's achievements. The set was included among "Reference Books of 1975" (*Library Journal*, April 15, 1976, p. 969). More current, but less useful, is *Authors in the News: A Compilation of News Stories and Feature Articles from American Newspapers and Magazines Covering Writers and Other Members of the Communications Media* (Gale, 1976). William C. Young's review in *ARBA 1977* (p. 537) noted that the biographical articles were largely from newspapers like the *Miami Herald*, with nothing from sources like the *New York Times*. Young also noted the preponderance of minor and obscure writers.

1051.   Borkland, Elmer. **Contemporary Literary Critics.** St. Martin's, 1978. 550p.
Part of the series edited by James Vinson and entitled Contemporary Writers of the English Language, this convenient biographical dictionary includes 113 modern British and American literary critics.

1052.   Browning, David Clayton. **Everyman's Dictionary of Literary Biography.** 5th ed. Dent, 1970.
Nearly 2,400 biographical sketches on both major and minor writers are included. Entries are unsigned and vary in length from a few lines to three or four pages. S. A. Allibone's *A Critical Dictionary of English Literature and British and American Authors, Living and Deceased* (Lippincott, 1858-71, 3v.; suppl., 1891, 2v.) may still occasionally be useful for an extended search because there are 46,000 authors in the basic set and 37,000 in the supplement. More specialized is *Directory of Irish Literature*, edited by Robert Hogan (Greenwood, 1979).

1053.   Burke, W. J., and W. D. Howe. **American Authors and Books, 1640 to the Present Day.** 3rd ed. Rev. by Irving and Ann Weiss. Crown, 1972. 719p.
About 17,000 short articles on authors, books, periodicals, newspapers, publishing firms, literary societies, regions, and localities are arranged in alphabetical order with cross references to related subjects. Limited to the continental United States, it is more inclusive than the *Oxford Companion to American Literature* (see item 1042), but the articles are shorter.

1054.   **Children's Authors and Illustrators: An Index to Biographical Dictionaries.** 2nd ed. Gale, 1978. 251p.
Approximately 15,000 authors are covered and references to some 55,000 biographical sketches are provided. There are no stated limitations by nationality or time period.

1055.   **Contemporary Authors: A Bio-bibliographical Guide to Current Authors and Their Works.** 1962- . S-Ann. Gale.
Living authors, mostly writing in English, are selected for initial inclusion. Cumulative indexes (e.g., the v. 77-80 index covering v. 1-80) are issued from time to time. There are now three series: *Original Series*, added to at regular intervals by new inclusions; *Revised Series*, an updating on active authors with new works; *Permanent Series*, deceased or inactive authors whose biographical sketches are updated for the final time. About 60,000 authors (many difficult to find in other sources) are now included in these series.

1056. **Dictionary of Literary Biography**, ed. by Matthew Bruccoli. Gale, 1978- . (In progress).
The purpose of this multi-volume series is to provide information that will reflect the changes since the publication of the *Dictionary of American Biography* (1928-36). A scholarly essay of some length is devoted to each literary figure selected for inclusion. Some retrospective coverage may be found in *Who Was Who among North American Authors, 1921-1939* (Gale, 1976, 2v.) and *Who Was Who in Literature, 1906-1934* (Gale, 1979, 2v.).

1057. Kirkpatrick, Daniel, ed. **Twentieth Century Children's Writers.** St. Martin's, 1978. 1507p.
Biographical, bibliographical, and critical data are provided for 630 children's writers. There is also a brief appendix on nineteenth-century children's authors.

1058. Kunitz, Stanley Jasspon, and Howard Haycraft, eds. **The Junior Book of Authors.** 2nd ed. Wilson, 1951. 309p.
This standard work has nearly 300 biographical sketches with many portraits. The first edition (1934) is still useful for over 100 authors omitted from the second. Supplementation and updating is provided in *More Junior Authors*, by Muriel Fuller (Wilson, 1963), *The Third Book of Junior Authors*, by Doris De Montreville and Donna Hill (Wilson, 1972), and *The Fourth Book of Junior Authors and Illustrators*, by De Montreville and Hill (1978). The last has a cumulative index to the four volumes.

1059. Kunitz, Stanley Jasspon, and Howard Haycraft, eds. **Twentieth Century Authors: A Biographical Dictionary of Modern Literature: Complete in One Volume, with 1,850 Biographies and 1,700 Portraits.** Wilson, 1942. 1577p. Suppl. 1955. 1123p.
International coverage was attempted, but Kunitz favored writers whose works were available in English. Biographies include major works with dates of original publication and sources of further information. This essential work is supplemented and updated by *World Authors, 1950-1970*, by John Wakeman and Stanley J. Kunitz (Wilson, 1975). Kunitz provided coverage for earlier periods in such works as *European Authors, 1000-1900* (Wilson, 1967), *American Authors, 1600-1900* (Wilson, 1938), *British Authors before 1800* (Wilson, 1952), and *British Authors of the Nineteenth Century* (Wilson, 1936).

1060. Millet, Fred Benjamin. **Contemporary American Authors: A Critical Survey and 219 Bio-bibliographies.** Harcourt, 1940. 716p.
A critical survey of more than 200 pages is followed by entries on individual authors. There are three indexes: index of authors, divided into 13 types; index of abbreviations of books and periodicals cited; and index of authors also included in *Contemporary British Literature* (3rd ed., Harrap, 1935; repr., Johnson, 1969).

1061. Rush, Theressa G., Carol F. Myers, and Esther S. Arata. **Black American Writers Past and Present: A Biographical and Bibliographical Dictionary.** Scarecrow, 1975. 2v.
Easily the most comprehensive work available, this was included in "Reference Books of 1975" (*Library Journal*, April 15, 1976, p. 468). Although the compilers have concentrated on poets, dramatists, novelists, children's writers, and critics, they have also included other writers whose works are likely to appear in black studies curricula and

writers from Africa and the West Indies if they live in the United States or have published here. *Living Black Authors: A Biographical Directory*, by Ann A. Shockley and Sue P. Chandler (Bowker, 1973), includes 450 authors and was compiled chiefly from questionnaires. Another work that should not be overlooked is *Selected Black American Authors: An Illustrated Bio-Bibliography* (Hall, 1977).

1062. Russell, Josiah-Cox. **Dictionary of Writers of Thirteenth Century England.** Longman, 1936; repr., Franklin, 1971. 210p.
Detailed biographical and bibliographical information is provided for 350 authors. Entries are under given names (rather than surnames).

1063. **Something about the Author**, 1971- . S-Ann. Gale.
Biographical entries typically give personal facts, careers, writings, works in progress, sidelights, and sources of additional information. There are many illustrations from children's and young adult books. More selective and critical coverage is given by Miriam Hoffman and Eva Samuels in *Authors and Illustrators of Children's Books* (Bowker, 1972). Supplemental coverage will be found in *The Who's Who of Children's Literature*, by Brian Doyle (Schocken, 1969).

1064. Woodress, James Leslie, ed. **Eight American Authors: A Review of Research and Criticism.** Rev. ed. Norton, 1972. 392p.
Individual scholars have contributed bibliographic essays on: Edgar Allen Poe, Ralph Waldo Emerson, Nathaniel Hawthorne, Henry David Thoreau, Herman Melville, Walt Whitman, Samuel Langhorne Clemens, and Henry James. A similar pattern (for different writers) is followed in *Fifteen Modern American Authors: A Survey of Research and Criticism*, edited by Jackson R. Bryer (Duke, 1969), and *Fifteen American Authors before 1900: Bibliographic Essays on Research and Criticism*, edited by Robert A. Rees and Earl N. Harbert (University of Wisconsin Press, 1971).

1065. **The Writer's Directory**, 1971/72- . Bi. St. James; St. Martin's.
The third edition (1976-78) contains brief biographies of 12,000 living writers in English from Australia, Canada, Ireland, New Zealand, South Africa, the United Kingdom, the United States, and other countries. The main part is arranged alphabetically by authors' surnames, with cross references from pseudonyms. A listing of authors by categories occupies over 150 yellow pages at the beginning and a list of publishers' addresses (subarranged by countries) is provided at the end.

1066. **Yesterday's Authors of Books for Children**, 1977- . Ann. Gale.
The subtitle of this attractive new series, which complements *Something about the Author* (see item 1063), reads as follows: "Facts and Pictures about Authors and Illustrators of Books for Young People, from Early Times to 1960." Profusely illustrated, each account gives biographical and career information, writings, and sidelights (often with liberal quotations from authors' diaries).

Reference Histories

1067. Baugh, Albert Croll, ed. **A Literary History of England.** 2nd ed. Appleton, 1967. 4v.
Baugh's work is very highly regarded by scholars and reference librarians. Contents: v. 1 — *The Middle Ages: The Old English Period (to 1100)*, by K. Malone; *The Middle*

English Period (1100-1500), by A. C. Baugh; v. 2 — *The Renaissance (1500-1660)*, by T. Brooke and M. A. Shaaber; v. 3 — *The Restoration and Eighteenth Century (1660-1789)*, by G. Sherburne and D. F. Bond; v. 4 — *The Nineteenth Century and After (1789-1939)*, by S. C. Chew and R. D. Altick.

1068. **Cambridge History of American Literature.** Ed. by William Peterfield Trent, John Erskine, Stuart P. Sherman, and Carl Van Doren. Putnam, 1917-21. 4v. (Repr. in 1933 in 3v. without bibliographies. Repr. of 1933 ed. in 1v. by Macmillan, 1967).
This is still a valuable work, especially thorough on the early period. Literary forms, subjects, writers, etc. are treated in great detail. Related topics (explorers, travelers, colonial newspapers, literary annuals, gift books, children's literature, oral literature, non-English writings, etc.) are also included. Although it is more recent, Martin S. Day's *Handbook of American Literature: A Comprehensive Study from Colonial Times to the Present Day* (Crane, Russak, 1976) is recommended "only as a supplementary reference" (see Bohdan S. Wynar's review in *ARBA 1977*, p. 577). *The South in American Literature, 1607-1900*, by Jay Broadus Hubbell (Duke, 1954; repr., 1973) is a major historical survey, with an extensive bibliography. Another important facet of American literary history was covered by Vernon Loggins in *The Negro Author; His Development in America to 1900* (Columbia, 1931; repr., Kennikat, 1964).

1069. **Cambridge History of English Literature**, ed. by A. W. Ward and A. R. Waller. Cambridge University Press, 1907-27; repr., 1976. 15v.
The most important general history of English literature, this major set covers the period from the earliest times to the end of the nineteenth century. Each chapter was written by a specialist. It includes extended and very useful bibliographies. Contents: v. 1 — *From the Beginnings to the Cycles of Romance*; v. 2 — *The End of the Middle Ages*; v. 3 — *Renaissance and Reformation*; v. 4 — *Prose and Poetry: Sir Thomas North to Michael Drayton*; v. 5, 6 — *The Drama to 1642*; v. 7 — *Cavalier and Puritan*; v. 8 — *The Age of Dryden*; v. 9 — *From Steele and Addison to Pope and Swift*; v. 10 — *The Age of Johnson*; v. 11 — *The Period of the French Revolution*; v. 12, 13, 14 — *The Nineteenth Century*; v. 15 — *Index*. (Reprinted in 1932 without bibliographies.) Planned for graduate students, *The English Romantic Poets and Essayists: A Review of Research and Criticism*, by Carlyn W. Houtchens and Lawrence H. Houtchens (2nd ed., MLA; distr., NYU Press, 1966), has chapters on Blake, Lamb, Hazlitt, Scott, Southey, Campbell, Moore, Landor, Leigh Hunt, DeQuincey, and Carlyle.

1070. Dobrée, Bonamy, ed. **Introductions to English Literature.** 3rd ed. Cresset Press, 1961-69. 5v.
V. 1 — *The Beginnings of English Literature to Skelton, 1509*, by W. L. Renwick and Harold Orton, 3rd ed. revised by Martyn F. Wakelin, 1966; v. 2 — *The English Renaissance, 1510-1688*, by V. de Sola Pinto, 3rd revised ed., 1966; v. 3 — *Augustans and Romantics*, by H. V. D. Dyson and John Butt, 3rd revised ed.1961; v. 4 — *The Victorians and After, 1830-1914*, by Edith C. Batho and Bonamy Dobrée, 3rd revised ed., 1962; v. 5 — *The Present Age, After 1920*, by David Daiches, 1958. LC classifies and catalogs separately but provides a series entry.

1071. Johnston, Grahame. **Annals of Australian Literature.** Oxford, 1970. 147p.
Johnston covers the period from 1789 to 1969 selectively, but he includes the principal publications. Alongside each year's tabulation, the compiler has included marginal

notes on such things as the founding of newspapers and journals, etc. The index has authors but not titles. The book is most useful in larger literature and specialized collections. Another important title is Henry Mackenzie Green's *A History of Australian Literature, Pure and applied: A Critical Review of All Forms of Literature Produced in Australia, from the First Books Published after the Arrival of the First Fleet until 1950, with Short Accounts of Later Publications up to 1960* (Angus and Robertson, 1961, 2v.).

1072. Klinck, Carl Frederick, and Alfred G. Bailey, eds. **Literary History of Canada: Canadian Literature in English.** 2nd ed. University of Toronto Press, 1976. 3v.
A broad survey of literature and closely related fields, this work has chapters by 30 different specialists and will probably remain the standard source for many years to come. A fresh individual approach is found in Desmond Pacey's *Creative Writing in Canada: A Short History of English-Canadian Literature* (new ed., Ryerson, 1967; repr., Greenwood, 1976) and in Margaret Atwood's *Survival: A Thematic Guide to Canadian Literature* (Anansi, 1972).

1073. Legouis, Émile Hyacinthe. **A History of English Literature: The Middle Ages and the Renascence (650-1600),** by Émile Legouis. Tr. from the French by Helen Douglas Irvine. **Modern Times (1660-1970),** by Louis Cazamian and Raymond Las Vergnas (Book 8). Rev. ed. Bibliographies by Donald Davie and Pierre Legouis. Dent, 1971. 1488p.
This standard one-volume history is useful as a text or for reference purposes.

1074. **Literary History of the United States,** ed. by Robert E. Spiller and others. 4th ed. Macmillan, 1974. 2v.
Contents: v. 1 — *History*; v. 2 — *Bibliography*. This is the first comprehensive history since the *Cambridge History of American Literature* (see item 1068). V. 1 presents a survey from colonial times to the present in a series of chapters written by experts and integrated by the editors. V. 2 consists of bibliographical essays organized to develop the treatment of the text. There are four main sections: 1) guide to resources; 2) literature and culture; 3) movements and influences; 4) individual authors. Each part has valuable critical comments on editions, biographies, etc. In the fourth edition, the history volume has been only minimally revised and the bibliography volume merely brings together the contents of the original (1948) and its two supplements (1963, 1972), though it does provide continuous paging and an inclusive index.

1075. Longaker, John Mark, and Edwin C. Bolles. **Contemporary English Literature.** Appleton, 1953. 526p.
Although now somewhat old, this book is still valuable for reference purposes because of detailed information about individual authors and their works.

1076. Mott, Frank Luther. **A History of American Magazines.** Harvard, 1938-1968. 5v.
This monumental study has detailed information about the history, editors, and contents of American magazines from the colonial period to 1930. V. 5 contains an index to the complete set.

1077. **Oxford History of English Literature,** ed. by Frank Percy Wilson and Bonamy Dobrée. Oxford, 1945- .
A long-range project, planned for completion in 12 volumes (some volumes with 2 parts). Each volume or part is written by a major scholar and includes extensive

bibliographies. LC catalogs each volume separately but also provides a common classification number and a series added entry. For an update on titles, check the "Series" section of the publisher's catalog. Titles issued to date include: v. 2, pt. 1, *Chaucer and the Fifteenth Century*, by H. S. Bennett; v. 2, pt. 2, *English Literature at the Close of the Middle Ages*, by E. K. Chambers; v. 3, *English Literature in the Sixteenth Century, Excluding Drama*, by C. S. Lewis; v. 4, pt. 1, *The English Drama, 1485-1585*, by Frank Percy Wilson; v. 5, *English Literature in the Earlier Seventeenth Century, 1600-1660*, by Douglas Bush; v. 6, *English Literature of the Late Seventeenth Century*, by James Sutherland; v. 7, *English Literature in the Early Eighteenth Century 1700-1740*, by Bonamy Dobrée; v. 9, *English Literature, 1789-1815*, by W. L. Renwick; v. 10, *English Literature, 1815-1832*, by I. Jack; v. 12, *Eight Modern Writers (Hardy, James, Shaw, Conrad, Kipling, Yeats, Joyce and Lawrence)*, by J. I. M. Stewart.

1078.　Sampson, George. **The Concise Cambridge History of English Literature.** 3rd ed. Rev. by R. C. Churchill. Cambridge, 1970. 979p.
The main portion of this classic work has been thoroughly revised and three essential new chapters have been added, giving fuller coverage to the literature in English from Ireland, India, Pakistan, Ceylon, Malaysia, Canada, Australia, New Zealand, West Indies, South Africa, and the new African states. Another standard history, by a noted scholar, is *A Critical History of English Literature*, by David Daiches (2nd ed., Ronald Press, 1970).

1079.　Ward, A. C. **Illustrated History of English Literature.** Longmans, Green, 1953-55; repr., McKay, 1961-62.
Contents: v. I — *Chaucer to Shakespeare*; v. II — *Ben Johnson to Samuel Johnson*; v. III — *Blake to Shaw*. A one-volume edition (without illustrations) has been issued under the title *English Literature: Chaucer to Bernard Shaw* (Longmans, 1958).

Recommended Collections

1080.　**Best American Short Stories and the Yearbook of the American Short Story,** 1915- . Ann. Houghton.
The title varies. Each volume contains a selection of short and brief yearbook information.

1081.　Emanuel, James A., and Theodore L. Gross. **Dark Symphony: Negro Literature in America.** Free Press, 1968. 604p.
More than simply an anthology, this vital work has extensive biographical and bibliographical information as well. *A Galaxy of Black Writing*, edited by R. Baird Shuman (Moore Publishing Co., 1970), should also be considered. Another anthology that will aid in answering requests for short pieces of fiction is *From the Roots: Short Stories by Black Americans*, by Charles L. James (Dodd, 1970). Two valuable anthologies of poetry in this important and growing area of interest are *The Poetry of the Negro, 1746-1970*, by Langston Hughes and Arna Bontemps (Doubleday, 1970), and *American Negro Poetry*, by Arna Bontemps (2nd ed., Hill & Wang, 1974).

1082.　**The New Oxford Book of English Verse: 1250-1950**, ed. by Helen Gardner. Oxford, 1972. 974p.
This admirable anthology is but one of a series issued by Oxford University Press. It

supersedes *The Oxford Book of English Verse: 1250-1918* (1939; repr., 1955). Other titles in this series that might be considered would include *The Oxford Book of American Verse* (2nd ed., 1950; repr., 1959); *The Oxford Book of American Light Verse*, edited by William Harmon (1979); *The Oxford Book of Canadian Verse, in English and French*, edited by A. J. M. Smith (1960; repr., 1970); *The Oxford Book of Children's Verse*, edited by Iona and Peter Opie (1973); and *The Oxford Book of Twentieth Century English Verse*, edited by Philip Larkin (1973). *The Oxford Anthology of Canadian Literature*, edited by Robert Weaver and William Toye (1973), would make a good addition where demand warrants.

1083.   Stevenson, Burton E. **The Home Book of Verse, American and English.** 9th ed. Holt, 1953; repr., 1971. 2v.
Complementary coverage is found in Stevenson's *Home Book of Modern Verse* (2nd ed., Holt, 1953; repr., 1966).

1084.   Untermeyer, Louis. **A Treasury of Great Poems, English and American.** Simon & Schuster, 1955. 1286p.
Many reference librarians regard this as a model anthology. Another excellent collection is Untermeyer's *Modern American Poetry and Modern British Poetry* (combined new and enl. ed., Harcourt, 1962). A more recent work, but one that ran afoul of critics for some of its omissions, is *The Norton Anthology of Modern Poetry*, edited by Richard Ellman and Robert O'Clair (W. W. Norton, 1973). Anthologies of poetry are reviewed by William Cole in "Poets and Anthologies" (*American Libraries*, June 1974, pp. 294-97). Many librarians are also guided in their selection of anthologies by inclusion in standard indexing tools like Granger's *Index to Poetry* (see item 1098).

1085.   Woods, Ralph. **A Treasury of the Familiar.** Macmillan, 1942. 751p.
There are three indexes: 1. Titles; 2. Familiar lines; 3. Authors. A useful sequel is *A Second Treasury of the Familiar* (Macmillan, 1950). The major reference value of these two books lies in their attention to lines of poetry other than to first lines.

Poetry

Introductory Works and Bibliographic Guides

1086.   Gershator, Phillis. **A Bibliographic Guide to the Literature of Contemporary American Poetry, 1970-1975.** Scarecrow, 1976. 124p.
Excellent coverage of reference works, literary criticism, anthologies, and textbooks is provided in this classified, well-annotated bibliography. There is a topical index as well as an author/title index.

1087.   Haviland, Virginia. **Children and Poetry: A Selective, Annotated Bibliography.** Rev. ed. Library of Congress, 1978.
Illustrations and examples of poetry are also included.

Bibliographies (Current and Retrospective)

1088.   **The Bibliography of Contemporary Poets.** Regency Press, 1973. 195p.
Arranged alphabetically by surnames, this useful book gives information on birthdates, pseudonyms, occupations, and other interests. Publications of each author are given

full bibliographical descriptions. Cross references from pseudonyms to real names are provided where needed. More specialized are *Index of Australian and New Zealand Poetry*, by E. L. Cuthbert (Scarecrow, 1963) and *Haiku in Western Languages*, by G. L. Brower and D. W. Foster (Scarecrow, 1972).

1089.   Davis, Lloyd, and Robert Irwin. **Contemporary American Poetry: A Checklist.** Scarecrow, 1975. 179p.
There are over 3,300 entries for poets, mainly from the 1950s and 1960s. The basic arrangement is alphabetical by surnames, and there is a 40-page title index. Vanity presses, translations, reprints, and children's books are excluded.

1090.   Deodene, Frank, and William P. French. **Black American Poetry since 1944: A Preliminary Checklist.** Chatham Bookseller, 1971. 41p.
"This brief bibliographic guide updates earlier works on black American poetry such as Dorothy Porter's *North American Negro Poets: A Bibliographical Checklist of Their Writings 1760-1944"—ARBA 1973*, p. 492.

1091.   Foxon, David Fairweather. **English Verse, 1701-1750: A Catalogue of Separately Printed Poems with Notes on Contemporary Collected Editions.** Cambridge University Press, 1975. 2v.
Contents: v. 1—*Catalogues*; v. 2—*Indexes*. Though highly specialized, this work is very well done and recommended for collections that support research in eighteenth-century English literature. For a detailed description, see Richard A. Gray's review in *ARBA 1976*, pp. 609-610. Also specialized, and useful primarily as an example of sources available for an exhaustive search, is *A Bibliography of English Poetical Miscellanies, 1521-1750*, by Arthur Ellicott Case (Oxford, 1935).

1092.   Kuntz, Joseph Marshall. **Poetry Explication: A Checklist of Interpretation since 1925 of British and American Poems Past and Present.** Rev. ed. Swallow, 1962. 331p.
"What does this poem mean?" is a familiar reference question. Kuntz indicates sources of explanation of meanings of poems in a selected group of books and periodicals. Useful supplementation and updating is provided in *An Index to Criticism of British and American Poetry*, by Gloria Stark Cline and Jeffrey A. Baker (Scarecrow, 1973).

Indexes, Abstracts, and Current Awareness Services

1093.   Brewton, John E., and Sara W. Brewton, comps. **Index to Children's Poetry: A Title, Subject, Author, and First-Line Index to Poetry in Collections for Children and Youth.** Wilson, 1942. 965p. Suppls. 1954, 1965, 1972, 1978.
Including the four supplements, well over 30,000 poems by more than 5,000 authors are indexed. The third and fourth supplements, edited with the aid of G. Meredith Blackburn, III, carry the title *Index to Poetry for Children and Young People*. The name of Lorraine A. Blackburn appears with the fourth supplement.

1094.   Brown, Carleton Fairchild, and Rossell Hope Robbins. **The Index of Middle English Verse.** Index Society; distr., Columbia, 1943. 785p. Suppl. by Rossell H. Robbins and John L. Cutler. University of Kentucky Press, 1965. 551p.
The main work indexes alphabetically by first line some 4,365 poems written before 1500. There is a subject and title index. A location list of private manuscripts is also

provided. The supplement follows the same basic arrangement, with corrections and updatings. Another specialized index, covering the next historical period, is *First-Line Index of English Poetry, 1500-1800: In Manuscripts of the Bodleian Library, Oxford*, edited by Margaret Crum (MLA, 1969, 2v.), which includes nearly 23,000 poems, reflects careful bibliographical scholarship, and is especially rich in seventeenth-century verse.

1095.   Bruncken, Herbert. **Subject Index to Poetry: Guide for Adult Readers.** ALA, 1940. 210p.
The purpose of this index to 215 anthologies is defined in the preface as "(1) the location of poetry on specific subjects, (2) the location of a poem, the topical matter or dominant idea of which is known, but not author, title, or first line, (3) the location of a poem whose author, title, or first line is not known, but a line or fragment of a line of which is known." A different kind of subject approach is provided by Peter Marcan's *Poetry Themes: A Bibliographical Index to Subject Anthologies* (Shoestring, 1978).

1096.   Chapman, Dorothy. **Index to Black Poetry.** G. K. Hall, 1974. 451p.
The first index of its kind, this excellent work, which was included among "Reference Books of 1975" (*Library Journal*, April 15, 1976, p. 969), covers 5,000 poems by almost 1,000 authors. There are three parts: title and first line index; author index; and subject index. For a detailed review, see Ann Allen Shockley's comments in *ARBA 1976*, p. 584.

1097.   **Chicorel Index to Poetry in Collections in Print, on Discs and Tapes: Poetry on Discs, Tapes and Cassettes.** Chicorel, 1972.
This computer-produced index has been followed by others in the Chicorel series. Those most pertinent here include: *Chicorel Index to Poetry and Poets — Literature* (1975); *Chicorel Index to Poetry in Anthologies and Collections in Print* (1974); and *Chicorel Index to Poetry in Anthologies and Collections: Retrospective* (1975).

1098.   Granger, Edith. **Index to Poetry.** 6th ed. Columbia, 1973. 2100p. Suppl. 1970-77, 1978. 635p.
Long the pre-eminent work in this field, the first edition was published in 1904. It covers the largest selection of standard and popular anthologies and poetry collections. Editions 1-3 included prose. In the fourth, fifth and sixth editions, title and first line indexes are combined, followed by an author index and subject index. Because of changes from edition to edition, most large libraries keep older editions for search questions. The sixth edition includes 121 new collections (15 of them anthologies of black poetry) and new subject headings like "Ecology," "Women's Liberation," etc. Better coverage of small press publications is provided in *Contemporary Poets in American Anthologies*, by Kirby Congdon (Scarecrow, 1978).

1099.   **Index of American Periodical Verse**, 1971- . Ann. Scarecrow.
Approximately 170 American periodicals are indexed. The main part is alphabetical by poets' surnames. There is also a title index.

1100.   Smith, Dorothy B. Frizzell, and Eva L. Andrews. **Subject Index to Poetry for Children and Young People, 1957-1975.** ALA, 1977. 1035p.
Poems from 263 collections of interest to various age groups from kindergarten through

senior high school are indexed in this valuable update to ALA's *Subject Index to Poetry for Children and Young People*, compiled by Violet Sell and others (ALA, 1957), which covered 157 poetry books.

Biographies

1101. Malkoff, Karl. **Crowell's Handbook of Contemporary American Poetry.** Crowell, 1973. 338p.
Malkoff concentrated on poets since 1940, and his book is a good supplement to older standard works. The introduction deals with movements, and the main work, with individual poets (in alphabetical order). More specialized is *Black American Poetry: A Critical Commentary*, by Ann Semel (Monarch, 1977).

1102. Murphy, Rosalie, ed. **Contemporary Poets of the English Language.** St. James, 1970; St. Martin's, 1971. 1243p.
Biographical and bibliographical information is provided, plus selective critical evaluations. Worldwide coverage of poets writing in English is attempted. Among the 1,000 poets included are many minor figures on whom information might otherwise be difficult to obtain.

1103. Poets and Writers, Inc. **A Directory of American Poets**, 1973- . Bi. Distr., Publishing Center for Cultural Resources.
This biennial directory provides names, addresses, special interests, and recent books published for between 1,500 and 2,000 poets. The basic arrangement is by states, then alphabetically by surnames. An alphabetical index of surnames and an alphabetical index of minority poets (arranged by minority groups) is also provided. Groups or institutions seeking a poet as a guest reader or speaker will find this most useful. The activities of Poets & Writers, Inc., are supported by grants from the National Endowment for the Arts. The *Directory* is supplemented and updated by *Coda: Poets & Writers Newsletter*, 1973- (5/yr.).

1104. **Poets of the English Language**, ed. by W. H. Auden and Norman Holmes Pearson. Viking, 1950. 5v.
Contents: v. I—*Langland to Spenser*; v. II—*Marlowe to Marvell*; v. III—*Milton to Goldsmith*; v. IV—*Blake to Poe*; v. V—*Tennyson to Yeats*.

History and Criticism

1105. Faverty, Frederic Everett, ed. **The Victorian Poets: A Guide to Research.** 2nd ed. Harvard University Press, 1968. 433p.
This useful source covers bibliography, editions, manuscripts, letters, biography, and criticism for each major poet and groups of minor ones.

1106. Hamer, Enid Hope Porter. **The Metres of English Poetry.** 4th ed. Methuen, 1951; repr., 1966. 340p.
A standard handbook for students and others interested in the technical aspects of the subject.

1107.   Jordan, Frank, ed. **The English Romantic Poets: A Review of Research and Criticism.** 3rd ed. Modern Language Association, 1972. 468p.
A handbook for graduate students, this is a companion volume to *The English Romantic Poets and Essayists*, by C. W. and L. H. Houtchens (rev. ed., MLA, 1964).

Fiction

Introductory Works and Bibliographic Guides

1108.   **Anatomy of Wonder: Science Fiction**, comp. by Neil Barron. Bowker, 1976. 471p. **(Bibliographic Guides for Contemporary Collections**, Peter Dorian, ed.).
This excellent guide covers the entire period from Plato to the present and is divided into two parts. The first deals with science fiction by period, with a separate section on juvenile fiction. The second deals with the reference and research tools in the field. Hans Weber (*ARBA 1977*, pp. 568-69) recommended purchase of both reference and circulating copies. One may still occasionally wish to consult Robert E. Briney's *SF Bibliographies: An Annotated Bibliography of Bibliographic Works on Science Fiction and Fantasy Fiction* (Advent, 1972), and the two published volumes of Donald H. Tucks' projected three-volume *Encyclopedia of Science Fiction and Fantasy through 1968* (Advent, 1974-). For other reference tools pertaining to science fiction, see items 1125n, 1131, and 1134.

1109.   Baskin, Barbara H., and Karen H. Harris. **Notes from a Different Drummer: A Guide to Juvenile Fiction Portraying the Handicapped.** Bowker, 1977. 288p.
The heart of the book is a bibliographic chapter in which over 400 juvenile titles are annotated. There are title and subject indexes.

1110.   Heninger, S. K., ed. **English Prose Fiction and Criticism to 1660: A Guide to Information Sources.** Gale, 1974. 255p.
This useful title in the Gale series covers the very earliest period, before the novel had really taken shape. The period when the novel assumed its modern form is covered in Jerry C. Beasley's *English Fiction, 1660-1800: A Guide to Information Sources* (Gale, 1978). A. E. Dyson's *The English Novel* (Oxford, 1974) consists of bibliographic essays written by specialists, on major writers. Robert J. Stanton covers 17 writers in *A Bibliography of Modern British Novelists* (Whitston, 1978, 2v.).

1111.   Kirby, David K. **American Fiction to 1900: A Guide to Information Sources.** Gale, 1975. 296p.
The first part of the book covers general aids, and the second deals with 41 individual writers. There are 1,430 entries in all. The succeeding period is covered by James Woodress in *American Fiction, 1900-1950: A Guide to Information Sources* (Gale, 1974). The period since 1950 is covered in *Contemporary Fiction in America and England, 1950-1970*, by Alfred F. Rosa and Paul A. Escholz (Gale, 1976).

1112.   Smith, Myron J., and Robert C. Weller. **Sea Fiction Guide.** Scarecrow, 1976. 256p.
This pioneer work covers more than 2,500 novels and anthologies for the period from 1700 to 1975.

1113. **Victorian Fiction: A Second Guide to Research**, ed. by George H. Ford. MLA, 1978. 401p.

Chaptes are contributed by specialists and deal with the major writers of the period. The first edition (1964) was edited by Lionel Stevenson.

Bibliographies (Current and Retrospective)

Bibliographies of Fiction

1114. Baker, Ernest Albert. **A Guide to Historical Fiction.** Macmillan, 1914; repr., Gale, 1975. 566p.

This standard work covers about 5,000 novels. It is arranged by country and then by historical period. Annotations give plots, settings, and characters. There is an index of authors, titles, historical names, places, events, etc.

1115. Baker, Ernest Albert, and James Packman. **A Guide to the Best Fiction, English and American, Including Translations from Foreign Languages.** New and enl. ed. Macmillan, 1932; repr., Barnes & Noble, 1967. 634p.

Arranged alphabetically by authors, this work has good annotations and an index of places, subjects, titles, characters, historical names, etc.

1116. Coan, Otis Welton. **America in Fiction: An Annotated List of Novels That Interpret Aspects of Life in the United States, Canada and Mexico.** 5th ed. Pacific Books, 1967. 232p.

Lists novels and collections of short stories by phase or aspect of American life, with brief annotations indicating subject matter and treatment. Recommended titles are starred. Other major works are A. T. Dickinson's *American Historical Fiction* (3rd ed., Scarecrow, 1971), which covers novels dealing with the entire period from colonial times to the present, but concentrates on books published since 1917, and Jeannette Hotchkiss's *American Historical Fiction and Biography for Children and Young People* (Scarecrow, 1973). More specialized in focus is Jack W. Van Derhoof's *A Bibliography of Novels Related to American Frontier and Colonial History* (Whitston, 1971).

1117. Fairbanks, Carol, and Eugene A. Engeldinger. **Black American Fiction: A Bibliography.** Scarecrow, 1978. 359p.

The basic arrangement is alphabetical by the surnames of about 600 black authors. Entries for prolific authors frequently have subdivisions (e.g., novels, short fiction, biography and criticism, reviews). There is a general bibliography at the end. There are no indexes.

1118. Fee, Margery, and Ruth Cawker. **Canadian Fiction: An Annotated Bibliography.** Peter Martin; distr., Books Canada, 1976. 170p.

Confined to items in print (but including some non-fiction), this annotated bibliography is arranged alphabetically by authors' surnames. Novels are indexed by title. Short stories are indexed by author and title. A subject index for novels is also provided.

1119. Gardner, Frank M. **Sequels.** 6th ed. Library Association; Chicorel, 1974-77. 2v. Contents: v. 1—*Adult Books*; v. 2—*Junior Books*. Especially useful in public library fiction departments where "What comes next?" books are often requested, this is much more comprehensive (for English-language authors) and vastly more up-to-date than *Bibliography of the Sequence Novel*, by Margaret Elizabeth Kerr (Minnesota, 1950; repr., 1971). Not identical but related in purpose is *Young People's Literature in Series: Fiction: An Annotated Bibliographical Guide*, by Judith K. and Kenyon C. Rosenberg (Libraries Unlimited, 1972) and *Young People's Literature in Series: Fiction, Non-Fiction, and Publishers' Series, 1973-75* (Libraries Unlimited, 1977).

1120.   Logasa, Hannah. **Historical Fiction.** 9th ed. McKinley, 1968. 383p.
Guide for junior and senior high schools. Also, general reader. Classified list, with author and title index. *A Guide to Historical Fiction for the Use of Schools, Libraries and the General Reader*, by Leonard Bertram Irwin (10th ed., McKinley, 1971), and *World Historical Fiction Guide: An Annotated Chronological, Geographical, and Topical List of Five Thousand Historical Novels*, by Daniel D. McGarry and Sarah Harriman White (2nd ed., Scarecrow, 1973), also give general coverage. *European Historical Fiction and Biography for Children and Young People*, by Jeannette Hotchkiss (2nd ed., Scarecrow, 1972), is more specialized.

1121.   O'Dell, Sterg. **A Chronological List of Prose Fiction in English, Printed in England and Other Countries, 1475-1640.** Massachusetts Institute of Technology, 1954; repr., Norwood, 1977. 147p.
Chronological arrangement is supplemented by author and anonymous title index. Gives locations in 69 libraries. Coverage of later periods is given in the following works: *English Prose Fiction, 1600-1700: A Chronological Checklist*, by Charles Carroll Mish (Bibliographical Society of Virginia, 1967); *A Check List of English Prose Fiction, 1700-1739*, by William Harlin McBurney (Harvard University Press, 1960); and *The English Novel, 1740-1850: A Catalogue Including Prose Romances, Short Stories, and Translations of Foreign Fiction*, by Andrew Block (2nd ed., Oceana, 1961).

1122.   U.S. Library of Congress. **Author Bibliography of English Language Fiction in the Library of Congress through 1950,** comp. by R. Glenn Wright. G. K. Hall, 1973. 8v.
Arranged by country and then alphabetically by author, this set includes both a list of authors whose works have been translated into English and an index of translators. An index of pseudonym identifications is also provided.

1123.   Wilson, H. W., Firm, Publishers. **Fiction Catalog,** ed. by Estelle A. Fidell. 9th ed. Wilson, 1976. 797p.
This standard lilbrary tool was first published in 1908. The main part is alphabetical by author, with a subject and title index and a directory of publishers. Recommended items are starred or double starred. There are annual supplements.

1124.   Wright, Lyle Henry. **American Fiction, 1774-1850.** 2nd rev. ed. Huntington Library, 1969. 411p.
First published in 1939, this standard work was revised in 1948 and thoroughly revised again in 1969. Some 600 titles were added, to make a total of 2,772 entries. There is a useful chronological index. Novels, romances, short stories, fiction, biographies, travels, allegories, and tract-like tales written by Americans are listed. Copies are located in 19 libraries and 2 private collections. Wright has also compiled *American Fiction, 1851-1875* (Huntington Library, 1965) and *American Fiction, 1876-1900* (Huntington Library, 1966). Books listed in Wright are being reproduced in microform

by University Microfilms. Wright has prepared *American Prose Fiction, 1774-1900: Cumulative Author Index* (University Microfilms, 1974) as well.

Bibliographies of Fiction Criticism

1125.   Adelman, Irving, and Rita Dworkin. **The Contemporary Novel: A Checklist of Critical Literature on the British and American Novel since 1945.** Scarecrow, 1972. 614p.
Novelists whose major works or recognition came after 1945 are included. Books and scholarly articles are cited in preference to reviews in this extremely useful reference tool. The period from 1900 to 1972 is covered in *The Twentieth Century English Novel: An Annotated Bibliography of General Criticism*, by A. F. Cassis (Garland, 1977). A more specialized focus is provided by Thomas D. Clareson in *Science Fiction Criticism: An Annotated Checklist* (Kent State University Press, 1972). For other science fiction coverage, see items 1108, 1131, and 1134.

1126.   Bell, Inglis Freeman, and Donald Baird. **The English Novel, 1578-1956: A Checklist of Twentieth-Century Criticism.** Swallow, 1958; repr., Shoe String, 1974. 168p.
Bell's work is a select list of twentieth century criticism of English novels from Lyly to 1956, including citations to books and periodicals. The arrangement is alphabetical by novelists' names and then by titles of novels. It is continued for the period from 1957 to 1972 in *English Novel Explication: Criticism to 1972*, by Helen H. Palmer and Anne Jane Dyson (Shoe String, 1973), and for the more recent period in *English Novel Explication: Supplement I*, by Peter L. Abernethy, Christian J. W. Kloessel, and Jeffrey R. Smitten (Bingley, 1976).

1127.   Gerstenberger, Donna L., and George Hendrick. **The American Novel since 1789: A Checklist of Twentieth Century Criticism.** Swallow, 1961-70. 2v.
Volume 1 covers criticism published prior to 1959, v. 2 covers criticism published from 1960 to 1968. The set is arranged alphabetically by novelists, with listings of criticism under individual novels. A second section lists general studies of the American novel by century. Parts of the period are covered more intensively by Clayton L. Eichelberger in *A Guide to Critical Reviews of United States Fiction, 1870-1910* (Scarecrow, 1971-74, 2v.) and by Douglas Messerli and Howard N. Fox in *Index to Periodical Fiction in English, 1965-1969* (Scarecrow, 1977).

1128.   Thurston, Jarvis A. **Short Fiction Criticism: A Checklist of Interpretation since 1925 of Stories and Novelettes (American, British, Continental) 1800-1958.** Swallow, 1960. 265p.
Confined to material in English, this handy work is a listing of critical articles published in books and periodicals, including "little magazines," on stories and novelettes up to 150 pages in length.

1129.   Walker, Warren S. **Twentieth Century Short Story Explication: Interpretations, 1900-1975, Inclusive, of Short Fiction since 1800.** 3rd ed. Bingley; Shoe String, 1977. 880p.
Except for recent items, many references duplicate those in Thurston. Because of its recency, however, the new edition is particularly valuable.

Indexes, Abstracts, and Current Awareness Services

1130.   Cook, Dorothy Elizabeth, and Isabel S. Monro. **Short Story Index; An Index to 60,000 Stories in 4,320 Collections.** Wilson, 1953. 1,553p. Suppls. 1950-54, 1956, 394p.; 1955-58, 1960, 341p.; 1959-63, 1965, 487p.; 1964-68, 1969, 599p.; 1969-73, 1974, 639p. Together, the main work and supplements index more than 100,000 short stories. Author, title, and subject entries are in one alphabet. Good, but now somewhat out of date, is *Subject and Title Index to Short Stories for Children* (ALA, 1955). Less comprehensive is *Chicorel Index to Short Stories in Anthologies and Collections* (Chicorel, 1974).

1131.   Contento, William. **Index to Science Fiction: Anthologies and Collections.** G. K. Hall, 1978. 608p.
Reviewers have noted that this work is more comprehensive than earlier efforts like *A Checklist of Science-Fiction Anthologies*, by William Coe (1964; repr., Arno, 1974) and *Science Fiction Short Story Index, 1950-1968*, by Frederick Siemon (ALA, 1971). For reviews, one can now consult the *Science Fiction Book Review Index, 1923-1973*, edited by H. W. Hall (Gale, 1975). For other science fiction coverage, see items 1108, 1125n, and 1134.

1132.   **Cumulated Fiction Index**, 1945/60- . Association of Assistant Librarians.
The main set, compiled by G. B. Cotton and A. Glencross, covers about 25,000 works of fiction (including short stories) under some 3,000 subject headings. The 1960-69 supplement was compiled by R. F. Smith and the 1970-74 supplement by R. F. Smith and A. J. Gordon.

1133.   Freeman, William. **Dictionary of Fictional Characters.** Rev. by Fred Urquhart, with indexes of authors and titles by R. F. Pennell. Dent, 1973; Writer, 1974. 579p.
This useful work is arranged alphabetically by the names of characters — approximately 22,000 from 2,300 novels, short stories, poems and non-musical plays by 500 British, American and Commonwealth authors in the last 600 years. The index enables one to find the names of principal characters when only the author or title is known. The English edition has the title *Everyman's Dictionary of Fictional Characters.* More specialized works dealing with fictional characters include *Black Plots and Black Characters*, by Robert Southgate (Gaylord, 1976), and *Plots and Characters of the Fiction of Eighteenth-Century English Authors*, by Clifford R. Johnson (Archon, 1977-78, 2v.).

Biographies

1134.   **Encyclopedia of Mystery and Detection**, comp. by Chris Steinbrunner and Otto Penzler. McGraw-Hill, 1976. 436p.
More than 500 mystery writers of the past and present are covered. Synopses of major works and full bibliographical details on all works are provided. There are some general articles in addition to the biobibliographies. Less well done but occasionally useful are three books published by Taplinger: *Who's Who in Science Fiction*, by Brian Ash (1976); *Who's Who in Horror and Fantasy Fiction*, by Mike Ashley (1978); and *Who's Who in Spy Fiction*, by Donald McCormack (1978). These follow a similar pattern, and each provides biographies for about 400 writers. For other science fiction coverage, see items 1108, 1125n, and 1131.

1135.   Poets and Writers, Inc. **A Directory of American Fiction Writers**, 1976- . Bi. Distr., Publishing Center for Cultural Resources.
The counterpart of *A Directory of American Poets* (see item 1103), this work is similar in purpose and design. It is also updated by *Coda: Poets and Writers Newsletter*, 1973- (5/yr.).

1136.   Vinson, James, and D. L. Kilpatrick, eds. **Contemporary Novelists.** 2nd ed. St. James; St. Martin's, 1976. 1636p.
Biographical and directory information and lists of publications are provided for 600 living novelists. There is also a signed critical essay on each writer. A short personal statement is included from each novelist who chose to make one.

History and Criticism

1137.   Baker, Ernest Albert. **The History of the English Novel.** Witherby, 1924-39; repr., Barnes & Noble, 1969. 11v.
This standard work covers the entire period from the beginnings of the novel to the early twentieth century. Each volume contains brief bibliographies and an index. V. 11, *Yesterday and After*, by Lionel Stevenson, supplements the original ten-volume set by Baker and was published in 1967. Coverage of the formative period will also be found in Ian Watt's *The Rise of the Novel: Studies in Defoe, Richardson and Fielding* (University of California Press, 1957; repr., 1971).

1138.   Bone, Robert A. **The Negro Novel in America.** Rev. ed. Yale University Press, 1965. 289p.
This valuable history covers a topic often overlooked until recently.

1139.   Forster, Edward Morgan. **Aspects of the Novel.** Harcourt, 1927; repr., 1955. 250p.
A classic source for discussion of such topics as plot, viewpoint, and characterization. Historical coverage of the viewpoints of major figures is provided by Phillip Stevick in *The Theory of the Novel* (Free Press, 1967).

Serials

1140.   **American Literature: A Journal of Literary History, Criticism, and Bibliography**, 1929- . Q. Duke.
Indexed: *A&HCI, Abstr.Engl.Stud., Hum.Ind., MLA Int.Bibliog., Am.Lit.Abstr., ARTbibliog.Mod., Bk.Rev.Ind., Bull.signal.:lit., MLA Abstr.Art.Sch.J.* V. 1-30 were also indexed by Thomas F. Marshall in *Analytical Index to American Literature, Volumes I-XXX, March, 1929-January, 1959* (Duke University Press, 1963). Book reviews and bibliographies are found in this scholarly official publication of the American Literature Section of the Modern Language Association.

1141.   **American Quarterly**, 1949- . 5/yr. University of Pennsylvania.
Indexed: *Abstr.Engl.Stud., Hum.Ind., MLA Int.Bibliog., Am.Lit.Abstr., MLA Abstr.Art.Sch.J., A&HCI.* Tries to do for American studies as a whole what *American Literature* does for literature.

1142. **The Antioch Review**, 1941- . Q. Antioch Press.
Indexed: *A&HCI, Abstr.Engl.Stud., Bk.Rev.Ind., Curr.Cont., Hist.Abstr., Hum.Ind., PAIS, Phil.Ind., Soc.Abstr., MLA Int.Bibliog., Bull.signal.:lit.* At one time, this was the leading vehicle for the "new criticism." Somewhat more general in scope than it was formerly, this periodical has struggled to survive and sometimes has been irregular in appearance.

1142a. **Ariel: A Review of International English Literature**, 1960- . Q. University of Calgary.
Indexed: *A&HCI, Hum.Ind., Br.Hum.Ind., MLA Abstr.Art.Sch.J.* This useful journal contains book reviews and bibliographies and was formerly entitled *Review of English Literature*.

1143. **Canadian Literature/Littérature canadienne: A Quarterly of Criticism and Review**, 1959- . University of British Columbia.
Indexed: *Can.Per.Ind., Hum.Ind., Abstr.Engl.Stud., MLA Int.Bibliog., A&HCI.* Review articles, bibliographies, and book reviews are found in this valuable periodical.

1144. **Criticism: A Quarterly for Literature and the Arts**, 1959- . Q. Wayne State University Press.
Indexed: *A&HCI, Abstr.Engl.Stud., Hum.Ind., MLA Int.Bibliog., Am.Lit.Abstr., Bk.Rev.Ind., Film Lit.Ind., MLA Abstr.Art.Sch.J.* Evaluations of writers and their works together with lengthy, critical book reviews will be found in this useful periodical.

1145. **Critique: Studies in Modern Fiction**, 1957- . 3/yr. Georgia Institute of Technology.
Indexed: *Abstr.Engl.Stud., Hum.Ind., MLA Int.Bibliog., Am.Lit.Abstr., MLA Abstr.Art.Sch.J., A&HCI.* Studies of individual authors (sometimes with bibliographies) are particularly useful.

1146. **ELH (English Literary History)**, 1931- . Q. Johns Hopkins.
Indexed: *A&HCI, Abstr.Engl.Stud., Hum.Ind., Am.Lit.Abstr.* Articles deal mainly with English literature.

1147. **The Explicator**, 1942- . 10/yr. Virginia Commonwealth University.
Indexed: *A&HCI, Hum.Ind., MLA Int.Bibliog., Abstr.Engl.Stud., Am.Lit.Abstr., MLA Abstr.Art.Sch.J.* V. 1-20, 1942-62, have been cumulated into *The Explicator Cyclopedia*. Issue no. 10 (June) is the *Index and Check List Issue*. There are three types of indexes: 1. list of authors treated in the current volume; 2. list of contributors; 3. list of explications found in other journals and books.

1148. **Modern Fiction Studies: A Critical Quarterly Devoted to Criticism, Scholarship and Bibliography of American, English and European Fiction since about 1800**, 1955- . Q. Purdue University.
Indexed: *A&HCI, Abstr.Engl.Stud., Hum.Ind., MLA Abstr.Art.Sch.J., MLA Int.Bibliog.* Studies of individual novelists (with bibliographies) and book reviews are useful features.

1149. **Nineteenth Century Fiction**, 1945- . Q. University of California Press.
Indexed: *A&HCI, Am.Lit.Abstr., Abstr.Engl.Stud., Hum.Ind., MLA Int.Bibliog., Bull.signal.:lit., MLA Abstr.Art.Sch.J.* Critical studies of authors and book reviews are major features.

1150. **The Partisan Review**, 1934- . Q. Partisan Review, Inc.
Indexed: *A&HCI, Am.Lit.Abstr., Abstr.Engl.Stud., Hum.Ind., Bk.Rev.Ind., Film Lit.Ind., MLA Int.Bibliog.* Book reviews and criticism of current literature are included.

1151. **Philological Quarterly**, 1922- . Q. University of Iowa.
Indexed: *A&HCI, Abstr.Engl.Stud., Hum.Ind., Folk Ind., Bk.Rev.Ind., Bull.signal.:lit., MLA Abstr.Art.Sch.J., MLA Int.Bibliog.* Primarily concerned with English literature, especially the eighteenth century.

1152. **Poetry**, 1912- . Mo. Modern Poetry Association.
Indexed: *A&HCI, Bk.Rev.Dig., RG, Abstr.Engl.Stud., Bk.Rev.Ind.* Original poetry, critical essays, book reviews, notices of new books received, announcements (e.g., poetry readings), and prizes are included in this highly respected periodical.

1153. **Review of English Studies: A Quarterly Journal of English Literature and the English Language**, 1925- . Q. Oxford.
Indexed: *A&HCI, Abstr.Engl.Stud., Br.Hum.Ind., Hum.Ind., Am.Lit.Abstr., LLBA, MLA Int.Bibliog.* Critical reviews, tables of contents of selected periodicals, and lists of new books received are useful reference features.

1154. **Sewanee Review**, 1892- . Q. University of the South.
Indexed: *A&HCI, Am.Lit.Abstr., Abstr.Engl.Stud., Hum.Ind., Bk.Rev.Ind., Bull.signal.:lit., MLA Int.Bibliog.* Review articles and book reviews are useful reference features.

1155. **Studies in English Literature, 1500-1900**, 1961- . Q. Rice University.
Indexed: *A&HCI, Abstr.Engl.Stud., Hum.Ind., Bull.signal.:lit., LLBA, MLA Int.Bibliog.* Each issue has a bibliographic survey of recent scholarship on some specific topic.

1156. **Studies in Romanticism**, 1961- . Q. Boston University.
Indexed: *A&HCI, Abstr.Engl.Stud., Hum.Ind., Bull.signal.:lit., MLA Abstr.Art.Sch.J., MLA Int.Bibliog.* This periodical concentrates on English literature of the early nineteenth century.

1157. **University of Toronto Quarterly: A Canadian Journal of the Humanities**, 1930- . Q. University of Toronto Press.
Indexed: *A&HCI, Abstr.Engl.Stud., Can.Per.Ind., CIJE, Hum.Ind., Abstr.Folk.St., Am.Lit.Abstr., Bull.signal.:lit., MLA Int.Bibliog.* Since 1935, this major journal has carried "Letters in Canada," an annual critical survey of Canadian literature and criticism for the preceding year.

1158. **Victorian Studies: A Journal of the Humanities, Arts and Sciences**, 1957- . Q. Indiana University.
Indexed: *A&HCI, Abstr.Engl.Stud., Hum.Ind., ARTbibliog.Mod., Bk.Rev.Ind., Bull.signal.:lit., MLA Abstr.Art.Sch.J., MLA Int.Bibliog.* Book reviews and an annual bibliography of current scholarship make this periodical especially useful to reference librarians.

LITERATURE IN OTHER LANGUAGES

Greek and Latin

1159. **American Journal of Philology**, 1880- . Q. Johns Hopkins.
Indexed: *A&HCI, Bk.Rev.Ind., Hum.Ind., Bull.signal.:lit., Phil.Ind.* Scholarly articles dealing with various aspects of classical studies are featured.

1160. **L'Année philogique; bibliographie critique et analytique de l'antiquité greco-latine**, 1924/26- . Ann. Societe d'Éditions "Les Belles Lettres."
Indexed: *Bull.signal.:hist.sci.tech.* Each volume has two parts. Part I is devoted to authors and their works. Part II is a classified subject bibliography. Four indexes: collections; name in antiquity; humanists; modern authors. Coverage begins with 1924-26.

1161. Avi-Yonah, Michael, and Israel Shatzman. **Illustrated Encyclopedia of the Classical World.** Harper, 1976. 509p.
This popular work has more than 2,000 articles and is profusely illustrated, with many photographs in full color. Articles are unsigned, and many do not have bibliographies.

1162. **Classical Philology: A Quarterly Journal Devoted to Research in the Languages, Literatures, History and Life of Classical Antiquity**, 1906- . Q. University of Chicago Press.
Indexed: *A&HCI, Abstr.Engl.Stud., Hum.Ind., Bull.signal.:lit., Bull.signal.:sci.lang.* Noted for its scholarly, technical articles on all aspects of classical studies.

1163. **Classical Review**, 1886- . 3/yr. Oxford.
Indexed: *A&HCI, Abstr.Engl.Stud., Br.Hum.Ind., Hum.Ind., Bull.signal.:lit., MLA Int.Bibliog.* Signed, lengthy book reviews and shorter notices are special features of this major periodical.

1164. Feder, Lillian. **Crowell's Handbook of Classical Literature.** Crowell, 1964. 448p.
This alphabetical dictionary of names, titles, mythological characters, etc. gives detailed summaries of individual works.

1165. Harvey, Sir Paul. **The Oxford Companion to Classical Literature.** Oxford, 1937; repr., 1974. 468p.
Frequently reprinted, this standard work has concise articles on classical writers, literary forms and subjects, individual works, names and subjects in Greek and Roman history, institutions, religions, etc.

1166. **International Guide to Classical Studies: A Quarterly Index to Periodical Literature**, 1961- . Q. American Bibliographic Service.
Section I, alphabetical by author, has full citations and individual item numbers; II is an alphabetical subject index which refers back to the full citations in Section I.

1167. **The Journal of Hellenic Studies**, 1880- . Ann. Society for the Promotion of Hellenic Studies.
Indexed: *Art Ind., Br.Hum.Ind., Bull signal.:lit., Phil.Ind., New Test.Abstr.* The book reviews are useful for collection development.

1168. **The Journal of Roman Studies**, 1911- . Ann. Society for the Promotion of Roman Studies.
Indexed: *A&HCI, Br.Arch.Abstr., Br.Hum.Ind., Bull.signal.:art et arch., Hum.Ind., New Test.Abstr.* The book reviews in this periodical are especially valuable for building a classical studies collection.

1169. **Oxford Classical Dictionary**. Ed. by N. G. L. Hammond and H. H. Scullard. 2nd ed. Oxford, 1970; repr., 1977. 1176p.
More scholarly than Avi-Yonah's *Illustrated Encyclopedia of the Classical World* (see item 1161), this standard work is strong in biography, literature, and civilization.

1170. Parks, George B., and Ruth Z. Temple. **The Greek and Latin Literatures: A Bibliography**. Ungar, 1968. (The Literatures of the World in English Translation, v. 1). 442p.
Covering translations of literature from any period made between 1645 and 1965, this volume begins with a general bibliography. After that, the arrangement is chronological and, within each period, alphabetical by author. There is an index of authors at the end, but no index of titles in translation or of Greek and Latin titles that have authors.

1171. Pauly, A. F. von, and G. Wissowa. **Pauly's Realencyclopädie der Classischen Altertumswissenschaft**. Metzler, 1894-1919. Suppl. 1903- . 2 reihe (R-Z), 1914- .
This monumental work covers the whole field of classical literature, history, antiquities, biography, etc. Long, signed articles by specialists have extensive bibliographies. Generally cited as Pauly-Wissowa, in German references, it is sometimes cited as RE. The arrangement and alphabetization are complicated. The supplement is geared to the main set.

1172. Stillwell, Richard, ed. **The Princeton Encyclopedia of Classical Sites**. Princeton University Press, 1976. 1019p.
This massive scholarly work has articles on 2,800 sites by 400 classicists and archaeologists. Articles vary in length from a few lines to several thousand words. Bibliographies refer to technical sources. Each site is shown on a map.

1173. Thompson, Lawrence Sidney. **A Bibliography of American Doctoral Dissertations in Classical Studies and Related Fields**. Shoe String, 1968. 250p. Suppl. 1976. 296p.
The main work covers classical studies from the beginnings of graduate work in the United States through 1963, with some for 1964 and 1965. The supplement covers 1964-72. Dissertations cover Greece and Rome from earliest times to 500 A.D. The main listing is by author. There is a good subject index—an average of four entries per dissertation—as well as a title entry for each dissertation. There are briefer indexes of Greek and Latin words of special importance.

Romance Languages

French

1174. Cabeen, David Clark, ed. **Critical Bibliography of French Literature**. Syracuse University Press, 1947- .
Contents: v. 1—*The Medieval Period*, ed. by U. T. Holmes, Jr. (1947); v. 2—*The Sixteenth Century*, edited by A. H. Schutz (1956); v. 3—*The Seventeenth Century*, edited

by N. Edelman (1961); v. 4 – *The Eighteenth Century*, edited by G. R. Havens and D. F. Bond (1951); supplement edited by R. A. Brooks (1968). This selective, evaluative, annotated bibliography, prepared by specialists, is a tool of prime importance for advanced graduate students and scholars. It is arranged by chronological periods and lists books, periodical articles, and dissertations. It also gives citations to reviews. Each volume has a good analytical index. More detailed coverage of the Middle Ages will be found in Robert Bossuat's *Manuel bibliographique de la littérature française du Moyen Age* (Librairie d' Argences, 1951; Suppls. 1955, 1961). The sixteenth century is covered by Alexandre Cioranescu's *Bibliographie de la littérature française du seizième siècle* (Klincksieck, 1959). Much more detail on the seventeenth century can be found in Cioranescu's *Bibliographie de la littérature française du dix-septième siècle* (CNRS, 1956-66, 3v.) and on the eighteenth century in Cioranescu's *Bibliographie de la littérature française du dix-huitième siècle* (CNRS, 1969, 3v.). An older work, now less vital, is Gustave Lanson's *Manuel bibliographique de la littérature française moderne (XVIe, XVIIe, XvIIIe, XIXe siècles)* (Hachette, 1931). Significant coverage since 1800 is provided by Hugo Paul Thieme's *Bibliographie de la littérature française de 1800 à 1930* (Droz, 1933, 3v.). The twentieth century is covered in great depth by Hector Talvart and Joseph Place in *Bibliographie des auteurs modernes de lange française* (Editions de la chronique des Lettres Française, 1928-), of which v. 1-15 (A-Mirbeau) were published between 1928 and 1963, while v. 16, 17 (1965, 1967) constitute an index. Twentieth-century criticism is covered in *Dictionnaire des critiques littéraires: guide de la critique française du XXe siècle*, by Laurent Le Sage and Andre Yon (Pennsylvania State University Press, 1969). The French novel has also received bibliographical treatment as a separate entity. The period from 1600 to 1800 is covered by the following works: *Bibliography of the Seventeenth Century Novel in France*, by Ralph C. Williams (MLA, 1931); *A List of French Prose Fiction from 1700 to 1750*, by Silas Paul Jones (Wilson, 1939); and *Bibliographie du genre romanesque français, 1751-1800*, by Angus Martin, V. G. Milne, and R. Frautsch (Expansion; Mansell, 1977). More recent coverage for the period from 1600 to 1750 is provided by Maurice Lever's *La fiction narrative en prose au XVIIème siècle: répertoire bibliographique du genre romanesque en France (1600-1700)* (CNRS, 1976) and Angus Martin's *Bibliographie du genre romanesque français, 1700-1750* (Mansell, 1977).

1175. Calvet, Jean, ed. **Histoire de la littérature français.** Nouv. ed. Del Duca, 1955-64. 10v.
Volume 1 – *Le Moyen Age*, par R. Bossuat (1955); v. 2 – *La Renaissance*, par R. Morcay et A. Muller (1960); v. 3 – *Le préclassicisme, d'après Raoul Morcay*, par P. Sage (1962); v. 4 – *Les écrivains classiques*, par H. Gaillard de Champris (1960); v. 5 – *La littérature religieuse de François de Sales à Fenelon*, par J. Calvet (1956); v. 6 – *De "Telemaque" à "Candide,"* par A. Cherel (1958); v. 7 – *De "Candide" à "Atala,"* par H. Berthaut (1958); v. 8 – *Le romantisme*, par P. Moreau (1957); v. 9 – *Le réalisme et le naturalisme*, par R. Dumesnil (1955); v. 10 – *Les lettres contemporaines*, par L. Chaigne (1964). These monographs by specialists follow a pattern similar to the *Oxford History of English Literature*. French-Canadian literature is covered by Gerard Tougas in *Histoire de la littérature canadienne française* (4th ed., Presses Universitaires de France, 1967).

1176. Harvey, Sir Paul, and Janet E. Heseltine. **The Oxford Companion to French Literature.** Oxford, 1959; repr., 1969. 771p.

This standard work covers French literature from the Middle Ages to the start of World War II (1939). The arrangement is alphabetical: 1) articles on authors, critics, historians, religious writers, scholars, scientists, etc.; 2) articles on individual works, allusions, places, and institutions; 3) general survey articles on phasess or aspects of French literary life, movements, etc. More recent coverage can be found in *The Concise Oxford Dictionary of French Literature*, edited by Joyce Mott Reid (Oxford, 1976), and in *Dictionnaire de littérature française contemporaine* (Delarge, 1977).

1177. Mahaffey, Denis. **A Concise Bibliography of French Literature.** Bowker, 1975. 286p.

This up-to-date guide is arranged by periods and then alphabetically. Entries are un-annotated. An index of authors is provided. More elementary is Robert Baker's *Intro-duction to Library Research in French Literature* (Westview, 1978), which is aimed at undergraduates, covers fewer titles, and provides annotations. Other works include *Research and Reference Guide to French Studies*, by Charles B. Osburn (Scarecrow, 1968; Suppl., 1972) and Osburn's *The Present State of French Studies: A Collection of Research Reviews* (Scarecrow, 1971). Some limited coverage may also be found in *A Bibliographical Guide to the Romance Languages and Literatures*, by T. R. Palfrey, J. G. Fucilla, and W. C. Holbrook (8th ed., Chandler's, 1971).

1178. **Modern French Literature: A Library of Literary Criticism,** ed. by Debra and Michael Popkin. Ungar, 1977. 2v.

Critical evaluations of some 160 modern French writers are contained in this collection of excerpts from the works of approximately 100 major literary critics. "A list of works mentioned in the excerpts, a cross-reference index to comparisons of authors made in the criticism, and an index to critics increases the usefulness of this important set" — Charles A. Bunge, "Current Reference Books," *Wilson Library Bulletin*, September 1977, p. 86.

Italian

1179. Bondanella, Peter, and Julia Conway Bondanella. **Dictionary of Italian Literature.** Greenwood, 1979. 608p.

This useful dictionary makes information about Italian literature readily available to a much wider audience than students and scholars. The latter will want to turn to *Dizion-ario enciclopedico della letteratura italiana* (Unedi, 1966-70, 6v.), which is similar in arrangement to Bompiani (v. 6 contains appendices and title and general indexes). Those who need an in-depth treatment of the history of Italian literature can use *Storia della letteratura italiana*, by Emilio Cecci and Matalino Sapegno (Garzanti, 1965-), which is similar in plan to the *Cambridge History of English Literature*. Those who do not read Italian but are interested in contemporary criticism will find some useful excerpts in *Modern Romance Literatures*, compiled by Dorothy Nyren Curley and Arthur Curley.

Spanish

1180. Bleznick, Donald W. **A Sourcebook for Hispanic Literature and Language: A Selected, Annotated Guide to Spanish and Spanish American Bibliography, Literature, Linguistics, Journals and Other Source Materials.** Temple University Press, 1974. 183p.

Reviewers have praised this work as an excellent starting point for research at various levels. *Manual of Hispanic Bibliography*, by David W. and Virginia Ramos Foster (University of Washington Press, 1970), covers primary and some secondary sources. Another bibliographical source is *Bibliografia de la literatura hispanica*, by Jose Simon Diaz (Consejo Superior de Investigaciones Cientificas, Instituto "Miguel de Cervantes" de Filologia Hispanica, 1950-), which includes Latin America as well as Spain. More specialized is *Dissertations in Hispanic Languages and Literatures, 1876-1966*, by James R. Chatham and Enrique Ruiz-Fornelis (University of Kentucky Press, 1969). For serving library users who do not read Spanish, *The Literature of Spain in English Translation: A Bibliography*, by Robert S. Rudder (Ungar, 1975), will be most valuable.

1181. Foster, David William, and Virginia Ramos Foster. **Modern Latin American Literature**. Ungar, 1975. 2v.
Another in Ungar's Library of Literary Criticism series, this one has been less well compiled than most and must be used in conjunction with other sources. The Fosters have also produced *Research Guide to Argentine Literature* (Scarecrow, 1970) and *The 20th-Century Spanish-American Novel: A Bibliographic Guide* (Scarecrow, 1975). Of higher quality but more limited scope is *Index to Anthologies of Latin American Literature in English Translation*, by Juan R. and Patricia M. Freudenthal (G. K. Hall, 1977), which covers works by 1,122 Spanish American and Brazilian authors from 20 countries, as represented in 116 anthologies.

1182. Ward, Philip, ed. **The Oxford Companion to Spanish Literature**. Oxford, 1978. 629p.
This welcome addition to a familiar series brings a vast wealth of information to the English-language reader. Scholars will wish to consult *Ensayo de un diccionario de la literatura*, by Federico Carlos Sainz de Robles (3rd ed., Aguilar, 1965-), which includes Latin America as well as Spain. Latin America and the Philippines are included in *Historia general de las literaturas hispanicas*, by Guillermo Diaz-Plaja (Barna, 1949-67, 6v. in 7), which is somewhat similar to the *Cambridge History of English Literature*.

Germanic Languages

1183. Garland, Henry, and Mary Garland. **The Oxford Companion to German Literature**. Oxford, 1976. 977p.
The period from 800 A.D. to the present is covered in alphabetically arranged entries for biographies, terms, trends, historical figures, and events. There are numerous cross references. Like the others in this series, it is a standard source for all types of libraries.

1184. Goedeke, Karl. **Grundriss zur Geschichte der deutschen Dichtung und den Quellen**. 2 ganz neubearb. Aufl. Ehlermann, 1884-1959. 14v. Index. Kraus-Thomson, 1975.
This is the most complete bibliography of German literature and very useful for an exhaustive search in a large library. Each volume has a detailed index, but there was no cumulative index for the set until 1975.

1185. **Introductions to German Literature**. Cresset Press, 1968- .
Contents: v. 1—*Literature in Medieval Germany*, by P. Salmon; v. 2—*German Literature in the Sixteenth and Seventeenth Centuries*, by R. Pascal; v. 4—*Twentieth Century German Literature*, by A. Closs. LC classifies and catalogs them separately, but also provides a series added entry.

1186. **Jahresbericht für deutsche Sprache und Literatur**, bearb, unter Leitung von Gerhard Marx. Akademie-Verlag, 1960- .
Combining two former series in which language and literature were separate, this work provides comprehensive coverage of books and articles dealing with all periods of German language and literature. A classified arrangement is used, with access through extensive indexes.

1187. Kosch, Wilhelm. **Deutsches Literatur-Lexikon: biographisch-bibliographisches Handbuch.** 3., vollig neu beard. Aufl. hrsg. von Bruno Berger und Heinz Rupp. Francke Verlag, 1968- .
Biographical and bibliographical information about German, Austrian, and Swiss authors is contained in this set, which is to be completed in 8 volumes.

1188. Köttelwesch, Clemens. **Bibliographisches Handbuch der deutschen Literaturwissenschaft, 1945-1969.** V. Klostermann, 1971- . (In progress).
This select bibliography of books, articles, theses, etc. on German literature will probably run to 10 volumes when complete. There is a very detailed subject classification. It is relatively easy to find material on specific subjects, even though author and subject indexes will not appear until the final volume. It will both cumulate and supplement *Bibliographie der deutschen Literaturwissenschaft* (v. 1-8, 1945/53 — 1968).

Slavonic Languages

1189. Akademiia Nauk SSSR. Institut Russkoi Literatury. **Istoriia russkoi literatury.** Izd-vo Akademiia Nauk SSSR. 1941-56. 10v.
This comprehensive history of Russian literature from the beginnings until 1917 is somewhat like the *Cambridge History of English Literature* in that individual chapters are written by specialists, but it differs in that it lacks bibliographies.

1190. Carlisle, Olga Andreyev, and Rose Styron, trs. and eds. **Modern Russian Poetry.** Viking, 1972. 210p.
An anthology with historical background information, this work concentrates on poets of World War II and of the Revolution of 1917. Reviewers have praised both the selections and the quality of the translations.

1191. Mihailovich, Vasa D., comp. **Modern Slavic Literature: A Library of Literary Criticism.** Ungar, 1972-76. 2v.
Contents: v. 1 — *Russian Literature*; v. 2 — *Bulgarian, Czechoslovak, Polish, Ukrainian and Yugoslav Literature*. A generally good selection of criticism has been made for a representative group of modern authors. Readers interested in the availability of these authors' works in English translation may consult *The Slavic Literatures*, by Richard C. Lewanski (Ungar, 1967). Information about individual authors, trends, movements, and literary criticism will be found in *Dictionary of Russian Literature*, by William Edward Harkins (Allen & Unwin, 1956). Separate chapters on major novelists from Pushkin to Pasternak will be found in *The Russian Novel*, by Franklin D. Reeve (McGraw-Hill, 1966). Readers interested in the novel may also wish to consult *Plots and Characters in Major Russian Fiction*, by Thomas Edwin Berry (Shoe String, 1977-). A more detailed search might usefully employ *A Guide to the Bibliographies of Russian Literature*, by Serge A. Zenkousky and David L. Armbruster (Vanderbilt, 1970).

1192. Struve, Gleb. **Russian Literature under Lenin and Stalin, 1917-1953.** University of Oklahoma Press, 1971. 454p.
The best book available in English for the literature of this period, both for courses and for reference work. A sequel dealing with the post-Stalin era is planned.

Oriental Languages

1193. Columbia University. Columbia College. **A Guide to Oriental Classics.** Prepared by the Staff of the Oriental Studies Program, Columbia college, and edited by W. T. DeBary and A. T. Embree. 2nd ed. Columbia University Press, 1975. 257p.
This useful guide has sections on Islamic, Indian, Chinese, and Japanese literatures.

1194. **Dictionary of Oriental Literatures,** ed. by Jaroslav Prusek. Basic Books, 1974. 3v.
Contents: v. 1 – *East Asia*; v. 2 – *South and Southeast Asia*; v. 3 – *West Asia and North Africa*. Reviewing this work in *Library Journal* (October 1974, p. 2592), Warren Collins wrote: "Articles cover individual authors, major anonymous works, most important literary forms and genres, important schools of writing, and literary movements. They are signed and each concludes with a brief bibliography. . . . " A more specialized work is *Biographical Dictionary of Japanese Literature*, by Sen' ichi Hisamatsu (Kodansha, 1976).

1195. Kravitz, Nathan. **3,000 Years of Hebrew Literature: From the Earliest Times through the Twentieth Century.** Swallow, 1972.
"Kravitz is an excellent scholar who writes with verve and authority. His is the only single-volume history of Hebrew literature, and it is excellent" – George Adelman, *Library Journal*, August 1972, p. 2606. Another useful source is Meyer Waxman's *A History of Jewish Literature* (Yoseloff, 1960, 5v.).

1196. Lang, David Marshall, ed. **A Guide to Eastern Literatures.** Weidenfield; Praeger, 1971. 501p.
Chapters by specialists cover 18 Oriental literatures, giving historical background, major literary trends, individual authors and their works, general bibliography, and English translations. Author, title, and subject index. More restricted geographically are *Guide to Japanese Prose*, by Alfred H. Marks and Barry D. Bort (G.K. Hall, 1975), *Guide to Japanese Poetry*, by J. Thomas Rimer and Robert E. Morrell (G. K. Hall, 1976) and *Classical Chinese Fiction: A Guide to Its Study and Appreciation*, by Winston L. Y. Yang and others (G. K. Hall, 1978).

African Languages

1197. **African Folktales and Sculpture.** 2nd ed. Pantheon, 1964.
The first edition was published by Princeton in 1952. The folktales were selected and edited by Paul Radin, with the collaboration of Elinore Marvel. The sculpture was selected and introduced by James Johnson Sweeney.

1198. Herdeck, Donald E. **African Authors: A Companion to Black African Writing.** 2nd ed. Inscape Corp., 1974- .
Also to be considered are *Black African Literature: An Introduction*, by J. P. Makouta-Mbaukon (Black Orpheus Press, 1973), *African Writers Talking*, edited by Dennis Duerden and Cosmo Pieterse (Africana Publishing Co., 1972), and *Perspectives on African Literature*, edited by Christopher Heywood (Africana Publishing Co., 1971).

1199. Jahn, Janheinz, and Claus Peter Dressler. **Bibliography of Creative African Writing.** Kraus-Thomson, 1971. 446p.
In this book, the compilers have updated and expanded the African section of *A Bibliography of Neo-African Literature from Africa, America and the Caribbean* (Praeger, 1965). Jahn has also written *Neo-African Literature: A History of Black Writing* (Grove, 1969). Both bibliographical and biographical information about black Africans south of the Sahara who write in English will be found in *A Reader's Guide to African Literature*, by Hans M. Zell and Helen Silver (Africana, 1971).

1200. Scheub, Harold. **African Oral Narratives, Proverbs, Riddles, Poetry and Song.** G. K. Hall, 1977. 393p.
This useful work was first published in 1971 under the title *Bibliography of African Oral Narratives*.

13 THE COMPUTER AND THE HUMANITIES*

The broadening definition of art, the waning distrust of technology among humanists, and the increasing facility of computer languages combine to make computer technology and the humanities increasingly compatible. To reflect this growing relationship this chapter has been divided into two parts. The first part will approach the role the computer plays and has played in the creation and understanding of works in the various fields of the humanities. The second part will provide a brief overview of on-line bibliographic data bases that are available to the reference librarian.

APPLICATIONS

General

Since World War II, great emphasis has been placed upon science and technology, and as a result, the humanities have been somewhat ignored. Yet, scholars still recognize a need for the humanities in society. William H. Cornog believes it is because of the "seeking of these deeper illuminations of human values and the human spirit that the humanities have special power to inform the mind and refresh the soul of man" ["Teaching Humanities in the Space Age," *School Review* 72 (Autumn 1964):393]. Sister Francis Tinucci sees humanistic disciplines as "the medium through which man's belief in himself will be restored" ["A Rationale for a Humanities-Centered Curriculum in a Cybernetic-Centered Society," *Catholic Educational Review* 66 (January 1969):634]. John Hurt Fisher defines the humanities as offering "unparalled methods and materials by which the mind can contemplate and examine the universal implications of both science and art" ["The Humanities in an Age of Science," *Journal of General Education* 18 (October 1966):190].

---

*This chapter was contributed by Cynthia McLaughlin, State Library of Ohio.

If the humanities are to fulfill any of the above purposes, they must stay abreast of research and maintain control over the printed material in their fields. Modern technology must be used to achieve these ends. But, until recently, humanists have tended to avoid the use of the computer for fear of dehumanizing the humanities. Automatic data processing machines, they argue, cannot duplicate the human aspect of research. But they can assist "in remembering and organizing external stimuli [and] in coordinating the tools which give us power over our environment" [*see* William H. Desmonde, *Computers and Their Use* (Prentice-Hall, 1964), p. 1]. Their major value for study of the humanities is precisely their ability to store a large amount of information and to arrange it systematically, so that it can be retrieved at a later date. This enables researchers to spend more time gathering information and to control this material efficiently.

Although the computer has had limited use in relation to the humanities for the past 20 years, significant advances have come about in the last decade, in part because of the great increase in material available. With this recent increase in interest has come the support for computer-oriented studies. Most significantly, studies done by the American Council of Learned Societies have helped to solve a problem that previously separated the humanities and the computer: because most humanists had no knowledge of mathematics, it was necessary to create computer program languages that non-mathematicians could use. This has now been accomplished. In addition, several universities have designed courses that explain these languages, and courses are also being offered in computer techniques relating to specific fields. Opportunities to become proficient in on-line searching of data bases are now offered by many library schools.

In view of the increasing involvement of the humanities with computers, it has been recognized that far more needs to be done to aid computer-oriented researchers. Computer scientists now regard the humanities as a new frontier. However, the field still lacks "an organization or human mechanism to make known and avalable to scholars and their professional organizations the capabilities of the computer in the field of bibliographical control" [see Theodore Stern, "Computers, Traditional Scholarship, and the ACLS," *Journal of Asian Studies* 27 (February 1968):330]. One of the existing projects of this nature is the ACLS Bibliographic Data-Processing Center. Other techniques of information dissemination include the biennial international conferences on computing in the humanities (Minneapolis, 1973; Los Angeles, 1975; Waterloo, 1977) and publications like *Computer-Assisted Research in the Humanities: A Directory of Scholars Active 1966-1972* (Pergamon, 1976).

Another aid has been the creation of new journals covering computer applications in the various fields of the humanities. *Computers and the Humanities*, which covers the whole scope of the humanities, was begun in 1967, is edited at Queens College of the City University of New York, and published quarterly by North-Holland Publishing Company. Its articles, covering all phases of computer technology and humanities research, include reports of conferences, lists of scholars active in research, annual bibliographies, book reviews, abstracts of related articles and other publications, lists and reviews of available programs in the humanities, and notices of new courses being offered in computer applications to the humanities. A more recently created journal is *Hephaistos*, published quarterly by St. Joseph's College, Philadelphia. It, too, covers the entire area. More specialized publications include the *Newsletter of Computer Archaeology*, and *Calculi*, the newsletter for computer-oriented classicists.

Although other fields may not have specific journals covering computer applications, many articles covering individual projects are found in the recent issues of prominent journals for specific fields. *English Studies*, for example, includes descriptions of computer-produced concordances as well as data bases and translations. The material in these journals must also be bibliographically controlled so that the researcher will be aware of other projects being done in his field and related areas; the computer's ability to store and manipulate large quantities of data in a very short time assists in maintaining this control. The scholar is free to cover broader areas in greater depth than ever before, and this extended research will result in the creation of a great variety of data bases in all fields.

Architecture

Few architecturally-oriented computer applications are available; computer applications to architecture did not begin until about 1960. Because of the complexity of design problems, architects had not utilized the computer to any appreciable degree in the design process. But, the computer can now be programmed to manipulate total design problems and various aspects of these problems. One such project is operation GREAT (Graphics Research with Ellerbe Architects Technology), constructed by Ellerbe Architects to develop software required for very elementary interactive manipulation of simple architectural space components used during the initial design stage [Sheldon Anonsen, "Interactive Computer Graphics in Architecture," *Computers and Automation* 19 (August 1970):28]. The computer's ability to deal simultaneously with a vast number of elements has made possible the storage of an entire building description. The principal justification for taking the effort to maintain a current description of a building in a computer throughout the design process is the fact that the computer can be used as a means of communication among all those concerned with design decisions. It is now being realized that the computer can perhaps actually enhance the architect's capabilities to determine aesthetic qualities by assisting him in many of the non-aesthetic design calculations that consume a great deal of his talent and time. The time saved by architects in the design process offsets the costs generated by computer equipment and software expenses.

Visual Arts

The field of art includes several very different computer applications. One application is that of computer graphics, which gained attention in the early 1960s. Computer graphics can be made using any of three peripheral devices: a computer-driven graphic plotter that follows instructions from a magnetic tape; a cathode ray tube (CRT) display on which designs can be drawn; and various printers that produce patterns composed of letters or symbols. The two primary applications of computer graphics are the utilitarian and the aesthetic. The utilitarian function had its beginnings with William Fetter, of the Boeing Company, who used computer graphics to simulate landings on the runway and determine possible movement of a pilot sitting in the cockpit. The greatest development in the aesthetic function has come about in large universities where artists have had access to a computer. One such artist is Charles Csuri, of The Ohio State University in Columbus, who is primarily responsible for aesthetic work in computer graphics. Other artists are also becoming involved in this art form and are exhibiting their creations. The yearly computer art contest held by *Computers and People* (formerly *Computers and Automation*) provides a gallery for their work; the August issue has published the results of this contest each year since 1962 [*see* Edmund C. Berkeley, "Computer Art: Turning Point," *Computers and Automation* 16 (August 1967):7]. The number of entries each year has grown, illustrating the advancing interest and development in the field.

The attraction of artists to computerized art forms proves that the computer can be used to enhance rather than destroy man's creative abilities: "Besides the challenge of breaking new ground, one might be able to learn something significant about pattern and design, about order and disorder, about general laws of aesthetics" [*see* L. Mezei, "Artistic Design by Computer," *Computers and Automation* 16 (August 1964):12]. Grace C. Hertlein believes that computer-aided graphics is an art form subject to the personal style of the artist. In fact, Hertlein goes on to say that "the computer has become the symbol of man's creative, affirmative use of science and technology for constructive, creative purposes," which are limited only by "the artist's imagination and the degree to which the artist accepts the computer as an aid in creation" [*see* "An Artist Views Discovery through Computer-Aided Graphics," *Computers and Automation* 19 (August 1970):25-26].

The computer has also been used in the creation of oil paintings and sculpture. Completely automatically-produced paintings were shown at the formal opening of the Chicago office for the Univac Division of Sperry Rand Corporation in 1968. These paintings were reproduced from programs recorded on magnetic tape by UNIVAC 1107 at the University of Notre Dame. Don Mittleman, Director of the Computing Center at Notre Dame, developed the software system, which uses the FORTRAN IV language, to process the instructions. Mittleman, who is a pioneer in the field, uses a variety of materials such as inks, water and vegetable colors [*see* Edmund C. Berkeley,

"Oil Paintings Produced with the Aid of the Computer," *Computers and Automation* 17 (Sept. 1968:56)]. An example of computer-aided sculpture is Alfred Duca's spheroid sculpture, which he created by using a numerically-controlled flame-cutting machine. His product is a sphere seven feet in diameter, made of 80 layers of one-inch thick steel. The computer program was developed and written by Andrew Wales, President of Brown-Wales, a steel distributing company in Cambridge, Massachusetts [*see* Roger Ives, "Computer-Aided Sculpture," *Computers and Automation* 18 (August 1969):33].

In addition, the computer has a variety of applications to filmmaking. An electronic microfilm recorder can be used to create computer-generated films. This technique was developed in the 1960s by Bell Telephone Laboratories using an IBM 7094 computer, Stromberg-Carlson 4020 microfilm, and the FORTRAN language to create a series of computer-produced movies. Kenneth C. Knowlton has devised a mosaic picture system that he and Stan Vanderbeek have used in making films like *Man and His World*. F. W. Siden has also used Knowlton's method to make the educational film, *Force, Mass, and Motion*.

Motion picture animation by computer is also possible. The computer generates visual displays that correspond to single frames of film. There are at least two organizations that use computers to produce animated films of professional quality: one is located in New York and produces commercials by means of an off-line operation; the other is an on-line system in Canada. Full descriptions and explanations of these computer applications are given in Jasia Reichardt's *The Computer in Art* (Van Nostrand Reinhold, 1971).

Most of the information retrieval in art is done by art museums. It is becoming more difficult for museums to maintain control of their holdings and at the same time to make the material available to their patrons. The Metropolitan Museum of Art has studied ways of adapting the computer's capabilities to this end. In fact, its first project involved pottery typography with the use of the CRT. (The CRT's extension of the computer's ability to visualize information has proved a great advantage to the fields in which so much depends upon sight.) The United States Museum Computer Network, established in 1967 by the National Gallery of Art and fifteen art museums in New York City, set up a trial data bank in relation to compiling a combined catalog. This project also considered the capabilities of the GRIPHOS macro language, existing museum records, and information needs of museums and their patrons [*see* David Vance, "A Data Bank of Museum Holdings," *ICRH Newsletter* 4 (March 1969):3].

Other examples of the work done in this area include the assembling of computerized data banks that cover distinct classes of museum information; the listing, by the International Council of Museums, of the records of single museums; and the development of automated documentation. The work in computer-oriented documentation falls primarily into three main categories: creation of comprehensive data bases, recording of museum collections in machine-readable form, and analysis of discrete bodies of data pertinent to a particular and narrowly defined problem [*see* Everett Ellin, "An International Survey of Museum Computer Activity," *Computers and the Humanities* 3 (November 1968):65]. The shift in recent years from philology to interpretation presents a clearer picture of the museum's educational function.

Music

The use of the computer in the control of music research allows the researcher to broaden the data base to include all pertinent material. The major result of information retrieval in music is thematic indexing, which is a common tool for musicological research. Use of the computer can decrease the amount of time necessary for production of the index while increasing its efficiency. Examples of thematic indexing include the development of a thematic locator for Mozart's works as contained in Köchel's *Werkverzeichnis*, developed by a research group in the Department of Music at New York University [*see* George Hill, "The Thematic Index to the Köchel Catalog," *ICRH Newsletter* 4 (March 1969):8]. Barry S. Brook and Murry Gould have developed "Plaine and Easie Code System for Musicke," described as a "Computer-oriented language for symphonic scores in print, in manuscripts, in libraries and in private hands collated where possible with available disc and tape recordings" [*see* Barry S. Brook and Harold Heckman, "Utilization of Data Processing Techniques in Musical Documentation," *Fontes Artis Musicae* 12 (May-December 1965):115].

The second major area of computer applications in music is stylistic analysis. Here the computer not only retrieves information but identifies, locates, counts, and codes the information. Projects in this area include a study of the stylistic properties of the Masses of Josquin Desprez and an analysis of Haydn's symphonies by Jan La Rue, at New York University. Closely related to stylistic analysis are analyses of theory and harmony. Examples include the theoretical possibilities of equally tempered musical systems done by William Stoney in 1966 and 1967, and Robert M. Mason's encoding algorithm which provides each harmony with an individual designation [*see* Robert M. Mason, "An Encoding Algorithm and Tables for the Digital Analysis of Harmony(I)," *Journal of Research in Music Education* 17 (Fall 1969):286; *see also* P. Howard Patrick and Karen Strickler, "A Computer-Assisted Study of Dissonance in the Masses of Josquin Desprez," *Computers and the Humanities* 12 (no. 4, 1978):341-64].

Like the visual arts, music has faced the problem of the conversion of information, to machine-readable form. In 1964, a programming language, MIR (Machine Information Retrieval), was developed at Princeton as part of a pilot project in the use of the digital computer for music research. Two other languages used with specific types of problems are ALMA (Alphameric Language for Music Analysis) and DARMS (Digital Alternate Representation of Music Symbols). A system for interactive encoding of music scores under computer control is being developed at Indiana University, using a sonic digitizer and an organ keyboard, both attached to a computer [*see* Garry Wittlich, Donald Byrd, and Rosalie Nerheim, "A System for Interactive Encoding of Music Scores under Computer Control," *Computers and the Humanities* 12 (no. 4, 1978):309-319].

The computer has changed the dimension of academic research within the field of music. Instead of individuals working alone with isolated data, teams of people have begun working together. In the near future, for instance, a catalog of the sound recordings of the Institute of Jazz Studies of Rutgers University will be accessible through OCLC [*see* "Special Report: Music Library Association Meets in New Orleans," *Library Journal*, May 15, 1979, pp. 1101-1102]. Total bibliographic control of all scholarly information about music past and present is the purpose of RILM (Répertoire International de la Littérature Musicale). Sponsored by the International Association of Music Libraries and the International Musicological Society, RILM is an international center in the United States where literature and computers are available. Its publication, *RILM Abstracts*, an abstracted-computer-indexed bibliography of scholarly literature on music, includes current literature and retrospective material, and in 1979 it became accessible for on-line searches through Lockheed's DIALOG system.

Language and Literature

The various fields of the humanities discussed above are isolated in their applications of the computer. However, the limited research done with computers in religion and philosophy overlaps that done in language and literature. Both the Old and the New Testament, for instance, are being studied for omissions from the standard text, substitution of one word or a group of words for another, additions, inversions of word order, spelling, itacisms, differences caused by case and tense endings which have made meaningful variations in the sentence, and nonsense spelling errors [*see* J. W. Ellison, "Computers and the Testaments," in *Computers and Humanistic Research*, ed. by Edmund A. Bowles (Prentice-Hall, 1967), p. 163]. J. W. Ellison, at the Harvard Computation Laboratory, carried out the first of these studies with a Mark IV computer. Another use of the computer has been for production of complete concordances to the *Revised Standard Version* and the *New American Bible*. A computer program for indexing the words in the Dead Sea Scrolls was developed by Paul Tasman and Robert Busa [*see* Edmund A. Bowles, *Computers and Humanistic Research* (Prentice-Hall, 1967), p. 119]. In addition, Joseph G. Devine and Joseph Seberz developed a program in 1964 for processing the works of the early Christian writers. The steps involved included preparation of the texts in machine-readable form, production of

"Text Tape" by a program called PROOFREADER, and production of the concordance by a program called CONCORDER. The format of the concordance was the IBM Key Word in Context indexing system. This type of product, which would mean hours of tedious work for the researcher, can be produced in a small amount of time with much less possibility of error.

Data processing in the field of literature had its first general use when Stephen Parrish at Cornell used an IBM 704 computer to develop automatic indexing techniques in 1957. The first product of this development was a concordance to Matthew Arnold's poetry. Since that time, computer-produced concordances have become commonplace. Two well-noted examples of computer-generated concordances for the classics are Louis Robert's *A Concordance to Lucretius*, and Alva Walter Bennett's *Index Verborum Sallustianus*. Three methods of publishing have been used for these concordances—normal typesetting methods, photo-offset directly from computer print-out, and photo-composition—but it is hoped that these products will soon be distributed on microfilm or magnetic tape.

The computer's ability to isolate words has also resulted in automatic textual editing, such as Vinton Dearing's editing of volumes of Dryden with the use of an IBM 7090 computer (UCLA) [*see* Edmund A. Bowles, *Computers and Humanistic Research* (Prentice-Hall, 1967), p. 121]. It has also been utilized for statistical analysis, such as the work done by Michael Levison, A. Q. Morton, and A. D. Winspean to support their theory that the Seventh Letter of Plato was written by someone else [*see* Stephen V. F. Waite, "Computers and the Classics," *Computers and the Humanities* 5 (September 1970):49].

Other applications that do not depend on the counting and sorting abilities of the computer include Louis Delatte's project to determine the mental attitudes of Roman lyric poets through location and restoration of papyrological fragments, and the use of familial relationships of the Greek pantheon to test programs for kinship structures. Medieval studies have also benefitted enormously from computer use. Indeed, a very extensive double issue of *Computers and the Humanities* (v. 12, nos. 1/2, 1978) was devoted entirely to this topic.

In order to enhance the awareness of computer applications in the classics, the American Philological Association has established a regular Advisory Committee for Computer Archives. One development has been the idea of a library of classical texts, accessed by teletype or computer, to serve as a distribution center for magnetic tape copies of the texts. Similar centers have been set up for the distribution of machine-readable material in language and modern literature. Details may be found in "Verbal Materials in Machine-Readable Form," which appears sporadically in *Computers and the Humanities*.

Another area of study in which the computer has been applied is stylistic analysis. The result of this type of application is described by Sally Y. Sedelow of the University of North Carolina as "a sequentially multidimensional view of the text" [*see* Edmund A. Bowles, *Computers and Humanistic Research*

(Englewood Cliffs, NJ: Prentice-Hall, 1967), p. 120]. Stylistic analysis consists of the "study patterns formed in the process of the linguistic encoding of information" [*see* Sally Yeates Sedelow and Walter A. Sedelow, Jr., "A Preface to Computational Stylistics," in *The Computer and Literary Style*, ed. by Jacob Leed (Kent State University Press, 1966), p. 1], but the term "stylistic analysis" encompasses the whole range of literary research and involves other types of analysis, including syntactic analysis, qualitative analysis, factor analysis, and content analysis. Any one of these analyses can be used either to define the particular stylistic study or as an end in itself. For example, factor analysis has been used by Hanan C. Selvin of the University of Rochester to determine poetic style of certain seventeenth century poets [*see* Josephine Miles and Hanan C. Selvin, "A Factor Analysis of the Vocabulary of Poetry in the Seventeenth Century," in *The Computer and Literary Style*, ed. by Jacob Leed (Kent State University Press, 1966), p. 116].

The two main results of stylistic analysis are attributive stylistics and interpretive stylistics. Attributive stylistics is the identification of a given work as the product of a given writer through the style of the work. Interpretive stylistics is used to gain deeper understanding of the writer, his mind, and his personality [*see* Louis T. Milic, "Unconscious Ordering in the Prose of Swift," in *The Computer and Literary Style*, ed. by Jacob Leed (Kent State University Press, 1966), p. 82]. A fairly well-known study in attributive stylistics is Frederick Mosteller and David L. Wallace's attempt to determine the authorship of the disputed *Federalist Papers* [*see* Ivor S. Francis, "An Exposition of the Statistical Approach to the *Federalist* Dispute," in *The Computer and Literary Style*, ed. by Jacob Leed (Kent State University Press, 1966, p. 83]. For full treatment of this field of scholarship, see *The Computer in Literary and Linguistic Studies*, edited by Alan Jones and R. F. Churchouse (University of Wales Press, 1976).

Conferences on the use of computers in literary research are now held biennially; the first was held at Cambridge in 1970, the second at Edinburgh University in 1972, and later conferences in Cardiff (1974), Oxford (1976), and Birmingham (1978). A selective and edited version of the 36 papers presented at the Edinburgh Conference has been prepared by W. J. Aitken, R. W. Bailey and N. Hamilton-Smith under the title, *The Computer and Literary Studies* (Edinburgh: Edinburgh University Press, 1973).

Still another application is the computer's manipulation of individual words to produce poetry. Computer-produced poetry has been described as being similar to computer-produced art; however, it has not received as much attention and the results have not encouraged others to pursue the area. But, the novel has also received some attention [*see* Edmund C. Berkeley, "Writing a Novel by Computer — Part 1," *Computers and People* 28 (March-April 1979):28-31].

But some of the most promising applications of the computer have been in lexicography. One very interesting example, because it relates to computer graphics as well as dictionary making, is Leonard H. Lesco's "The Berkeley

Late Egyptian Dictionary" [*Computers and the Humanities* 11 (May-June 1977):139-45] which describes the use of a computer to produce camera-ready copy for the hieroglyphics. A system which can help lexicographers store and edit texts for production of dictionaries and concordances was developed at the University of Wisconsin-Madison with the aid of a grant from the National Science Foundation [*see* Richard L. Venezky, Nathan Relles and Lynne Price, "LEXICO: A System for Lexicographic Processing," *Computers and the Humanities* 11 (May-June 1977):127-37].

In linguistics, information retrieval is primarily used for machine translation, which has been the object of study for a number of years. The many programs developed for its use include the production of foreign language textbooks. Nevertheless, other linguistics research, such as phonological typology, has also employed computers. All computer-oriented linguistics studies have been aided greatly by the development of COMIT, a program language designed for natural language process. A problem still remains, however, since this language has not been standardized; the only area in which an attempt at standardization has been made is Old English studies for which interchangeable programs have been developed in order that all workers will use compatible programs. Aided by the Research and Development Office of the Central Intelligence Agency, Wayne W. Zachary has conducted a recent state-of-the-art review [*see* "A Survey of Approaches and Issues in Machine-Aided Translation Systems," *Computers and the Humanities* 13 (no. 1, 1979):17-28].

The problem of standardization is one that plagues all fields of the humanities. FORTRAN (Formula Translation), one of the most universally used programming languages, is less than ideally suited for application to humanistic disciplines. Languages have been developed within specific fields to satisfy the needs of that particular discipline, such as MIR for music. IBM has developed PL/1, which contains a set of characters large enough to make it applicable to fields other than language and literature. Another programming language, used primarily to process text material mechanically, is SNAP (Stylized Natural-Language Process), developed by Michael P. Barnett and used in a course on information processing at Columbia. The program runs on computers made by several manufacturers and its procedure consists of simple English sentences [*see* Michael P. Barnett, "SNAP — A Programming Language for Humanists," *Computers and the Humanities* 4 (1969-70):225]. Another natural language system which was recently developed has the enchanting name "GIPSY" (General Information Processing System). Applications in the humanities have included linguistics and museum catalogs. It is described as follows:

> . . . a question-oriented General Information Storage and Retrieval System. . . . By making the entire content of each document available as selection criteria and not merely some predetermined keywords or index terms, GIPSY permits the user to

answer "ad hoc" inquiries and also to "browse" through an information collection [Patricia A. Tracy, "Software Review: GIPSY," *Computers and the Humanities* 12 (no. 4, 1978):365-66].

Until recently each field in the humanities required a different language, and each type of computer required a different program. This resulted in the isolation not only of each field but also of individual data bases within these fields. With the development both of programming languages applicable to all fields and of intermediate programs or compilers which make existing languages transparent to otherwise incompatible computer systems, data bases will be available to anyone interested in their contents.

In order that the humanities may maintain their place in our society, they need extensive research and development. This can be accomplished through the interrelated use of data bases, but the availability of these data bases must be made known. Directories of these data bases must be made accessible, and until compatability of programming languages and equipment is achieved, individual differences must be noted. Support for research is now available from the National Endowment for the Humanities [*see* Gerald P. Tyson, "Funding Computer-Aided Research in the Division of Research Grants at the National Endowment for the Humanities," *Computers and the Humanities* 12 (no. 3, 1978):247-51] and scholars are identifying projects which should receive funding [*see* Simone Reagor and W. S. Brown, "The application of Advanced Technology to Scholarly Communication in the Humanities," *Computers and the Humanities* 12 (no. 3, 1978):237-46].

In addition to the numerous articles on specific projects already cited, some general surveys, or state-of-the-art reviews, are beginning to appear in such places as the *Annual Review of Information Science and Technology* [*see* Joseph Raben and R. L. Widman, "Information Systems Applications in the Humanities," *Annual Review of Information Science and Technology* 7 (Washington, DC: American Society for Information Science, 1972):439-69; see later volumes for updating].

BIBLIOGRAPHIC DATA BASES AND REFERENCE SERVICE

A data base is a collection of records, organized in such a way that the records, or the data they contain, may be accessed and retrieved for use when needed. A library may be considered a data base, but current use of the term is usually restricted to mean a structured set of records in machine-readable form. A computer program (a set of instructions) communicates to the computer exactly how the information in the data base is to be processed in order to produce the desired results.

If data exist in machine-readable form, different programs may be written which will allow the same data to be accessed and retrieved for uses other than that of the original design. For example, many of the bibliographic data bases which are now searchable on-line in academic, special, and public libraries were originally constructed to realize the economies of computer printing in the production of indexes and abstracts. Advances in computer technology and in telecommunications capabilities have made it possible for commercial firms (vendors) to buy or lease data bases from many suppliers and to make them publicly available for searching on-line using a standardized command language.

Consequently, the computer has allied humanities reference librarians and humanities researchers by providing a flexible tool for bibliographic control of information. As mentioned above, a literature search conducted on-line can be accomplished with greater speed and accuracy than the identical search done manually. But the most significant advantage of a machine-aided search is that, by discretely combining and manipulating terms and concepts, citations specific to the demands of the individual researcher may be retrieved. As a result, the library profession has become very deeply involved with on-line searching of data bases. Indeed, good reference service to a research-oriented clientele can no longer be given without such access. Extensive coverage of this topic is given by William Katz ["Reference Service and the Computer," in *Introduction to Reference Work; V. II, Reference Service and Reference Processes* (3rd ed., McGraw-Hill, 1978), pp. 123-241]. The section in Chapter 6 entitled "Social Sciences and Humanities Data Bases" (pp. 166-71) is especially pertinent.

The rapidity of the change in reference service can be noted by comparing *Computer-Based Reference Service*, by M. Lorraine Mathies and Peter G. Watson (ALA, 1973), with *The On-Line Revolution in Libraries: Proceedings of the 1977 Conference*, edited by Allen Kent and Thomas J. Galvin (Dekker, 1978). The necessity of this change has been underscored by F. W. Lancaster in *Toward Paperless Information Systems* (Academic, 1978).

Public libraries appear to be less affected by these developments than academic and special libraries [*see* James M. Kusack, "On-Line Reference Service in Public Libraries," *RQ* 18 (Summer 1979):331-33], but the trend is accelerating and the literature is replete with discussions of such issues as user fees [e.g., P. J. Crawford and J. A. Thompson, "Free Online Searches Are Feasible," *Library Journal* 104 (April 1, 1979):793-95], reference interviews [e.g., Sara D. Knapp, "Reference Interview in the Computer-Based Setting," *RQ* 17 (Summer 1978):320-24], and student usage [e.g., Pamela Kobelski and Jean Trumbore, "Student Use of Online Bibliographic Services," *Journal of Academic Librarianship* 4 (March 1978):14-18].

When we turn to the actual data bases in the humanities that are available for on-line searching, the literature is not plentiful. Data bases in the humanities are fewer in number than those in either the social sciences or the pure and applied sciences. Commercial vendors such as Bibliographic Retrieval Service (BRS), Lockheed Information Systems (LIS), and Systems Development Corporation (SDC) indicate the intention of adding files in the humanities, but those described here are data bases that are currently available. Prices for use, determined by the amount of royalties the vendor pays to the supplier, the number of records in the file, and the complexity of the file structure, vary considerably.

America: History and Life
The online data base corresponds to the printed *America: History and Life*, Parts A,. B, and C. Covered are American studies, folklore, and popular culture, appearing from 1964 to the present. The file contains 43,000 records, and is updated quarterly. Available through LIS.

Art Modern
References are to all modern art and design literature in books and to dissertations, exhibition catalogs, and approximately 300 periodicals. 21,000 records include abstracts covering art history; biographies of artists; and media such as sculpture, ceramics, and printing in the nineteenth and twentieth centuries. Dates are 1974 to the present, and the file is updated quarterly. Available through LIS.

Comprehensive Dissertation Abstracts
This is a subject, title, and author guide to dissertations accepted at American universities since 1861, to many Canadian dissertations, and to some papers submitted to foreign institutions. The data base comprises 600,000 citations and monthly updates. Available through BRS and LIS.

Historical Abstracts
Contains abstracts and indexes to world periodical literature in the humanities from more than 2,000 journals published in 90 countries in 30 languages. Some 54,000 citations cover 1973 to the present, and updating is quarterly. Available through LIS.

Language and Language Behavior Abstracts
This data base provides abstracts of articles from approximately 1,000 domestic and foreign journals covering language and language behavior. The approximately 27,000 records are updated quarterly and cover articles appearing between 1973 and the present. Available through LIS.

LIBCON

Provides coverage of monographic literature and some nonprint literature in all Roman alphabet languages and transliterated items cataloged by the Library of Congress, including MARC records. Approximately 130,000 items are added per year, and updating is weekly. Available through SDC.

MLA Bibliography

Indexes books and journal articles published on modern languages, literature, and linguistics. This is the on-line version of the printed *MLA Bibliography* (see item 951), beginning with 1976. The approximately 40,000 records are updated annually. Available through LIS.

Philosopher's Index

Provides citations and abstracts of major U.S. philosophical works appearing since 1940, and of works of the Western world published since 1967. The file contains 60,000 records with approximately 4,400 added in annual updates. Available through LIS.

RILM
(Répertoire International de la Littérature Musicale)

Provides international coverage of historical musicology, ethnomusicology, instruments and voice, performance practice and notation, theory and analysis, and interdisciplinary music studies. The approximately 50,000 records from 1967 to the present are updated irregularly. Available through LIS.

In 1979, both the *Philosopher's Index* (see item 29) and *RILM Abstracts* (see item 561) became available for on-line searching through Lockheed's DIALOG Information Retrieval Service. *ARTbibliographies Modern* (see item 252) and *MLA Bibliography* became available through Lockheed in 1976. (In addition, *Language and Language Behavior Abstracts* [see item 910] and *Arts and Humanities Citation Index* [see item 3] can also be searched through DIALOG.)

Certain other data bases are not yet available through vendors but may be searched by making direct arrangements with the producers. Examples include the COMMPUTE (Computer-Oriented Music Materials Processed for User Transformation or Exchange) Program of the Center for Contemporary Arts and Letters, State University of New York at Stony Brook, and the Choral Music Bibliography in the Gustavus Adolphus College Performance Library. The former is available only to members, but membership is open to qualified institutions on a worldwide basis.

The professional societies are attentive to the needs of librarians engaged in on-line searching, and independent publishers offer materials designed for this audience. The American Society for Information Science (ASIS) has a Special Interest Group for arts and humanities, and the Machine Assisted Reference Section (MARS) of ALA's Reference and Adult Services Division has experienced phenomenal growth (its members are kept informed through the newsletter, *Messages from MARS*). *Online Review* (edited by Martha E. Williams and Alex Tomberg), *Online* and its companion *Database* (edited by Jeffrey K. Pemberton), are quarterly publications which analyze individual data bases, offer advice on search technique, and present special features and general surveys of the field. Information about additional data bases in the humanities may be found in Anthony Kruzas's *Encyclopedia of Information Systems and Services* (3rd ed., Gale, 1978), in Martha E. Williams's *Computer-Readable Data Bases: A Directory and Data Sourcebook* (2nd ed., Knowledge Industry Publications, 1979), and in *Information Marrketplace* (annual, R. R. Bowker Company).

Inevitably the advantages of speed, accuracy, and flexibility in on-line searching are balanced by certain negative aspects. Some of these problem areas are inherent in the manner in which the individual files are organized, and can be expected to be corrected in time. Other difficulties, however, are specific to the way in which research in the humanities is conducted, leading to occasional incompatibility between scholarly needs and available computer-based information sources.

Research in the humanities, unlike that in the sciences, is less concerned with the "most recent" materials: there may be equal interest in publications of the last century as in those of the last month. Although the printed sources from which the data base is derived may have indexed retrospective works, the machine-readable version often covers only the last five to ten years. Data bases dedicated to documents in the humanities may not be sufficiently inclusive to produce adequate citations for certain questions. Therefore, knowledge of the contents of files outside a given discipline is often necessary. For example, the *Monthly Catalog Online* may need to be accessed to trace publications of the Library of Congress, the National Endowment for the Humanities, or the Smithsonian Institution.

Each of these two difficulties involves a third problem. Humanities researchers are more likely to conduct their research individually, forming complex and subtle relationships between concepts as documents are examined and research progresses. This method poses restraints on the formulation of search strategies essential for effective on-line information retrieval – especially so when further complicated by the vagaries of indexing vocabularies between data bases.

Obviously, then, humanities reference librarians conducting on-line searches require an orientation somewhat different from their counterparts in the sciences. This orientation, however, is entirely consistent with good reference service, regardless of the form of the tools ultimately utilized. The reference interview in particular takes on added importance in preparing for an on-line search [*see* William Katz, "Reference Service and the Computer," in *Introduction to Reference Work, V. II: Reference Service and Reference Processes* (3rd ed., McGraw-Hill, 1978), pp. 123-241; and Sara D. Knapp, "Reference Interview in the Computer-Based Setting," *RQ* 17 (Summer 1978):320-24]. The librarian, always an intermediary between information sources and patrons, is even more so in computer-based reference service. As indicated earlier, a thorough knowledge of many files is essential, and file structures vary in depth of indexing and kind of vocabulary required for access. Each commercial vendor has a different command language peculiar to the data bases available on its own system. While these languages are similar and not difficult to learn, they cannot be considered standardized. Changes and improvements in each system are frequent, and on-line searching skill, like any acquired skill, requires practice to maintain proficiency. For the present time, at least, the searcher/intermediary is essential, but the humanities researcher using on-line search services may feel quite removed from the information being sought. The librarian-as-searching-specialist must determine, as in any reference situation, the appropriateness of the tools to be used; computerized data bases offer another choice, not a universal answer.

AUTHOR AND TITLE INDEX TO BIBLIOGRAPHICAL CHAPTERS

Each item (whether book or periodical) that has been given a separate entry has also been given an item number. These numbers run consecutively from the beginning of the first bibliographical chapter through the final bibliographical chapter. The index refers to item numbers — not to page numbers. Books and serials mentioned in the annotations but not given separate entries are also indexed. The number in each such case refers to the main entry under which an annotation makes reference to the book or serial in question and is followed by the designation "n."

The following guidelines were used in alphabetizing index entries. Articles which occur at the beginning of titles have been omitted in the index. Lengthy titles have been shortened where this could be done without ambiguity. Entries have been arranged in accordance with the "word by word" or "nothing before something" method of filing. Names beginning with "Mc" have been filed as though spelled "Mac." Acronyms (e.g., ARLIS, UNESCO) have been treated as regular words rather than abbreviations. Numbers have been arranged as though written in word form. Works by one author alone have been placed before those by two or more joint authors if the surname and initials of the first author are identical with those of the single author.

SUBJECT INDEX

The purpose of this index is to provide access to more or less broad topics that have received more than simple mention in the text. Consequently, only those organizations associated with more than one discipline are listed here. More specialized organizations will be found in the "Accessing Information" chapter for each discipline.